# THE WORKS OF JONATHAN EDWARDS

VOLUME 11

*Harry S. Stout, General Editor*

Plate XIV (Ps. 84:1) by William Marshall from Francis Quarles, *Emblemes* (1693). Beinecke Rare Book and Manuscript Library, Yale University.

JONATHAN EDWARDS

# Typological Writings

*"IMAGES OF DIVINE THINGS"*
*"TYPES"*

EDITED BY
WALLACE E. ANDERSON
LATE ASSOCIATE PROFESSOR OF PHILOSOPHY
OHIO STATE UNIVERSITY

*"TYPES OF THE MESSIAH"*

EDITED BY
MASON I. LOWANCE, JR.
PROFESSOR OF ENGLISH
UNIVERSITY OF MASSACHUSETTS

WITH
DAVID H. WATTERS
PROFESSOR OF ENGLISH
UNIVERSITY OF NEW HAMPSHIRE

New Haven and London

YALE UNIVERSITY PRESS, 1993

*Published with assistance from Pew Charitable Trusts, Lilly Endowment, and Exxon Education Foundation*

*Printed in the United States of America by Vail-Ballou Press, Binghamton, New York.*

*Library of Congress Cataloging-in-Publication Data*

Edwards, Jonathan, *1703–1758*.
[Selections. 1993]
Typological writings / Jonathan Edwards.
  p.  cm. — (The Works of Jonathan Edwards ; v. 11)
Includes bibliographical references and index.
Contents: Images of divine things / edited by Wallace E. Anderson — Types / edited by Wallace E. Anderson — Types of the Messiah / edited by Mason I. Lowance with David H. Watters.
  ISBN 0-300-05352-5
  1. Analogy (Religion)—Early works to 1800.
2. Typology (Theology)—Early works to 1800.
3. Jesus Christ—Messiahship—Early works to 1800.
I. Title.  II. Series: Edwards, Jonathan, 1703–1758.  Works.  1957 ; v. 11.
BX7117.E3  1957 vol. 11.
[B1210]
285.8 s—dc20
[220.6′4]          93-9689
                 CIP

*A catalogue record for this book is available from the British Library.*

*The paper in this book meets the guidelines for permanence and durability of the Committee on Production Guidelines for Book Longevity of the Council on Library Resources.*

*10  9  8  7  6  5  4  3  2  1*

Dedicated to Wallace E. Anderson

# CONTENTS

# ILLUSTRATIONS

# FOREWORD

$\mathbf{V}$OLUME 11 of the Yale Edition of *The Works of Jonathan Edwards, Typological Writings*, represents many years of labor by several editors. In order to help the reader understand the content and organization of the pieces in this collection, the General Editor and the Executive Committee have thought it helpful to provide a brief explanation of the history and format of the volume.

The late Wallace E. Anderson, editor of volume 6 of the Yale Edition, *Scientific and Philosophical Writings*, had originally planned to include the texts of "Images of Divine Things" and the "Types" notebook, along with introductory notes to each, in volume 6. Considerations of length, however, precluded having these documents in that volume. Consequently, it was agreed to combine the work done by Anderson with that of Mason I. Lowance, Jr., who had been working on a new edition of "Types of the Messiah" as part of a separate project. Shortly after this decision was made, David H. Watters came on as Lowance's assistant. Thus converged the pieces for this particular volume.

This volume of Edwards' typological writings took shape during a time when scholarship focused especially on typology in American literature, an endeavor in part attributable, coincidentally, to Perry Miller's introduction to his 1948 edition of "Images of Divine Things," which he entitled *Images or Shadows of Divine Things*. The late 1960s and 1970s witnessed a burst of scholarly activity in the field, which had the effect of demonstrating how important typology was to shaping American perceptions and imaginations.[1]

The untimely death of Anderson in 1982 brought progress on this

1. See, for instance, Ursula Brumm, *American Thought and Religious Typology* (New Brunswick, N.J., Rutgers, 1963); Sacvan Bercovitch, ed., *Typology and Early American Literature* (Amherst, Univ. of Massachusetts Press, 1972), which contains a useful annotated bibliography; and Mason I. Lowance, Jr., *The Language of Canaan: Metaphor and Symbol in New England from the Puritans to the Transcendentalists* (Cambridge, Harvard Univ. Press, 1980). See above p. 166, n. 8.

volume to a standstill. Anderson and Lowance had each agreed to do
the introduction to the documents they were editing, departing from
the Edition's usual practice of having a single "Editor's Introduction"
at the beginning of each volume. Lowance's introduction appears at
the beginning of the second half of the volume. Though Anderson
had completed notes on the manuscripts of "Images" and "Types," he
left only fragments of a draft for an introduction for these pieces. The
Executive Committee of the Edition, out of respect to the interpretative work done by Anderson, decided to use as much of this material as
possible in composing an introduction to "Images" and "Types." Anderson's material is arranged according to his original outline with
some alterations and additions that attempt to make the introduction
reflect current scholarship.

The introductions at the beginning of each half of the volume are
not comprehensive interpretations. Rather they attempt to cover the
main issues involved in Edwards' conception of typology, to address
the problems that the manuscripts present, and to suggest avenues for
further research into this area of Edwards' thought. The introduction
to "Images" and "Types" places Edwards' typological views within the
context of the early eighteenth century; it also ties his defense of
typology to his metaphysical system and to his general theory of being
and nature. The introduction to "Types of the Messiah" demonstrates
the relationship of the document to the rest of Edwards' corpus and
also situates Edwards in the American literary canon.

This volume is dedicated to the memory of Wallace E. Anderson,
formerly Associate Professor of Philosophy at the Ohio State University. Besides editing *Scientific and Philosophical Writings*, he edited the
texts of "Images of Divine Things" and the "Types" notebook that are
included in this volume. Anderson had a rare talent; he combined the
searching eye of the historian with the insight of the philosopher, and
he contributed, among other things, to our understanding of Edwards' relation to the thought of John Locke and to the writings of Sir
Isaac Newton. Anderson's death was a great loss both to the laborers in
the Edwards vineyard and to the philosophical community at large.

*Preparation of the Text*

In this edition, the text of Jonathan Edwards is reproduced as he
wrote it in manuscript or, if he published it himself, as it was printed in
the first edition. In order to present this text to modern readers as

practically readable, several technical adjustments have been made. Those which can be addressed categorically are as follows:

1. All spelling is regularized and conformed to that of *Webster's Third New International Dictionary*, a step that does not involve much more than removing the "u" from "colour" or "k" from "publick" since Edwards was a good speller, used relatively modern spelling, and generally avoided "y" contractions. His orthographic contractions and abbreviations, such as ampersands, "call'd," and "thems." are spelled out, though pronounced contractions, such as "han't" and "ben't," are retained.

2. There is no regular punctuation in most of Edwards' manuscripts and where it does exist, as in the earliest sermons, it tends to be highly erratic. Editors take into account Edwards' example in punctuation and related matters, but all punctutation is necessarily that of the editor, including paragraph divisions (especially in some notebooks such as the "Miscellanies") and the emphasizing devices of italics and capitalization. In reference to capitalization, it should be noted that pronouns referring to the deity are lower case except in passages where Edwards confusingly mixes "he's" referring to God and man: here capitalization of pronouns referring to the deity sorts out the references for the reader.

3. Numbered heads designate important structures of argument in Edwards' sermons, notebooks, and treatises. Numbering, including spelled-out numbers, has been regularized and corrected where necessary. Particularly in the manuscript sermon texts, numbering has been clarified by the use of systematic schemes of heads and subheads in accordance with eighteenth-century homiletical form, a practice similar to modern analytical outline form. Thus the series of subordinated head number forms, 1, (1), *1*, a, (a), in the textual exegesis, and the series, I, *First*, 1, (1), *1*, a, (a), in Doctrine and Application divisions, make it possible to determine sermon head relationships at a glance.

4. Textual intervention to regularize Edwards' citation of Scripture includes the correction of erroneous citation, the regularizing of citation form (including the standardization of book abbreviations), and the completion of quotations which Edwards' textual markings indicate should be completed (as in preaching).

5. Omissions and lacunae in the manuscript text are filled by insertions in square brackets ([ ]); repeated phrases sometimes represented by Edwards with a long dash are inserted in curly brackets ({ }). In all cases of uncertain readings, annotation gives notice of the problem.

Markings in the text designate whole word units even when only a few letters are at issue.

6. Minor slips of the pen or obvious typographical errors are corrected without annotation. Likewise, Edwards' corrections, deletions, and internal shifts of material are observed but not noted unless of substantive interest.

7. Quotations made by the editor from the Bible (AV) and other secondary sources are printed *verbatim ac literatim*. Edwards' quotations from such sources are often rather free but are not corrected and are not annotated as such unless significant omissions or distortions are involved.

Other conditions of textual preparation are related to differences of genre and factors unique to particular texts or manuscripts. For information on such matters please consult the note on the text in each volume or the first volume of each series within the Edition.

*Acknowledgements*

Primary funding for this volume was provided by the Pew Charitable Trusts and the Lilly Endowment. Wallace Anderson received financial support from Ohio State University, while Mason Lowance's work benefited from a Guggenheim Fellowship. A grant from the Exxon Foundation subsidized printing costs.

The Executive Committee would like to thank Ruth Mastin Anderson for her assistance in the publication of her husband's work. In addition, the counsel and expertise of Judith Calvert and James Mooney of Yale University Press were instrumental in the production of this volume.

PART ONE
# "IMAGES OF DIVINE THINGS"
## "TYPES"

*Edited by*
*Wallace E. Anderson*

## EDITOR'S INTRODUCTION TO "IMAGES OF DIVINE THINGS" AND "TYPES"

T HE documents in this volume present Jonathan Edwards' major statements on the exegetical discipline of typology. Traditionally, typology involved the exercise of matching biblical "types"— prophetic figures, events, or circumstances—in the Old Testament with their "antitypes" or fulfilling figures, events, or circumstances in the New. In Edwards' hands, however, typology took on a broadened significance that comprehended not only Scripture but also nature and history. "So it is God's way in the natural world," he writes in an early entry in "Images of Divine Things," no. 19, "to make inferior things in conformity and analogy to the superior, so as to be images of them." For Edwards, types were found not only in the Old Testament; the phenomenal world also declared divine truths.

The two manuscripts that comprise the first half of this volume Edwards labelled "Images of Divine Things" and "Types," and the one in the second half is "Types of the Messiah." "Images of Divine Things" and "Types" are to be distinguished from "Types of the Messiah" in that the former are separate notebooks Edwards kept on an occasional basis, adding to them as needed, while the latter is entries in his "Miscellanies" written in a relatively brief period of time.[1] "Types of the Messiah" is devoted almost exclusively to Edwards' reflections on Old Testament persons and events, "Types" contains general principles as well as many New Testament proofs, and "Images" is more concerned with the things of nature and the world in which he lived. To understand the pieces fully, it is necessary to examine them as responses to the views of typology with which Edwards was most familiar, and as components within his philosophical theology.

1. However, the concluding entries in both the "Types" notebook and "Types of the Messiah" are similar in ink, hand, and content, dating from the Stockbridge period.

*Edwards and the History of Typology*

The theory and terminology of Christian typology hark back to the earliest days of the church, when it was used as a way of interpreting passages of Scripture. In part, the conception of typological interpretation derives from certain passages in the New Testament in which particular persons, institutions, and events mentioned in the Old Testament are viewed as figures, types, or foreshadowings of Christ. In Rom. 5:14, for example, the apostle Paul states that Adam was the "figure of him that was to come," or Christ. These passages gave Christians a way to interpret the Old Testament in light of the New. Events mentioned or described in the former as belonging to the history of the Jews had a significance beyond their actual and historical reality. They were ordained by God to stand as prophetic representations of what was to come, namely, God's full revelation of himself in the person of Christ.

Some early Christian exegetes, notably Origen, were greatly influenced by Hellenistic and Jewish modes of allegorical interpretation—particularly those of Philo of Alexandria—which were used to explain covert meanings of obscure passages or to account for statements that were considered unworthy, incredible, or even contradictory when taken literally.[2] Allegory recommended itself to Christian apologists when challenged by difficult passages of Scripture. It also afforded a way of exploiting the rich descriptive details of the biblical record by reading them as signifying hidden moral or spiritual meanings.

Allegorical methods of interpretation provided an expansion of exegetical possibilities beyond that afforded by the prophetic scheme of scriptural typology. The latter, employed by adherents of the Antiochene literalist school, notably the fourth-century theologian Basil, was restricted to the interpretation of signs that were historically verifiable and antecedent to their referents, and that were reported or described as such in the Old Testament.[3] The meaning of these signs was limited to the subsequent manifestations of Christ in the New Testament. The allegorists, on the other hand, could apply their method to any text that supplied a sensible image, regardless of whether it was presented as a historical report, a dream or vision, a

2. Joseph A. Galdon, S.J., *Typology and Seventeenth-Century Literature* (The Hague, Mouton, 1975), p. 35.

3. Thomas H. Davis, "The Traditions of Puritan Typology," in Bercovitch, ed., *Typology and Early American Literature*, p. 25.

prophetic warning, or something else. In all cases, the "truth" of the text was found in the invisible, spiritual, and eternal things signified by the text. The spiritual meaning of these signs was not restricted to the New Testament record of Christ, but could be supplied from any part of the theological system.

Allegory came to dominate Christian hermeneutics at an early stage and remained dominant through the medieval period. It was first effectively systematized by the Latin Fathers; later scholastic exegetes developed an elaborate and subtle schematization of levels of meaning. By the time of the Henrician reforms in sixteenth-century England, preachers were measured by their ability for creative allegorization. John Langland, Bishop of Lincoln, derided the historical sense as fit only "for the nourishment of babes"; allegory, however, was for "apter wits."[4]

During the Protestant Reformation, the allegorical method came under severe criticism. The reformers were repelled by the excessive invention that the traditional method allowed and objected to perceived mishandling of the text. William Tyndale, the sixteenth-century English reformer, criticized the schoolmen for tearing biblical texts out of context to suit their purposes. "The literal sense," he complained, "is become nothing at all: for the pope hath taken it clean away, and hath made it his possession."[5] The notion that in any given text there was embedded a profusion of meanings, discoverable only to those who had mastered exegetical theory, was for the reformers fraught with the danger of introducing human additions and errors into the divinely inspired Word. There was a general agreement among them that modes of scriptural interpretation that failed to recognize the primacy of the literal and historical and that were not based on the direct testimony of Scripture itself were to be discarded as capricious and arbitrary. In particular, they objected to treating the Bible as "mere" allegory.

But the reformers did not entirely reject the validity of typological interpretation. John Calvin, who called the Old Testament a "book of promises," insisted that many passages had to be interpreted typologically. One fundamental difference between "the Old and New Testaments," Calvin wrote, "consists in figures; that, in the absence of the reality, it showed but an image and shadow in place of the substance;

---

4. Quoted in J.W. Blench, *Preaching in England in the Late Fifteenth and Sixteenth Centuries* (Oxford, Blackwell, 1964), p. 22.

5. *Ibid.*, p. 20.

the New Testament reveals the very substance of the truth as present."[6] It was to this tradition that Edwards belonged. Like the reformers, he saw that the New Testament writers declared that the Old Testament contained figurative prophecies of Christ. Even as the Old Testament presented types that should be interpreted prophetically in relation to the Christ who was to come, so these types could be interpreted as signifying truths that Christ made manifest and which are revealed through the New Testament. The Protestant hermeneutic that came down from sixteenth-century Europe to eighteenth-century New England emphasized a literal and historical interpretation of Scripture, but it also accepted and employed both prophetic or typological interpretations as well as allegorical interpretations of certain texts, at least so far as these were warranted by the Bible.[7]

*Edwards on Types*

Superficially, Edwards' "Images of Divine Things" and "Types" notebook appear to be collections of apt metaphors and illustrations gathered for use in ornamenting his sermons. Phenomena of common experience and various objects in nature are found to be fit, or suitable, or "lively" representations of certain moral, spiritual, and theological points. With a more attentive reading of the entries, however, it becomes clear that Edwards' intentions were quite different. In most of the entries, he positively states that the natural things he describes were established by God to be representations, or types, or images, of those moral and spiritual matters. In many cases he asserts that the one was specifically created and ordained to signify and "shadow forth" the other. He often adds specific reasons and cites passages of Scripture to support these claims. From these features of substance and language it is evident that Edwards devoted this series, not to the exercise of literary imagination alone, but to a certain investigation of fact.

Edwards summed up these points during late 1728, in a general statement in "Miscellanies" no. 362. He apparently considered the

6. Davis, "Traditions of Puritan Typology," pp. 38–39; *Institutes*, bk. II. ch. XI, §4. See also Barbara K. Lewalski, *Protestant Poetics and the Seventeenth-Century Religious Lyric* (Princeton, Princeton Univ. Press, 1979).

7. For a related discussion of JE's incorporation of typology into his view of sacred history, see the "Editor's Introduction" in *The History of the Work of Redemption*, ed. John F. Wilson, in *The Works of Jonathan Edwards* (New Haven, Yale Univ. Press, 1989), 9, 40–50.

passage to be an appropriate prologue to "Images," for he jotted a reference to it next to his original title at the beginning of the whole series. The passage begins:

> For indeed the whole outward creation, which is but the shadows of beings, is so made as to represent spiritual things. It might be demonstrated by the wonderful agreement in thousands of things, much of the same kind as is between the types of the Old Testament and their antitypes, and by spiritual things being so often and continually compared with them in the Word of God.[8]

The central thesis of "Images," as expressed in these lines, is that all "outward" and created things are specifically designated by God to "represent spiritual things." This thesis, he maintains, can be justified, even demonstrated, both from the testimony of Scripture and from independently discoverable facts concerning the agreement between natural objects and spiritual things.

Among modern readers, at least, any such claims that all the objects of the natural world signify other things, and that we can discover or confirm moral and spiritual truths by examining their representations in observable things, would probably be received with open scepticism. Neither did Edwards suppose that his own contemporaries were ready to endorse such a view. Several passages in "Images" and in the "Types" notebook indicate that he planned to publish some systematic exposition and defense of it. In "Types" he outlines his intended position: "To show how there is a medium between those that cry down all types, and those that are for turning all into nothing but allegory and not having it to be true history; and also the way of the rabbis that find so many mysteries in letters, etc."[9] Later in the same document, he frankly admits the critical reception he expected to receive:

> I expect by very ridicule and contempt to be called a man of a very fruitful brain and copious fancy, but they are welcome to it. I am not ashamed to own that I believe that the whole universe, heaven and earth, air and seas, and the divine constitution and history of the holy Scriptures, be full of images of divine things, as full as a language is of words; and that the multitude of those things that I

8. Excerpts from the "Miscellanies" that appear in this volume were provided by the editor, Thomas A. Schafer.

9. See below p. 151.

have mentioned are but a very small part of what is really intended to be signified and typified by these things.[1]

There is no evidence that Edwards went any further in the actual preparation of a treatise than to write the materials in these manuscripts, but even in them the need to defend his claims was never far from his thoughts. "Types" is almost entirely devoted to composing general principles and assembling scriptural testimony for the belief he is "not ashamed to own." A number of entries throughout "Images" are concerned with sketching philosophical and scriptural arguments to support the general thesis that all natural things are designed and ordained to represent spiritual or divine things. In several entries Edwards copies substantial passages from the works of contemporary English philosophers such as George Turnbull, Andrew Ramsey, and others that seem to lend support to the thesis. Even his particular correlations of natural objects and phenomena with spiritual interpretations are often defended with more specific reasons and scriptural evidence. The polemical character of all these passages leaves little doubt that Edwards tried to anticipate the major objections his readers would raise at every point. He was attempting in these documents to develop convincing replies and provide appropriate illustrations.

One major source of objections can easily be found in the exceptionally wide variety of the things, both natural and spiritual, that Edwards claimed to be correlated. In "the whole outward creation" described in "Miscellanies" no. 362, he includes the entire fabric of history as recorded in the Old Testament, at least some of the things recorded in the New Testament, and beyond this the order and constitution of the physical world. This also includes the kind of objects the physical world contains, the laws that govern them, and the regular and recurrent phenomena they exhibit. Human arts and established institutions, as varied as husbandry and the Olympic games, common human experiences such as scaling a hill, and natural human affections and dispositions, as of a man's strong love for a woman, are claimed to represent spiritual truths.

Another source of objections lies in Edwards' shifting use of terms such as *image, shadow, type, correlation, representation,* and *symbol,* a practice which apparently stems from his efforts to describe the variety of phenomena he thought to be correlated. This range of terminology

---

1. See above p. 179.

reflects at once Edwards' willingness to view typology in a more expansive way than his contemporaries and to give the discipline a metaphysical component. His manuscripts readily exhibit his sometimes indeterminate usage. The collection of observations that he initially called "Shadows of Divine Things" he later (in late 1737) renamed "Images of Divine Things." Some time after writing "Images" no. 45, Edwards emended the third sentence, which originally read, "The type is only the representation of the thing," adding "or shadow" after "representation." These examples suggest how, over time, Edwards experimented with different terms to describe the multivalent relations he perceived.

Edwards formulated his view of typology to conform to his perception of how God manifested himself and his work of redemption in the corporeal realm. He began the notebook that he eventually entitled "Images of Divine Things" concurrently with a 1728 sermon on Luke 16:24, a terrifying sermon that deals with the eternal torments of hell. In the application, he discusses how temporal death is a type of the eternal death that the damned are to experience in hell. The first entry of "Images" records this observation. Thus Edwards' entries pertain as much to the foreshadowed miseries of sinners as to the anticipated happiness of the saints. Storms, for example, signify misery and wrath, and ravens, devils, while the simple act of breathing represents "how the spiritual life is constantly maintained by the Spirit of God entering into the soul" (no. 62).

By themselves, these natural types were illustrative of Edwards' inventive imagination, but they also were elements of a much larger and all-encompassing system. For Edwards, the end of creation was God's communication of himself—and thereby of his glory—to the understanding and will of his creatures.[2] The universe itself was part of that divine self-communication, an act performed every moment by the power of the sovereign God. Edwards' efforts to rehabilitate Calvinist doctrine led him to conceive of a new manner of incorporating the creation into redemptive history. In Edwards' hands, the natural world, its processes, inhabitants, and history, contained more than simple allegories from which we learn lessons or gain reminders of the moral life; rather, the universe itself became prophetic of future redemption and judgment. Not content with the linear typical correspondences of the two testaments, Edwards saw types as transcending

2. "Miscellanies" no. 243.

time. Along with Scripture, things in nature and human experience became types, shadows, or forerunners, not only of what was but what was *to be*, so as to apply to the attributes and offices of the ultimate antitype, Christ, and to things pertaining to the final states of heaven and hell.

Edwards found in this unique formulation of typology what he thought was the key to explaining the profound harmony with which God infused creation. He writes in "Images" no. 8,

> There is a wonderful resemblance in the effects which God produces, and consentaneity in his manner of working in one thing and another, throughout all nature.... Therefore 'tis allowed that God does purposely make and order one thing to be in an agreeableness and harmony with another.

As the growth of a plant, or the development of a fetus in the womb, or conversion, are "growing things," so Edwards perceived the world to be in a "progressive state" because of the unfolding of the work of redemption—a major idea behind his History of Redemption discourse. The "Jewish church" of the Old Testament could not see this clearly because God spoke to it only in veiled language. With the revelation of Christ, however, God's purpose was made increasingly clear to the church, and the heightened perception of God's purpose in creation was a function of the coming of the new heaven and the new earth.

The Reformed tenet of *sola scriptura* depended upon a view of scriptural interpretation that was guided by what Luther and Calvin called the "witness of the Spirit," which identified the presence of grace in the soul as the basis for interpretational circumspection and authority. Typological interpretation was also subject to this principle. Unregenerate readers of God's Word and observers of nature could derive some vague idea of God's power, but only the regenerate knew of God's beauty or "excellency," as Edwards called it. Likewise, the full meaning of the types was closed to the reprobate. For Edwards, the "light" in the soul imparted by the Holy Spirit in conversion enabled the regenerate to comprehend more fully the harmony or "agreeableness" of creation, human experience, and the work of redemption as given in Scripture.

The spiritual truths represented by the array of natural things comprehended the temporal unfolding of the divine plan of salvation. These included the attributes and ordinances of God; his dispositions and actions in the administration of providence; the work of Christ as savior; the operations of the Holy Spirit in the work of redemption; Satan and his influences; and the spiritual and moral condition and destiny of human beings in general and of the saints and the damned in particular. In short, Edwards' domain of spiritual things encompassed all that properly pertained to the order and constitution, the members, and the history of the spiritual kingdom of God, as it was revealed in the New Testament and systematically presented in Calvinist theology.

## Edwards and Contemporary Thought on Typology

In "Types," Edwards sought a "medium" between those who "cry down all types," those who "are for turning all into nothing but allegory," and "the way of the rabbis." Those who "cry down all types" were the advocates of natural theology, Enlightenment rationalism, and Deism in particular. Those who tended to turn "all into nothing but allegory" can most readily be identified as the Catholic and Anglican inheritors of the ancient Alexandrian approach, who spurned the literalist approach in favor of allegorism. Edwards also deemed worthy of consideration Cabalism, the Jewish mystical tradition that included ciphering meaning from words. Among these poles stood a variety of viewpoints, most important of which for Edwards was that of the inheritors of the Puritan dissenting tradition.

### THE RATIONALISTS AND DEISTS

Most vocal and controversial in their use of Scripture were those who claimed that Christianity had to be based ultimately on the principles of reason. These included the adherents of natural theology, the rationalist disciples of John Locke, and the "Freethinkers," or Deists. Their goal was to purge religion—homiletics, theology, and piety—of extravagance and enthusiasm. However, each group was willing to go to different lengths. While Latitudinarians like Locke saw revelation as confirming the "reasonableness of Christianity" so long as faith and reason were kept within their proper "boundaries," the Deists did not.[3] In his seminal work, *De Veritate* (1624), Lord Edmund Herbert de Cherbury had separated "Revealed truth" from self-evident truth,

---

3. Gerald R. Cragg, *The Church and the Age of Reason, 1648–1789* (New York, Penguin, 1970), pp. 75–77; Locke, *An Essay Concerning Human Understanding*, ed. Peter H. Nidditch (Oxford, Clarendon, 1975), bk. IV, ch. XVIII, §7–11.

thereby relegating revelation to a subsidiary, and therefore doubtful, status. Those influenced by Herbert sought to rest their definition of true religion on the epistemological foundations of human reason and the laws of nature. Whatever was beyond the ken of these was ultimately of no force.[4]

The beginning of the eighteenth century saw the beginning of a new age in biblical hermeneutics, which impacted on the relevance of typology.[5] As a result of their emphasis on the rationality of religion, rationalists and Deists adopted a sceptical method of scriptural interpretation. They attacked the credibility of the Old Testament prophecies and the miracles of Christ. Edwards was familiar with certain of these writers, either through having read their works or through secondary sources, such as Ephraim Chambers' *Cyclopedia*. Prominent among them were William Whiston, John Toland, Matthew Tindal, and Anthony Collins, who called for doing away with those scriptures that partook of mysticism and irrationality.[6] Miracles were derided as contradicting the natural laws of the universe, and any notions of the fulfillment of Old Testament prophecies—literal, figural, or typological—were either false because they could not be applied literally or nonsensical because allegorical methods were purely arbitrary. Portraying the Old Testament as a collection of tales, the sceptics sought to demonstrate that the obscurity of the prophecies made them liable to manipulation. Allegorical interpretations, they stated, could so twist the Scripture out of shape as to render them misleading.

Edwards affirmed both the literal meaning and historical reliability of the biblical narratives in response to deistical criticism. He held that it was improper to separate what a sacred author intended from any supposedly "real" or allegorized meaning of a given text that existed apart from that intention. By the 1740s, Edwards was therefore assembling evidence in his notebooks to defend "the historicity of the Old Testament narratives" and to demonstrate the fulfillment of proph-

4. John Leland, *A View of the Principal Deistical Writers* (2 vols., London, 1754, rep. 1807), *1*, 1–15.

5. On hermeneutics in the early eighteenth century, see Sir Leslie Stephen, *English Thought in the Eighteenth Century* (2 vols., London, 1876), *1*, 186–227; S. L. Greenslade, ed., *The Cambridge History of the Bible: The West From the Reformation to the Present Day* (Cambridge, Cambridge Univ. Press, 1963), pp. 238–49; and Hans W. Frei, *The Eclipse of Biblical Narrative: A Study in Eighteenth and Nineteenth Century Hermeneutics* (New Haven, Yale Univ. Press, 1974), pp. 51–85.

6. Stephen, *English Thought in the Eighteenth Century*, *1*, 214–17.

ecies.[7] These notebooks are related to the larger work that Edwards was working on toward the end of his life that he called "The Harmony of the Old and New Testament," which was to include sections on the prophecies of the Messiah, the fulfillment of those prophecies, and the types of the Messiah.[8] Edwards' gathering these materials in one work shows how in his opinion prophecy and typology, though different modes of discourse, could not be arbitrarily separated. The trustworthiness of the Old Testament and its prophetic content was essential to his view of typology.

Edwards' view of typology, as part of a larger system, was based on a specific scriptural interpretation but also depended on metaphysical principles. For the express thesis of "Images" and "Types"—that *all* the objects of nature consist of representations of spiritual things—went beyond any of the scriptural evidence that Edwards presented and which pertained only to a certain limited number of correlations. By its very nature, Edwards' general view required an independent and philosophical defense based upon principles of reason and well-attested facts of experience. Passages pertaining to such a defense, both of particular cases of representation and of his general thesis, are found throughout "Images" and "Types." As in the case of his arguments from Scripture, however, these passages do not form a full and systematic demonstration of his claims. They seem rather to be directed to persuading sceptics within the philosophical and scientific community of his time, and to avoiding or answering the main objections that he expected from these groups.[9]

Among the first and most radical of the philosophical opponents of

7. See the notebooks entitled "The Harmony of the Genius, Spirit, Doctrines and Rules of the Old and New Testaments," "Defense of the Authenticity of the Pentateuch as a Work of Moses and the Historicity of the Old Testament Narratives," and "Scripture Prophecies of the Old Testament" (Beinecke Rare Book and Manuscript Library, Yale University, f. 33, 41.1, and 42).

8. "Miscellanies" nos. 1067–1069; "Types of the Messiah" was originally conceived as part of this larger work. In "Things to be Particularly Inquired Into" (Beinecke Library, f. 41.5), JE wrote an entry contemporaneous with "Types of the Messiah," which reads: "Read the Scripture—at least such parts as are most likely—in order to observe how the visible things of the creation are made use of as representations and TYPES of spiritual things, that I may note them in my book about 'Images of Divine Things.'"

9. For an authoritative treatment of the developments in his early metaphysical and philosophical thought, see "Editor's Introduction," in *Scientific and Philosophical Writings*, ed. Wallace E. Anderson, in *The Works of Jonathan Edwards* (New Haven, Yale Univ. Press, 1980), 6, 52–136.

Edwards' natural typology were those who, like Thomas Hobbes, defended some form of metaphysical materialism. The whole of observable nature, according to these critics, involved no other objects but bodies, and no other causes except matter and motion. The claim that anything in nature represented spiritual things presupposed that there actually were such spiritual entities, and that they were distinct from and independent of those material things. But the facts of experience gave no evidence for the existence of immaterial spirits in animals or human beings, and the assumption that they existed otherwise in the system of reality was contrary to the principles of reason.

The central point in Edwards' response to this objection is indicated in "Miscellanies" no. 362: "The whole outward creation, *which is but shadows of beings*, is so made as to represent spiritual things."[1] Long before he wrote these words, he had launched a philosophical attack upon materialism, and had proved to his own satisfaction that, so far from being the only substances that exist, only God was "proper substance."[2] Bodies were not themselves substances in the sense of being self-subsistent at all, but were the result of the exercise of God's power. His earliest philosophical writings in "Natural Philosophy" present arguments from which he concludes that the actual and continued existence of every body depends upon the infinite power of an immaterial, voluntary, and infinite being—that is, God. "All material existence," Edwards writes in "The Mind" no. 40, "is only idea."[3] Although his earlier metaphysical views were modified in important respects during subsequent years while he studied the works of Newton, Locke, More, and others, he continued to hold this conclusion as a rationally demonstrable principle in his philosophical system. That outward and created things were only "shadows" of other beings may be understood in part as reaffirming that the entire system of physical objects subsisted only in immediate and continual dependence on God. And this claim in turn was a central support for Edwards' belief that everything in nature represented spiritual things.

But even if it were granted that all physical objects subsisted only in dependence upon God, this would not be sufficient to justify Edwards' claim that nature was a system of representations of spiritual or divine things, nor would it answer the most widespread and pressing philosophical objections his contemporaries would advance against it. Des-

1. Ed. italics.
2. "Of Atoms," prop. 2, corol. 6, in *Works, 6,* 215.
3. *Ibid.,* 356.

cartes, Newton, Locke, and most of their contemporaries and immediate successors were prepared to acknowledge that the real existence and immateriality of God, and the dependence of the physical world upon God, were rationally demonstrable. Many of these philosophers and scientists went on to argue that from the properties and constitution of the physical world we may derive further knowledge concerning the nature and attributes of the Creator. From the immeasurable vastness and complexity of the entire system of bodies, for example, we may conclude that God's power is inconceivably immense. The orderliness of the system in accordance with general laws of nature showed the perfection of God's wisdom, and the special contrivance of certain parts of the system to fit them for particular ends gave evidence of God's purposefulness and beneficence towards humanity in ordering the works of creation.

So far forth, the proponents of natural theology would have concurred with Edwards' thesis that the entire physical world "shadows forth" spiritual things. But the arguments they offered in support of this general thesis hardly would have confirmed the particular instances of *typical* representation that Edwards claimed to find. Neither observation of the facts nor evident principles of natural reason would have seemed adequate to establish that the serpent's art of luring prey was a shadow of Satan's wiles, that the invention of the telescope predicted the approach of a general spiritual enlightenment, or that the principles of hydrostatics revealed truths about human moral powers.

In the standard Newtonian view, bodies—the basic furniture of the physical world—were individual substances or combinations of individual substances, each endowed with certain properties, both common and special, and each exerting various attractive and repulsive forces upon the others so as to determine the exact manner in which they moved and changed their motions. The substances themselves, Newton maintained, and their essences and real properties, even the real nature and foundation of the forces they exerted upon each other, could not be discerned by our senses nor discovered by logical analysis or intuitive insight.[4] But the actual existence of bodies was an obvious implication of ordinary sense experience; and the existence of forces and the manner in which they acted upon bodies was discoverable by careful observation and measurement of the phenomena that bodies exhibited to the senses. The order and operations of the laws of

4. *Principia* (London, 1713), p. 483.

nature were thus taken to be true descriptions of the effects of those forces that were universally present in material substances.

In "Natural Philosophy," Edwards attacked this conception of bodies through an analysis of that solidity or resistance which was counted as a universal and essential property of matter. He concluded that this infinite power of resistance could not reside in an underlying substance, but must be a constant exercise of the infinite power of God, so that

> it follows that the certain unknown substance, which philosophers used to think subsisted by itself, and stood underneath and kept up solidity and all other properties, and which they used to say it was impossible for a man to have an idea of, is nothing at all distinct from solidity itself; or, if they must needs apply that word to something else that does really and properly subsist by itself and support all properties, they must apply it to the divine Being or power itself. And here I believe all those philosophers would apply it, if they knew what they meant themselves.[5]

Edwards thus came to replace the standard Newtonian conception of bodies in their real nature with a wholly phenomenalistic view of the physical universe which nevertheless retained and emphasized its character as a Newtonian system. As Edwards developed his view he elaborated with increasing fullness the points that bodies were nothing but the ideas we immediately perceived by our senses, and that the essence of bodies consisted in their *relations* among these ideas as they were presented to us, and in the general laws governing these relations, their order and harmony, and their successive changes throughout the course of time.[6] "The secret lies here," Edwards writes in "The Mind" no. 13, a grand summary of his position:

> That which truly is the substance of all bodies is the infinitely exact and precise and perfectly stable idea in God's mind, together with his stable will that the same shall gradually be communicated to us, and to other minds, according to certain fixed and exact established methods and laws: or in somewhat different language, the infinitely exact and precise divine idea, together with an answerable, perfectly exact, precise and stable will with respect to corre-

5. "Of Atoms," prop. 2, corol. 11, in *Works, 6,* 215.
6. As discussed in Sang H. Lee, *The Philosophical Theology of Jonathan Edwards* (Princeton, Princeton Univ. Press, 1988), esp. pp. 48–55.

spondent communications to created minds, and effects on their minds.[7]

The ideas we perceive by our senses, Edwards held, are "excited" in our minds by God; and the laws of nature which govern the order of these ideas are the manner in which God determines to communicate his own perfect and stable ideas. Hence the regularities discoverable by a careful inspection of the order among observable phenomena are not evidence of the presence of unperceivable forces residing in the unknowable substrata of material things; they are the very essences of material things. The progress of science consists in the further discovery of such regularities and of the relations among them, until, in the end, every perceived fact about any material thing is to have its full and adequate explanation according to its place in the "complete ideal system of the world." And again, when we inquire into the causes of the phenomena and their apparent order, we are mistaken in supposing them to be unknown material substances acting upon our material sense organ. Their cause is the divine Being, who continually excites ideas in our minds in such a constantly changing series, but always according to fixed laws determining their order. In so doing, God constantly and variously communicates to us an idea that is fixed and entirely unchanging and eternal. It was thus that Edwards came to conceive the manner in which the physical sciences were to be perfected, and thus that he thought the perfection of them would issue in a fuller and more perfectly understood divinity.[8]

For Edwards, then, the similarity or dissimilarity between objects was due to their "proportion" or relation. Being was ultimately proportion, that is, the correspondence of mind and its modes of opera-

---

7. *Works*, 6, 344.

8. Perry Miller's assertion that the system of physical objects as treated and explained by Newton and Locke had equal authority for JE with Scripture needs clarification. (See the "Introduction" to *Images or Shadows of Divine Things* [New Haven, Yale Univ. Press, 1948], pp. 17ff.). When JE referred to the "perfection" of the arts and sciences that would issue in divinity, Miller understood him specifically to mean the arts and sciences of the eighteenth-century Enlightenment. More particularly, when JE referred to material things as types of the spiritual, Miller interpreted him as meaning the system of bodies and events that were properly understood only through Newtonian physics and were truly apprehended only in the manner explained by Locke. Miller overstated the influence of Newton and Locke upon JE's thought. His misunderstanding distorted his interpretation of the whole of JE's writing, but more particularly JE's claim that material and visible things were images, shadows, and types of spiritual ones.

While JE rejected Deism and Arminianism, he did not reject the arts and sciences of the Enlightenment in favor of the scholasticism of these antecedents—the physics of qualities

tion. And this was the basic point in Edwards' view that the physical
world existed as a "representation" or "shadow" of the spiritual world.
God, he held, created and governs the world according to established
rules of order and proportion, and in so doing he manifests his nature
and purpose in creation itself. Early on he refers to this notion of
"correspondency" in "The Mind" no. 1:

> That sort of beauty which is called "natural," as of vines, plants,
> trees, etc. consists of a very complicated harmony; and all the natu-
> ral motions and tendencies and figures of bodies in the universe
> are due according to proportion.... As bodies are shadows of be-
> ings, so their proportions are shadows of proportion.[9]

Edwards later incorporates this conviction in "Images" no. 79, where
he makes gravity itself integral to his relational view: "The whole
material universe is preserved by gravity, or attraction, or the mutual
tendency of all bodies to each other. One part of the universe is hereby
made beneficial to another.... This is a type of love or charity in the
spiritual world."[1]

Edwards' response to the "moral sense" writers, primarily Shaftesbury and Hutcheson, also illuminates how his view of the natural
world as analogous to the spiritual fit into his larger metaphysical
system. As such, it composed an important element in Edwards' defense of his thesis against the rationalists. The moralists' epistemology
posited that the reasoning mind could through nature discover what
Shaftesbury in his *Characteristicks* (1711) called "first beauty," or
"forming power," identified as the immediate recognition of true virtue.[2] But in later works such as *The Nature of True Virtue*, written in the

---

and powers and the psychology of faculties. When JE spoke of the perfection of the arts and
sciences, he did not suppose that Newton had achieved the perfection of physics. Even less
did he believe that Locke had established a true psychology and epistemology. In both cases,
he saw the perfection of the arts and sciences as requiring a major advance beyond Newton
and especially beyond Locke. It was through this further perfection that they would issue in
and coincide with the true divinity—that of the Westminister Confession and JE's Puritan
forebears. And it was to lay the foundation for this future perfection that JE devoted so
much of his writings. In fact, his thesis that material things were types of spiritual things
rested upon conceptions of the nature of both material and spiritual worlds that JE developed in his advance beyond Newton and Locke.

9. *Works, 6,* 335.
1. See above p. 81.
2. See Norman Fiering, *Jonathan Edwards's Moral Thought and Its British Context* (Chapel
Hill, Univ. of North Carolina Press, 1981), pp. 106–27; and Stanley Grean, *Shaftesbury's
Philosophy of Religion and Ethics: A Study in Enthusiasm* (Columbus, Ohio State Univ. Press,
1967), pp. 50–51, 65.

1750s but published after his death, Edwards sought to demonstrate his long-standing conviction that the "moral sense" that was being described was actually a secondary sort of cognition, and that naturalist aesthetics pertained merely to the world of types.[3] What Edwards considered to be "first," or "primary," beauty was the spiritual world that the typical world shadowed forth, and the ability to discern primary beauty given only to the regenerate. His distinction of beauty into primary and secondary was characteristic of his theology: Being-in-general was primary, spiritual, and, ultimately, divine; being-as-manifest was secondary, corporeal, and only a reflection of God. Edwards subsumed Hutcheson's aesthetics into his larger view, characterized by the aesthetic of consent or relation, that the entire material world could be interpreted in terms of spiritual reality. In short, what the moralists attributed to the moral sense, or nature, Edwards attributed to the new spiritual "sense," or grace, given in regeneration.[4]

One of the alternative names that Edwards gave to "Images of Divine Things" was "The Book of Nature and *Common* Providence,"[5] implying that nature was not the repository of saving grace, nor to be worshipped as an "image" of God, but was full of the "emanations, or shadows, of the excellencies of the Son of God."[6] Hence Edwards had no difficulty in positing the representative beauty and significance of the natural world in "Images" and "Types," while elsewhere, especially in his weekly sermons, describing in an eminently Calvinist manner how creation and humanity were forever despoiled by sin. The apparent contradiction can be resolved in his perception of bodies as not subsisting as separate realities. The beauties of the natural world, as they were the "shadows of being" or reflections of the divine beauty of God, could be used as guides to the presence and purpose of God, for God's intention in creating was to exercise and communicate his perfections to spirits, which were "properly beings."[7] Edwards concludes in "Images" no. 212, "The immense magnificence of the visible world,

---

3. In *Ethical Writings*, ed. Paul Ramsey, in *The Works of Jonathan Edwards* (New Haven, Yale Univ. Press, 1989), *8*, 35–37, 561–74, esp. 561–62.

4. For more on "spiritual understanding" in JE, see Fiering, *Jonathan Edwards's Moral Thought*, pp. 123–29; and "Editor's Introduction," *Religious Affections*, ed. John E. Smith, in *The Works of Jonathan Edwards* (New Haven, Yale Univ. Press, 1959), *2*, 30–35. On the elect's heightened capacity to read types, see Lowance, *The Language of Canaan*, pp. 253–72.

5. Ed. italics.

6. "Miscellanies" no. 108.

7. Roland A. Delattre, *Beauty and Sensibility in the Thought of Jonathan Edwards* (New Haven, Yale Univ. Press, 1968), pp. 176–83.

its inconceivable vastness, the incomprehensible height of the heavens, etc. is but a type of the infinite magnificence, height and glory of God's work in the spiritual world...."[8]

## THE ANGLO-CATHOLIC TRADITION

At another point on the field, at a far remove from the Deists and rationalists, were the Catholic and Anglican exegetes who, to Edwards' mind, were "for turning all into nothing but allegory and not having it to be true history." Catholic dogma was perceived by Reformed exegetes as interpreting the whole of Scripture as mere divine pedagogy, or the mere presentation of truths, rather than the fulfillment of promises and the effective introduction of a new dispensation for humanity through Christ's sacrifice and resurrection. Edwards' knowledge of Catholic exegesis was probably drawn from secondary sources rather than actual exposure to the works of Catholic writers, but that was enough to confirm him in his opinions of Catholicism. In his scriptural and apocalyptic notebooks, Edwards, a vigorous anti-Catholic, collected evidence of the supposedly declining state of the Catholic church as it related to the progress of redemptive history.[9]

A source related to Catholic exegesis, and more accessible to Edwards, was the literature of the High Church Anglicans, those who, since the Henrician reforms, had been in favor of restoring the Church of England in conformity with pre-Nicean Catholicism. In Edwards' time, the early seventeenth-century preachers such as Lancelot Andrewes, John Donne, and the other "witty" writers were still highly regarded, though their influence was being challenged by the ethical preaching of Archbishop John Tillotson and his emulators. With their emphasis on metaphysical interpretation and the "four senses" of exegesis—the "letter," the analogic, the moral, and the prophetic—the High Church Anglicans represented a return to the allegorizing of the Old Learning in reaction to the literal exposition that had characterized the Puritan Commonwealth.[1] It is possible,

---

8. See above pp. 129–30.

9. See, for instance, Stephen J. Stein, "Cotton Mather and Jonathan Edwards on the Number of the Beast: Eighteenth-Century Speculation about the Antichrist," *Proceedings of the American Antiquarian Society*, 84 (1974), 293–315; see also his introduction to *The Works of Jonathan Edwards, 5, Apocalyptic Writings* (New Haven, Yale Univ. Press, 1977), 48–74.

1. W. Fraser Mitchell, *English Pulpit Oratory From Andrewes to Tillotson: A Study of Its Literary Aspects* (London, Society for Promoting Christian Knowledge, 1932), pp. 146–48.

therefore, that if Edwards did not specifically intend this tradition as those who are "for turning all into nothing but allegory," he most likely would have included it under such a rubric.

Finally, Edwards could also have had in mind the general direction that scriptural exegesis and pulpit discourse was taking in the early eighteenth century. The definite emphasis in England—and the growing one in New England—was on rational, ethical homiletics; commentators and preachers sought a way between the dogmatism that had characterized the Puritan era and the enthusiasm of more recent evangelicals. For preachers of the Tillotsonian approach, eschewing the literal historical verity of Scripture encouraged a spirit of tolerance—a key theme of Anglo-American exegesis and preaching in this period.[2]

Edwards' response to the Catholic and High Church Anglican writers was largely shaped by the principles of the Reformation. Granted that allegory was called for in interpreting certain books of the Bible— for example, Puritans produced a substantial number of works on Canticles alone, and the book was one of Edwards' favorites—but Scripture and the historical sense had to be the touchstone in drawing any conclusions. Edwards would have found forced and full of "human invention" the tropes and allegories of such preachers as Lancelot Andrewes, Jeremy Taylor, and John Donne. Their approach violated the parameters of the typological method as Edwards knew it and, in his opinion, was ineffective in plumbing the true depths of divine meaning and communication to be found in natural phenomena.

The rhetorical excesses that the allegorical method gave rise to also disturbed Edwards. In the stylistic notes that he wrote on the cover of "Natural Philosophy," for instance, Edwards directed himself to "use as few terms of art as possible"; later, in the preface to his first volume of published sermons, he rejected "elegance of style" for an "unpolished dress."[3] His own approach fused the Ramistic simplicity of the Cambridge Platonists and the "primitive purity" found in the sermons of Tillotson,[4] without question the most copied preacher in early

---

2. James Downey, *The Eighteenth-Century Pulpit: A Study of the Sermons of Butler, Berkeley, Secker, Sterne, Whitefield and Wesley* (Oxford, Clarendon, 1969), pp. 1–29, esp. pp. 13–15.

3. Cover-leaf memoranda in "Natural Philosophy," *Works*, 6, 195; *Discourses on Various Important Subjects, Nearly concerning the great Affair of the Soul's Eternal Salvation* (Boston, 1738), p. v.

4. Mitchell, *English Pulpit Oratory From Andrewes to Tillotson*, pp. 308–12; Harold P. Simonson, *Jonathan Edwards: Theologian of the Heart* (Macon, Georgia, Mercer Univ. Press, 1982), pp. 93–95.

eighteenth-century English homiletics. Tillotson's rhetoric represented a resurgence of the "plain style," the old Puritan mode of pulpit
discourse that had emphasized an unadorned and non-academic rhetoric. It was these stylistic standards that Edwards brought to his elu-
cidation of the types.

The plain style no longer dominated the New England of Edwards'
day as it had in the days of early preachers like John Cotton, Thomas
Shepard, and Thomas Hooker. Because such important figures as
these had employed typology, through the years a range of typological
and figural innovations were introduced into the literature of the
province. Just as the early reformers had allowed allegorical readings,
so those who shared with Edwards his Puritan heritage experimented
with other "senses" besides the strictly literal. For example, divines like
Increase Mather and laypersons such as Samuel Sewall considered
certain events—earthquakes, epidemics, and other traumatic natural
occurrences—as "illustrative providences," or means by which God
made his will known to his covenant people. In addition, third-
generation New England leaders, notably Cotton Mather in his *Magnalia Christi Americana* (1702), reasserted the typological method originated by founders such as John Cotton and John Winthrop to show
that the settlers of New England were antitypes of the biblical Israel.
These approaches constituted evident—and permissible—expansions
of the prevalent patterns of interpretation.[5]

Other New England clergymen tested the bounds of the method in
attempting to formulate their own typological perspective. Edward
Taylor, the parson-poet of Westfield, Massachusetts, avoided the New
Israel typology of his contemporaries in favor of the stricter exegesis
of exact correspondences between the testaments. But in seeking a
typological language in his sermons and poetry that was metaphysical,
personal, and meditative, he employed not only the conventional historical method but also allegory and tropology.[6] Beside the figurative
prophesies of Scripture, he had no qualms about employing a system
of extra-prophetic, but divinely ordained, figures and emblems, on
the order of the poems of the seventeenth-century English writer,
Francis Quarles.

5. Sacvan Bercovitch, "New England Epic: Cotton Mather's *Magnalia Christi Americana*,"
*English Literary History*, 33 (1966), 337–51, and Mason I. Lowance, Jr., "Typology and the
New England Way: Cotton Mather and the Exegesis of Biblical Types," *Early American
Literature*, 4 (1969), 15–37.
6. Edward Taylor, *Upon the Types of the Old Testament*, ed. Charles W. Mignon (2 vols.,
Lincoln, Univ. of Nebraska Press, 1989), *1*, xl–xliii.

In a related vein were the "spiritualizers" to whom Edwards referred and whose works were popular in early eighteenth-century Anglo-America. Chief among the spiritualizers was the nonconformist divine John Flavel, whose writings Edwards respected and used but did not accept unquestioningly. In his most famous work, *Husbandry Spiritualized*, Flavel began not with Scripture but with nature as a place to find God's revealed will. *"The irrational and inanimate, as well as rational creatures,"* he wrote, *"preach unto man the wisdom, Power, and goodness of God."*[7] One conspicuous attempt to emulate Flavel was Cotton Mather's *Agricola* (1727), which combined the use of metaphorical analogies with traditional biblical typology.[8] Edwards, however, sufficed with only a note to himself (in "Images" no. 164) to make use of some of Flavel's specific scriptural illustrations.

But Edwards' favorable attitude towards the figural use of nature was not only the result of his Reformed emphasis on scriptural verity, his efforts to achieve the new plain style of the Tillotsonian sermon, or the diversity of an evolving New England Puritanism; it also stemmed from his study of Locke's empiricist psychology and his accompanying view of language.[9] In Book III of the *Essay Concerning Human Understanding*, Locke stated that words were assigned to represent certain ideas for the sake of convenience and expediency. *"Words in their primary or immediate Signification,"* he wrote, *"stand for nothing, but the Ideas in the Mind of him that uses them."* However, the ideas that a given word excited in one person's mind could be different from what it excited in another's. Because we concentrate more on words than on the ideas behind them, the ability to convey our thoughts concisely and accurately is hampered. "Nay," Locke continued, "because Words are many of them learn'd, before the *Ideas* are known for which they stand: Therefore some, not only Children, but Men, speak several Words, no otherwise than Parrots do."[1]

Edwards agreed with Locke that the meanings of words could easily degrade, but he thought Locke's conception of language was wrong-

7. John Flavel, *Husbandry Spiritualized: Or, the Heavenly Use of Earthly Things* (3rd ed. London, 1654; rep. Boston, 1709), "Epistle Dedicatory."

8. Lowance, *The Language of Canaan*, p. 176.

9. On JE, Locke, and language, see Perry Miller, "The Rhetoric of Sensation," in *Errand into the Wilderness* (Cambridge, Belknap Press, 1956), pp. 167–83; Edward H. Davidson, "From Locke to Edwards," *Journal of the History of Ideas*, 24 (1963), 355–72; and Paul M. Baumgartner, "Jonathan Edwards: The Theory Behind His Use of Figurative Language," *Proceedings of the Modern Language Association*, 78 (1963), 321–25.

1. *An Essay Concerning Human Understanding*, bk. III, ch. II, §1, 7.

headed. Addressing Locke's arguments, Edwards writes in "The Mind" no. 43:

> Many of our universal ideas are not arbitrary. The tying of ideas together in genera and species is not merely the calling of them by the same name, but such an union of them that the consideration of one shall naturally excite the idea of others. But the union of ideas is not always arbitrary, but unavoidably arising from the nature of the soul, which is such that the thinking of one thing, of itself, yea, against our wills, excites the thought of other things that are like it.[2]

Edwards departed from Locke when he stated that ideas were excited in us by God, rather than by external bodies acting on our organs of sense. Moreover, when used correctly, Edwards affirmed, words could excite not only ideas in the mind but also affections in the heart.

Edwards goes on in "The Mind" no. 43 to argue for certain innate, even semiotic capacities of the mind to arrange sensory experiences and make associations between them. His integrative psychology led him to posit that the interpretation of words or images, when based on actual experience and the guidance of the Spirit, could be done not only literally but also anagogically.[3] Because of a pre-existent "agreement in things," words as images had the power to excite a chain of associations. This power enabled the mind to make the imaginative and aesthetic connection between the material world—the world of types—and the spiritual world. In short, it was through the typological application of words and images based on actual experience that Edwards saw a more effective means to demonstrate spiritual truths than by more and more extravagant figures and allegories.

### THE CABALISTS

Yet another reference point for Edwards in defending his typology was Cabala, a Judaic discipline that involved ciphering mystic meanings from particular letters that composed names. This method of interpretation, which can be traced to the seventh century, was experiencing its last period of productivity during Edwards' lifetime. Cabala's precise impact upon Christianity is difficult to assess, but the

---

2. *Works*, 6, 361.
3. See Simonson, *Jonathan Edwards: Theologian of the Heart*, 95–110.

similarities it shares with Christianity are understandably numerous, among them, belief in a triune God, creation *ex nihilo*, the immortality of the soul, and future rewards and punishments.

Edwards could draw on a long line of Christian scholars with more than passing familiarity with cabalistic teachings and techniques, including Erasmus, Thomas More, and Jean Bodin. During the seventeenth century, the English university-men Edward Pocoke and John Lightfoot were instrumental in translating cabalistic works, and John Donne, who was fascinated with cabalistic interpretation, incorporated them frequently in his sermons; on the continent, the elder and younger Buxtorf likewise produced translations, and Leibniz shared an interest in Cabalism. Closer to Edwards' own time, Jacque Basnage's *History of the Jews* (1708), a work cited several times in "Types of the Messiah," contains a lengthy account of Cabala. And in his *Religion of Nature Delineated* (1724)—another book on Edwards' reading list— William Wollaston demonstrated his accomplishments as a scholar of rabbinism.[4]

It is important not to over-emphasize the explicit influence of Cabala and related traditions on Edwards. Cabalistic ideas were often acquired through second- or third-hand sources, and were so mingled with the general intellectual attitudes and approaches of the period that scholars often did not recognize or inquire after their origins. Yet Cabalism as a discipline was attractive to theologians with a mystical bent, such as Boehme in Germany and the Cambridge Platonists in England. In New England, it is not surprising to find the versatile Cotton Mather dabbling in numerical significations. While Edwards himself had little use for such techniques, his statement in "Types" demonstrates his familiarity with rabbinical teachings, and doubtless he utilized them when they conformed to his own Christian worldview.[5]

4. See Bernard Pick, *The Cabala: Its Influence on Judaism and Christianity* (Chicago, Open Court Pub., 1913), pp. 3–4; and Alexander Altman, "William Wollaston: English Deist and Rabbinical Scholar," in *Studies in Religious Philosophy and Mysticism* (Ithaca, N.Y., Cornell Univ. Press, 1969), pp. 210–45. In supplementing his studies of "Prophecies of the Messiah" and "Fulfillment of the Prophecies of the Messiah" with instances of rabbinical interpretation, JE also relied on Johannes Stapfer's *Institutiones Theologiæ Polemicæ* (5 vols., Tiguri, 1743–47; rep. 1757) and Hugo Grotius' *De Veritate Christianæ* (Amsterdam, 1622).

5. Joseph P. Schultz, "The Lurianic Strand in Jonathan Edwards' Concept of Progress," *Judaica*, 30 (1974), 126–34. See also Schultz' "The Religious Psychology of Jonathan Edwards and the Hassadic Masters of Habad," *Journal of Ecumenical Studies*, 10 (1973), 716–27.

Edwards' conviction of the power and significance of words helps explain why he felt it necessary to consider Cabala·in formulating his "medium" way. His notebooks give evidence of his interest in this and related traditions as well as his own application of the mystical approach. For example, an early entry in the "Catalogue," under the heading "Books to be inquired for," reads, "the best that treats of the cabalistic learning of the Jews" (p. 4, no. 56). Entries elsewhere in his reading list include such standards as the Hebrew Bible, "the Chaldee Paraphrast," and the works of Moses Maimonides (p. 2, nos. 26–27, 29). The presence of Philo (p. 2, no. 28) and Josephus (p. 11, no. 4) in Edwards' reading even hints at an interest in Hermeticism, which taught that the Greeks had inherited their philosophy from the Jews and so anticipated Christian teachings. Edwards was by no means alone in this pursuit, for the Puritan tradition cultivated the hermetic approach.[6]

Edwards did attach certain import to the permutation of names in the Old and New Testament. He states in "Images" nos. 30 and 132 that God teaches "divine mysteries by the signification of persons' names." In addition, the third section of "Types of the Messiah" is devoted to supplying examples of such significations.[7] Reflective of his renewed interest in linguistics late in life, Edwards even kept a book of "Hebrew Idioms."[8]

As we have noted, Edwards differed at some points with Locke in his conception of language. By contrast, it is easy to see how Edwards was interested in the cabalistic approach, since its views of reality and language had affinities with his own in several respects. Like the cabalists, Edwards portrayed reality as the emanation, the "breathing forth," of God. He no doubt was attracted to the cabalistic apprehension that word and idea were somehow unified in an epistemological, metaphysical, and even ontological sense, and conveyed the larger, underlying unity of God and creation. As Edwards writes in an important passage in the "Types" notebook, "Types are a certain sort of language, as it were, in which God is wont to speak to us."[9] For Edwards, whose metaphysics verged on an outright rejection of Aris-

---

6. See Frances A. Yates, *The Occult Philosophy in the Elizabethan Age* (London, Routledge and Kegan Paul, 1979); and Daniel Walker Howe, "The Cambridge Platonists of Old England and the Cambridge Platonists of New England," *Church History*, 57 (Dec. 1988), 472.

7. See above pp. 294–305.

8. Beinecke Library, f. 34.

9. See above p. 150.

totelianism, cabalistic techniques may well have provided some intriguing clues towards conceptualizing the subsistence of everything in God.

## THE DISSENTERS

Among the main objections to his extensive system of representations that Edwards could anticipate, some would come from the community of dissenting and Reformed theologians to which he and his fellow New England ministers belonged. According to the theory of scriptural typology that was commonly shared among them, certain persons, objects, places, institutions, and events that have had an actual place in history were in fact ordained by God to signify and represent Christ and his work of spiritual redemption. This was assured, they held, by the testimony of the New Testament, in which certain things in the Old Testament record were specifically referred to as types of the gospel revelation. Hence Edwards was on firm ground when he asserted in "Images" no. 48 that the Jewish tabernacle was a type of the spiritual gospel tabernacle, and that the manna with which God sustained the Israelites in the desert was a type of the Christ.

The fundamentally divergent hermeneutical approaches that separated Deists from Reformed did not obtain between Edwards and the Dissenters, but there were differences nonetheless. According to the established view, the domain of types did not extend beyond the history presented in the Old Testament. Samuel Mather, whose *Figures or Types of the Old Testament* (1683) was accepted in New England as a standard authority, and was listed in Edwards' "Catalogue" (p. i, no. 43), incorporated this restriction into his very definition: "*A Type is some outward or sensible thing ordained of God under the Old Testament, to represent and hold forth something of Christ in the New.*" Every type, Mather held, must be interpreted not only as a figure having a spiritual meaning, but as a figurative prophecy that was to be fulfilled in the person of Christ and the New Testament gospel. "We must look beyond the Shadow, to the Substance, to the Truth and the Mystery of it: And this is Christ and the Gospel, as future, and hereafter to be exhibited." Mather formed this account of the types from passages of Scripture, and argued that it was essential to a correct understanding of the relation between the Old and New Testament revelations of the gospel, and between the Old and the New Dispensations of God toward humankind. "Men must not *indulge their own Fancies*," he cautioned, "as the Popish Writers use to do, with their Allegorical Senses, as they call them; except we have some Scripture ground for it. It is not safe to make any thing a Type meerly upon our own fansies and imaginations...."[1]

In light of Mather's restriction, Edwards would have been charged with erroneous excess by many of his New England colleagues when he asserted, for instance, that vines as found in nature were types of Christ, and that the risings and settings of the sun, as they daily occurred, were types of the death and resurrection of Christ. Not only were these and many other expressions contrary to Mather's understanding of the express teaching of Scripture concerning the types, but Edwards' wholesale extension of the typological system would be understood as implying that much of nature and human experience had an equal footing with the Old Testament, and with some of the New Testament, as authoritative and authentic revelations of the tenets of the Christian faith. Despite Edwards' efforts to establish his extended typology on scriptural bases, his general thesis would most likely have been construed as inviting and even demanding that exegetes abandon the guidance of Scripture in their search for interpretations, especially in cases of natural phenomena that were nowhere discussed in the Bible.

Reformed theologians also would have viewed Edwards' thesis as tenuous with regard to the dogmatic Calvinist view of creation. They allowed that the universe bore the "stamp" of God, but the ability of the human mind to discern the image of God in creation had been disrupted by the Fall of Adam. Because the creation was marred by the introduction of sin, the reliability of nature as a means of understanding God and his ways was extremely suspect. Only to the converted was the "book of nature" laid open, but even then sin prevented the complete comprehension that would be made plain at the day of judgment. Edwards' private writings reveal his efforts to make his expanded typology, couched in the language of relation, conform with doctrine. In the list of "Scriptures" appended to "Images," for example, water at one time represents trouble, while at another divine grace (nos. [12], [28]). In "The Beauty of the World"[2] and "Miscellanies" no. 108, Edwards portrays things in nature as so many transparent "emanations of the sweet benevolences of Jesus Christ" by virtue of their "mutual consents" and "agreeablenesses." But in "Miscellanies" no.

1. Samuel Mather, *The Figures or Types of the Old Testament*, ed. Mason I. Lowance, Jr. (New York, Johnson Reprint Corp., 1969), pp. 52, 55.
2. Printed in *Works*, 6, 305–07.

182, recognizing that sin entails the lack of consent, he qualifies his view by stating that beauty is necessarily obscured in being embodied: "hereby the ravishingness of the beauty is much obscured, and our sense of it flattened and deadened."

The "Types" notebook, along with "Types of the Messiah," seems especially geared toward answering the objections of the literalist and historicist critics of Edwards' view. Edwards agreed with Samuel Mather that the explicating of types must always be done with an eye towards Scripture. Echoing Mather, he recognized the danger of untrained persons designating and interpreting types drawn from nature. In the "Types" notebook, he explicitly cautioned that "persons ought to be exceeding careful in interpreting of types, that they don't give way to a wild fancy; not to fix an interpretation unless warranted by some hint in the New Testament of its being the true interpretation...."[3]

While Scripture remained Edwards' guide for designating types, it nonetheless left certain avenues open, and he affirmed that it was not untoward to explore them. The literal sense itself comprehended a variety of meanings, most important of which was the "spiritual."[4]

> When we are sufficiently instructed that all these things were typical and had their spiritual significance, it would be on some accounts as unreasonable to say that we must interpret no more of them than the Scripture has interpreted for us, and than we are told the meaning of in the New Testament, as it would be to say that we must interpret prophecy, or prophetical visions and types, no further than the Scripture has interpreted it to our hand.[5]

If, Edwards argued, types are "a certain sort of language" that God has taught believers in Scripture, then believers need not confine themselves to explicit correspondences. Even more, such literalism would have prevented believers under the Old Dispensation from searching for the meanings of the types.

> If we may use our own understandings and invention not at all in interpreting types, and must not conclude anything at all to be

3. See above p. 148.
4. See Stephen J. Stein, "The Quest for the Spiritual Sense: The Biblical Hermeneutics of Jonathan Edwards," *Harvard Theological Review*, 70 (1977), 99–113; and "Jonathan Edwards and the Rainbow: Biblical Exegesis and Poetic Imagination," *New England Quarterly*, 47 (1974), 440–56, esp. pp. 453–56.
5. See above pp. 146–47.

types but what is expressly said to be and explained in Scripture, then the church under the Old Testament, when the types were given, were secluded from ever using their understanding to search into the meaning of the types given to 'em; for God did, when he gave 'em, give no interpretation.[6]

Such were the objections Edwards had in mind when he assembled and interpreted evidence from Scripture to support his view. He took it as undisputed that certain things in the Old Testament were indeed types of the New Testament revelation; they were expressly pointed out by the New Testament authors themselves. But, he argued, it would be unreasonable to say "that we must not say that such things are types of these and those things unless the Scripture has expressly taught us that they are so."[7] But what kind of evidence was to be found in the New Testament to assure that the objects and phenomena of nature at large were indeed types of spiritual and divine things? Edwards' most explicit answer to this question seems to be that given in "Miscellanies" no. 362: the evidence consists in "spiritual things being so often and continually compared with them in the Word of God."

Many passages in "Images" and "Types" are devoted to presenting and discussing scriptural evidence of this sort. Edwards, for example, cites several texts that compare God's goodness with a river in "Images" no. 15, and others that compare misery with water in no. 27. From this and other instances it is clear that he was prepared to accept a wide range of scriptural metaphors and similes as evidence of the typological import of natural phenomena. Other passages, however, indicate that Edwards distinguished between purely illustrative metaphors and genuine types. He pointed out that certain comparisons in Scriptures were not used merely to illustrate a spiritual meaning, but were introduced as evidence and argument for a spiritual reality or truth.[8] In "Images" no. 45, Edwards quotes several passages from the New Testament which he considers as evidence that "natural things were ordered for types of spiritual things." The central clue he found in these passages lay not in any explicit or implied reference to the Old Testament history, nor in the fact alone that spiritual things were compared with natural ones, but in the further point that the spiritual things in these comparisons were said to be "true" with respect to the

6. See above p. 150.
7. See above p. 152.
8. "Images" nos. 7, 20, 22, and 26.

natural ones. "This was the true light," or "I am the true vine," are such examples. Edwards comments, "Things are thus said to be true in Scripture in contradistinction to what is typical. The type is only the representation or shadow of the thing, but the antitype is the very substance and is the true thing."[9]

Whereas more conservative exegetes like Samuel Mather would deny that God had ordained the objects in nature at large to be types, Edwards argued the contrary from certain metaphors in Scripture. The evidence did not consist in Scripture's use of them to assert and argue for the substantial reality and truth of those spiritual things. Whatever the intrinsic merits of these arguments, it was clear that they ignored the point that a type was essentially prophetic, and that it anticipated and promised the antitype that was to come. In Edwards' view, so far as these arguments reveal it, the essence of a type consisted instead in a certain metaphysical relation to its antitype. The type actually and literally existed, but it was not, by itself, a true and substantial thing. It was only a representation or "shadow" of some real and spiritual thing—its antitype. The scriptural metaphors and other comparisons that Edwards cited in his arguments were evidence for a typological connection just because, as he interpreted them, they expressed or implied such a metaphysical connection between the "true" spiritual realities and the "shadowy" natural things that were compared.

It is an open question, of course, how far the Reformed critics of Edwards' typology would have been satisfied with such arguments or with the metaphysical interpretation of Scripture upon which they seemed to depend. But even if they had no objections upon these points, it is evident that they would have found Edwards' arguments from the testimony of Scripture to be insufficient for his conclusions. At best, such arguments would only have shown that certain kinds of objects and phenomena in nature, those which were variously alluded to in Scripture, were types of spiritual things pertaining to Christ. In a number of cases in "Images of Divine Things," Edwards correlates spiritual things with objects and phenomena that are not alluded to in the Bible at all. For conservatives like Mather, the suggestion that the way in which serpents lured their prey represented the way in which Satan captured human souls, or that the invention of the telescope was a harbinger of the approaching glorious times of the Christian church,

9. "Images" no. 45.

or that the fact that water cannot rise by itself above the level of its source signifies a limited human capacity for self-improvement, went beyond the testimony of Scripture.[1] If such cases were to be considered more than the fictions of a "very fruitful brain and copious fancy," Edwards had to depend for their justification upon independent facts of observation and principles of reasonable inference.

*   *   *

In "Images of Divine Things" and "Types," Edwards set down and amplified biblical, natural, and historical examples of correspondence between the material and natural world. From scattered statements in the entries it is clear that he was developing a conception of typology that conformed to his view of the natural world: just as "the whole outward creation... is but the shadow of beings," so it also represents "spiritual things."

Edwards anticipated that his view would be challenged on all sides. In formulating his position, he explicitly identified three distinguishable groups, each with its own interpretative orientation. The first included the rationalists, Lockeans, and Deists, all part of the new and growing "fashionable" divinity. Due to their disparagement of revelation and prophecy in favor of reason, those under this rubric dismissed typology out of hand as illogical. Secondly were Catholics and High Church Anglicans, who desired to perpetuate the old methods of allegorization in their sermons. Finally came those from the cabalist tradition. With its mystical recognition of the unity of God and creation, "the way of the rabbis" no doubt held a certain intellectual curiosity for Edwards. Another group that Edwards implicitly addressed was the Reformed evangelicals, those who shared with him his heritage of Puritan dissent. With their typological approach based on the literal, historical sense, those in this camp would have objected to Edwards' expansion of types beyond Scripture into the natural world.

Edwards answered each group according to their own devices. With the rationalists he discoursed in a philosophical and logical manner, delineating the nature of being and seeking to demonstrate that God was the only real substance, of which the entire natural world was an analogue. He critiqued the failure of the Catholics and Anglicans to understand the nature of language as a guide to spiritual truth. The

---

1. "Images" nos. 11, 63, 87, and 95.

cabalists he could fault for what he held to be their exaggerated apprehensions of the signification of reality. And to the Reformed, Edwards responded with scriptural arguments, showing that the Bible itself sanctioned interpretation beyond explicit types.

Edwards' approach, as preserved most fully in "Images of Divine Things" and the notebook on "Types," represented an important innovation in Christian typology and philosophy. Edwards attempted to free typology from the narrow correspondences of the two testaments without reverting to exaggerated medieval allegory. In the process, he transcended philosophical dualism, linking the natural and the supernatural in a compelling and dynamic unity in God.

# NOTE ON THE MANUSCRIPT OF
## "IMAGES OF DIVINE THINGS"

"I MAGES of Divine Things" belongs to the Yale collection of Edwards' manuscripts. It is a 48-page folio volume, sewn into a cover of heavy gray paper. The main series of 212 numbered entries is contained on pages 3–38 of the volume; the separately numbered list of seven scripture images that follows is found on page 41. Except for the jottings on the inside of the front cover, the other pages of the volume are blank. There are also two tables or indexes prepared by Edwards for the main series, which are kept loose inside the rear cover. The earlier of these is on a shortened folio leaf, the later on a folded full sheet of paper. The manuscript volume has been paginated, but the two tables are not; the page numbers are in pencil, and have apparently been added by a recent hand.[1]

"Images of Divine Things" is the latest of the titles Edwards adopted for the work. The abbreviated forms of "Images of Div." and "Images of D." are written in four places on the outside of the cover of the volume, and Edwards used this title in other writings when referring to later entries in the series.[2] He began the work, however, with the title "Shadows of Divine Things," which is written at the top of the first page of entries. This earlier title was used at least as late as the writing of "Images" no. 58 in late 1737, for it is found in the reference to no. 58 which Edwards added to "Miscellanies" no. 370.[3] The fact that "Images" no. 118, probably written in 1741, is introduced with the formal heading, "Images of Divine Things," suggests that this was the point at

1. According to Thomas Schafer, the MS still lacked page numbers in 1945. It was probably paginated for Perry Miller when he was preparing his edition of the notebook.

2. E.g. in three notes in JE's "Blank Bible" which he cross-referenced with "Images" no. 141. The "Blank Bible" is a MS composed of the pages of the Old and New Testament separated and rebound between leaves of foolscap on which he wrote notes upon the texts of Scripture. The MS is in the Beinecke Library.

3. The passage in question is quoted below, p. 51, n. 6. JE's "Blank Bible" note on Luke 23:44 also gives the earlier title in citing "Images" no. 54 (see below, pp. 64–65, n. 2).

which Edwards changed the title of the series. Two other titles are among the jottings on page 2 of the manuscript: "The Book of Nature and Common Providences," and "The Language and Lessons of Nature." The hand and ink of these two approximate that in "Images" no. 123, which was probably written during the winter of 1741–42. Neither of these titles appears to have been used by Edwards in referring to this series. He probably jotted them down at a time when he was only contemplating possible titles for the series, or for a work he might have thought of publishing from it.

The Andover collection contains a hand-written transcription, in the hand of Sereno Dwight, of seventy-five "Images" selected from the series.[4] Dwight did not publish these selections, however, and nowhere mentions the manuscript. In 1940 Harvey Townsend published several substantial excerpts from the manuscript,[5] but the only complete edition of "Images of Divine Things" published previous to this one was edited by Perry Miller, and it appeared in 1948.[6]

Like most of Edwards' other manuscript notebooks, this volume was formed by successive additions of paper from time to time as needed for continuing the series. In some cases, the new paper was inserted between leaves of the already formed component. The final arrangement of the sheets and leaves of the manuscript, with their distinguishing watermarks, is shown in Fig. 1.

The stages by which Edwards produced the manuscript are as follows: He began on a single folded sheet of English/GR$^{wr}$ paper, writing "Images" nos. 1–57.[7] Then he added a second separately folded sheet of London/GR paper for nos. 58 through the first part of no. 77. The shortened folio leaf he used for the first table has the countermark of this paper. By the time the second sheet was filled, Edwards had formed a quire of four infolded sheets of London/GR$^{wr}$ paper, and inserted the two separately folded sheets in their original order between the first and second leaves of this quire. The series from the second part of no. 77 through the beginning of no. 97 fills the second, third, and fourth leaves to the center of the quire, where Edwards

4. Heavy "X" marks in the margins of the MS, both through the main series and next to many of the subject entries in the two tables, correspond to the entries in Dwight's transcription.

5. Harvey Townsend, "Jonathan Edwards' Later Observations of Nature," *New England Quarterly*, 13 (1940), 510–18. Hereafter cited as "JE's Later Observations."

6. *Images or Shadows of Divine Things*, which is a composite of JE's earlier and later titles.

7. The sheet is of the same mold as the two sheets of that paper in the "Miscellanies," containing nos. 328–358.

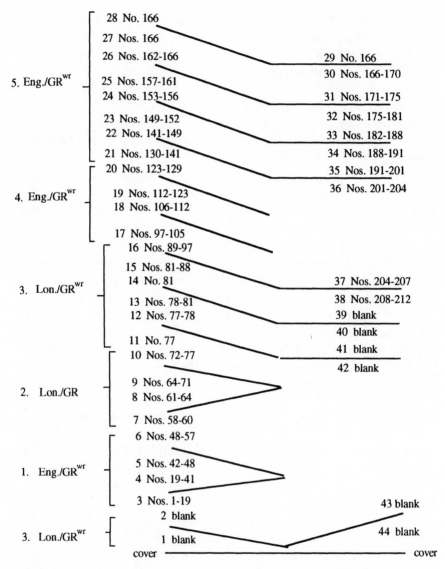

28 No. 166
27 Nos. 166
26 Nos. 162-166
29 No. 166
30 Nos. 166-170
5. Eng./GR$^{wr}$
25 Nos. 157-161
24 Nos. 153-156
31 Nos. 171-175
23 Nos. 149-152
32 Nos. 175-181
22 Nos. 141-149
33 Nos. 182-188
21 Nos. 130-141
34 Nos. 188-191
20 Nos. 123-129
35 Nos. 191-201
36 Nos. 201-204
4. Eng./GR$^{wr}$
19 Nos. 112-123
18 Nos. 106-112
17 Nos. 97-105
16 Nos. 89-97
15 Nos. 81-88
3. Lon./GR$^{wr}$
14 No. 81
37 Nos. 204-207
13 Nos. 78-81
38 Nos. 208-212
12 Nos. 77-78
39 blank
40 blank
11 No. 77
41 blank
10 Nos. 72-77
42 blank
9 Nos. 64-71
2. Lon./GR
8 Nos. 61-64
7 Nos. 58-60
6 Nos. 48-57
5 Nos. 42-48
1. Eng./GR$^{wr}$
4 Nos. 19-41
3 Nos. 1-19
43 blank
2 blank
3. Lon./GR$^{wr}$
44 blank
1 blank
cover ————————————————— cover

Fig. 1. "Images of Divine Things": Structure of the Manuscript.
The diagram gives an exploded view of a lateral cross-section of the MS with the leaves fanned out. The entries on each page are indicated. Groupings to the left are according to watermarks, which are numbered in the order in which JE added the paper to the MS. The earliest apparent period from which each group dates is as follows: 1) late 1728, 2) late 1737, 3) mid-1738, 4) early 1740, and 5) early 1742. The MS also includes two tables (not pictured here), inserted at the rear of the volume but never stitched in: the earlier is a shortened folio made of the same London/GR paper as no. 2; the latter is a folded sheet made of the same English/GR$^{wr}$ paper as in nos. 4 and No. 5.

made his last additions of paper. These consist of two single leaves followed by five infolded full sheets, a mixture of various sorts of English/GR[wr] papers.[8] From their appearance in his dated sermons, Edwards had a supply of all these papers on hand at about the same time; he might have added the two leaves and the five sheets to "Images" at the same time. The two single leaves contain entries from the middle of no. 97 through no. 129; nos. 130–212 are written on the first nine leaves of the infolded sheets following. As this account indicates, the order of Edwards' text in the manuscript as it now stands corresponds to the chronological order in which the entries were written.

Edwards did not number his entries until he had filled the first two pages of text. He then numbered them in order from the beginning, and thereafter numbered each entry at the time that it was written. Most of the entries after the first two pages, and especially the longer ones, appear to have been copied into the volume from an earlier draft. Corrections and deletions are relatively infrequent, and are almost always for the sake of style. Many of the citations and cross-references were inserted after the entry was written, but there are only a few cases where Edwards added discursive text to an entry after it was originally written. The additions in all such cases are very brief, and in only one case, in no. 18, was it clearly made at a much later time.

Except for Thomas Schafer's investigation of the beginning of the series, there has been little effort to determine the specific dates of entries in "Images." Townsend argues that the work was begun after Edwards settled in Northampton in 1727.[9] Miller judges, from the number and diversity of pens and shades of ink used in the manuscript, that Edwards continued to write entries in the series throughout his life.[1] They were both right. By comparisons of the paper, the hand and ink, and the contents of entries in the earliest portion of "Images" with that of other manuscripts, Schafer has confirmed that Edwards began the work within the first few years of his Northampton pastorate. Using Schafer's methods, similar comparisons of succeed-

8. The first of the two single leaves has the countermark of four of the full sheets following. The watermark on the second leaf was stretched out of shape when the paper was made, but it appears to be the same as that on the fifth full sheet following. Another sheet of this paper was used for the second table to the series.

9. "JE's Later Observations," p. 512. Townsend rests his case on the fact that "Images" no. 58 cites Ephraim Chambers' *Cyclopedia, or an Universal Dictionary of Arts and Sciences* (2 vols., London, 1728).

1. *Images or Shadows*, p. 1.

ing portions of the text of "Images" with Edwards' sermons and other manuscripts indicate that he continued to add entries from time to time throughout his Northampton and Stockbridge pastorates. The final entries were probably written within a few years of his death.

"Images" nos. 1–19, those on the first page of text, are the most difficult to date with precision, for none of the writings with which they are chronologically parallel are themselves dated or directly datable. These entries were clearly written before the beginning of 1733, when Edwards started regularly to date his sermons by month and year. The English/GR$^{wr}$ paper on which he began the series is found in only four sermons, all of them undated, but all apparently written in his early Northampton period. The same paper is found in several other manuscripts of about the same time; most important for the present purpose, Edwards added a total of nine sheets of it to the first book of "Miscellanies," for the writing of "Miscellanies" nos. 329–475. Several passages among the earlier entries in this group are closely related in content, as well as in hand and ink, to entries on the first page of "Images." No. 19 begins with a reference to "Miscellanies" no. 362; and another reference to the same discussion is written next to the title at the top of the page, though Edwards jotted it there after the series was begun. Most of the sermons which correspond in hand and ink with these "Miscellanies" and "Images" entries belong to a group of twenty for which Edwards used a London/PD paper that is not found in either the "Miscellanies" or the "Images" manuscripts. Passages in some of these sermons reflect ideas which are expressed in "Miscellanies" entries in the 300s. One of the London/PD sermons seems to be directly related to the beginning of "Images."

The sermon on Luke 16:24 is organized as a series of arguments by which Edwards defends the doctrine, "The torments of hell are exceeding great," against more moderate views of hell that certain freethinkers had advanced. The fifth argument, from "the metaphors and similitudes that the Scripture makes use of to signify" hell, turns on Edwards' reply to the claim that scriptural imagery is often hyperbolical: it is so in relation to the temporal things that are signified; but these temporal things are images of spiritual things, and the metaphors "fall short of the truth" when considered in relation to the spiritual things.[2] Edwards' point not only contains the central thesis of

---

2. JE, Sermon on Luke 16:24, c. 1728 (Beinecke Library). The thesis, as expressed in the sermon, is, "Where the Scripture uses metaphors and similitudes about temporal things, it

"Images of Divine Things," that natural and temporal objects are mere images and shadows of spiritual and eternal ones, but it expresses the relation between this general thesis and Edwards' particular interest in the interpretation of scriptural images and types. This interest is manifested throughout "Images," but shows itself more openly and regularly in the earlier entries.

The seventh argument of this sermon, based on the "images and types" of hell which are found in the natural world, is even more closely related to the beginning of "Images." Temporal death is the first of the natural types Edwards considers, in a passage which is nearly parallel with "Images" no. 1.[3] Despite some differences in his treatment of the theme in the two places, many similarities in phrasing indicate that both passages resulted from the same course of reflection. Because they are also nearly identical in hand and ink, it is very probable that both were written at nearly the same time.

Schafer assigns the London/PD sermons, as a group, to the period between early 1728 and early 1729; this was the last year of Solomon Stoddard's life, when Edwards assumed the major responsibility for pastoral duties in the Northampton parish. Schafer estimates that Stoddard's death on February 11, 1729, corresponds with Edwards' writing of "Miscellanies" entries in the 370s or 380s, and that those in the 330s were written in late 1728. The sermon on Luke 16:24 is nearest in ink color to "Miscellanies" nos. 338–344.[4] Since "Images" nos. 1–6 also agree in the shade and condition of ink with "Miscellanies" nos. 346 and 347, it is most likely that Edwards began "Images of Divine Things" in late September or early October 1728.

Edwards made the next several entries in rapid succession. Comments on the typology of Canticles, which include mention of Christ as spouse of the church, is the basis of "Images" no. 5 and the last paragraph of "Miscellanies" no. 359. "Images" nos. 7 and 8, the first in the series to deal with the basis of the concept of an image, are similar in hand and ink to miscellanies in the latter 350s. A review of "Images" nos. 7 and 8, as well as "Miscellanies" no. 359, may have inspired

---

does it for the beauty of expression; and oftentimes, taken literally, they express more than is intended because they allude to some spiritual thing that temporal thing was the image of."

3. The relevant passage is quoted below, p. 52, n. 8.

4. Schafer has noted that the intense dark-brown ink at the beginning of the sermon has a grayish cast that appears on "Miscellanies" nos. 338 and 339 but not before. The gray cast is gone from the ink of no. 340, and that in no. 344 is indistinguishable from that of the last pages of the sermon.

Edwards to write "Miscellanies" no. 362, an important typological statement.[5] Since this entry is cited twice on the first page of "Images," Edwards evidently considered it at the time to be a definitive statement of his doctrine. The first part of "Miscellanies" no. 362 is an early statement of the notion that heavenly bodies represent persons of the Trinity. Edwards rewrote the passage in "Miscellanies" no. 370, and this entry is referred to in "Images" no. 58,[6] which was written several years later. The idea is a recurrent theme in later writings, and especially in "Images"; it is anticipated by no. 4, and found more explicit in no. 14. "Images" nos. 13–15 are comparable in ink, and related in content, to "Miscellanies" no. 364 and the November 1728 thanksgiving sermon on Ps. 64:9, which describes rain as a type of God's overflowing bounty. Nos. 16 and 17 have the same ink as miscellanies in the 380s, and so can be dated to January or early February 1729.

Prevented by increased pastoral responsibilities and a mid-summer illness from making regular entries, Edwards did not return to the notebook until September 1729, when he wrote nos. 18 and 19. No. 18 seems to have been based on a rereading of "Miscellanies" no. 369, while no. 19 refers to "Miscellanies" no. 362 but compares best in hand and ink with "Miscellanies" no. 370. After writing no. 19, Edwards again laid the series aside for a considerable period of time. Nos. 20–23 compare in ink and hand with "Miscellanies" nos. 470ff., and no. 24 contains an integral reference to "Miscellanies" no. 487. These parallels indicate that nos. 20–24 were probably no sooner than the latter half of 1730, with no. 24 coming in November or December. "Images" nos. 25–33 are contemporaneous with miscellanies in the early and middle 490s, written between March and June 1731. On July 8, 1731, Edwards delivered his sermon, *God Glorified in the Work of Redemption* for the public lecture in Boston.

After a period of relative activity from mid-1730 to mid-1731, writing in the notebook progressed very slowly during the next several years. Whereas Edwards took about nine months to fill the first page of "Images," four years would elapse before he had filled the second page with nos. 20–41. "Images" nos. 36–38 are used for citations of undated notes in the "Blank Bible." No. 39 refers to "Miscellanies" no. 635, and no. 40 refers to no. 638. The "Miscellanies" entries probably

5. The second part of "Miscellanies" no. 362 is given below, p. 51, n. 6.
6. JE introduced "Images" no. 58 with the note, "Join this to 'Miscellanies' no. 362 and 370." "Miscellanies" no. 370 is cited later in the entry, and the relevant passage will be found quoted below, p. 51, n. 6.

belong to the latter half of 1733. After writing "Miscellanies" no. 635, Edwards added a reference in the entry to his sermon on Jer. 8:11, which is dated October 1733. The doctrine of this sermon, "'Tis greatly to be desired that we should have a thorough and not only a slight and deceitful cure of our spiritual wound," expresses a central point in the image in question in "Miscellanies" no. 635. "Images" no. 39, then, might have been added as late as October, at the time the sermon was written, and when Edwards had occasion to reread the "Miscellanies" entry. This supposition is supported by the fact that the short note added to the citation in no. 39 is almost identical in ink to the sermon.

In the fall of 1733, according to Edwards' own account, the first stirrings of the coming revivals were felt in Northampton.[7] The greater portion of "Images" after no. 39 was written during the next fifteen years, when his activities and writings were dominated by the concerns of the Great Awakening. The entries in this portion of the series are longer and more fully and carefully developed. The moral and spiritual truths which are represented are familiar themes in sermons of the 1730s and 1740s, and many of the entries are written in a style comparable to passages in these sermons. His writings in "Images" continued to be sporadic during the earlier years of the revival, but by 1740 he was adding entries quite regularly. Nos. 41–44 are written in a dark brown ink with grainy black solids, closest in appearance to that of sermons dated in late 1735 and early 1736. In "Images" nos. 45–57, the remaining entries on the first sheet of the series, the ink has a very different texture and consistency. It is a thick dark ink which failed to penetrate into the fibers of the paper, similar to that found in sermons beginning in November 1736. The muddy brown ink of the Thanksgiving sermon on Ps. 136:1 is most similar to "Images" nos. 45 and 46. The slightly bleeding ink of nos. 52–57 compares with that of the sermons on Ezek. 20:21–22 of March 1737, and on Matt. 18:8–9 of April 1737.

With no. 58, Edwards added a second sheet of paper to "Images"; the London/GR watermarks of this sheet are also found in sermons from March 1737 to July 1738. The entries on this sheet, no. 58 through the beginning of no. 77, are in a thick ink similar in texture to that used in late 1736, but the hand is decidedly larger and bolder. In

---

7. See *A Faithful Narrative of the Surprising Work of God*, ed. C. C. Goen, in *The Works of Jonathan Edwards, 4, The Great Awakening* (New Haven, Yale Univ. Press, 1972), 147.

hand and ink, no. 58 compares best with sermons in November and December of 1737; probably the most similar is that on Hag. 2:7–9, which is inscribed, "After the finishing of the new meeting house, December 25, 1737." In this sermon, the glory of Solomon's temple is mentioned as a type of Christ's beauty,[8] while in no. 58 the beautiful colors of the precious stones in Solomon's temple are used as an image of divine and spiritual excellencies. The sermon on Acts 7:9 to which Edwards refers in no. 58 is unfortunately not extant.

"Images" nos. 59–76 were probably written during the winter and spring of 1737–38. Before he began no. 77 on the last verso of the London/GR sheet, Edwards made a quire of four infolded sheets of London/GR$^{wr}$ paper, and inserted his first two sheets with nos. 1–76 between the first and second leaves of this quire, to make pp. 3–10 of the volume thus formed. The first leaf of the quire (pp. 1–2) was left blank, and no. 77 was continued on the recto of the second (p. 11). The London/GR$^{wr}$ paper used for the quire is also found in Edwards' sermons beginning in July 1738. Nos. 77–78 were probably written not long after this date, for they compare in the shade of ink with sermons dated from August through December 1738. "Images" no. 80 agrees in ink and hand with sermons in January 1739, and no. 87 with sermons of midsummer of that year. No. 89 is nearly identical in ink and hand with the sermon on John 1:47, dated September 1739.

"Images" no. 90 is written in a distinctive brown ink with a considerable quantity of a thick translucent substance which gives it a tallowy sheen, even to the naked eye. Closely related inks, which vary in basic color and in the amount and consistency of the tallowy material, are found in "Images" nos. 91–157. This ink first appears in sermons of September 1739, and continues with comparable variations until the spring of 1743. These years saw the climax of the Great Awakening, with George Whitefield's tour of New England in 1740. Edwards' sermon on Deut. 32:35, *Sinners in the Hands of an Angry God*, is dated June 1741. *The Distinguishing Marks of a Work of the Spirit of God* appeared the same year, and *Some Thoughts Concerning the Present Revival of Religion in New England* was published in 1742. "Images" nos. 90–94 belong to the early months of this period: no. 90 is nearly identical in ink and hand to a sermon written in three units on Luke 22:44 of October

8. See below, p. 68, n. 1.

1739, and nos. 91–94 compare with the Thanksgiving sermon on Luke 8:2–3 of November 1739.

Before beginning no. 97 on the verso page at the center of his quire of London/GR^wr paper (p. 16), Edwards inserted two single leaves (pp. 17–20) at that point in the manuscript. These were followed by five more infolded sheets, which contain the remainder of the series. The paper of these latest additions is a mixture with two different English/GR^wr watermarks, both of which Edwards seems to have had on hand at about the same time. Samples of each are found, together with pieces of the earlier London/GR^wr paper, in sermons of the spring and summer of 1740. Probably the earliest of these is the funeral sermon on Matt. 14:12, dated April 14, 1740, which contains paper of both English watermarks. "Images" in the early 100s correspond in ink and hand to sermons through that year, with nos. 106–08 probably belonging to the fall of 1740. A series of six sermons on the Parable of the Sower (Matt. 13:3–7), dated November 1740, agree in ink and hand with nos. 109–12. Nos. 108, 110, and 112 might have been suggested by reflections on that parable. Nos. 113–21 appear to have been written in the following year, between June and November 1741. No. 125 is similar in ink and hand to sermons in March and April 1742, and nos. 143–44 compare with sermons of September 1742. No. 148 refers to Abraham Hellenbroek's sermon on Cant. 2:15, which was translated from the Dutch and published in Boston in 1742.

Nos. 156 and 157 are the last entries in "Images" with ink containing any noticeable quantity of the tallowy substance which first appeared at no. 90. The latest sermons with this ink are found in April 1743; a similar change of ink occurs in "Miscellanies" no. 999. A reference to "Miscellanies" no. 1000 in "Images" no. 155 was added after the entry was written. Nos. 158 and 159 compare in ink with the sermon on Ps. 78:57, dated June 1743. Nos. 169 and 170 are similar in ink and hand to the last unit of a sermon series on The Rich Young Man (Mark 10:17–27), dated October 1743. At the beginning of no. 171 Edwards wrote and then deleted a reference to the sermon on Rev. 14:15, which is dated January 1744; from the hand and ink of the two, the entry was probably written shortly after the sermon.

Nos. 172–87 were probably written during the next three years, between the beginning of 1744 and the beginning of 1747. They all have basically the same brown ink with heavy black solids. The intense black ink of no. 188 is found in sermons of January and February

1747, for example, the sermons on Heb. 6:7 and Heb. 6:8. The former
of these is mentioned in Edwards' second table to "Images."[9] Exact
comparisons with the ink and hand of sermons of this period are quite
unreliable, however. Through the middle and late 1740s, Edwards
made his sermon booklets almost entirely out of scraps of used and
low-grade paper, on which the ink seems to have a quite different
appearance. Also, many of these sermons are mere outlines for extem-
poraneous delivery, and are written in a smaller and more rapidly
formed hand than is found in entries in the 170s and 180s in "Images."
The fact that nos. 177–79 make use of John Spencer's *Things New and
Old* is of little help, since the book was published in 1658, and it is not
mentioned in Edwards' "Catalogue."[1] His notes in the first column of
p. 14 of the "Catalogue," however, are in an ink and hand very similar
to that of "Images" nos. 172–80. None of these notes contains a current date—they record books Edwards found mentioned and com-
mended in the first volume of Philip Doddridge's *The Family
Expositor*[2]—but the last item on p. 14 contains a citation of *The Boston
Gazette* for July 15, 1746. A much earlier item on p. 12 of the "Catalogue" cites *The Daily Gazette* for February 18, 1744 (nos. 4b, 5). The
notes in the first column of p. 14, then, probably belong to the year
1745; and "Images" nos. 172–80 can reasonably be assigned to the
same period.

On the basis of the ink, "Images" no. 188 was almost certainly written no earlier than the end of 1746. The intense black ink of nos. 189–
93 is similar to that found in dated sermons and letters of 1747 and
early 1748. In nos. 194–98 the ink takes on a brown tint comparable to
that found in many of his writings from mid-1748 through early 1750,

9. See below, pp. 138, 139.
1. JE's "Catalogue," his personal record of his reading and reading interests, is in the
Beinecke Library. The first three pages of this quarto volume contain, for the most part, a
simple list of titles; from p. 4 on the entries are longer memoranda in which he mentions not
only the titles that had come to his attention, but the books, magazines and newspapers,
letters, and even personal conversations from which he learned about them. Many of these
references include dates from which one may infer the time of the hand and ink of the
entries, and the time of JE's reading of published works, where these are cited as read. The
"Catalogue" is therefore a valuable instrument for dating others of JE's writings, especially
for the later years of his life. References to the "Catalogue" here will cite the page number of
the MS, and the number of the entry on the page. Where an entry mentions more than one
published work or other written document, each will be further designated by "a," "b," "c,"
etc., in the order of their occurrence.
2. Philip Doddridge, *The Family Expositor* (6 vols., London, 1739–56); cited in "Catalogue,"
p. 13 (no. 5a) and p. 14 (nos. 1b, 2b, 3b).

which were connected with the dissension in Northampton. Edwards' citation of Hervey's *Meditations and Contemplations*[3] in no. 198 gives a further basis for dating this entry, for the work is also cited in seven nearly consecutive entries in his "Catalogue" (p. 20, no. 7c; p. 21, nos. 2b, 3b, 5b, 6b, 7b, 9b). The nearest following "Catalogue" entry containing a date is 1a, in the first column on p. 23. It reads, "Mr. McLaurin in his letter to me dated Aug. 14, 1750, p. 3, speaks of Mr. Hervey's preparing for the public some composure in favor of sound doctrine." On the other hand, the nearest dated entries preceding the citations on Hervey are found on p. 19 (nos. 4b, 7b), where Edwards refers to an unnamed newsletter of January 1750 and to *The Scot's Magazine* for November 1749. He probably did not acquire Hervey's work much earlier than this, for on p. 18 (no. 6b), he recorded John Erskine's commendation of it to him in a letter of February 14, 1749. These points of evidence from the "Catalogue" indicate that Edwards read Hervey's book during the spring and summer of 1750. "Images" no. 197 was probably written during this time.

Edwards preached his farewell sermon in Northampton on July 1, 1750. In October 1751 he removed his family to Stockbridge. The event is probably reflected in "Images" in the change of hand and ink between nos. 198 and 199. Nos. 199–202, in a fainter gray ink with a large quantity of coarse black particles, seem to have been written within a short time, probably during 1752 or early 1753. No. 203 quotes extensively from George Turnbull's *The Principles of Moral Philosophy* and *The Principles of Christian Philosophy*, which Edwards evidently read during 1753:[4] they are cited in the "Catalogue" on pp. 32 (nos. 7b, 8b, 9b, 10b, 11, 12b, 13b, 14a) and 33 (no. 1b), preceded by an entry on p. 31 referring to *The Monthly Review* for January 1753 (no. 2b), followed on p. 34 by an entry dated January 1754 (no. 4).

"Images" no. 206, in which Edwards quotes from the second volumes of Andrew Ramsay's *The Philosophical Principles of Natural and Revealed Religion*,[5] can be dated on similar grounds. On p. 27 of the "Catalogue" (no. 7a), Edwards notes it advertised in issues of *The Monthly Review* for March and April 1751. It is cited as read on p. 36

---

3. James Hervey, *Meditations and Contemplations* (2 vols., London, 1748).

4. George Turnbull, *The Principles of Moral Philosophy, An Enquiry into the Wise and Good Government of the Moral World* (2 vols., London, 1740). The title page of the second volume reads: *The Principles of Moral and Christian Philosophy*.

5. Andrew Ramsay, *Philosophical Principles of Natural and Revealed Religion* (2 vols., Glasgow, 1748).

(nos. 2a, 3b, 4a). The two entries preceding these were taken from "a catalogue of books published in London, brought from New York by my wife, June 1754" (no. 1b).

Johann Stapfer's *Institutiones Theologiae Polemicae Universae*,[6] which Edwards quotes from in "Images" no. 207, is cited or mentioned in twelve entries on pp. 40–42 of the "Catalogue." The ink and hand of no. 207 is almost identical to that found on these pages of the "Catalogue." An earlier entry on p. 39, which has a comparable ink and hand, is dated March 1756 (no. 6b). An entry on p. 42, second after the last of those citing Stapfer's work, refers to a letter written by Mr. Hopkins with the date January 13, 1757 (no. 4b).

The last entries in "Images," nos. 208–12, almost certainly belong to the last year of Edwards' Stockbridge pastorate. Ralph Cudworth's *The True Intellectual System of the Universe*,[7] which he quotes in nos. 208–10, is not cited as read in the "Catalogue," though commendations of the work are recorded on p. 25 (no. 10a), and p. 36 (no. 2b). On p. 33 (no. 6a) is an advertisement for the second edition. The smooth light brown ink of the last entries in "Images," however, is the same as that in the final entries in the "Catalogue," including that which cites Hopkins' letter of January 13, 1757, and all the five that follow it. The same hand and ink is found in the latest entries, nos. 1358–60, in Edwards' "Miscellanies." "Miscellanies" no. 1359 includes extensive extracts from Cudworth's *Intellectual System* also; it was probably one of the last major works he read before going to Princeton in February 1758. He died there on March 22 of the same year.

The seven numbered scriptural images, with the general heading "Scriptures," are written on p. 41 of the "Images" manuscript. Edwards divided the page with a vertical line for two columns of such items. These seven fill only part of the first column, however, and what seems to be Edwards' draft of a continuation of the list is found on a separate folded sheet, now located in the Andover collection. The pages of this sheet are also double columned, and the entries fill the first recto and verso, and continue on the tops of both columns of the second recto. These items are not numbered, but in other respects they seem to be entirely similar to those in "Images of Divine Things." They are included in the text below as an addition to the numbered set

---

6. See above p. 25, n. 4.
7. Ralph Cudworth, *The True Intellectual System of the Universe* (London, 1678).

of seven in "Images," and are given numbers in brackets continuous with them.

All these scriptural images were written during the later period of Edwards' composition in "Images of Divine Things." The first six of the numbered items in the "Images" manuscript are in an ink and hand comparable to that in "Images" nos. 203–05, and so should probably be assigned a date during the year 1753. The seventh of this list, and all those on the separate sheet, are written in the ink of "Images" no. 207; they were probably written in 1756 or the first part of 1757.

## Editing "Images of Divine Things"

The text presented here is based upon Edwards' manuscript. Readings have been compared systematically with those of Sereno Dwight, Harvey Townsend, and Perry Miller. There prove to be many discrepancies in readings, but in most cases a careful inspection of the passage in the manuscript has established the correct reading beyond reasonable doubt. In the few cases where doubt remains, alternate possible readings have been given in footnotes.

Throughout the "Images" Edwards includes references to passages in his other manuscript writings. Except where the writing has been lost, the passages referred to are paraphrased, and the most relevant portions of them are quoted directly, in footnotes to the text. Passages quoted from Edwards' "Blank Bible," "Notes on the Scripture," and from his sermons have been transcribed and edited directly from the manuscripts. Passages from the "Miscellanies" are taken from Thomas Schafer's transcriptions for the Yale edition.

The text has been edited in accordance with the style manual of the Yale edition. Spellings and capitalization have been corrected and punctuation added. Special problems are encountered in punctuating Edwards' "Images," especially where he gives a detailed explanation of his image and of what is represented by it within the grammatical confines of a single complex sentence. In some cases, the reader is confronted with a sequence of dependent clauses set off by commas before coming to the main verb, which is usually "represents" or "is an image of."

Edwards made few changes or corrections on the manuscript. Most of the emendations are of no interest, and have been incorporated without comment. But a few show his concern with style, and others suggest some change or development in the thought he intended to express. In one or two cases the change of words produced a particularly awkward or obscure phrase structure. In all these cases the nature of Edwards' emendation is explained in footnotes.

The seven scriptural images at the back of the manuscript are a separate series, apparently Edwards' beginning for a kind of index of natural objects and processes, together with what he takes to be the correct typological interpretations of their use in Scripture. Because the notes on the separate sheet in the Andover collection are of an exactly similar sort, they are presented below as a continuation of this series. And because they are not numbered in the manuscript, they are given numbers in brackets, [8] to [45], continuous with the initial seven scriptural images.

The two tables Edwards drew up for his "Images" have been combined and organized alphabetically to give the reader a useful index to the entries. His list of Scripture citations in "Images," which he organized in double columns on the last verso of his second table, is also printed below at the end of the text.

*"IMAGES OF DIVINE THINGS"*

# IMAGES OF DIVINE THINGS[1]

## The Book of Nature and Common Providence
## The Language and Lessons of Nature[2]
See Spencer's *Similes and Sentences*;[3]
see Mr. Mason's *Remains*, p. 49, etc.[4]

1. The latest of JE's titles for the series. It is written in abbreviated form on the cover of the MS, but probably was not adopted much earlier than the writing of "Images" no. 118, where JE used it for the heading of his entry. See above, pp. 34–35.

2. These two titles are found on p. 2 of the MS. The sheet was probably not added to the MS before the writing of "Images" no. 77, and the titles are similar in hand and ink to "Images" no. 123. JE might have jotted them down while casting about for a new title for his series, before settling on the one above.

3. John Spencer, *Things New and Old: Or, A Storehouse of Similes, Sentences, Allegories, Apophthegms, Adagies, Apologues, Divine, Morall, Politicall, etc. With their severall Applications* (London, 1658). This and the following reference are found on p. 2 of the MS. JE quotes and cites Spencer's book in "Images" nos. 177–79.

4. John Mason, *Select Remains of the Reverend John Mason ... Recommended by ... Isaac Watts* (3rd ed. Boston, 1743). Ch. 2 (pp. 49–54) is headed, "Containing some Religious Observations, by way of Simile." With the possible exception of "Images" no. 171, the series shows no direct influence of Mason's similes.

# SHADOWS OF DIVINE THINGS[5]

U NDER the head of Creation, vid. "Miscellanies" [no.] 362.[6]

1. Death temporal is a shadow of eternal death. The agonies, the pains and groans and gasps of death, the pale, horrid, ghastly appearance of the corpse, its being laid in the dark and silent grave, there putrifying and rotting and becoming[7] exceeding loathsome, and being eaten with worms (Is. 66:24), is an image of the misery of hell. And

---

5. This title, the one with which JE began the series, is found at the top of the first page of text, p. 3 of the MS. He continued to use this title at least as late as the writing of "Images" no. 58 (see above, pp. 34–35).

6. The reference is jotted next to the title at the top of p. 3 of the MS. JE added it soon after the series was begun, probably at about the time he wrote "Images" nos. 7 and 8. The first portion of "Miscellanies" no. 362, under the head "Trinity," was rewritten as "Miscellanies" no. 370. The second portion of the entry, to which JE here refers, expresses the basis upon which this series was conceived: "For indeed the whole outward creation, which is but the shadows of beings, is so made as to represent spiritual things. It might be demonstrated by the wonderful agreement in thousands of things, much of the same kind as is between the types of the Old Testament and their antitypes, and by spiritual things being so often and continually compared with them in the Word of God. And it's agreeable to God's wisdom that it should be so, that the inferior and shadowy parts of his works should be made to represent those things that are more real and excellent, spiritual and divine, to represent the things that immediately concern himself and the highest parts of his work. Spiritual things are the crown and glory, the head and soul, the very end and Alpha and Omega of all other works: what therefore can be more agreeable to wisdom, than that they should be so made as to shadow them forth?

"And we know that this is according to God's method which his wisdom has chosen in other matters. Thus, the inferior dispensation of the gospel was all to shadow forth the highest and most excellent, which was its end; thus almost everything that was said or done that we have recorded in Scripture from Adam to Christ, was typical of Gospel things: persons were typical persons, their actions were typical actions, the cities were typical cities, the nation of the Jews and other nations were typical nations, the land was a typical land, God's providences towards them were typical providences, their worship was typical worship, their houses were typical houses, their magistrates typical magistrates, their clothes typical clothes, and indeed the world was a typical world. And this is God's manner, to make inferior things shadows of the superior and most excellent, outward things shadows of spiritual, and all other things shadows of those things that are the end of all things and the crown of all things. Thus God glorifies himself and instructs the minds that he has made."

7. MS: "become."

the body's continuing in the grave and never rising more in this world, is to shadow forth the eternity of the misery of hell.[8]

2. (Vid. [no.] 46.)[9] We are all clothed with the fleeces of sheep. We are clothed with the righteousness of the Lamb. Acts 8:32, "As a lamb dumb before his shearers." We were all Christ's crucifiers; our sins crucified him, and we are his shearers. We, by his sufferings, which our sins brought on him, get his fleece to clothe ourselves withal.

3. Roses grow upon briers, which is to signify that all temporal sweets are mixed with bitter. But what seems more especially to be meant by it, is that true happiness, the crown of glory, is to be come at in no other way than by bearing Christ's cross by a life of mortification, self-denial and labor, and bearing all things for Christ. The rose, the chief of all flowers, is the last thing that comes out. The briery prickly bush grows before, but the end and crown of all is the beautiful and fragrant rose.

4. The heaven's being filled with glorious, luminous bodies, is to signify the glory and happiness of the heavenly inhabitants; and amongst these, the sun signifies Christ and the moon, the church.

5. Marriage signifies the spiritual union and communion of Christ and the church, and especially the glorification of the church in the perfection of this union and communion forever. *[1] Vid. [nos.] 9, 12, 56.

8. A parallel passage is found in JE's sermon on Luke 16:24 (Beinecke Library). The sermon gives a series of arguments to defend the doctrine, "The torments of hell are exceeding great." The seventh argument presents types and images of hell; the first of these is temporal death: "Temporal death is but the image and shadow of [hell].... Death is very awful and terrible in its circumstances; in its forerunners, concomitants and consequences. The pains, languishings, the groans and convulsions that go before it are awful. And it is dreadful and shocking to nature to see that nature break, and the dying person gasping and catching for breath, the eyes fixing and the countenance changed with pale death. And its consequents have an awful aspect: the body is laid in the dark and silent grave, and there putrefies and rots, becomes exceeding loathsome and filthy—it is awful to think of it. 'Tis very emphatically and livelily set forth, Job 10:21–22.... But, however, this is but the shadow of eternal misery. They are both called "death" in the Scripture, not because they are anything of the same nature one with another, but because one is the shadow of the other, as is very common in Scripture." JE did not date the sermon, but extensive comparisons of it with other MSS indicate that it was probably written near the beginning of 1728. "Images" no. 1 was probably written at about the same time (see above, p. 39).

9. The reference is inserted above the line, in a shade of ink comparable to no. 46.

1. The asterisk here is intended to refer the reader to no. 12, which begins with the mark. Before the asterisk are the deleted words, "we are expressly." The same words stand at the

6. The blood comes from the heart, to intimate that "out of the heart are the issues of life" (Prov. 4:23).

7. That the things of the world are ordered [and] designed to shadow forth spiritual things, appears by the Apostle's arguing spiritual things from them. I Cor. 15:36, "Thou fool, that which thou sowest is not quickened, except it die." If the sowing of seed and its springing were not designedly ordered to have an agreeableness to the resurrection, there could be no sort of argument in that which the Apostle alleges; either to argue the resurrection itself or the manner of it, either its certainty, or probability, or possibility. See how the Apostle's argument is thus founded (Heb. 9:16–17) about the validity of a testament.[2]

8. Again, it is apparent and allowed that there is a great and remarkable analogy in God's works. There is a wonderful resemblance in the effects which God produces, and consentaneity in his manner of working in one thing and another, throughout all nature. It is very observable in the visible world. Therefore 'tis allowed that God does purposely make and order one thing to be in an agreeableness and harmony with another. And if so, why should not we suppose that he makes the inferior in imitation of the superior, the material of the spiritual, on purpose to have a resemblance and shadow of them? We see that even in the material world God makes one part of it strangely to agree with another; and why is it not reasonable to suppose he makes the whole as a shadow of the spiritual world? Vid. [no.] 59.

9. Again, as to marriage, we are expressly taught that that is a designed type of the union between Christ and the church (Eph. 5:30–32). Vid. nos. 5, 12, 56.

---

beginning of no. 9; JE probably would have added the content of no. 9 to this entry if he had left enough space between it and no. 7.

2. Nos. 7 and 8 were probably written at about the same time as the second part of "Miscellanies" no. 362 (quoted above, p. 51, n. 6), i. e. near the beginning of 1729. JE's appeal to Scripture, both here and elsewhere, presupposes the validity of typological interpretations of Scripture itself. He was aware of the dangers of such interpretations, especially in texts where the context provides no explicit explanation. The problems of finding and justifying correct typological interpretations are the subject of an eight-page octavo MS entitled "Types" in JE's hand (Trask Library, Andover Newton Theological School, Newton, Massachusetts). The text of this pamphlet is presented below, pp. 146–53.

10. Children's coming into the world naked and filthy, and in their blood, and crying and impotent, is to signify the spiritual nakedness, pollution of nature and wretchedness of condition with which they are born.

11. The serpent's charming of birds and other animals into their mouths, and the spider's taking of the fly in his snare, are lively representations of the devil's catching our souls by his temptations.

12.*[3] We are told that marriage is a great mystery, as representing the relation between Christ and the church (Eph. 5:32). By "mystery" can be meant nothing but a type of what is spiritual. And if God designed this for a type of what is spiritual, why not many other things in the constitution and ordinary state of human society, and the world of mankind? Nos. 5, 9, 56.

13. Thus I believe the grass and other vegetables growing and flourishing, looking green and pleasant, as it were rejoicing, blossoming and bearing fruit from the influences of the heavens, the rain and wind, and light and heat of the sun, to be on purpose to represent the dependence of our spiritual welfare upon God's gracious influences and the effusions of his Holy Spirit. I am sure there are none of the types of the Old Testament are more lively images of spiritual things. And we find spiritual things very often compared to 'em in Scripture.

14. The sun's so perpetually, for so many ages, sending forth his rays in such vast profusion, without any dimunition of his light and heat, is a bright image of the all-sufficiency and everlastingness of God's bounty and goodness.[4]

15. And so likewise are rivers which are ever-flowing, that empty vast quantities of water every day and yet there is never the less to come. The Spirit communicated and shed abroad, that is to say, the

3. Another asterisk at the end of no. 5 indicates that this was intended as a continuation of that entry.
4. At the end of the entry JE deleted the beginning of another sentence, "We have shown already that the rays of the sun are ... to represent." No earlier entries in "Images" discusses the rays of the sun. JE might have had in mind the first part of "Miscellanies" no. 362, where the sun is treated as an image of the Trinity, its rays representing the Holy Ghost. The passage was later rewritten as "Miscellanies" no. 370.

goodness of God, is in Scripture compared to a river; and the trees that grow and flourish by the river's side through the benefit of the water, represent the saints who live upon Christ and flourish through the influences of his Spirit.[5] Jer. 17:8, Ps. 1:3, Num. 24:6.

16. I don't know but that there are some effects commonly seen in the natural world that can't be solved by any of the general laws of nature, but seem to come to pass by a particular law for this very end, to represent some spiritual thing: particularly[6] that of serpents' charming of birds and squirrels into their mouths. #[7] Vid. no. 43.

17. In its being so contrived, that the life of man should be continually maintained by breath, respect was had to the continual influence of the Spirit of God that maintains the life of the soul. No. 62.

18. Women travail and suffer great pains in bringing children [forth],[8] which is to represent the great persecutions and sufferings of the church in bringing forth Christ and in increasing the number of his children; and a type of those spiritual pains that are in the soul when bringing forth Christ.[9]

19. (Vid. "Miscellanies" [no.] 362.)[1] So it is God's way in the natural world to make inferior things in conformity and analogy to the superior, so as to be the images of them. Thus the beasts are made like men:

5. This and the two preceding entries reflect JE's interest in scriptural images of the Holy Spirit, which is also expressed in several "Miscellanies" entries on the Trinity written during the first years of his Northampton pastorate. "Miscellanies" nos. 334, 336, and 364 all mention the metaphor of a river in this connection. "Miscellanies" no. 364 was probably written at nearly the same time as "Images" no. 15, in early 1729.

6. JE deleted "the strange influence of that luminous vapor that sometimes appears in the night called Jack-with-a-lantern."

7. This cross-hatch mark also appears at the beginning of no. 43, which JE apparently regarded as a continuation of no. 16. Similar marks are found at the ends of later entries, but their significance is not evident.

8. MS: "fo."

9. In "Miscellanies" no. 369 JE makes use of "the frequent comparisons made [in Scripture] between the church's spiritually bringing forth Christ and a woman in travail." This entry and "Images" no. 18, except for its final clause, were probably written at about the same time, early in 1729. The final clause of no. 18, which makes a new use of the image, was probably added in 1733, when JE added a parallel passage to "Miscellanies" no. 635.

1. Quoted above, p. 51, n. 6. From similarities in ink and hand, no. 19 is probably contemporary with "Miscellanies" no. 370, in which JE rewrote the first part of "Miscellanies" no. 362.

in all kinds of them there is an evident respect had to the body of man, in the formation and contrivance of their bodies, though the superior are more in conformity and the inferior less. Thus they have the same senses, the same sensitive organs, the same members—head, teeth, tongues, nostrils, heart, lungs, bowels, feet, etc. And from the lowest animal to the highest you will find an analogy, though the nearer you come to the highest, the more you may observe of analogy. And so plants, that are yet an inferior set of beings, they are in many things made in imitation of animals. They are propagated by seed which produce others of the same kind. The earth answers to the womb. There is something that answers to generation in the flower; there is a male part that impregnates the female part. The time of blossoming is as it were the time of love and pleasure, being the time of generation, when the seed and fruit are as it were conceived. They are like animals in their growing by nourishment running in veins, in suffering and dying by wounds, and [in] some of them there is an image of sensitiveness.

20. See how the Apostle argues, I Cor. 15, from the thirty-sixth to the forty-second verse.[2]

21. The purity, beauty, sublimity and glory of the visible heavens as one views it in a calm and temperate air, when one is made more sensible of the height of them and of the beauty of their color, when there are here and [there] interposed little clouds, livelily denotes the exaltedness and purity of the blessedness of the heavenly inhabitants. How different is the idea from that which we have in the consideration of the dark and dire caverns and abyss down in the depths of the earth. This teaches us the vast difference between the state of the departed saints and of damned souls: it shows the ineffable glory of the happiness of the one and the unspeakable dolefulness and horrors of the state of the other. See no. 212.

2. In JE's "Blank Bible" note on I Cor. 15:42, he speaks of the Apostle's "arguments" that the fallen body differs from the glorified body as terrestial bodies differ from celestial bodies, and that glorified bodies differ among themselves as celestial bodies differ among themselves. In calling them arguments, JE understands these analogies to be both illustrations of the meaning, and also evidence of the truth of the statements about glorified bodies (see below, no. 26). From the hand and ink of the entries, nos. 20 and 21 were probably not written before late 1730, more than a year later than no. 19 (see above, p. 40).

22. The wise man argues from an image in the natural world, Eccles. 1:7, "All the rivers run into the sea; yet the sea is not full." See it by me explained.[3]

23. Vid. John 12:24, "Verily, verily, I say unto you, Except a corn of wheat fall into the ground and die, it abideth alone: but if it die, it bringeth forth much fruit."

24. The head is after a peculiar manner the seat of the soul, though the soul be also in the whole body.[4] So the Godhead dwells in the man Christ Jesus bodily. He dwells also in believers, by way of participation with the Head. Vid. "Miscellanies" [no.] 487.[5]

25. There are many things in the constitution of the world that are not properly shadows and images of divine things, that yet are significations of them; as children's being born crying is a signification of their being born to sorrow.[6] A man's coming into the world after the same manner as the beasts is a signification of the ignorance and brutishness of man, and his agreement in many things with the beasts.

26. Christ often makes use of representations of spiritual things in the constitution of the [world] for argument, as that the tree is known by its fruit [Matt. 12:33]. These things ben't merely mentioned as illustrations of his meaning, but as illustrations and evidences of the truth of what he says.

---

3. Probably in the "Blank Bible" note on Eccles. 1:5–10, which is cited later in no. 36 (see below, pp. 59–60, n. 1); the note is similar in hand and ink to this entry. "Notes on the Scripture" no. 461, on Eccles. 1:9, gives a similar treatment of the text, but was written at a much later date. "Notes on the Scripture" (hereafter "Scripture"), which is at the Beinecke Library, is a set of notebooks containing numbered entries treating scriptural texts that JE used before he obtained the "Blank Bible."

4. MS: "body the."

5. No. 24 is substantially taken from "Miscellanies" no. 487, where JE uses the metaphor to explain how God dwells alike in the man Christ, and in believers of whom Christ is head, "as in one body, one Christ, and one church"; but with the difference that "God dwells in the man Christ as the Head, and in us as the members, as the head is the seat of the soul after a peculiar manner; 'tis the proper seat of the soul, though the soul also dwells in the members, but 'tis by derivation from and participation with the head." Both "Miscellanies" no. 487 and "Images" no. 24 were probably written in late 1730 (see above, p. 40).

6. JE deleted the unfinished clause, "or as we said before, the beauty and glory of the visible heavens"; the reference is probably to no. 21.

27. The waves and billows of the sea in a storm and the dire cataracts there are of rivers have a representation of the terrible wrath of God, and amazing misery of [them] that endure it. Misery is often compared to waters in the Scripture—a being overwhelmed in waters. God's wrath is compared to waves and billows (Ps. 88:7, Ps. 42:7). Job 27:20, "Terrors take hold as waters." Hos. 5:10, "I will pour out my wrath upon them like water." In Ps. 42:7, God's wrath is expressly compared to cataracts of water: "Deep calleth unto deep at the noise of thy waterspouts." And the same is represented in hail and stormy winds, black clouds and thunder, etc.

28. As thunder, and thunder clouds, as they are vulgarly called, have a shadow of the majesty of God, so the blue sky, the green fields and trees, and pleasant flowers have a shadow of the mild attributes of goodness, grace and love of God, as well as the beauteous rainbow.

29. When we travail up an hill 'tis against our natural tendency and inclination, which perpetually is to descend; and therefore we can't go on ascending without labor and difficulty. But there arises a pleasant prospect to pay us for our labor as we ascend, and as we continue our labor in ascending, still the pleasantness of the prospect grows. Just so is a man paid for his labor and self-denial in a Christian course. Vid. [no.] 67.

30. If God had so much regard to the names of persons, that they might signify things chiefly remarkable concerning them, why should we think he would not, in his ordering the nature of things, have respect to spiritual things, so as to signify and represent them?[7]

31. I do believe that it is so ordered, that such an extraordinary degree of heat should be necessary in order to refine metals, that it might represent the exceeding fierceness of God's wrath and the extremity of the sufferings by which the dross of the world is consumed and the saints (who are the gold) are saved. As the metal is delivered from its ore and dross by the heat of the furnace, so the saints are saved

7. On the typological significance of names, see also "Images" no. 132 and "Types of the Messiah," pp. 294–305.

from their sins by their suffering, in their Head, Jesus Christ, the due wrath of God.[8]

32. It is ordered so that there should be, in man's nature, a foundation laid for so strong and dear a love towards a woman, if a suitable object and occasion presents, to represent the exceeding love of Christ to his church; and that man's jealousy of unchastity in the woman beloved should be so violent and cruel a passion, to represent the jealousy of Christ towards his people, when he sees they give that to other lovers which belongs to him alone.[9]

33. The extreme fierceness and extraordinary power of the heat of lightning is an intimation of the exceeding power and terribleness of the wrath of God.

34. Young twigs are easily bent and made to grow another way, old trees most difficultly. So persons in youth are more easily turned than others. Again, a young plant is much more easily plucked up by the roots, than after it hath long stood and is rooted deep in the ground. So is it more easy to forsake sin in the beginning, than after a long continuance in it.

35. The silkworm is a remarkable type of Christ, which, when it dies, yields us that of which we make such glorious clothing. Christ became a worm for our sakes, and by his death finished that righteousness with which believers are clothed, and thereby procured that we should be clothed with robes of glory. Vid. [no.] 46. See II Sam. 5:23–24 and Ps. 84:6; the valley of mulberry trees.

36. See notes on Eccles. 1:5–10.[1]

8. No. 31 is similar in hand and ink to JE's sermon on Matt. 13:41–42, with the doctrine, "The wicked hereafter will be cast into a furnace of fire." JE dated the sermon May 1733.
9. No. 32 is similar in ink and hand to the sermon on Cant. 1:3, "Jesus Christ is a person transcendently excellent and lovely," which JE marked as preached in Boston in June 1733. In its opening passage, the Song of Songs is described as "treating of the divine love, union and communion of the most glorious lovers, Christ and his spiritual spouse, of which a marriage union and conjugal love ... is but a shadow."
1. "Blank Bible" note on Eccles. 1:5–10, in part: "'The sun also ariseth,' etc. These kind of vicissitudes in earthly things shows the great imperfection of earthly good in these respects: 1. 'Tis good that is sought by this labor of the creature.... But by their restlessness, their still

37. See notes on Job 41:34.[2]

38. See notes on Gen. 15:5.[3]

39. See "Miscellanies" no. 635, concerning searching and lancing a wound in order to a cure.[4]

40. The gradual vanishing of stars when the sun approaches is a type [of] the gradual vanishing of Jewish ordinances as the Gospel dispensation was introduced. Vid. "Miscellanies" no. 638.[5]

41. Children's coming to their inheritance by the death of their parents, and by their will and testament which becomes of force by their death, is a designed type and shadow of believers receiving their inheritance by the free and sovereign disposal and gift of God in his

---

continuing to labor, it appears that they don't fully attain their end. They don't attain any sufficient good.... As what the rivers aim at by their running is to fill up the sea, but by their still continuing to run, they go back to the same place and run the same course again. It appears they do not do it (v. 7). 2. By their doing the same work over and over it appears that they not only don't attain any sufficient good, but they don't make progress towards it.... The rivers not only don't fill up the sea, but they don't gain upon it.... 3. It shows the unsatisfying nature of earthly good thus, that when one kind has been enjoyed a little while there is need of change.... 4. And as it shows the unsatisfying nature of earthly good, so it shows its exceeding fleeting, fading nature."

2. "Blank Bible" note on Job 41:34: "'King over all the children of pride.' I. e. mystically, he whom the leviathan was made to be a type of, viz. Satan, is king over all the children of pride."

3. "Blank Bible" note on Gen. 15:5: "The stars were designed by the Creator to be a type of the saints, the spiritual seed of Abraham; and the seeming multitude of them, which is much greater than the real multitudes of visible stars, was designed as a type of the multitude of the saints."

4. "Miscellanies" no. 635, in part: "Conviction. Humiliation. Bad wounds must be searched to the bottom; and oftentimes when they are very deep, they must be lanced and the core laid open, though it be very painful, before they can have a good cure. The surgeon may skin them over so that it may look like a cure, without this, without much hurting the patient, but it will not do the patient much good.... This figures forth to us the case of our spiritual wound, the plague of our hearts, which is great and deep and must be searched, must be lanced with painful conviction. The core must be laid open; we must be made to see that fountain of sin and corruption there is, and what a dreadful state we are in by nature, in order to a thorough and saving cure."

JE's sermon on Jer. 8:11 has the doctrine, "'Tis greatly to be desired that we should have a thorough and not only a slight and deceitful cure of our spiritual wound." The sermon is dated October 1733; "Miscellanies" no. 635 was probably written at approximately the same time.

5. "Miscellanies" no. 638, headed "Lord's Day," develops the idea of "Images" no. 40: "So when the day of the gospel dawned, the ceremonies of the Old Testament and ordinances of the law of Moses, that were only appointed to give light in the absence of the Sun of

Word; which is his testament or declaration of his will with respect to the disposal of his goods, or the blessings he has in store for men. And believers come to the possession thereof by the death of Christ. This is evident by the Apostle's arguing from it, Heb. 9:15–17.

42. The gradual progress we make from childhood to manhood is a type of the gradual progress of the saints in grace, and the gradual progress the church makes towards perfection of knowledge, holiness and blessedness; as seems by the Apostle's arguing in[6] I Cor. 13:11, "For when I was a child, I spake as a child, I understood as a child: but when I became a man, I put away childish things."

43. #[7] (Vid. no. 16.) 'Tis a great argument with me that God, in the creation and disposal of the world, and the state and course of things in it, had great respect to a showing forth and resembling spiritual things; because God in some instances seems to have gone quite beside the ordinary laws of nature in order to it, particularly that in serpents' charming birds and squirrels and such animals. The material world, and all things pertaining to it, is by the Creator wholly subordinated to the spiritual and moral world. To show this, God, in some things in providence, has set aside the ordinary course of things in the material world to subserve to the purposes of the moral and spiritual, as in miracles. And to show that all things in heaven and earth, the whole universe, is wholly subservient, the greater parts of it as well as the smaller, God has once or twice interrupted the course of the greater wheels of the machine, as when the sun stood still in Joshua's time. So to show how much he regards things in the spiritual world, there are some things in the ordinary course of things that fall out in a manner quite diverse and alien from the ordinary laws of nature in other things, to hold forth and represent spiritual things.

---

Righteousness, or until Christ should appear, and shone only with a borrowed and reflected light like the planets, they were gradually abolished one after another; and the same ordinance gradually ceased, and those ordinances that were principal (one of which was the Jewish sabbath) continued the longest. There were a multitude of those ceremonies, which was a sign of their imperfection, but all together did but imperfectly supply the place of the Sun of Righteousness; but when the Sun of Righteousness is come, there is no need of any of them."

6. MS: "in the."

7. JE added a similar mark after no. 16, indicating that no. 43 is to be considered a continuation of that entry.

44. Vid. notes on Is. 28:23–29.[8]

45. That natural things were ordered for types of spiritual things seems evident by these texts: John 1:9, "This was the true Light, which lighteth every man that cometh into the world"; and John 15:1, "I am the true vine." Things are thus said to be true in Scripture, in contra-distinction to what is typical. The type is only the representation or shadow of the thing, but the antitype is the very substance, and is the true thing. Thus heaven is said to be the true holy of holies, in opposi-tion to the holy of holies in the tabernacle and temple. Heb. 9:24, "For Christ is not entered into the holy places made with hands, which are figures of the true; but into heaven itself, now to appear in the pres-ence of God for us." So the spiritual gospel tabernacle is said to be the true tabernacle, in opposition to the legal typical tabernacle which was literally a tabernacle. Heb. 8:2, "A minister of the sanctuary, and of the true tabernacle, which the Lord pitched, and not man." And that, though the legal tabernacle was much more properly a tabernacle, according to the literal meaning of the word, than the other. So Christ is said to be the true bread from heaven, in opposition to the manna that was typical, though that was literally bread from heaven. John 6:32, "Then Jesus said unto them, Verily, verily, I say unto you, Moses gave you not that bread from heaven; but my Father giveth you the true bread from heaven." So, in those forementioned texts, 'tis evi-dently in the same sense that Christ is said to be the true vine and the true light of the world; and is the true vine in opposition to vines literally so called, which are types, the union and dependence of whose

8. "Blank Bible" note on Is. 28:23–29, in part: "Here, first, God deals with his people as a prudent husbandman deals with his field. First he plows his field and breaks the hard clods, and makes smooth the roughnesses of it, makes plain the face of it, and so fits and prepares it, and then sows his seed. So God, by the afflictions he brings on his people, he doth as it were plow and mellow the hard ground, and breaks the hard clods and evens their rough-nesses to fit them to receive the seed and to bring forth good fruit. And as the plowman plows the ground no more and no longer than is needful to fit it for the seed ... so God will afflict his people no more, and hold 'em under affliction no longer than to fit them for spiritual good. And as the husbandman suits his seed to his ground ... so God deals with his people. He deals with everyone according to their needs, deals forth those blessings that are most fit for them.... If the husbandman has this discretion in managing his field, much more shall he have in dealing with his people who gives the husbandman that discretion, and is the fountain of all wisdom and prudence.

"Secondly, God deals with his people in the afflictions he brings upon them, as the husbandman deals with his grain when he threshes it. The end of his threshing it is not to

branches on the stock and root is a type of the union and dependence of Christ's members on him. So he is the true light of the world in opposition to the sun, the literal light of the world, that is a type of the Sun of Righteousness. See Dan. 7:16. #[9]

46. We, in our fallen state, need garments to hide our nakedness (having lost our primitive glory) which were needless in our state of innocency. And whatsoever God has provided for mankind to clothe themselves with, seems to represent Jesus Christ and his righteousness: whether it be anything made of skin, as the coats of skins that God made our first parents represented the righteousness of Christ; or the fleeces of sheep do represent[1] the righteousness of him who is the Lamb of God, and who was dumb as a sheep before his shearers. And the beautiful clothing from the silkworm, that that worm yields us at his death, represents the glorious clothing we have for our souls by the death of him who became a man, who is a worm; and the son of man, who is a worm, and who said he was a worm and no man [Ps. 22:6].

And the flax with which we are clothed seems well to represent the spiritual clothing we have by Christ. That small, weak, feeble and unadorned plant well represents him who grew up as a tender plant, as a root out [of] a dry ground, wherein was no form or comeliness [Is. 53:2]. It is exceedingly bruised and broken, and beaten with many blows, and so yields us its coat to be our clothing. And Christ, through exceeding great sufferings, yields us his righteousness, that is as fine linen, clean and white, and presents us without spot to the Father. Vid. [nos.] 2 and 35.

---

break or bruise the grain, but to cleanse it, to separate it from the husk and fit it for the owner's use. So God's end in the afflictions he brings on his people is not to injure his people, but to purify them and to separate them from their sins, and wean them from the world, and fit them for God's use. And as the husbandman uses discretion in threshing his grain, one sort of grain he threshes in one manner and another in another, as shall best suit the several sorts of grain and tend most to separating of it from the husk without bruising it; and the husbandman shows his discretion also in the degree of his threshing ... so God deals wisely with his people in the degree and kind of afflictions he brings on them. He will bring various afflictions on various sorts of persons, such [as] are suitable for them, and he will afflict them no more than is for their good."

9. Similar cross-hatch marks are also found at the ends of nos. 59, 114, 123, 125, and 155. Their significance is not evident, and it is not certain they were added by JE. The hand and ink of nos. 45 and 46 are like the sermon on Ps. 136:1, JE's Thanksgiving sermon for November 1736 (see discussion above, p. 41).

1. MS: "Represented."

47. That the earth is so small a thing in comparison of the distance between us and the highest heaven, that if we were there, that not only the high palaces and highest mountains would look low whose height we gaze and wonder at now, but the whole earth would be less than nothing—nothing could be seen of it. Yea, if it were many million times bigger than it is, yea, probably many millions of millions times, it would probably be too small a speck to be seen, i.e. it would still be less than nothing. It seems to typify how that worldly things, all worldly honor and pleasure and profit, yea, the whole world or all worldly things put together, is so much lower and less than heavenly glory, that when the saints come to be in heaven, all will appear as it were infinitely less than nothing.

48. Corn must be first ground to powder before 'tis fit for our food. So Christ must first suffer very extremely, even to death, and a very dreadful death, before we can receive spiritual nourishment by him. The execution of God's wrath is compared to this very thing by Christ, viz. grinding to powder by a stone (Matt. 21:44). Hence meal is used as a type of Christ. II Kgs. 4:41, Elisha cast meal into the poisoned pottage and healed it. So corn must be baked in the oven or by the heat of the fire before 'tis fit for our nourishment, and all our food almost is prepared by fire; which has respect to Christ, our spiritual food, his being prepared for to be our food by suffering the fire of God's wrath. Vid. [no.] 68.

49. The trial of gold and silver in the fire is a type of the trying of saints and their graces by persecution and other occasions of suffering and self-denial for God's sake. Hereby the gold and silver is not only found to be true, but is refined and purified more from dross and made much better. So those trials of the saints don't only prove their sincerity, but refines them, purges away their dross, strengthens their graces and purges 'em from impure mixtures.

50. The rising and setting of the sun is a type of the death and resurrection of Christ. Vid. notes on Deut. 21:23 and Luke 23:44.[2]

2. "Blank Bible" note on Deut. 21:23, in part: "But 'tis very probable that one reason why those that were hanged and accursed were to be taken down and buried as soon as the sun was down, was that the sun was a type of Christ, and its setting was a type of the death of Christ (vid. note on Luke 23:44). The curse was to be removed and buried as soon as the sun was set, to signify that the curse is removed by the death of Christ. For he, in dying, was made

51. As the death of the body is a type of the second death, spiritual and eternal death, so the stinking of a dead corpse is a type of that said in Prov. [10:7], "The name of the wicked shall rot." 'Tis a type of that everlasting shame and contempt and abhorrence that the damned shall be the subjects of, signified by that, Is. 66:24, "And they shall go forth, and look upon the carcasses of the men that have transgressed against me: for their worm shall not die, neither shall their fire be quenched; and they shall be an abhorring to all flesh." Nos. 1, 61.

52. The flame of a candle or lamp, the manner of its burning, when first lighted up, with a feeble light; the ways of extinguishing of it; its being so easily put out by a breath or blast of wind; its being drowned by its own oil that feeds it, when there is an excess of it; the manner of lighting one by another; the manner of its going out when burnt out: seems designed by providence to represent the life of man. I Kgs. 11:36, "That David may always have a lamp" (or "candle") "before me in Jerusalem." I Kgs. 15:4, "Nevertheless for David's sake did the Lord his God give him a lamp," or *candle*, "in Jerusalem." So II Kgs. 8:19; II Chron. 21:7. Job 18:6, "His candle" (or "lamp") "shall be put out with him"; Job 21:17, "How oft is the candle" (or "lamp") "of the wicked put out! and how oft cometh their destruction upon them!" So Prov. 13:9, 24:20 and 20:20.

53. The different glory of the sun, moon and stars represents the different glory of Christ and the glorified saints. The sun represents Christ. The moon well represents the glory of the prophets and apostles and other ministers of Christ that have been improved as great

---

a curse for us; and the curse, by his death, is taken from the earth, or at least from the land of Israel, or the land of the church, so that that land is not defiled. God's people have not the curse remaining amongst them to render them abominable to God and to cause him to depart from them. Their sins and abominations are buried forever out of his sight by Christ's death. Indeed, it was so ordered that the body of Christ, though it was hanged on a tree, was taken down and buried before sun-setting: the Jews took it down before, that it might not remain in the open air on the sabbath day (John 19:31). This seems to be so ordered because Christ, though made a curse, was not such a curse as was removed by what was typified by the setting of the sun, but he was the antitype itself."

"Blank Bible" note on Luke 23:44, in part: "That the sun is a type of Christ was probably one reason why Christ's resurrection was about the time of the rising of the sun, i. e. its first rising by its light; because the rising of the sun is a type of the resurrection of Christ, as the sun's setting is a type of the death of Christ (vid. note on Deut. 21:23). And though the rising of the sun happens so often, 'tis no sign that it is not a type of the resurrection of Christ that is but once; for 'tis fit that the type should be repeated often but that the antitype should be but once, as the daily sacrifices of old.... Vid. "Shadows of Divine Things" no. 54."

lights of his church and instruments of promoting and establishing his kingdom and glory, and so have been luminaries to enlighten the world by reflecting the light of the sun, that is, of Christ, and conveying his beams to them; and possibly the Blessed Virgin who, in another respect, was the instrument of bringing this light to the world—but yet, in such a respect that the other is compared:[3] for they are called Christ's mother, they travail in birth till Christ is formed and brought forth, they are the great instrument of bringing forth the man-child, in the sense in which it is spoken in Rev. 12:5. See notes on Cant. 3:11, the second part of that note;[4] see note on I Cor. 15:42.[5]

54. As the sun, by rising out of darkness and from under the earth, raises the whole world with him, raises mankind out of their beds, and by his light as it were renews all things and fetches 'em up out of darkness, so Christ, rising from the grave and from a state of death, he, as the first begotten from the dead, raises all his church with him; Christ the first fruits, and afterwards they that are Christ's at his coming. And as all the world is enlightened and brought out of darkness by the rising of the sun, so by Christ's rising we are begotten again to a living hope; and all our happiness and life and light and glory and the restitution of all things is from Christ rising from the dead, and is by his resurrection.

55. That the works of nature are intended and contrived of God to signify and indigitate spiritual things is particularly evident, concerning the rainbow, by God's own express revelation.

3. "The other," i. e. the prophets, apostles, and other ministers of Christ. The subject is treated in two "Blank Bible" notes cited in the entry (see below, notes 4 and 5), and in "Scripture" no. 314, on Luke 1:35.

4. In the second part of the "Blank Bible" note on Cant. 3:11, both the bride and the mother in the Song are taken to refer to the church, but with a distinction: "By 'his mother' here seems especially to be meant the church as holding forth the word of Christ and administering the ordinances of Christ, whereby souls are converted and brought forth and brought to an union and spiritual marriage with Christ. And therefore the ministers of the gospel seem especially to be intended by 'his mother,' for they travail in birth with souls till Christ be formed in them (Gal. 4:19)."

5. In the "Blank Bible" note on I Cor. 15:42, the glory of the sun represents the glory of Christ's "resurrection" body, and the glory of the moon represents the glory of those of the apostles, prophets, and other lights of the church, as well as that of the Virgin Mary: "She was the instrument of conveying this light to the world in a way to which the way in which the apostles and other ministers do is compared; for they travail in birth till Christ is formed and brought forth, and are the great instruments of bringing forth the man-child, in the sense spoken of, Rev. 12:5."

56. (Vid. nos. 5, 9, 12.) Eph. 5:30–32, "For we are members of his body, of his flesh, and of his bones. For this cause shall a man leave his father and mother, and shall be joined unto his wife, and they two shall be one flesh. This is a great mystery: but I speak concerning Christ and the church." By this passage of Scripture it is evident that God hath ordered the state and constitution of the world of mankind as he has to that end, that spiritual things might be represented by them. For here the Apostle tells us that 'tis so ordered of God that a man should "leave his father and his mother and cleave to his wife" for this cause, viz. because Christ is so closely united to the church (for 'tis much the most natural so to understand it). And then in the next words says, "This is a great mystery: but I speak concerning Christ and the church": a great mystery, i.e. a mysterious typical representation, which refers ultimately to the union between Christ and the church. God had respect to Adam and Eve as a type of Christ and the church, when he took Eve out of Adam and gave this institution mentioned in Genesis.

57. 'Tis very fit and becoming of God, who is infinitely wise, so to order things that there should be a voice of his in his works instructing those that behold them, and pointing forth and showing divine mysteries and things more immediately appertaining to himself and his spiritual kingdom. The works of God are but a kind of voice or language of God, to instruct intelligent beings in things pertaining to himself.[6] And why should we not think that he would teach and instruct by his works in this way as well as others, viz. by representing divine things by his works, and so pointing them forth, especially since we know that God hath so much delighted in this way of instruction?

58. (Join this to "Miscellanies" nos. 362 and 370.)[7] 'Tis a sign that the beautiful variety of the colors of light was designed as a type of the various beauties and graces of the Spirit of God, that divine and spiritual beauties and excellencies are so often represented in Scripture by beautiful colors. Thus particularly, the colors of the rainbow are made use of, as has been shown ("Miscellanies" nos. 362 and 370).[8] So it was

6. For further comments on God's works as a language, see text of JE's MS notebook, "Types," below, pp. 146–53.

7. Because this note begins the first line of text in the MS, JE must have written it before proceeding with the entry itself. It does not indicate, therefore, that JE had intended actually to write this entry in the "Miscellanies" rather than "Images."

8. The first portion of "Miscellanies" no. 362, under the head "Trinity," was rewritten as "Miscellanies" no. 370. The passage referred to here is substantially the same in both places.

in the colors of the precious stones of the breastplate of the high priest, in which were red, yellow, green, blue and purple, and by the colors of the precious stones of the foundations and gates of the new Jerusalem, in which were all those same colors (see Chambers' *Cyclopedia*).[9] The foundations, gates, windows and borders of the church, of the City of God, are said to be of such precious stones in Is. 54:11–12; and God there promises to lay her foundations on fair or beautiful colors. So the temple of Solomon was beautified with precious stones of various beautiful colors (I Chron. 29:2).[1] God's appearance is said to be as of a jasper and sardine stone (Rev. 4:3): a jasper is green, sometimes red, sometimes purple, sometimes of many colors (see Chambers),[2] and a sardine, which is red. So the light of the new Jerusalem is said to be as of "a stone most precious, even a jaspar stone" (Rev. 21:11). The streets of the city were as "pure gold, like unto clear glass" [v. 18]. So the hangings of the tabernacle and temple, and the ephod and breastplate, were of blue, purple [and] scarlet. Thus the amiable beauties and graces of the Spirit of God are represented by various beautiful colors to the eye, in the same manner as by the various sweet spices of the holy anointing oil, and the sweet incense and the various sweet odors of the

---

In the version of no. 370 it is as follows: "The various sorts of rays of the sun and their beautiful colors do well represent the Spirit, or the amiable excellency of God, and the various beautiful graces and virtues of the Spirit.... Therefore, I suppose, the rainbow was chosen to be a sign of the covenant; and St. John saw a rainbow round about the throne of God (Rev. 4:3) ... so Ezekiel saw a rainbow round about the throne (Ezek. 1:28). And I believe the variety that there is in the rays of the sun, and their various beautiful colors, were designed in the creation for this very purpose. See 'Shadows of Divine Things' no. 58." In "Scripture" no. 348, JE discusses at length the typological import of the rainbow.

9. Chambers, *Cyclopedia*, 2, 860. In the article, "Precious, or Pretious Stones," Chambers summarizes Bp. John Wilkins' classification of precious stones according to their transparency and color: "The *more transparent* he distinguishes into such as are colourless, as the Diamond and white Saphir; and colour'd, which are either red, as the Ruby, Carbuncle, and Granate; yellow, as the Chrysolite, and Topaz; green, as the Emerald, Smaragd, and Beryl; blueish, as the Saphir; and purple or violaceous, as the Amathist and Hyacinth."

1. In the sermon on Hag. 2:7–9, JE takes Solomon's temple as a type of Christ: "The beauty and excellency of Christ, where it is discovered, is a glorious sight. Christ is the antitype of Solomon's temple that was so exceeding costly and magnificent, and therefore his beauty is the antitype of the beauty and magnificence of that temple. But the antitype exceeds the type, inasmuch as it is the substance of which the type is only the shadow.... He that sees Christ's excellency in an house of worship sees that of which the glory of Solomon's temple was but a dark shadow." This sermon is inscribed, "After the finishing of the new meeting house, Dec. 25, 1737." Comparisons of paper watermarks, hand, and ink indicate that "Images" no. 58 was probably written within a short time of this date (see above, pp. 41–42).

2. *Cyclopedia*, 2, 367. In his article, "Jasper," Chambers mentions these colors in describing the "florid" jasper found in the Pyrenees.

different spices and sweet fruits so often spoken of in Solomon's song. Joseph's coat of many colors represents the various spiritual beauties and graces of his robe of righteousness; see sermon on Acts 7:9ff.[3]

The various colors of the light of the sun signifies the various beauties of the Spirit of God in two respects, and are so made use of in Scripture: first, to represent the moral goodness of God (which, as it is in God, is the same with the Holy Ghost), as variously expressed and manifested in several attributes, as justice, truth, goodness, mercy, patience and the like; second, to represent the virtues and graces in the saints, that are the various exercises and fruits of the Spirit in their hearts.

White, which comprehends all other colors, is made use of in Scripture often to signify holiness, which comprehends all moral goodness and virtue: sometimes to denote the holiness of God (as Rev. 19:11, Matt. 17:2, Rev. 20:11 and elsewhere), and sometimes the holiness or righteousness of the saints, either imputed or inherent (Rev. 3:4–5, 18; 4:4; 7:9, 13; 15:6; 19:8, 14).

There is a variety in light: one and the same white light, though it seems to be an exceeding simple thing, yet contains a very great variety of kinds of rays, all of so many different excellent and lovely appearance. So the same simple Spirit of God seems to contain a great variety, and therefore he is in Revelation called "seven Spirits." There is one body, one Spirit, and yet a vast variety of gifts. I Cor. 12:4, "Now there are diversities of gifts, but the same Spirit"; and v. 11, "All these worketh that one and selfsame Spirit."

59. (Add this to no. 8.) If there be such an admirable analogy observed by the Creator in his works throughout the whole system of the natural world, so that one thing seems to be made in imitation of another, and especially the less perfect to be made in imitation of the more perfect, so that the less perfect is as it were a figure or image of the more perfect—so beasts are made in imitation of men, plants are [a] kind of types of animals, minerals are in many things in imitation of plants—why is it not rational to suppose that the corporeal and visible world should be designedly made and constituted in analogy to the

---

3. This foregoing sentence, with the reference, was inserted later at the end of the paragraph. Neither the Beinecke nor Trask libraries contains a sermon on Acts 7:9ff. In the "Blank Bible" note on Acts 7:9, and in other places, JE takes Joseph to be a type of Christ. Cf. "Types of the Messiah," pp. 146–53, above.

more spiritual, noble and real world? 'Tis certainly agreeable to what is apparently the method of God's working./[4]

60. That of so vast and innumerable a multitude of blossoms that appear on a tree, so few come to ripe fruit; and that so few of so vast a multitude of seeds as are yearly produced, so few come to be a plant; and that there is so great a waste of the seed of both plants and animals, but one in a great multitude ever bringing forth any things, seem to be lively types: how few are saved out of the mass of mankind, and particularly how few are sincere, of professing Christians, that never wither away but endure to the end, and how, of the many that are called, few are chosen.

61. Ravens that with delight feed on carrion seem to be remarkable types of devils who with delight prey upon the souls of the dead. A dead, filthy, rotten carcass is a lively image of the soul of a wicked man that is spiritually and exceeding filthy and abominable. Their spiritual corruption is of a far more loathsome savor than the stench of a putrefying carcass. Such souls the devil delights in; they are his proper food. Again, dead carcasses are types of the departed souls of the dead, and are so used (Is. 66:24). Ravens don't prey on the bodies of animals till they are dead; so the devil has not the souls of wicked men delivered into his tormenting hands and devouring jaws till they are dead. Again, the body in such circumstances, being dead and in loathsome putrefaction, is a lively image of a soul in the dismal state it is in under eternal death. See nos. 1, 51.

Ravens are birds of the air that are expressly used by Christ as types of the devil in the parable of the sower and the seed [Matt. 13:3–8]. The devil is "the prince of the power of the air," as he is called [Eph. 2:2]; devils are spirits of the air. The raven by its blackness represents the prince of darkness. Sin and sorrow and death are all in Scripture represented by darkness or the color black; but the devil is the father of sin, a most foul and wicked spirit, and the prince of death and misery.

62. (Vid. [no.] 17.) The natural life is continually supported by the breath that enters into the vitals, by which is represented how the spiritual life is constantly maintained by the Spirit of God entering into

---

4. The significance of the mark here is not evident.

the soul. And therefore one is used as a type of the other in the Scripture, as particularly in Ezek. 37:9–10, "Prophesy unto the wind, prophesy, son of man, and say unto the wind, Thus saith the Lord God; Come from the four winds, O breath, and breathe upon these slain, that they may live. So I prophesied as he commanded me, and the breath came into them, and they lived, and stood up upon their feet, an exceeding great army"; together with vv. 13–14, "And ye shall know that I am the Lord, when I shall have opened your graves, O my people, and brought you up out of your graves, And shall have put my spirit in you, and you shall live." John 20:22, "He breathed on them, and saith unto them, Receive ye the Holy Ghost."

63. In the manner in which birds and squirrels that are charmed by serpents go into their mouths and are destroyed by them, is a lively representation of the manner in which sinners under the gospel are very often charmed and destroyed by the devil. The animal that is charmed by the serpent seems to be in great exercise and fear, screams and makes ado, but yet don't flee away. It comes nearer to the serpent, and then seems to have its distress increased and goes a little back again, but then comes still nearer than ever, and then appears as if greatly affrighted and runs or flies back again a little way, but yet don't flee quite away, and soon comes a little nearer and a little nearer with seeming fear and distress that drives 'em a little back between whiles, until at length they come so [near] that the serpent can lay hold of them: and so they become their prey.[5]

Just thus, oftentimes sinners under the gospel are bewitched by their lusts. They have considerable fears of destruction and remorse of conscience that makes 'em hang back, and they have a great deal of exercise between while, and some partial reformations, but yet they don't flee away. They won't wholly forsake their beloved lusts, but return to 'em again; and so whatever warnings they have, and whatever checks of conscience that may exercise 'em and make [them] go back a little and stand off for a while, yet they will keep their beloved

5. Of the rattlesnakes of New England, Judge Paul Dudley wrote, "I dare not answer for the Truth of every Story I have heard, of their charming, or Power of Fascination; but yet I am abundantly satisfied from many Witnesses, both *English* and *Indian*, that a Rattlesnake will charm both Squirrels and Birds from a Tree into his Mouth.... When they charm, they make a hoarse Noise with their Mouths, and a soft Rattle with their Tails, the Eye at the same time fixed on the Prey" ("An Account of the Rattlesnake," *Philosophical Transactions*, 32 [1723], 293–94).

sin in sight, and won't utterly break off from it and forsake [it], but will return to it again and again, and go a little further and a little further, until Satan remedilessly makes a prey of them. But if anyone comes and kills the serpent, the animal immediately escapes. So the way in which poor souls are delivered from the snare of the devil is by Christ's coming and bruising the serpent's head.

64. Hills and mountains are types of heaven, and often made use of as such in Scripture. These are difficultly ascended. To ascend them, one must go against the natural tendency of the flesh that must be contradicted in all the ascent, in every step of it, and the ascent is attended with labor, sweat and weariness, and there are commonly many hideous rocks in the way. 'Tis a great deal easier descending into valleys.

This is a representation of the difficulty, labor and self-denial of the way to heaven; and how agreeable it is to the inclination of the flesh to descend into hell. At the bottom of valleys, especially deep valleys, there is water—either a lake or other water. But water, as has been shown elsewhere in "Notes on Scripture,"[6] commonly signifies misery, especially that which is occasioned by the wrath of God. So in hell is a lake or gulf of misery and wrath.

65. Eccles. 3:21, "Who knoweth the spirit of man that goeth upward, and the spirit of a beast that goeth downward to the earth?" The Wise Man there seems to have evident respect to the manner of the breath's going forth in death, in men and beasts, by the posture they are commonly in when dying, as a type that the spirit or soul of man returns to God that gave it (ch. 12:7), and the spirit of a beast to the earth where the body goes, that is, ceases to be, comes to nothing, as the body does that putrifies and turns to earth.

66. (Vid. [no.] 64.) Hills and mountains, as they represent heaven, so they represent eminence in general, or any excellent and high attainment. And as hills, especially high mountains, are not ascended with-

---

6. JE probably refers to "Scripture" no. 297, on Gen. 7:1–7, in which the company in Noah's Ark is seen as a type of the church of Christ. "The ark was made for the salvation of the church, and for the saving the church from the destruction ... which all the rest of mankind were to be the subjects in an overflowing deluge of God's wrath.... So the way by which we are saved by Christ is by flying from the deluge of God's wrath, and taking refuge in Christ, and being in him."

out difficulty and labor, and many rocks and steep places are in the way, so men don't attain to anything eminent or of peculiar excellence without difficulty.

67. (Vid. [no.] 29.) He that is traveling up a very high mountain, if he goes on climbing, will at length get to that height and eminence, as at last not only to have his prospect vastly larger, but he will get above the clouds and winds, and where he will enjoy a perpetual serenity and calm. This may encourage Christians constantly and steadfastly to climb the Christian hill. The perfect and uninterrupted serenity and calm there is on some very high mountain is also a type of the heavenly state. See [no.] 159.

68. (Vid. [no.] 48.) As wheat is prepared to be our food to refresh and nourish and strengthen us, by being threshed, and then ground to powder, and then baked in the oven, whereby it becomes a type of our spiritual food, even Christ, the bread which comes down from heaven, which becomes our food by his sufferings; so the juice of the grape is a type of the blood of Christ, as it is prepared to be our refreshing drink to exhilarate our spirits and make us glad, by being pressed out in a wine press. The pressure of a winepress is that to which the suffering of the wrath of God is often compared in Scripture. And because our bread made of wheat, and our wine made of the juice of the grape, are thus types of Jesus Christ, as given for our meat and drink by his sufferings and the sacrifice of himself, therefore this bread and wine in Deut. 32:14 is called "the fat of the kidneys of wheat" and "the pure blood of the grape," in an evident allusion to those parts of slain beasts that were offered to God in sacrifice, that were by God's law appropriated to him and wholly offered to him as being the most essential parts of the sacrifice. For the fat of the kidneys and the blood of their sacrifices were things which, by divine appointment,[7] were parts of their sacrifices so appropriated. So oil, that great type of the grace of the Holy Spirit, is procured by treading and pressing the olives (Mic. 6:15). But this Holy Spirit is the sum of all the benefits of Christ, procured for us by his sufferings.

*Corol.* Hence we learn how fitly bread and wine were chosen to represent the body and blood of Christ in the Lord's Supper. See further concerning that text in Deut. 32:14, no. 149; see [no.] 189.

---

7. MS: "appointed."

69. Some of the most poisonous sorts of serpents have their tongue for their weapon, wherewith they mortally sting others, and serpents commonly threaten with their tongues, to represent the venomous nature of the tongues of wicked men, and how much the corruption of the heart flows out by that member, and in how venomous and deadly a manner it is put forth thereby. And therefore 'tis said of wicked men that the poison of asps is under their tongues [Rom. 3:13], and the apostle James says the tongue is "full of deadly poison" (Jas. 3:8), and that it is "a fire, a world of iniquity" and sets together "on fire the course of nature; and is set on fire of hell. For every kind of beasts, and of birds, and of serpents, and of things in the sea, is tamed, and hath been tamed of mankind: But the tongue can no man tame; it is an unruly evil, full of deadly poison" [Jas. 3:6–8]. And[8] Ps. 140:3, "They have sharpened their tongues like a serpent."

70. If we look on these shadows of divine things as the voice of God, purposely, by them, teaching us these and those spiritual and divine things, to show of what excellent advantage it will be, how agreeably and clearly it will tend to convey instruction to our minds, and to impress things on the mind, and to affect the mind. By that we may as it were hear God speaking to us. Wherever we are and whatever we are about, we may see divine things excellently represented and held forth, and it will abundantly tend to confirm the Scriptures, for there is an excellent agreement between these things and the Holy Scriptures.

71. It is from littleness of soul that the mind is easily disturbed and put out of frame by the reproaches and the ill treatment of men; as we see that little streams of waters are much disturbed in their course by small unevennesses and obstacles that they meet with, and make a great deal of noise as they pass over them, whereas great and mighty streams would pass over them calmly and quietly,[9] smooth and unruffled. Prov. 16:32, "He that is slow to anger is better than the mighty; and he that rules his spirit than he that takes a city."

72. When God began to make the world and put it into order and cause light to shine, it was a chaos, in a state of utter confusion, "with-

8. MS: "and the."

9. MS: "with." JE at first wrote "with a smooth and unruffled"; then he deleted the article "a," but not the preposition "with." Hence Miller: "with smooth and unruffled [surface]."

out form and void, and darkness was upon the face thereof" [Gen. 1:2]. So commonly things are in a state of great confusion before God works some great and glorious work in the church and in the world, or in some particular part of the church or world, and oftentimes towards particular persons. Any very great and remarkable work of God is in Scripture commonly compared to a work of creation; and before God appears in such a work, and so causes light to shine, things are commonly in a most dark, confused and woeful state, and appear most remote from anything that is good, and as if there was no hope of their ever coming to rights. So we may expect it should be before the beginning of the glorious times of the church of God, and after this confusion, light will be the first thing that will appear—light, clearly to explain and defend the truth. The doctrines of the gospel will begin to shine forth with clear and irresistible light.

This lower world, being without form and void, at first was an image of what it was afterwards to be: a world of confusion and emptiness, vanity of vanities.[1] See "Notes on Scripture" no. 342.[2]

73. The way of a cat with a mouse that it has taken captive is a lively emblem of the way of the devil with many wicked men. A mouse is a foul, unclean creature, a fit type of a wicked man. Lev. 11:29, "These also shall be unclean unto you among the creeping things that creep upon the earth; the weasel, and the mouse." Is. 66:17, "Eating swine's flesh, and the abomination, and the mouse." The cat makes a play and sport of the poor mouse; so the devil does as it were make himself sport with a wicked man. The cat lets the mouse go, and it seems to have escaped. It hopes it is delivered, but is suddenly catched up again before it can get clear. And so, time after time, the mouse makes many vain attempts, thinks itself free when it is still a captive, is taken up again by the paws and into the jaws of its devourer, as if it were just going to be destroyed, but then is let go again, but never quite escapes; till at last it yields its life to its enemy, and is crushed between his teeth and totally devoured. So many wicked men, especially false professors of religion and sinners under gospel light, are led captive by Satan at his will, are under the power and dominion of their lusts; and though they have many struggles of conscience about their sins, yet never

1. This sentence, and the following reference, are a later addition to the entry.

2. "Scripture" no. 342, on Gen. 1:2, repeats the substance of the last sentence of this entry, and adds: "So in the first state of man in his infancy, is an image of what man always is in himself, a poor, polluted, helpless worm."

wholly escape them. When they seem to escape, they fall into them again, and so again and again, till at length they are totally and utterly devoured by Satan.

74. Lightning more commonly strikes high things such as high towers, spires and pinnacles, and high trees, and is observed to be most terrible in mountainous places; which may signify that heaven is an enemy to all proud persons, and that especially makes such the marks of his vengeance. Is. 2:12–17, "For the day of the Lord shall be upon every one that is proud and lofty, and upon every one that is lifted up; and he shall be brought low: And upon all the cedars of Lebanon, that are high and lifted up, and upon all the oaks of Bashan, And upon all the high mountains, and upon all the hills that are lifted up, and upon every high tower, and upon every fenced wall, And upon all the ships of Tarshish, and upon all pleasant pictures. And the loftiness of man shall be bowed down, and the haughtiness of men shall be made low: and the Lord alone shall be exalted in that day."

75. That balm that came chiefly from Gilead, that was used in the land of Israel and in all those eastern parts of the world, and so is to this day, as the chief and most sovereign medicine for healing wounds, was procured by piercing the balsam tree; whereby the tree is caused to bleed, and this blood of the tree is the balm, which, if done with iron nails, the tree dies (see Chambers).[3] So the blood of Christ, the sovereign balm for healing the wounds of our souls, is procured by piercing of Christ.

76. Concerning the moon, her revolution and changes, and especially conjunction with the sun, see notes on Num. 10:10.[4] Con-

3. *Cyclopedia, 1,* 78. In "Balm of Gilead," Chambers reports several opinions: Theophrastus', that the incision must be made with iron nails; Pliny's, that iron makes the tree die; and Tacitus', that the sap does not flow through incisions made with iron.

4. "Blank Bible" note on Num. 10:10, in part: "The moon is a lively image of the church; as she borrows all her light from the sun, so doth the church receive light from Christ, the Sun of Righteousness. The old moon represents the church under the Old Testament, which looks to, depends upon, and receives light from Christ yet to come, and is drawing nearer and nearer to the time of Christ's coming, as the old moon [looks towards the sun] and receives light from it yet to come, whose conjunction with the moon is yet future. The new moon represents the church under the New Testament, which receives light from Christ already come and having already united himself to the human nature, as the new moon looks towards and receives light from the sun as having already been in conjunction with her. The conjunction of the sun and moon in the time of the change seems to represent the

cerning eclipse of the sun and moon, see "Notes on Scripture" no. 315.[5]

77. There is a wonderful analogy between what is seen in RIVERS: their gathering from innumerable small branches beginning at a great distance one from another in different regions, some on the sides or tops of mountains, others in valleys, and all conspiring to one common issue, all after their very diverse and contrary courses which they held for a while, yet all gathering more and more together the nearer they come to their common end and ultimate issue, and all at length discharging themselves at one mouth into the same ocean. Here is livelily represented how all things tend to one, even to God, the boundless ocean, which they can add nothing to, as mightiest rivers that continually disembogue themselves into the ocean add nothing to it sensibly. The waters of the ocean are not raised by it; yea, all the rivers together, great and small, together with all the brooks and little streams, can't raise the waters of the ocean in the least degree.

The innumerable streams, of which great rivers are constituted, running in such infinitely various and contrary courses, livelily represent the various dispensations of divine providence. Some of them begin at the greatest distance from the common mouth, others nearer

---

coming of Christ, whereby Christ actually united himself to the church by uniting himself to the human nature, the church's nature."

5. "Scripture" no. 315, on Num. 10:10, in part: "The sun is sometimes eclipsed in his conjunction with the moon, which signifies two things, viz. 1. The veiling of his glory by his incarnation.... As the moon proves a veil to hide the glory of the sun, so the flesh of Christ was a veil that hid his divine glory. 2. It signifies his death. The sun is sometimes totally eclipsed by the moon at her change; so Christ died at the time of the change of the church from the old dispensation to the new. The sun is eclipsed at his conjunction with the moon in her darkness; so Christ, taking our nature upon him in his low and broken state, died in it.... The moon, that receives all her light from the sun, eclipses the sun and takes away his light; so Christ was put to death by those that he came to save. He is put to death by the iniquities of those that he came to give life to; and he was immediately crucified by the hands of some of them, and all of them have pierced him in the disposition and tendency of that sin that they have been guilty of; for all have manifested and expressed a mortal enmity against him. 'Tis an argument that the eclipse of the sun is a type of Christ's death, because the sun suffered a total eclipse miraculously at that time that Christ died.

"The sun can be in a total eclipse but a very little while, much less than the moon, though neither of them can always be in an eclipse; so Christ could not, by reason of his divine glory and worthiness, be long held of death, in no measure so long as the saints may be, though it ben't possible that either of them should always be held of it.

"The sun's coming out of his eclipse is a figure of his resurrection from the dead. As the sun is restored to light, so the moon that eclipsed him begins to receive light from him, and so

to it, multitudes of them meeting first to constitute certain main branches of the river before they empty themselves into the main river and so into the ocean. Some of the first constituent streams never empty themselves into any of the branches at all, but empty themselves directly into the main river. Others first empty themselves into other branches, and those into others, and those still into others, and so on many times, before they yield their tribute to the main river. Several springs first constitute a brook, and then many of those brooks constitute a small river, and then several of those small rivers meet to constitute a main branch of the main river, and then all together empty into that main river. Some of the constituent branches of the main river have their head or source at the greatest distance from the mouth, others take their source much nearer the mouth: and so all along there are new heads or new sources, beginning from the head to the mouth of the main river. Some of these branches run directly contrary to others, and yet all meet at last. And the same branches don't keep the same course: their course is not continually in a right line, that which appears to us the directest course to the main river, but sometimes they run one way, sometimes another. Sometimes their course is directly contrary to what it is at others. Sometimes instead of going towards the main river they tend to, they run for a considerable space right from it. But yet nothing is lost by this, but something gained: they nevertheless fail not of emptying themselves into the main river in proper times and due place, and bring the greater tribute of waters for their crooked and contrary courses.

And so it is with the main river itself. Its course is not directly the shortest way towards the ocean to which its waters are due, but tends thither by degrees, with many windings and turnings, sometimes seeming to run from the ocean and not towards it. If a spectator were to judge by the appearances of things before his eyes, he would think

---

to partake of his restored light. So the church, for whose sins Christ died, and who has pierced Christ, rises with Christ, is begotten again to a living hope by the resurrection of Christ from the dead, and is made partaker of the life and power of his resurrection, and is partaker of the glory of his exaltation, is raised up together and made to sit together in heavenly places in him....

"The moon is eclipsed when at the full, in its greatest glory, which may signify several things. That God is wont to bring some great calamity on his visible church, when [in] its greatest glory ... and that his people may not lift up themselves against him, that he alone may be exalted. 2. That 'tis often God's manner to bring some grievous calamity on his saints, at times when they have received the greatest light and joys, and have been most exalted with smiles of heaven upon them.... he is wont to bring with it some calamity to eclipse it, to keep them [from] being exalted in their prosperity, and trusting in it."

that the river could [not] reach the ocean. There appears such an innumerable multitude of obstacles in the way, many hills and high mountains which a person that views at a distance sees no way between. He don't discover those ways through the hideous forests, and the openings between the mountains are not to be seen till we come to them. The winding passages through mountainous countries are not to be discovered but by tracing the course of the waters themselves. But yet amidst all these obstacles these rivers find their way, and fail not at last of an arrival at the ocean at last, though they pass through so many vast regions that all seem to be full of obstacles for so long a course together. And 'tis observable that those very hills and mountains that appear like the most insurmountable obstacles, instead of obstructing the course of these rivers, do afford the greatest supplies and additions. These rivers will at last come to the ocean, and 'tis impossible to hinder; 'tis in vain for men to attempt to turn back the stream or put a stop to it. Whatever obstacles are in the way, the waters will either bear them away before them, or will find a passage round them, under them or above them.

I need not run the parallel between this and the course of God's providence through all ages, from the beginning to the end of the world, when all things shall have their final issue in God, the infinite, inexhaustible fountain whence all things come at first, as all the rivers come from the sea, and whither they all shall come at last: for of him and to him are all things, and he is the Alpha and Omega, the beginning and the end. God hath provided a watercourse for the overflowing of the waters and he turns the rivers of water whithersoever it pleaseth him.[6]

By what has been spoken of, is it particularly livelily represented and shown, after what manner all the dispensations of providence, from the beginning of the world till the coming of Christ, all pointed to Christ: all had respect to his coming, and working out redemption and setting up his kingdom in the world, and all finally issued in this great event. From time to time in the different successive ages of the world, there began new dispensations of providence, tending to make way and forward this great event; as there are heads of new branches all along as we come nearer and nearer to the mouth of the main river. Thus in Noah began a new series of dispensations of providences, in addition to what had been begun before, making further preparation

6. See Rev. 21:6, Job 38:24, and Prov. 21:1.

for the coming of the Messiah. Again in Abraham began another
remarkable course of providences to make way for the same event,
which held till Christ came. So again, in the redemption out of Egypt,
and in David and in the Babylonish captivity.

The course of divine providence seems to be represented by a river
in Gen. 41:1–3 and Ezek. 1:1. It was near a river that Ezekiel saw the
wheels of providence, so v. 3; so again, Dan. 8:2–3, 16, and Dan. 10:4–
5 and ch. 12:6–8. See the next.[7]


78. (See the last.) We see the reverse in TREES of what we do in
[rivers]. In these, all comes from one common stock and is distributed
into innumerable branches, beginning at the root where the trunk is
biggest of all, and ending in the extremities of the smallest twigs. The
water here, in the sap of those trees, has a contrary course from what it
has in rivers, where the course begins in the extremities of the smallest
branches, and ends in the mouth of the river where the river is largest,
and all the waters are collected into one body.

What is observable in trees is also a lively emblem of many spiritual
things, as particularly of the dispensations of providence since the
coming of Christ. Christ is as it were the trunk of the tree, and all the
church are his branches: "I am the vine, ye are the branches," says
Christ [John 15:5]. Christ, rising from the dead, is as it were the trunk
of the tree, which appears coming out of the ground. And how do we,
from this one rising Head, see the body of Christ multiplied. The
Christian church, as distinguished from the Jewish, began in Christ's
resurrection. And how many branches shot forth soon after Christ's
resurrection. The apostles, after that, were endowed with power from
on high; these were as it were main branches, whence all the lesser
branches came. The apostle Paul, who was a branch that shot forth
later than the rest, exceeded all in thirstiness and fruitfulness, so that
the bigger part of the future tree came from this branch. The tree
went on growing, and the further it proceeded in its growth, the more
abundantly did its branches multiply; till the tree filled the Roman
Empire in a few hundreds of years, and will fill the whole earth at last.
Thus the parable of the grain of mustard seed is verified. This tree will
appear more and more glorious, till it shall appear in the greatest glory

7. The last paragraph was added somewhat later; otherwise, no. 77 appears to have been
copied out at once from a previously written draft. From the paper JE added to the MS to
complete the entry, and from its hand and ink, it was probably written in the last half of 1738
(see above, p. 42).

of all at the end of all things, and its full ripe fruits shall be gathered in. And though there have been many winters, and may be more, wherein this tree has ceased growing, and has been in a great measure stripped of leaves and fruit and seemed to be dead or dying, yet springs and summers are appointed to follow these winters, wherein the tree shall flourish again and appear higher and larger and more abundantly multiplied in its branches and fruit than ever before.

This tree is sometimes represented as first beginning in Abraham and sometimes in David, and Christ himself as the branch of these roots, but Christ is most properly the trunk or body of the tree. Indeed, the course of the sap of the tree, from its beginning in the extremities of the roots to its end in the extremity of the branches, is an emblem of the whole series and scheme of divine providence, both before and after Christ, from the beginning to the end of the world. The sap in the roots is like the water of a river, gathering from small branches into a common body; and this, as was said before, represents the course of divine providence during the times of the Old Testament, when the designs of providence as they related to Christ and the work of redemption—which is as it were the summary comprehension of all God's works of providence—was hid as it were underground. All was under a veil, and the scheme of redemption was a mystery, kept secret from the foundation of the world. But after this the mystery was revealed, and the scheme of providence was like a tree above ground, gradually displayed as the branches successively put forth themselves. Hence we may observe that God's calling of Abraham and anointing David was as it were the planting the root whence the tree should grow, and Abraham and David were main roots whence the tree grows; but Christ himself is the sprout or branch from these roots, which becomes the tree whence all other branches proceed.

79. The whole material universe is preserved by gravity, or attraction, or the mutual tendency of all bodies to each other. One part of the universe is hereby made beneficial to another. The beauty, harmony and order, regular progress, life and motion, and in short, all the well-being of the whole frame, depends on it. This is a type of love or charity in the spiritual world.

80. When the sun sets in red, 'tis a sign that it will bring a fair day when it rises. So Christ, the Sun of Righteousness, set in blood. The sun is a type of Christ, and his setting is a type of his death, which was

with blood and dreadful sufferings, and thereby [he] rose with a fair day. By this means he rose, without clouds, in clear light, blessedness and honor for himself and all on whom he shines.

81. The Roman triumph was a remarkable type of Christ's ascension. The general of the Roman armies was sent forth from Rome, that glorious city and metropolis of the world, by the supreme Roman authority, into remote parts and the enemies' country, to fight with the enemies of the Roman state; as Christ, the captain of the Lord's hosts, was sent forth from Heaven, the head city of the universe, by the supreme authority of Heaven into this remote country, the country of Heaven's enemies, to conflict with those enemies. And on obtaining some very signal and great victory, he returned in triumph to the city whence he came out; entered the city in a very glorious manner. So Christ, having gone through the terrible conflict and obtained a complete and glorious victory, returned again to Heaven, the city whence he came, in a glorious triumphant manner. When the authority of Rome heard of his victory, they sent him the title of Imperator. So when Christ had conquered his enemies, he was invested with the greatest honor of rule and command; all power was given him in heaven and on earth.

As the Roman general was coming towards the city of Rome, the Roman people, and even the Senate themselves, went forth to meet him, and marched in order before him to the capitol, the principal building of the whole city, wherein was their chief temple of Jupiter, and where was the place of the sitting of the Senate. So when Christ was ascending to heaven, the inhabitants of heaven came forth to meet him, even the most glorious angels and archangels, the nobles and princes of that city, and joyfully conducted him to the highest and most honorable part of that city. The Roman general was richly clad in a purple robe, embroidered with figures of gold setting forth his glorious achievements. His buskins were set with pearl; he wore a crown of laurel or of gold. Which livelily represents the glory of Christ's ascension, when he came from the slaughter of his enemies, red in his apparel, traveling in the greatness of his strength and glorious in his apparel (Is. 63:1). He was drawn in a chariot adorned with ivory and plates of gold; so Christ is represented as ascending in the chariots of God after glorious victories over his enemies. Ps. 68:17–18, "The chariots of God are twenty thousand, even thousands of angels: the Lord is among them, as in Sinai, his holy place. Thou hast ascended on high," together with other parts of the psalm.

At the feet of the triumphing general were his children. So Christ, when he ascended into glory, did as it were carry up with him his children. He went into glory and took possession of it as their head, and not only for himself, but also for them, and actually carried a number of them with him; and at his second ascension, after the day of judgment, will carry all of them with him.

The cavalcade was led up by musicians. So God went up with a shout and the most high with the sound of a trumpet [Ps. 47:5]. Christ's ascension was attended with the joyful and glorious praises and songs of the heavenly hosts, represented by the joyful music and songs that attended the carrying up the ark into Mt. Zion, and the hosannas that attended Christ's entry into Jerusalem. And as then they strewed their garments in the way, and cut down branches of palm trees and strewed them in the way, singing praises to him as he passed, so, before the triumphal chariot as it passed, they all along strewed flowers, the music playing in praise of the conqueror, amidst the loud acclamations of the people crying, "*Io Triumphe.*"

The cavalcade was followed by the spoils taken from the enemy—their horses, arms, gold, silver, machines, tents, etc. After these came the kings, princes or generals subdued, loaden with chains and followed by mimics and buffoons who insulted over their misfortunes. Which is very agreeable to what is said of Christ, with an evident allusion to the Roman triumphs, in Col. 2:15, "And having spoiled principalities and powers, he made a show of them openly, triumphing over them in it." Next came the officers of the conquering troops with crowns on their heads. So the disciples of Christ, especially those that have had the greatest share with Christ in his conflict, such as the holy martyrs and those that Christ has improved as the chief ministers of his kingdom, shall triumph with him and be crowned and glorified together, and shall reign with him.

The triumphal chariot was followed by the Senate, clad in white robes, and the Senate by such citizens as had been set at liberty or ransomed; as Christ, in his triumph, is attended by the glorious angel principalities and powers in heavenly places, together with those saints, citizens of heaven, that have been ransomed and set at liberty by Christ, and these all as it were clothed with white robes (Rev. 19:13–14, ch. 7:9, 3:5, 18 and 6:11).

The procession in the Roman triumphs was closed by the sacrificers and their officers and utensils, with a white ox led along for the chief victim. In this order they proceeded through the triumphal gate along the Via Sacra to the capitol, where the victims were offered. In the meantime, all the temples were open and all the altars loaden with offerings and incense, which represent Christ at his ascension entering into the holiest of all, with his own blood, with his sufficient and perfect sacrifice, and the abundant incense of his merits, to present them there to God, the consequence of which is the abundant opening the temple of God to the giving free access to all.

These Roman triumphs were attended with games in public places and rejoicings everywhere, representing the unspeakable joy there was in heaven on occasion of Christ's ascension, which was attended with the utter confusion of Christ's enemies and their entire overthrow, as in the Roman triumphs. The captives, when arrived at the forum, were led back to prison and strangled. The rites and sacrifices being over, the triumpher treated the people in the capitol; as Christ, when he ascended on high, received gifts for men.

See notes on Ps. 68, concerning the removal of the ark, "Notes on Scripture" no. 319.[8]

82. There are three sorts of inhabitants of this world inhabiting its three regions, viz. the inhabitants of the earth, and the animals that inhabit the waters under the earth, and the fowls of heaven that inhabit the air or firmament of heaven. In these is some faint shadow of the three different sorts of inhabitants of the three worlds, viz. earth, heaven and hell. The birds represent the inhabitants of heaven. These appear beautiful above the beasts and fishes; many of them are decked with glorious [plumage].[9] Whereas others do but go on the earth or move in the waters, these fly with wings and are above all kinds of animals; employ themselves in music, many of them as it were sweetly praising their Creator. The fishes in the waters under the earth represent the inhabitants of hell. The waters in Scripture is represented as the place of the dead, the Rephaim, the destroyers; and whales and sea monsters that swim in the great deep are used in

8. In "Scripture" no. 319, on Ps. 68, the bringing up of the Ark into Jerusalem is developed as a parallel to the ascension of Christ. See also "Types of the Messiah," p. 218. For JE's use of van Mastricht's *Theoretica-Practica Theologia* and Chambers' *Cyclopedia* in this entry, see Miller, *Images or Shadows*, pp. 145–46, n. 9.

9. JE evidently omitted a word in copying from his draft; Miller interpolates "colors."

Scripture as emblems of devils and the wrath of God. And the miseries of death and God's wrath are there compared to the sea, to the deeps, to floods and billows, and the like.

83. The sun makes plants to flourish when it shines after rain; otherwise it makes them wither. So clouds and darkness and rains of affliction fit the soul for the clear shining of the Sun of Righteousness. Light and comfort, if the heart is not prepared by humiliation, do but make the heart worse. They fill it with the disease of pride, and destroy the welfare of the soul instead of promoting it. II Sam. 23:4.

84. The torrents and floods of liquid fire that sometimes are vomited out from the lower parts of the earth, the belly of hell, by the mouths of volcanoes, indicate or shadow forth what is in hell: viz. as it were a lake of fire and brimstone, deluges of fire and wrath to overwhelm wicked men, and mighty cataracts of wrath to come pouring down out of heaven on the heads of wicked men, as mighty torrents of liquid fire have sometimes come pouring down from Mount Etna and Vesuvius on cities or villages below. Such things do forebode the general conflagration.

85. Concerning the rising of the sun, see notes on Ps. 19:4–6, "Notes on Scripture" no. 328.[1]

86. As it is in the analogy that is to be observed in the works of nature, wherein the inferior are images of the superior, and the analogy holds through many ranks of beings, but becomes more and more faint and languid (thus, how many things in brutes are analogous to what is to be observed in men: in some the image is more lively, in others less, till we come to the lowest rank of brutes, in whom it is more faint than others; but if we go from them to plants, still the analogy and similitude holds in many things, and in different degrees in different plants, till we come to metals and some other inanimate things, wherein still is to be seen some very faint representations[2] of things

1. In "Scripture" no. 328, on Ps. 19:4–6, JE holds it is likely that the Holy Ghost uses expressions about the rising of the sun with "an eye to the rising of the Sun of Righteousness from the grave." The times of the Old Testament are night in comparison to the Gospel day, and the beginning of the Gospel dispensation is called the rising of the Sun of Righteousness in Mal. 4:2.
2. MS: "Represent."

appertaining to mankind); so it is with respect to the representations there are in the external world, of things in the spiritual world.[3] Thus the visible heavens are a type of the highest heavens, but in a lower degree mountains are types of heaven. The great deep under the earth is a type of hell, but in a lesser degree valleys, and the water that is in valleys, is so. The stars are types of saints in glory, and in a fainter degree the singing birds that fly in the firmament of heaven are so. And so in innumerable instances; and the same is to be observed of the types of Scripture.

87. He that is bitten with a poisonous serpent is exceedingly inclined to sleep, and is averse to a being kept awake; but if he sleeps in such circumstances, it is very mortal to him. So it is with respect to those that are bitten with the old serpent, the devil.

88. Multitudes of things, when they are good for nothing else, are good to be burnt, and that is the use men put them to. So it is said of barren branches, John 15:6, they are cast forth "and men gather them, and cast them into the fire, and they are burned." 'Tis the way men dispose of useless refuse, timber of barren trees, briers and thorns and bushes in clearing of land. So it is in spirituals.

89. 'Tis because the providence of God is like a wheel, as a machine composed of wheels, having wheels in the midst of wheels, that 'tis so ordered in the constitution of nature and in the dispositions of God's providence, that almost all the curious machines that men contrive to do any notable things or produce any remarkable effect, are by wheels, a compage of wheels, revolving round and round, going and returning, representing the manner of the progress of things in divine providence.[4]

90. A corn of wheat is sown, then arises and flourishes considerably; but before it rises to its height, before the perfect plant arises or the

---

3. JE deleted, "Thus in a child's being nourished at the breast of its mother," before proceeding to write the next sentence.

4. In the first of his series of sermons on Is. 51:8 (published as *A History of the Work of Redemption* [Edinburgh, 1774]), JE makes incidental use of the image of the machine composed of wheels to represent God's providence. The thirty sermons in the series are dated from March to August 1739. "Images" no. 89 was probably written during this same period. The distinctive ink of no. 90 is found in sermons beginning in September 1739. (See above, p. 42).

proper and perfect fruit produced, a long winter comes upon it and stunts[5] it. And then, when those many days of severe cold and frost are past, when the spring comes on, it revives and flourishes far beyond what it did before, and comes to its height a perfect plant, then comes the harvest. So is it with Christ: he was slain, and arose; and his church flourished glorious in the days of the apostles and afterwards. Then succeeded those many days of affliction, persecution, and darkness and deadness; but we hope the spring is coming.

91. The constitution of the Roman polity, which flourished in the time of Christ and his apostles, was in many respects a lively image of the constitution of the spiritual polity of the heavenly Jerusalem, or the church of Christ, and among other things in this: that there were many that were called and treated as Roman citizens—that were free of that city, and enjoyed the privileges of the city, and were looked upon as properly belonging to that city—that dwelt in other cities at a great distance from Rome, yea, and never saw Rome. So, many properly belong to the heavenly. They have their citizenship in heaven, that hitherto dwelt at a great distance from heaven, and never as yet have been in heaven, but dwelt here, in another country.

92. How much sooner and easier is undoing than doing in everything, and how much of a moral does this carry in it.

93. Blue, that is, the color of the sky, fades not, intimating that the beauty and luster of heavenly things is unfading.

94. A gathering time or harvest is succeeded by a threshing and winnowing, to separate the wheat from the straw and chaff, and grinding and sifting, to separate from the bran. So, many trials and afflictions are wont to follow the elects' being brought home to Christ, to separate between them and their remaining corruptions. And particularly, very commonly a time of great persecution very commonly follows a remarkable harvest in the church of God. So it was after that great ingathering soon after Christ's ascension, and so it was after that great ingathering at the Reformation. Hence Christ compares the trials of the godly to the sifting of wheat (Luke 22:31).

5. MS: "stunds." Alternative reading: "stuns."

95. That place in Genesis, "upon thy belly shalt thou go, and dust shalt thou eat" [Gen. 3:14], as it undoubtedly in part has respect to the manner of the serpent's going, which is by crawling on his belly, so it shows that that manner of going of the serpent was so ordered on purpose (partly, at least) to be a representation of some curse intended on the devil, who undoubtedly is the principal subject of the curse here denounced. And therefore it proves that outward things are ordered as they be, to that end that they might be images of spiritual things.

96. The heat of the sun in summer is to many things as trials and sufferings are to the souls of professors of godliness. It dries up the puddles of snow water. Though for a while they seem to run very freely, they dry up because they have no fountain sufficient for their supply; they are not fed by living springs. So those herbs and plants that have no deepness of earth, they wither away. So, many fruits though the blossom in the spring looked as fair as any, and the fruit seemed at first to be promising, yet as the heat of the summer comes on they wither up; whereas the more sound fruits receive no damage by this heat, but are rather bettered and brought to their proper ripeness and perfection by it.

97. The beams of the sun can't be scattered, nor the constant stream of their light in the least interrupted or disturbed, by the most violent winds here below; which is a lively image of what is true concerning heavenly light, communicated from Christ, the Sun of Righteousness, to the soul. 'Tis not in the power of the storms and changes of the world to destroy that light and comfort; yea, death itself can have no hold of it. The reasons why the sun's light is not disturbed by winds is two-fold: first, the light is of so pure and subtle a nature that that which is so gross as the wind can have no hold of it; and second, the sun, the luminary, is far above, out of the reach of winds. These things are lively images of what is spiritual.

98. Man is made with his feet on the earth, and with his posture erect, and countenance towards heaven, signifying that he was made to have heaven in his eye and the earth underfoot. See Mr. Henry on Gen. 1:1.[6] See no. 133.

6. Matthew Henry, *Exposition of the Old and New Testament* (London, 1708–10). Perry Miller notes that this popular commentary owed its success in great part to its being the first to incorporate the new science into Protestant orthodoxy (*Images or Shadows*, p. 146, n. 11).

99. A tree that has so many branches from one stock and root, that gradually increases more and more, becomes so great in so manifold branches, twigs, leaves, flowers, fruit, from so small a seed and a little twig, appearing so beautiful and flourishing under the light of the sun and influences of the rain, is a lively image of the church of God, which is often compared to it in the Scripture. It is represented by an olive tree, and vine, and a palm tree, and the bush on Mt. Sinai, trees of lignaloes, cedar tree, etc. The church in different ages is lively represented by the growth and progress of a tree; and the church in the same age, in Christ its head and stock, is like a tree. The various changes of a tree in different seasons, and what comes to pass in its leaves, flowers and fruit in innumerable instances that might be mentioned, is a lively image of what is to be seen in the church. The ingrafting of a tree and the various things done about it by the husbandmen also represent what is to be seen in the church. There is a marvelous representation of the abundant profusion of God's goodness and lovely grace in what is to be seen in a tree, therein representing what is to be seen in the church. Some particular sorts of trees do more represent the church on some accounts, and others on others, as the vine, the olive, the palm, the apple tree, etc. A tree also is many ways a lively image of a particular Christian, with regard to the new man, and is so spoken of in Scripture.

*Corol.* Hence it may be argued that infants do belong to the church.

100. By the vicissitudes of day and night in this world, God teaches that we are to expect changes here, and must not expect always to enjoy a sunshine of prosperity, but must have a vicissitude and mixture of prosperity and adversity.

101. Olympic games. See Turrentine, vol. 2, p. 546 at top.[7]

---

Commenting on Gen. 1:1, Henry writes that variety, beauty, accuracy, power, order, and mystery are all easily observed in the visible world. He goes on: "But from what we see of *Heaven and Earth* we may easily enough infer the Eternal Power and Godhead of the Great Creator, and may furnish our selves with abundant Matter for his Praises. And let our Make and Place, as Men, mind us of our Duty, as Christians, which is always to keep *Heaven in our Eye*, and the *Earth under our Feet*."

7. Franciscus Turretinus, *Institutio Theologiæ Elencticæ* (3 vols., Geneva, 1680–83). The passage referred to occurs in vol. 2, ch. 14, "de Vocatione et Fide," under question 1, "Quid sit Vocatio?": "What is vocation, how manifold is it, and how do external and internal vocation differ?

"III. Hence it is at one time called Holy Vocation (II Tim. 1:9), not only by reason of its beginning, because God is the holy author of Vocation (I Pet. 1:15), but also by reason of its

102. Grasshoppers and other insects that are idle and don't lay up food in summer against winter, as the ant and the bee does, but spend the time in singing, are never so brisk a-singing as on the approach of winter or just before they are destroyed by the frost; which represents what is spoken of in Matt. 24:37–39, "But as it was in the days of Noe, so shall also the coming of the Son of man be. For as in the days that were before the flood they were eating and drinking, marrying and giving in marriage, until the day that Noe entered into the ark, And knew not until the flood came, and took them all away; so shall also the coming of the Son of man be." See no. 136.

103. God shortens the night, or time of darkness, by the refraction of the atmosphere, so the sun is longer before it sets and sooner in rising than otherwise it would be, and partly by the reflection of the atmosphere in the morning and evening twilight, so that we have less darkness than light through the year. Which represents God's shortening the days of tribulation for the sake of his church. So God gives light in the time of darkness by the moon and stars, which represents those divine supports God gives his people in the day of their trouble, so that they shall not be in total darkness, nor be utterly cast down, but shall have many cordials and comforts—light sufficient to guide and direct them in what is absolutely necessary. They shall have comfort from innumerable promises and declarations of God's Word, as from so many stars; and shall have great comfort in God's ordinances in his church, which is the antitype of the light of the moon.

104. There is the tongue and another member of the body that have

---

end, because it tends toward sanctity; at another time κλῆσις ἐπουράνιος (Heb. 3:1), (that is, heavenly), and Philip. 3:14 ἡ ἄνω κλῆσις, (that is, supernal), because it is from heaven (*caelo*) and calls to heaven; alluding to the Olympic Games in which, not only was the prize suspended above the goal, but the athletes used to run below, but were crowned in a higher place, where the judges and officials sat; from whence the voice of the herald summoned the runners to the race.

"IV. If it is asked, why the Holy Spirit wished to use this nomenclature to describe its work, manifold reasons can be supplied. 1. To make the misery of man, because, separated from God by sin, and far distant, he must be recalled from his errors that he may return to God, in the way that God sought and called Adam in his flight, 'Adam, where are you?' 2. To denote the means which God uses to convert men, namely the voice of the Evangelist, and the announcement of the Word, since nothing more fitting or more suitable can be given to a rational being, so that man, who is λόγικος, might be harmonious with λόγῳ (the Word)" (Pp. 545–46; trans. courtesy of Dr. Carl Schlam).

a natural bridle, which is to signify to us the peculiar need we have to bridle and restrain those two members.[8]

105. When men stand on very high things, they are ready to grow giddy and are in great danger of falling, and the higher they are the more dreadful is their fall. Especially are those in great danger that are not used to be on high things. Which represents the danger men are in, when lifted up on high on the pinnacle of honor and prosperity, of having their eyes dazzle, of being very discomposed and erroneous in their notion of things, especially themselves and their own standing, and the great danger they are in of falling; and how that those that are most highly exalted in pride have the most dreadful fall.

106. If a building be built very high, it must have its foundation laid answerably deep and low, and must have its lower part answerably great and broad, or else it will be in danger of falling. So if a man be lifted up high in honor and prosperity, he will be in great danger of being overset unless his foundation be answerably strong and his heart be answerably established in knowledge and faith, etc. and unless his lower part, viz. his humility, be answerably great and his foundation be laid answerably low and deep in self-abasement. The same thing is represented by this: if a ship has great sails, much of that which is displayed in the air and lifted up on high, it must have ballast answerable to sink it answerably deep, otherwise it will be in danger of being overset.

107. That high towers and other high things are commonly smitten with thunder, and mountainous places more subject to terrible thunder and lightning, shows how that pride and self-exaltation does peculiarly excite God's wrath. See Is. 2:11–17.

108. Bread-corn is much used in Scripture to represent the saints. The wicked are represented by the clusters of the vine, but the godly by bread-corn. They are called Christ's wheat, that he will gather into

---

8. Cf. John Ray, *Wisdom of God Manifested in the Works of Creation* (London, 1709), pt. II, p. 446: "There are but two Members in the Body that have a natural Bridle, both which do very much need it; the Tongue, and another I shall not name. The Signification whereof may be, that they are not to be let loose, but diligently curbed and held in." JE also refers to a "natural bridle" of the tongue in "Images" no. 120.

his barn and into his garner, and we are all said to be that one bread.[9] Now this is remarkable of wheat and other bread-corn: that it is sown and grows before winter, and then is as it were killed, and long lies dead in the winter season, and then revives in the spring and grows much taller than before, and comes to perfection and brings forth fruit; which is a lively image of the resurrection of saints—as well as the grain's being first buried in the earth and dying there before it comes up—and that often comes to pass, concerning the saints in this life, that is livelily represented by it. After their conversion they have a falling away, and long continue in a cold and dead carnal state, and then revive again and grow much taller than before, and never fail again till they bring fruit to perfection. 'Tis also a lively image of what comes to pass with respect to the Christian church, which after it was planted by the apostles and flourished a while, then fell under a wintry season, a low and very suffering state, for a long while, and so continues till about the time of the destruction of Antichrist, and then revives and grows and comes to a glorious degree of prosperity and fruitfulness, which is what is called in Scripture "the first resurrection" [Rev. 20:5–6]. Therefore 'tis said of Israel, Hos. 14:7, "They shall revive as the corn." The reviving of the church after a low state and a time of trouble is compared to the reviving of corn from under the earth in the spring in Is. 37:30–31.[1]

109. The inside of the body of man is full of filthiness, contains his bowels that are full of dung, which represents the corruption and filthiness that the heart of man is naturally full of. See [no.] 115.

110. The awaking and crowing of the cock, to wake men out of sleep and to introduce the day, seems to signify the introducing the glorious day of the church by ministers preaching the Gospel. Many shall be awakened and roused to preach the Gospel with extraordinary fervency, to cry aloud and lift up their voices like trumpets. Peter's being awakened out of that deep sleep he had fallen into, and brought to repentance by the crowing of the cock at break of day, signifies the awakening of Christ's church that is built upon Peter; the rousing of the wise virgins out of that dull slumbering and backsliding state, in

9. See Matt. 3:12 and I Cor. 10:17.

1. The Beinecke Library contains a series of six sermons on Matt. 13:3–7, on the Parable of the Sower, dated November 1740. From hand and ink, "Images" nos. 106–108 were probably written during the fall of 1740 (see above, p. 43).

many respects denying their Lord, and bringing them to repentance by the preaching of the Gospel, to introduce the morning of the glorious times.

The introducing of the spring by the voice of spring birds signifies the same thing.

111. The morning of the day and the spring of the year are remarkable types of the commencement of the glorious times of the church. See note on Job 38:13.[2] See also Cant. 2:11–17.

112. As corn is not fit for our use till it is threshed and ground and baked in an oven, therein representing the way in which the bread that came down from heaven is fitted to nourish us, so most kinds of fruits are not fit to be eaten till they are red or till their juice is become like blood, representing the way in which the fruit of the tree of life is fitted for us, viz. by Christ's death, by his shedding his blood.

113. MILK represents the Word of God from the breasts of the church, that is not only represented as a woman, but of old was typified by heifers, she-goats, etc. Milk, by its whiteness, represents the purity of the Word of God. It fitly represents the Word because of its sweetness and nourishing nature, and being for the saints in this present state wherein they are children.

This is as it were the natural food of a new nature, or of the creature newly come into the world. By its whiteness and purity, it represents

2. "Blank Bible" note on Job 38:13, in part: "'That the wicked might be shaken out of it.'] 'Tis probable that one reason why God says this of the morning is because he has in his eye that glorious morning of the light and prosperity of the Christian church, when the Sun of Righteousness shall arise with healing in his wings [Mal. 4:2], and God shall say to his church, 'Arise, shine, for thy light is come, for the glory of the Lord is risen upon thee' [Is. 60:1]; which morning will be accomplished with that earthquake that we read of, Rev. 16:18, by which the wicked shall be shaken; of which morning the morning of the natural day is a type.

"What is said in the next verse is applicable to the morning of that glorious day more aptly than to the morning of the natural day. For though the face of the earth and the visible objects upon it are as it were turned and changed and put on a beautiful form at the rising of the natural sun, so that the sun is as it were the seal and they the clay, and they stand or appear as a beautiful garment that covers the earth, yet in the morning of that glorious day of the church, when the Sun of Righteousness shall arise, the world of mankind, the inhabitants of the earth (which seem especially to be intended by the pronoun 'they' in the verse), shall be turned or changed by the appearance of that sun much more properly as clay to the seal. They shall receive [the] impression from him as clay from the seal, and shall be changed into the same image."

holiness, that is the natural food and delight of the new spiritual nature; for it is this is the direct object of a spiritual relish and appetite.[3]

114. The blue color of the serene sky, which is a pure pleasant color, yet is a feeble color. 'Tis by a reflection of the weakest and least rays of the sun's light, hereby representing admirably not only the purity of the happiness of the saints in heaven, but that blessed humility and as it were holy pusilanimity that they are of. #[4]

115. Man's inwards are full of dung and filthiness, which is to denote what the inner man, which is often represented by various parts of his inwards—sometimes the heart, sometimes the bowels, sometimes the belly, sometimes the veins—is full of: spiritual corruption and abomination. So as there are many foldings and turnings in the bowels, it denotes the great and manifold intricacies, secret windings and turnings, shifts, wiles and deceits that are in their hearts. See [no.] 109; Prov. 20:27, 18:8, 26:22, 20:30 and 22:18.

116. This world is all over dirty. Everywhere it is covered with that which tends to defile the feet of the traveler. Our streets are dirty and muddy, intimating that the world is full of that which tends to defile the soul, that worldly objects and worldly concerns and worldly company tend to pollute us.

117. The water, as I have observed elsewhere,[5] is a type of sin or the corruption of man, and of the state of misery that is the consequence of it. It is like sin in its flattering appearance. How smooth and harmless does the water oftentimes appear, and as if it had paradise and heaven in its bosom. Thus when we stand on the banks of a lake or river, how flattering and pleasing does it oftentimes appear, as though under were pleasant and delightful groves and bowers, or even heaven itself in its clearness, enough to tempt one unacquainted with its nature to descend thither; but indeed, it is all a cheat. If we should descend into it, instead of finding pleasant, delightful groves and a garden of pleasure, and heaven in its clearness, we should meet with

3. The last paragraph was added between the lines at a somewhat later time.
4. The significance of the mark here is not evident.
5. See "Images" nos. 27 and 64. JE might also be referring to the passage "elsewhere in 'Notes on Scriptures,'" which is mentioned in no. 64.

nothing but death, a land of darkness, or darkness itself, etc. See Prov. 5:3–6.

118. IMAGES OF DIVINE THINGS.[6] It is with many of these images as it was with the sacrifices of old. They are often repeated, whereas the antitype is continual and never comes to pass but once. Thus sleep is an image of death that is repeated every night. So the morning is the image of the resurrection. So the spring of the year is the image of the resurrection, which is repeated every year. And so of many other things that might be mentioned. They are repeated often, but the antitype is but once. The shadows are often repeated to show two things: viz. that the thing shadowed is not yet fulfilled; and second, to signify the great importance of the antitype, that we need to be so renewedly and continually put in mind of it.[7]

119. See note on Prov. 30:15–16.[8]

120. TONGUE. God hath fixed to it a natural bridle and fenced it in with a strong wall as it were, even the double row of teeth, to intimate how it ought to be restrained and strongly guarded.

121. When persons lay themselves down to sleep in the night, they are wont to put off their garments. So it is when persons fall into a spiritual sleep. Therefore it is said, "Blessed is he that watches and keepeth his garments" (i.e. by keeping them on) "lest he walk naked and they see his shame" [Rev. 16:15]. So when God's people were

6. This entry might have been written on the occasion of JE's changing his title for the series from "Shadows of Divine Things" to "Images of Divine things" (see above, pp. 34–35).

7. This entry develops a point JE made earlier in his "Blank Bible" note on Luke 23:44 (quoted above, pp. 64–65, n. 2)

8. "Blank Bible" note on Prov. 30:15–16: "'These are three things,' etc.] This is said to the reproach of worldly-minded men, or those whose hearts are under the power of these two daughters of the horseleech, ambition and sensuality: that they are like 'the grave,' etc. These things were designed images and types of worldly-minded men, and therefore they show how mean and hateful they are, and how dreadful their case is upon other accounts. They are like the grave; they are in a state of death; their souls are like sepulchres full of dead men's bones and all uncleanness. They are like the barren [womb], greedy, taking in, sucking up the strength of the earth, the best the world can afford, and yet bringing forth no fruit and on whom the seed of the Word is spread in vain. They are like the earth; they are earthly, vile and base in their nature, as the dirt we tread under our feet. They are like the fire, by the rage of their lusts consuming all things, full of violent principles of enmity against God and men, that render 'em dangerous and exceeding hurtful to those that come near 'em."

building Jerusalem in troublous times, they did not put off their clothes (Neh. 4:23).

122. Men, as they are born all over filthy, proceeding out of that which is filthy and being begotten in filthiness, so they are born backward into the world, with their backs upon God and heaven and their faces to the earth and hell, representing the natural state of their hearts. See nos. 10, 25.[9]

123. The glory of the face of the earth is the grass and green leaves and flowers. These fade away; they last but a little while and then are gone. After the spring and summer, a winter comes that wholly defaces and destroys all; and that which is most taking and pleasant of [all], and as it were the crown of its glory, viz. the flower of the trees and the field, fades soonest. The glory of the heavens consists in its brightness, its shining lights, which continue the same through winter and summer, age after age. This represents the great difference between earthly glory, riches and pleasures, which fades as the leaf and as the grass and flower of the field, and the glory and happiness of heaven which fadeth not away, which is agreeable to many representations in the Scriptures. #[1]

124. The exceeding height of heaven above the earth, even above its highest towers or mountains, denotes the unspeakable and inconceivable height of the happiness of heaven, above all earthly happiness or glory.

125. There are many things between the young birds in a nest and a dam, resembling what is between Christ and his saints. The bird shelters them; so Christ shelters his saints, as a bird does her young under her wings. They [are] brought forth by the dam; so the saints are Christ's children. They are hatched by the brooding of the dam; so the soul is brought forth by the warmth and heat and brooding of Christ,

---

9. This entire entry has been deleted, not in a manner characteristic of JE's deletions, but by several pen strokes made diagonally down across the lines of text. The ink of these strokes is a glossy dark brown very similar to that found in MSS of JE's son, Jonathan Edwards, Jr. JE, Jr. used a similar ink in other emendations in his father's MSS, particularly in the "Miscellanies." It is very probable, therefore, that this entry was deleted by JE, Jr.

1. The significance of the mark is not evident.

by the Heavenly Dove, the Holy Spirit. They dwell in a nest of the dam's providing, on high out of the reach of harm, in some place of safety; so are the saints in the church. They are feeble and helpless, can neither fly nor go, which represents the infant state of the saints in this world. The manner of the dam's feeding the young, giving every one his portion, represents the manner of Christ's feeding his saints. When the dam visits the nest, all open their mouths wide together with a cry, and that is all that they can do. So should the saints do, especially at times when Christ makes special visits to his church by his Spirit. They don't open their mouths in vain. So God says, "Open thy mouth wide and I will fill" [Ps. 81:10]. The birds grow by this nourishment till they fly away into heaven to sing in the firmament. So the saints are nourished up to glory. #²

126. As these later ages have discovered the greatness of the heavenly bodies, and their height, and the smallness of the earth in comparison of the heavens, to be vastly beyond what it used to be imagined to be, so are eternal and heavenly things beyond what the church of God formerly imagined them to be.

127. Poisonous and hurtful animals, such as serpents [and] spiders, incline for the most part to hide themselves or lurk in secret places. Herein they are types of devils and the lusts of men.

128. As the SUN is an image of Christ upon account of its pleasant light and benign, refreshing, life-giving influences, so it is on account of its extraordinary fierce heat, it being a fire of vastly greater fierceness than any other in the visible world. Hereby is represented the wrath of the Lamb. This is a very great argument of the extremity of the misery of the wicked, for doubtless the substance will be vastly beyond the shadow. As God's brightness and glory is so much beyond the brightness of the sun, his image, thus the sun is but a shade and darkness in comparison of it, so his fierceness and wrath is vastly beyond the sun's heat.

129. That a child needs correction, and the benefit of correcting children, is a type of what is true with respect to God's children.

2. The significance of the mark is not evident.

130. The Apostle argues after such a manner,[3] from what is in the body of man to what should be in the mystical body of Christ or church of God, [to] show that something further than mere illustration is intended. It shows that [one] is a real type or intended representation of the other; otherwise his arguments can't be so forceable from these things as his manner of speaking supposes them to be.

131. The exceeding terribleness of the lion, tiger, crocodile and some other beasts teaches the infinite horror and amazement of those that fall a prey to the devil.

132. The Holy Ghost intends to teach divine mysteries by the signification of persons' names that were given accidentally, i.e. without any special command from God or any such design in them who gave the name. This seems manifest by Heb. 7:2. To signify divine things by the constitution of the world is no mere trifling.[4]

133. The beasts are so made that they commonly go with their heads down to the earth, seeking their food with their mouths in the dust, or down to the very ground. But how very different is man made from them, with his head towards heaven. Which shows that the highest good of the beasts is earthly, but that man's proper happiness is heavenly. See [no.] 98.

134. The very wiser heathens seemed to be sensible that the divine Being, in the formation of the natural world, designed to teach us moral lessons: so Ovid, concerning the erect posture of man.[5]

135. That trees were made to represent men, see note on Deut. 20:19.[6]

3. JE gives no reference, nor did he leave space to add one later. He might have had in mind I Cor. 12:4–31 or Rom. 12:4–5.

4. See "Images" no. 30 and "Types of the Messiah," pp. 294–305.

5. *Metamorphosis*, bk. I, ll. 84–86: "And, though all other animals are prone, and fix their gaze upon the earth, he gave to man an uplifted face and bade him stand erect and turn his eyes to heaven" (trans. F.J. Miller [Loeb Library, Cambridge, 1966]).

6. "Blank Bible" note on Deut. 20:19, concerning the injunction against cutting the trees of a city, and particularly the fruit-bearing trees, when the city is put under seige (in part): "It was God's will that a fruitful tree should not be cut down, but only trees that yielded no meat; because trees, with respect to their barrenness or fruitfulness, represented man, and therefore he would men deal with them as he deals with man. This is an argument in the law of Moses itself that its commands were given from some typical respect."

136. The destruction of the face of the earth in winter is a type of the end of the world, as is evident by the appointment of the Feast of Tabernacles, which was at the end of the year, just before the tempestuous season began. See notes on the Feast of Tabernacles.[7]

137. When we first get up in the morning, we rake open and kindle up the fire. So Christians, when they awake out of a spiritual sleep, re-enkindle their graces.

138. 'Tis the manner of princes to enstamp on their coin their image and their name; thus Christ speaks of Caesar's image and superscription on their pieces of money. Which is a type of what God doth to his saints that are his peculiar treasure, his jewels, and that are compared to pieces of money (Luke 15:8–10). He stamps his image on their hearts and writes on them his name, as is often represented in Revelation. He owns them for his; he challenges them as his special propriety.

139. The moon, which is the highest thing that belongs to the earthly system, and is the top of this lower world, and as it were the height and brightness and glory of it, is a lively image of earthly glory and all the good of this system: very changeable, waxing and waning, one while appearing in full splendor and soon after totally extinct,[8] constantly rising and falling. When it is come to full glory, then 'tis near a declension. It continues not in the full very long, and then when it is in full brightness is the time for an eclipse; it often suffers a total eclipse at that time.[9] See Rev. 12, at the beginning.

7. In "Scripture" no. 396, on Zech. 14:16–19, JE finds the Feast of Tabernacles spoken of in the text is "the glorious spiritual feast that God shall provide for all nations in the last ages of the world, and in the expected glorious state of the Christian church, which is spoken of, Is. 25:6. The Feast of Tabernacles was the last feast of the year, before the tempests of winter; as the last spiritual feast of the church will be followed by the destruction of the world."

8. MS: "extinctly."

9. In "Scripture" no. 315, the eclipse of the moon is taken to signify some calamity, either in the visible church or in the life of the saints, which God gives in times of great prosperity (see above, p. 77, n. 5). "Scripture" no. 271 develops the idea that the moon, as used in Rev. 12:1, is "a type of the revelation God made, and the ordinances he instituted, under the Old Testament, or of the Old Testament constitution and administration." Here the changes of the moon, first waxing and then waning, are compared with the course of Old Testament history. The Jewish nation began with God's covenant with Abraham, emerged to its greatest power in Solomon's time, and then declined until the time of Christ. And again, Christ's revelation began with Moses, "when the gospel light, or the revelation of Christ, and the great truths respecting him, was but very small and dim, being almost wholly hid under types

140. The influences of the stars on the earth and earthly things is a type of the government which God has assigned to the angels over earthly things.

141. The breath of man is as it were his life, hereby showing what man's life is, even a blast of wind that goeth away and cometh not again. To this the Scripture seems to have reference in several places, as Job 7:7, "O remember that my life is wind"; Ps. 78:39, "He remembered that they were but flesh; a wind that passeth away, and cometh not again," alluding to the breath's going forth when a person is dying. And that thin, vanishing vapor that is in the breath, that at some seasons appears but vanishes away as it were in a moment, is a type of the very thing expressed, Jas. 4:14, "What is your life? It is even a vapor, that appeareth a little while, and then vanisheth away." While the breath continues warm, the vapor appears, but when that warmth is gone, the vapor disappears. This represents how suddenly our vital heat or warmth, that maintains the life of the body, will be gone, and cold death will succeed. See note on Jas. 4:14 and Job 7:7 and Ps. 78:39.[1]

142. The silkworm is a remarkable type of Christ. Its greatest work is weaving something for our beautiful clothing, and it dies in this work. It spends its life in it, it finishes it in death, as Christ was obedient unto death; his righteousness was chiefly wrought out in dying. And then it rises again, a worm, as Christ was in his state of humiliation, but a more glorious creature. When it rises, it leaves its web for our glorious clothing behind, and rises a perfectly white [butterfly], denoting the purity from imputed grace[2] with which He rose as our surety, for in His resurrection He was justified.

143. The superior heavens are much more immovable and less subject to change than these inferior heavens that are nearer to the earth. For in these, the planets wander and change their places and are

---

and shadows." The clarity of the revelation gradually increased in later prophets until it reached a height in Isaiah, and then declined until Christ.

1. "Blank Bible" notes on Jas. 4:14, Job 7:7, and Ps. 78:39. Each of these brief notes explains that the words "wind" and "vapor" in the texts allude to breath. Each note also refers to "Images of Divine Things" no. 141.

2. "Grace" is a conjectural reading.

unsteady in their motion, and are in themselves opaque and shine with far less brightness, and are subject to wax and wane, some of them, in their light; and some of them subject to eclipses, as the two greater lights, the sun and moon; and besides, in them appear many comets of a most unsteady motion, variable appearance and short continuance. But in the superior heavens, the innumerable multitude of stars are all fixed immovable, and shine with a vastly superior brightness, and without waxing or waning, or eclipses, representing the durableness and brightness of the glory of the highest heavens as a kingdom that cannot be moved, the things of which are things that cannot be shaken.

144. As the worm's dying, and remaining in its aurelia state, and then rising a glorious flying creature, represents the resurrection of a saint, so the spots of gold that are on the aurelia represent the preciousness of the dust of the saint,[3] even while it remains in a state of death being still united to Christ and precious to him.

145. If persons have dirt in their eyes, it exceedingly hinders their sight. This represents how much it blinds men when their eyes are full of the world or full of earth. In order to the clearness of our sight, we had need to have our eyes clear of earth, i.e. our aims free from all things belonging to this earthly world, and to look only at those things that are spiritual, agreeable to what Christ says: "If thine eye be single, thy whole body shall be full of light. But if thine eye be evil, thy whole body shall be full of darkness" [Matt. 6:22–23].

146. The late invention of telescopes, whereby heavenly objects are brought so much nearer, and made so much plainer to sight, and such wonderful discoveries have been made in the heavens, is a type and forerunner of the great increase in the knowledge of heavenly things that shall be in the approaching glorious times of the Christian church.

147. The changing of the course of trade, and the supplying of the world with its treasures from America, is a type and forerunner of what is approaching in spiritual things, when the world shall be supplied with spiritual treasures from America.

3. MS: "stai."

148. Foxes are remarkable types of devils and other enemies of the church of God. See Mr. Hellenbroek's sermon on Cant. 2:15, pp. 4 to 12.[4] See also note on Cant. 2:15.[5]

149. (Add this to [no.] 68.) These two things, the blood and the fat, as they were those parts of animals that were especially appropriated for sacrifice, so they were the only parts of beasts which they were forbidden to eat, and particularly the fat of the kidneys. Lev. 3:15–17, "And the two kidneys, and the fat that is upon them, which is by the flanks, and the caul above the liver, with the kidneys, it shall he take away. The priest shall burn them upon the altar: it is the food of the offering made by fire for a sweet savor: all the fat is the Lord's. It shall be for a perpetual statute for your generations throughout all your dwellings, *that ye eat neither fat nor blood.*" And so Lev. 7:23–27: they are there forbidden to eat either of these with the greatest strictness, with awful curses added. And therefore, these being things in brute beasts that never were their food at all, but were things that they were to abominate the thoughts of eating, they were the most unlikely of any part of the animals they used for food to be made use of as metaphorical representations of their vegetable food, unless it were upon some mystical or typical consideration. If it was the design to represent their vegetable food by a metaphor taken from their animal food only for the sake of elegancy of speech, surely the metaphor would have been taken from that which was indeed some part of their animal [food],

4. *A Sermon by Abraham Hellenbroek, sometime Minister of the Gospel at Rotterdam, from Canticles, chap. 2, v. 15* (trans. from the Dutch [Boston, 1742]). On pp. 4–12, Hellenbroek argues that the text uses foxes as an emblem for heretics, who injure the church. They, like the philosophers who defend heresies, use cunning, wit, and deceit in their arguments. In particular, foxes conceal themselves below ground in holes and caverns; their holes have narrow and well-concealed entrances, but these holes have many passages from which the foxes may come out. They are very hard to catch; and they avoid capture by running from side to side rather than straight forward. They invade the holes of other animals and take possession of their dens; and they dissemble in order to make prey of other animals. In all these respects, the arguments of heretics may be compared with the behavior of foxes.

5. "Blank Bible" note on Cant. 2:15 (in part): "'Take us the foxes, the little foxes that spoil the vines, for our vines have tender grapes.'] Which represent either, first, the sins that spoil the graces of the saints in their present infant state, in which their graces are like tender grapes, easily damnified. These sins that spoil the graces are represented by foxes because [of] their sly, deceitful manner, ... and little foxes because the sins that are intended are not what are called gross sins, but other sins which the saints are more incident to. Or, secondly, they represent sly deceivers who don't appear as open and declared enemies of the church, nor their wickedness so great as to be plain and manifest and tends at first sight to shock the minds of the saints, which sly deceivers do corrupt and spoil young and tender converts in a time of great revival of religion."

and not those parts of the [animal] only singled out which never were their food, and which they were to abhor the thoughts of eating, and were forbidden on any account to eat, under pain of God's most fearful curses.

150. It was the manner at the time that Christ appeared in the world, and in the preceeding and following ages, for kings to wear robes of purple and scarlet[6] which was some representation of the apparel of him that God had appointed as King over the earth, who was, in a mystical sense, red in his apparel, having his garments stained first with his own blood and then with the blood of his enemies, as Is. 63. Therefore Christ him[self], in the time of his last suffering, had on him a scarlet and purple robe, which was to represent the same thing, though they that put it on meant not so.

151. (Vid. [no.] 29 and no. 67.) As one ascends a mountain, they get further and further from this lower world, and the objects of it look less and less to him. So it is in one that ascends in the way to heaven. Commonly near the foot of an high mountain there is a deep valley, which must be descended in order to come to the mountain. So we must first descend low by humiliation to fit us for spiritual exaltation.

152. The changes that pass on the face of the earth by the gradual approach of the sun is a remarkable type of what will come to pass in the visible church of God and world of mankind, in the approach of the church's latter-day glory. The latter will be gradual, as the former is. The light and warmth of the sun in the former is often interrupted by returns of clouds and cold, and the fruits of the earth kept back from a too-sudden growth, and a too-quick transition from their dead state in winter to their summer's glory, which in the end would be hurtful to them and would kill them. So it is in the spiritual world. If there should be such warm weather constantly without interruption, as we have sometimes in February, March and April, the fruits of the earth would flourish mightily for a little while, but would not be prepared for the summer's heat, but that would kill 'em. This is typical of what is true concerning the church of God, and particular souls. The earth being stripped of its white winter garments, in which all looked clean but all was dead, and the making of it so dirty, as it is early in the

6. MS: "scarlet robes."

spring, in order to fit it for more beautiful clothing in a living state in summer, is also typical of what passes in the spiritual change of the world, and also, a particular soul. The surface of the earth is as it were dissolved in the spring. The ground is loosened and broke up, and softened[7] with moisture, and its filthiness never so much appears as then; and then is the most windy turbulent season of all.

153. "Plutarch observes of the ass, which is of all creatures the dullest, that it has the fattest heart; thence the expression in Scripture, 'Go make their hearts fat,' i.e. gross and dull.

"There is a fish that they call 'Ovos,' the ass-fish, which hath its heart in its belly; a fit emblem of a sensual epicure" (see Manton on James, p. 535).[8]

154. The revolutions of the spheres of the heavens are a great representation of the revolutions of the wheels of providence. And in the system of the world there is a wheel in the midst of a wheel, the lesser spheres within the greater making several revolutions while the greater makes one; and there are the revolutions also of the satellites, that are like a lesser wheel joined to a greater, making many lesser revolutions while the greater makes one: very aptly representing the manner of things proceeding in divine providence (see note on Ezekiel's wheels, "Notes on Scripture" no. 398).[9] The revolutions of

7. MS: "soften."

8. Thomas Manton, *A Practical Commentary, or an Exposition with Notes on the Epistle of James* (London, 1653), p. 535.

9. "Scripture" no. 389, on Ezek. 1, contains an extended application of the image of wheels revolving within wheels to the progress of divine providence in the history of the world. JE writes, "All is the motion of wheels; they go round and come to the same again. And the whole series of divine providence, from the beginning to the end, is nothing else but the revolution of certain wheels, greater and lesser, the lesser being contained within the greater." The entire history of the visible world is represented by a great wheel performing a single revolution: "In the beginning of this revolution all things come from God, and are formed out of a chaos; and in the end all things shall return into a chaos again, and shall return to God." This contains a lesser wheel performing two revolutions, the first beginning with the creation and the second with the coming of Christ: "The first revolution began with the creation of the world; so the second revolution began with the creation of new heavens and a new earth." So the first revolution of this wheel is from Christ the creator of man, to Christ the redeemer of man. Another wheel revolves twice in the same period, from the covenant of grace to Adam to the calling of Abraham, and from Abraham to "the coming of Christ, the promised seed of Abraham and his antitype, in whom all the families of the earth are blessed, and in whom the church was planted anew, and in a far more glorious manner." This in turn contains yet other wheels, whose revolutions represent other significant periods and themes in Old Testament history and the history of the church.

the wheels of providence are fitly represented by the revolutions of the heavenly bodies, for they are those that rule the times and seasons, and are given "for times and for seasons and for days and for years" [Gen. 1:4]; and hereby, and by their secret influence on sublunary things,[1] represent the angels, the ministers of God's providence. The changes of time by the revolutions of the wheels of providence are fitly represented by those heavenly bodies that God has made to be the great measurers of time by their revolutions.

155. The spring season is spoken of in Scripture as representing a season of the outpouring of the Spirit of God. As it is so on many other accounts, so in these:

In the spring, the seed that is sown in stony places sprouts and looks as fair as that in good ground, though in the summer, for want of moisture and deepness of earth, it withers away. In the spring, innumerable flowers and young fruits appear flourishing and bid fair that afterwards drop off and come to nothing. (See "Miscellanies" no. 1000.)[2]

In the spring, many streams flow high, many from snow water—though not every day, even in the spring, but only in warm days by fits, and are frozen up betweenwhiles, like hypocrites' affections by pangs during a great outpouring of the Spirit. And in the spring also, those streams that flowed from living fountains, and run all winter and summer, are greatly increased. But when the spring is over, all streams are totally dried up but those that are supplied by living springs.

So a shower of rain is like an outpouring of the Spirit. It makes water flow abundantly in the streets, and greatly raises streams from living fountains, and when the shower is over, the streams in the streets are dried up and the streams from fountains are diminished. So a shower

1. In "Things to be Considered and Fully Written About" (LS) no. 56, JE offers the hypothesis that each heavenly body gives off an effluvium which is diffused into the atmospheres of the planets, thereby producing various effects upon them. *Works*, 6, 248–53.

2. "Miscellanies" no. 1000: "Blossoms may look fair, and not only so but smell sweet and send forth a pleasant odor, and yet come to nothing. It is the fruit, therefore, and neither leaves nor blossoms, is that by which we must judge of the tree. So persons' talk about things of religion may appear fair and may be exceeding savory, and the saints may think they talk feelingly; they may relish their talk, and may imagine they perceive a divine savor in it... and yet all may prove nothing."

No. 155 was probably written near the beginning of 1743 (see above, p. 43); the reference to "Miscellanies" no. 1000 was added somewhat later. It is inserted above the line in an ink comparable to that of "Miscellanies" no. 1000 itself. Similar ink is found in "Images" nos. 169ff.

causes mushrooms suddenly to spring up, as well as good plants to grow, and blasts many fruits as well as brings others to perfection.

(In the spring of the year, when the birds sing, the frogs and toads also croak. So at the same time that the saints sing God's praises, hypocrites sing also, but the voice is as different in God's ear as the sweet singing of birds and the croaking of toads and frogs.) #[3]

156. The Book of Scripture is the interpreter of the book of nature two ways: viz. by declaring to us those spiritual mysteries that are indeed signified or typified in the constitution of the natural world; and secondly, in actually making application of the signs and types in the book of nature as representations of those spiritual mysteries in many instances.

157. The earth, or this earthly world, does by men's persons as it does by their bodies. It devours men and eats 'em up. As we see, this our mother, that brought us forth and at whose breasts we are nourished, is cruel to us. She is hungry for the flesh of her children, and swallows up mankind, one generation after another, in the grave, and is insatiable in her appetite. So she does, mystically, [to] those that live by the breasts of the earth and depend on worldly things for happiness. The earth undoes and ruins them; it makes them miserable forever. It devours and eats up the inhabitants thereof, according to the evil report that the spies brought up of the land of Canaan (Num. 13:32).

158. The way in which most of the things we use are serviceable to us and answer their end is in their being strained, or hard-pressed, or violently agitated. Thus the way in which the bow answers its end is in hard straining of it to shoot the arrow and do the execution; the bow that won't bear straining is good for nothing. So it is with a staff that a man walks with: it answers its end in being hard-pressed. So it is with many of the members of our bodies, our teeth, our feet, etc.; and so with most of the utensils of life, an ax, a saw, a flail, a rope, a chain, etc. They are useful and answer their end by some violent straining, pressure, agitation, collision or impulsion, and they that are so weak not to bear the trial of such usage are good for nothing.

3. The significance of the mark is not evident.

Here is a lively representation of the way in which true and sincere saints (which are often in Scripture represented as God's instruments or utensils) answer God's end, and serve and glorify him in it: by enduring temptation, going through hard labor, suffering, or self-denial or such service or strains hard upon nature and self. Hypocrites are like a broken tooth, a foot out of joint, a broken staff, a deceitful bow, which fail when pressed or strained.

159. The higher anything is raised up in the air, the more swift and violent is its fall. The higher the place is that anyone falls from, the more fatal is his fall. And the higher any body falls from, if it falls into water, the more violently and deeply is it plunged. Thus it is in religion. Thus it is with backsliders and hypocrites and them that are raised high in knowledge, wealth and worldly dignity, and also in spiritual privileges and in profession, and religious illuminations and comforts.

160. As spiders, when shut up together so that they can't catch flies, devour one another, so the devils, after the day of judgment, when they shall be shut in their consummate misery and can devour the miserable children of men no more, will be each others' tormentors.

161. Water in artificial waterworks rises no higher than the spring from whence it comes, unless by a super-added strength from some other cause. So nothing in man can rise higher than the principle from whence it comes. Nature can't be improved by men themselves so as to bring them to any qualification higher than natural principles more excellent in their kind than self-love, etc.

162. True grace is like true gold: it will bear the trial of the furnace without diminishing. And it is like the true diamond: it will bear a smart stroke of the hammer and will not break.

163. The ore in which the gold and silver naturally [are] till refined by fire, the stone in which the gem naturally is bedded till separated by hard blows, the husk and chaff in which the good grain is till separated by threshing and winnowing, the shell and pod in which the kernel is till beaten off, are all representations of the mixtures that attend grace in the hearts of saints in this world, which are separated more and

more by affliction, as by a furnace or threshing, etc. (to which it is
compared in Scripture),[4] and finally, by the pains of death. This mixture is called "dross" and "tun."

164. For texts confirming observations that may be made, see innumerable places of Scripture representing spiritual things by things
appertaining to husbandry: fields, vineyards, trees, corn, fruit, etc.
See texts in Mr. Flavel's *Husbandry Spiritualized*.[5]

165. The seed that is sown in the ground, from the very time that it is
sown till it be fully ripe, is ever exposed to one thing or other that tends
to annoy and destroy it. When it is first sown, it is liable to be picked up
by the fowls. When it first puts forth, 'tis liable to be soon eaten by
worms, either above or underground, or to be scorched by the summer sun; and if it bears this, 'tis liable to be choked with weeds or
thorns. And when it is grown tall, and the fruit put forth but yet green,
'tis liable to be greatly injured by honey-dews. So it is with seeming
grace, and in some respects with real grace, in the soul.[6]
    There are various kinds of apostates and hypocrites. Some are over-
come and overthrown by one trial, others by another. Some hold out
for a shorter, and others for a longer time. Some bear trials that others
are overset by, and yet at last comes a trial that overthrows them. But of
all trials, great worldly prosperity and great seeming spiritual prosperity and honor is the greatest. This, like a honey-dew, may kill those that
have borne other trials. So true grace is assaulted and annoyed in all its
different stages with various enemies. And even when the saints are
arrived at a great height in religion, and are tall Christians, and near to
God, and their fruit put forth but not yet become solid and ripe, are
greatly in danger by a honey-dew, i.e. their great spiritual prosperity,

---

4. See, for example, I Chron. 21, I Cor. 9:10, Deut. 4:20, and Is. 48:10.
5. Flavel, *Husbandry Spiritualized*. Pts. I and II are concerned with the husbandry of fields
and orchards. It is probably to these parts in general, and to the texts of Scripture cited in
them, that JE refers. Pt. III spiritualizes the husbandry of animals. Each of Flavel's chapters
is introduced with a topical rhymed couplet, e.g. "Seeds dye and rot, and then most fresh
appear,/ Saints bodies rise more orient than they were." There follows an "Observation," in
which the analogy is explained, and an "Application" in which the appropriate lessons are
drawn. JE appears to have used Flavel's book as a source in several Images. For a further
discussion, see Miller's "Introduction" to *Images or Shadows*, pp. 13–14.
6. Flavel's chapter "Upon the Dangers incident to Corn from seed time to Harvest," is
introduced with the couplet, "Fowl, Weeds, Blastings do your Corn annoy;/ even so Corruptions would your Grace destroy."

and sweet joys and comfort, prove to bring 'em into a languishing sorrowful state through spiritual pride.

166. There are two quite different things intended by the God of nature and disposer of all things to be signified by the GRAFTING of trees; and therefore, some things in grafting by no means agree with one of these things, and other things that by no means agree with the other.

1. The first thing signified is the ingrafting the soul into Christ. In this Christ is the stock, and the believer is the scion or branch who is cut out of its natural stock, taken out of the stock of the first Adam, wherein he grew by nature; sin, or corrupt nature, is mortified. He is cut off from his own stock and root, emptied of himself, brought to self-denial and renunciation of his own righteousness and dignity, and is weaned from the world; is cut off from that stock by which it naturally grew in the earth, and this as it were by a keen knife, by the cutting work of the law and of repentance; and is brought to a Christ as a scion is to a new stock and root, and united so to him as to have a vital union with him and become a member or branch in him; and has a new head of vital influence, derives vital influence from Christ and lives by his life, and flourishes and increases, and looks fair and brings forth fruit by virtue of union with him. In these things the change made in the state of a soul at conversion is livelily represented by the ingrafting of trees.

But then there are some things in the ingrafting of trees that by no means agrees to this, viz. this stock conforms to the scion, and not the scion to the stock. The sap of the stock is changed and meliorated by the scion, and not the scion by the stock. The scion is taken out of a good tree that bears good fruit, and grafted into a bad tree that is wild by nature, that is barren or bears barren and useless fruit; and 'tis the stock that is changed for the better, and not the scion. The good fruit that the grafted tree bears is the scion's fruit, and not the fruit of the stock and root. And therefore, this be not all that is intended to be signified by ingrafting, but,

2. There is another great thing intended that God aimed at no less, which these latter things agree to, wherein Christ is not the stock but the branch; as he is often the "Branch," or the "tender twig," as the word in the original signifies.[7] He is the man whose name is the

---

7. I. e. the Hebrew word *tsemach*, especially as used in Zech. 6:12 and Ezek. 17:22; also in Jer. 23:5 and 33:15, Zech. 3:8, and Is. 4:2, etc.

BRANCH. And the thing signified is the union of Christ, the heavenly branch, with mankind. And particularly,

*1*. Christ's incarnation, whereby this divine person, this branch of paradise, was taken as it were from heaven, its natural soil, taken out of the bosom of his Father from whom he eternally proceeded or sprang, and was as it were cut off from him, from the glory he had with him before the world was; and emptied himself in his humiliation, to be ingrafted into the mean, inferior race of mankind, that may fitly, by reason of the manner of its propagation, be compared to a tree with many branches from one seed or root, and is often compared to a tree in Scripture. (See "Miscellanies" no. 991.)[8] Christ was as it were cut off from his natural stock in his humiliation. He emptied himself. He was, in some sense, cut off from the glory that he had with the Father before the world was, during his humbled state. And he took the human nature, that was comparatively a mean, worthless, barren stock. This human nature was not changed by Christ's taking it upon him, though it be dignified and its fruit exceedingly changed, even as the stock is not changed by the scion's being grafted upon it. It remains human nature still, and will forever; Christ is true man still, as well as God, and so will remain to all eternity. But this nature is infinitely dignified, and its fruit infinitely changed for the better, by virtue of the scion that is implanted into it. The nature of neither stock nor scion is changed, but both remain the same they were before, though both are united into one tree and live by one life. So neither the human nature [nor the

---

8. "Miscellanies" no. 991, in part: "PROGRESS OF THE WORK OF REDEMPTION. The race of mankind are like a tree, that comes from one seed, but runs out into many millions of branches, these branches still multiplying, each one into a multitude of branches. Some part of this tree is holy; there is evermore a holy branch in the tree that belongs to God, which is called 'The branch of God's planting' (Is. 60:21), though sometimes it be but a little twig. In all its successive productions and multiplied ramifications there is an holy line of branches that do in some respect grow one out of another, and commonly in the natural ramification or ordinary generation. And in other parts of the tree that are not actually holy branches, i. e. those parts that are already actually put forth are not holy, yet they have an holy or elect seed in them or an holy bud, though in some so deeply enfolded that 'tis a great way off from putting forth or unfolding. There yet remains a great number of successions of germinations or ramifications before its turn comes to put forth. Those branches that had the holy seed in them have in past ages of the world been but few, and all other branches, but only those, the great Husbandman cuts off from one age to another." "Miscellanies" no. 991 continues with a discussion of the biblical history of the tree of the race of mankind, with particular attention to those branches which were cut off, and to Christ, the Branch, who was maintained through successive ages until he should put forth. Much of the basis for JE's development of this image may be found in his remarks on the propagation of plants in "Things to be Considered and Fully Written About" (LS) no. 48, in *Works, 4*, 242–46.

divine] are changed one into the other, though both are united in one person.

2. Another thing intended is Christ's being ingrafted into the church of Christ, which was by his uniting himself with believers in his incarnation, whereby he became a member of the church, a branch of the church, a son of this mother, and a brother of believers, agreeable to the church's wish. Cant. 8:1, "O that thou were as my brother that sucked the breasts of my mother." The church of Christ is often represented by a tree in Scripture. The tree was planted in Abraham; every member of the church is a branch of that tree, and Christ is the seed of Abraham. He is the great *seed* of Abraham, to whom and in whom the promise was made (Gal. 3:19, 16). And 'tis by this seed or this BRANCH that the blessing is to the tree. All the fruit of the tree is by the ingrafting this tender twig into it. This ingrafted branch bears all. The tree in itself bears no good fruit; it is very sour, but this ingrafted branch sweetens it. This fruit, or ability to bear fruit, is the blessing: there is fruit to God and his glory, and that we receive ourselves, in a harvest of joy and comfort, and in everlasting life. The stock remains the same but the fruit is altered. So, by Christ being ingrafted, the faculties of the soul are the same. There is the same human nature still, but there is now fruit of grace, holy exercises and practice and true blessedness. The stock is the same, but the sap, by the union to the scion, is changed and made better. So the soul, by a vital union with Christ and by the faculties being as it were swallowed up in Christ, are altered, sanctified and sweetened.

'Tis observable that a good scion flourishes best in a sour stock. So Christ has more glory in saving the sinful and miserable, for the sick need a physician, and Christ came not to call the righteous, but sinners, to repentance.

3. Christ, by his incarnation and union with man, was ingrafted into David's royal stock. He is often represented as the branch of his family whence it should have all its glory and bear all its fruit. 'Tis by this branch that the royal family of Israel feeds all the world with its fruit, as was said in some sense of Nebuchadnezzar, under the type of a great tree. This is that tender twig of the royal family of David spoken of [Ezek. 17:22].

This blessed branch in the stock of Abraham and David, though it grows on the stock and flourishes from the root, yet proceeds not thence in the way of natural propagation, as the natural branches do, but is ingrafted in.

*4*. Christ is ingrafted into every believer. Every believer is ingrafted into Christ, and Christ is ingrafted into every believer. For the believer is not only in Christ, but Christ in him. Christ is born in the soul of the believer, and brought forth there, and every believer is a mother of Christ. Grace in the soul is the infant Christ there, a tender twig ingrafted from an heavenly stock, in the soul, by which it bears all its fruit. The nature is sanctified, the sap sweetened and the tree made fruitful. Christ is ingrafted by the Word's being ingrafted, which is able to save the soul. Not only the written or spoken Word is ingrafted, but the personal Word, which eminently is able to save the soul. Grace in the soul is Christ there. This is represented as a seed implanted there, and may as fitly be represented as a twig or bud ingrafted there, which sprouts and flourishes and brings forth fruit. In order to this ingrafting both must be cut off, the stock and the branch. The stock must be cut off; its natural produces, branches and fruit of its own righteousness must be cut off that Christ may be ingrafted in the room of them, and the fruit of worldly enjoyments and carnal happiness must be cut off. And Christ, the scion, is cut off from his natural stock, in his humiliation, to make way for his being vitally united to the vile and miserable sinner.

The change made in the stock, when the scion is ingrafted into it, fitly represents the change made in man by regeneration. Something is destroyed, and that which is new put into the room of it, and something remains. The old branches and fruit are all cut off and perish; new branches, and fruit entirely new, succeed. This fitly represents the change of dispositions, affections and practices. But the old stock and root remains: this fitly represents the same faculties remaining, the same human nature, that is as it were the substance or substratum of these properties, both old and new, and on which both old and new fruits do grow.

Upon the whole it is to be noted that when a tree that is bad by nature is grafted, or has a good scion inserted into it, all the old branches are cut off and do perish (though not at once, if the tree is grown to any bigness and has many branches) when the ingrafting is done. But as the ingrafted branch grows and flourishes, so the husbandman gradually cuts away the other branches to make room for it, till at length none are left but the ingrafted branch, and all the sap of the tree runs into that, and the tree becomes wholly a new tree. So it is Christ, the heavenly Branch, is ingrafted into the bad tree of the race of mankind, and all other branches perish, but only this ingrafted branch and the branches that grow from it [remain]. All perish in hell, and by degrees there is a visible destruction of them in this world, till at length only this scion and the branches that grow from it shall remain, and all things shall be made new. There was, soon after this scion was ingrafted, a great destruction of the nation of the unbelieving Jews; and after that, a great destruction of the heathen in the Roman Empire in Constantine's time, when the branch was grown much bigger. And hereafter will there be a yet vastly greater destruction of the wicked all over the world, and the earth shall be everywhere in a great measure emptied of wicked men, and this ingrafted branch shall spread and fill the earth. And after this, at the end, every branch and twig that don't proceed from this scion shall be perfectly destroyed, and the whole tree shall be made [new]. God shall say, "Behold I make all things new" [Rev. 21:5], and there shall be a new heaven and a new earth.

And so it shall be in the tree of Abraham, the visible church of God. Christ was the scion that was ingrafted into this tree, and other branches must all be cut off, but only they which grow from this scion [remain]. At the first insertion of the scion there was a great cutting of old branches of this tree in the destruction of the Jews, and there will be a still greater at the destruction of Antichrist, and all remains of the old branches shall be cut off at the end of the world. So it was with respect to the tree of the royal family of David. When this scion was ingrafted,[9] every other branch of that family was as it were cut off, by putting an end to the genealogy or perishing of all records of their families. And in a particular soul, when this heavenly seed is implanted in it, or this heavenly twig or bud ingrafted, the old nature is at once mortified, and old branches and fruits cut off by conviction and repentance; and the remains of them are more and more cut off and cleared away as this new branch increases, till at length there remains no other branch, and no fruit is brought forth but what grows on this branch, and so the tree is entirely renewed.

This latter signification of ingrafting seems to be chiefly intended by the Author of nature because he thought that great and glorious mystery of Christ's incarnation and union with mankind most worthy to be much showed forth and observed.

167. The manner of taking and destroying almost all kinds of wild

9. The phrase "when this scion was ingrafted" is inserted above the line. JE gives no indication whether the words were to be punctuated with the preceding clause, as in Miller, or with the following one, as here.

beasts and birds in traps, pits, snares and nets, by bait, laying before the creature that is to be taken and destroyed what is agreeable to its appetite, is a lively representation of what comes to pass in the moral and spiritual world.

168. There are most [lively] representations of divine things in things that are most in view, or that we are chiefly concerned in: as in the sun, his light and other influences and benefits; in the other heavenly bodies; in our own bodies; in our state, our families and commonwealths; and in that business that mankind do principally follow, viz. husbandry.

169. IMAGES of divine things. There are some types of divine things, both in Scripture and also in the works of nature and constitution of the world, that are much more lively than others. Everything seems to aim that way; and in some things the image is very lively, in others less lively, in others the image but faint and the resemblance in but few particulars with many things wherein there is a dissimilitude. God has ordered things in this respect much as he has in the natural world. He hath made man the head and end of this lower creation; and there are innumerable creatures that have some image of what is in men, but in an infinite variety of degrees. Animals have much more of a resemblance of what is in men than plants, plants much more than things inanimate. Some of the animals have a very great resemblance of what is in men, some in some respects and others in others, and some have much less. Some are so little above plants that there is some difficulty in determining whether they be plants or animals. And among plants there are numberless [degrees]: in some things there seems to be as it were only some feeble attempts of nature towards a vegetable life, and 'tis difficult to know what order of beings they belong to. There is a like difference and variety in the light held forth by types as there is in the light of the stars in the night. Some are very bright, some you can scarcely determine whether there be a star there or no; and the like different degrees, as there is the light of twilight signifying the approaching sun.

170. It is in the natural world as it is in the spiritual world, in this respect: that there are many imitations of, and false resemblances of, those things that are the more excellent in the natural world. Thus there are many stones that have a resemblance of diamonds, that are

not true diamonds. There are many ways of counterfeiting gold. The balm of Gilead, and many others of the most excellent medicines, are many ways sophisticated. So is grace counterfeited.

171. Concerning the blossoming and ripening of fruits and other things of that nature.[1] The first puttings forth of the tree in order to fruit make a great show and are pleasant to the eye, but the fruit then is very small and tender. Afterwards, when there is less show, the fruit is increased. So it often is at first conversion: there are flowing affections, passionate joys, that are the flower that soon falls off, etc. The fruit when young is very tender, easily hurt with frost, or heat, or vermin, or anything that touches it. So it is with young converts. Cant. 2:15, "Take us the foxes, the little foxes, that spoil the vines: for our vines have tender grapes."

Fruit on the tree or in the field is not in its fixed and ultimate state, or the state where it properly answers its end, but in a state wholly subordinate and preparatory to another. So it is with the saints. The fruit, while it stands in the field, or hangs on the tree till fully ripe and the time of gathering comes, is in a progressive state, growing in perfection. So it is with grace in the saints.

Many kinds of fruit have a great deal of bitterness and sourness while green, and much that is crude and unwholesome, which as it ripens becomes sweeter, the juices purer, the crude parts are removed. The burning heat of the summer sun purges away that which is crude, sour and unwholesome, and refines the fruit and ripens it, and fits it more for use; which burning heat withers and destroys those fruits that han't substance in them.

So young converts have a remaining sourness and bitterness. They have a great mixture in their experiences and religious exercises, but as they ripen for heaven they are more purified. Their experiences become purer, their tempers are more mollified and sweetened with meekness and Christian love; and this by afflictions, persecutions and occasions of great self-denial, or in one word, by the cross of Christ. Whereas these trials bring hypocrites to nothing.[2]

1. JE deleted, "See many things in sermon on Rev. 14:15, there especially the explication of the subject." The sermon on Rev. 14:15 is on the subject, "The saints grow ripe for heaven." In his explication he makes use of the image of ripening fruit in substantially the same way as in "Images" no. 171. From the hand and ink, no. 171 was probably written soon after the sermon, which JE dated January 1744.

2. This paragraph might have been inspired by the simile of John Mason: "As the sun ripens and sweetens Fruits by shining upon them, without which they would be sour and

Green fruit hangs fast to the tree, but when it is ripe it is loose and easily picked. Wheat, while it is green in the field, sucks and draws for nourishment from the ground, but when it is ripe, it draws no more. So a saint, when ripe for heaven, is weaned from the world.

172. Husbandmen are wont to PRUNE their trees after the dead time of winter, a little before the spring, when the time approaches for them to put forth and blossom with new life and rejoicing. So God is wont to wound his saints a little before he revives them, after falls and long seasons of deadness, and to purge them and prepare them for revival and comfort. So he is wont to wound and purge his church, and to lead them into sorrows. He will bring them into the wilderness and speak comfortably to them [Hos. 2:14].

173. Tears flowing from the eyes in sorrow typifies godly sorrow, flowing from spiritual sight or knowledge.

174. Observe the danger of being led by fancy; as he that looks on the fire or on the clouds, giving way to his fancy, easily imagines he sees images of men or beasts in those confused appearances.

175. There is nothing here below that reaches heaven—no, not the highest things—but all fall immensely short of it. Many things, before we experience [them], seem to reach heaven. The tops of high mountains seem to touch the sky, and when we are in the plain and look up to their tops, it seems to us as though, if we were there, we could touch the sun, moon and stars; but when we are come, we seem as far off from these heavenly things as ever. So there is nothing here below by which we can attain to happiness, though there be many of the high and great things of the world that seem to others that don't enjoy them as though happiness was to be reached by them. Yet those that have experience find happiness as far from them as from those that are in a lower state of life.

176. A HOG is in many respects an image of an earthly, carnal man; and among others, in this, that he is good for nothing till death: not

___

unsavory; so it is the Sunshine of God's Love and Favour that sweetens all earthly Blessings, without which they would be but Crosses and Curses to them that possess them." *Select Remains*, p. 52. JE jotted a reference to the book on p. 2 of "Images."

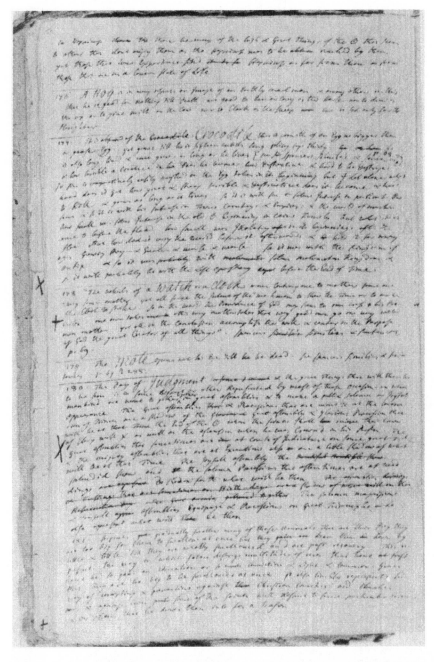

Manuscript page 32 of "Images of Divine Things," containing entries 176–181. Beinecke Rare Book and Manuscript Library, Yale University.

good to bear or carry as the horse, nor to draw as the ox, or to give milk as the cow, nor to clothe as the sheep, but is fed only for the slaughter.

177. It is observed of the CROCODILE that it cometh of an egg no bigger than a goose egg, yet grows till he is fifteen cubits long; Pliny says thirty. He is also long-lived and grows as long as he lives. (See Spencer's *Similes and Sentences*, p. 68.)[3] And how terrible a creature does he become, how destructive, and hard to be destroyed.

So sin is comparatively easily crushed in the egg, taken in its beginning; but if let alone, what head does it get, how great and strong, terrible and destructive does it become, and hard to kill, and grows as long as it lives.

So it is with sin, or Satan's interest in particular persons; and so it is with his interest in towns, countries and empires, and the world of mankind. How small was Satan's interest in the old world, beginning in Cain's family, but what did it come to before the Flood. How small was idolatry, in its beginnings after the Flood, but how did it carry the world before it afterwards, and hold it for many ages, growing stronger and greater, and worse and worse. So it was with the kingdom of Antichrist, and so it was with Satan's Mahometan kingdom, and so it will probably be with the last apostasy before the end of time.

178. "The wheels of a WATCH or a CLOCK move contrary one to another, some one way, some another, yet all serve the intent of the workman, to show the time, or to make the clock to strike. So in the world, the providence of God may seem to run cross to his promises, one man takes this way, another takes that way; good men go one way, wicked men another, yet all in the conclusion accomplish the will, and center in the purpose, of God the great Creator of all things" (Spencer's *Similes and Sentences*, p. 69).

179. The MOLE opens not his eyes till he be dead. See Spenser's *Similes and Sentences*, p. 69, no. 288.[4]

3. Spencer, *Things New and Old*, no. 282, p. 68. The preceding passage is virtually a direct quotation. Spencer continues: "This setteth forth the manner of *encreasing* of *Sathan's Kingdome*, and how *cunningly* he disposeth of his *temptations*; First he *beginneth* with *small matters*, and so by degrees to *greater*, from *thought* to *consent*, from *consent* to *action*, from *action* to *custom*, from *custom* to *habit of sin.*"

4. Spencer writes: "A wicked man believes not there is a Hell till he be in it. Tostatus [Tacitus] observeth out of *Pliny*, that the *Mole*, after he hath long lived *under ground*, beginneth to *see* when he *dyeth* ... he beginneth to *open* his eyes in dying, which he alwaies had shut

180. The day of JUDGMENT, and the great things that will then be to be seen, is in some respect or other represented by most of those occasions in which mankind are wont to gather together in great assemblies, and to make a public solemn or joyful appearance. The great assemblies and processions that are wont to [gather] at the coronation of princes are a shadow of the great assembly and glorious procession that will be at the end of the world, when the saints shall receive their crown of glory with Christ; as well as the ascension, when he was crowned in his person.

The great assemblies that sometimes are at courts of judicature on some great trial, and the mighty assemblies that are at executions, also are a little shadow of what will be at that time. The joyful assembly, the splendid show, and the solemn processions that oftentimes are at weddings do shadow forth what will be then.[5] The solemn, magnificent and joyful assemblies, equipage and processions on great triumphs do also represent what will be then.

181. Serpents gradually swallow many of those animals that are their prey. They are too big for them to swallow at once, but they draw them down, by little and little, till they are wholly swallowed and are past recovery. This represents the way in which Satan destroys multitudes of men that have had so good an education, or so much conviction and light and common grace, that they are too big to be swallowed at once. It also livelily represents his way of corrupting and prevailing against Christian countries and churches; and against even some of the saints, with respect to some particular errors and corruptions that he draws them into for a season.

182. When summer has continued uninterrupted for some time, then begin to come many flies and other insects that are hurtful and noisome. But after they are come, they remain long after the weather grows cool, and it must be a very hard frost to kill. A small frost may

---

whilst he lived: This is the true State of a *wicked earthly-minded man*, he neither seeth *Heaven*, nor thinketh of *Hell*: tell him that the *wicked shall be turned into Hell, and all that forget God*, it is but as *brutum fulmen*, a meer scare-crow, he feareth not *God* nor man all his *life-time*, till he approacheth *to Judgement*, and then *too soon* he beginneth to *feel* that which he could not be brought to *believe*."

5. JE deleted, "The assemblies, rejoicings and feastings that are sometimes on birthdays are a shadow of what will on the resurrection day," before proceeding in the composition of the sentence.

chill 'em and restrain 'em, but they will revive again at the return of every warm day.

So a long continuance of a summer of prosperity, of outward or spiritual comforts, breeds hurtful and noisome and corrupting insects as it were in the soul. Many evil things, contrary to the humility and simplicity that is in Christ, gradually creep in till they swarm. So it is in a particular person, and so it is in the church of God. And after they have got in, and have got foothold, 'tis a hard thing to root 'em out. If the prosperity and comforts are withdrawn, there must be very much of the contrary before they will be killed. These insects in summer signify the same with the worms in the manna.

183. The spiritual restoration of the world is compared to the renewing of the face of the earth in the SPRING in Ps. 147:18, with the context.

184. That dominion of the stars in the earth spoken of (Job 38:31–33) is an image of the dominion of angels in the earth.

185. That the sun is designed by God as a type of Christ may be argued from Scripture, not only by Christ's being frequently represented by it, being called the Sun, the Sun of Righteousness, the Light of the World, etc.; but also by the sun's withdrawing its light when Christ was crucified, as it were conforming to its antitype; as the veil of the temple did at the same time, that rent when Christ's flesh (which by the Apostle's testimony is its antitype [Heb. 10:20]) was rent, or his animal nature destroyed. And at the same time, the light of the sun was extinguished when the life of Christ, its antitype, was extinguished. Christ rising with the sun at his resurrection, is another argument of the same thing.

186. When the sun withdraws, beasts of prey go forth to destroy, and that is the time for caterpillars and noisome insects, and hurtful vermin in general, to go forth to prey upon the trees and plants. But when the sun rises they retire, well representing the nature of evil spirits, and the corruptions of the heart, and wicked men, and the enemies of our souls and the church of God in general.

187. BREAD. It seems to be because that those things which grain as it were suffers before 'tis fit for our food, and particularly threshing,

represents the sufferings of Christ, that God ordered that the altar of Israel should be built by David on a threshing floor [I Chron. 21:18]; which was the place where the Temple was built, and all the sacrifices of Israel thenceforward were offered. And therefore also, the same instruments that were used in threshing, in burning the sacrifice, because in both they typified the instruments of Christ's sufferings. And the oxen, who by their labors trod out the corn, were offered on the altar; because they represented Christ, who was not only the sacrifice but the priest too, was active in his own sufferings, and so provided us heavenly bread. Hence also Gideon was ordered to build an altar to God at or by the place where he threshed wheat, and also near the wine press (Judg. 6:11, 19–21, 26). The manner of procuring wine in a wine press representing the shedding the blood, as the threshing wheat for our bread signifies the sufferings inflicted on his body. See no. 197.

188.[6] As all the good and happiness of mankind comes by redemption and salvation, all his light arises out of darkness, all his happiness out of misery, all his wealth out of the most extreme poverty, and his life out of death. Agreeable to these circumstances of mankind, and the great designs and methods of God's grace towards him through the Savior, it is ordered that so many of our outward mercies and good things are given in a way of deliverance, protection or remedy from some calamity we have been the subjects of, or are exposed to.

Thus God rather gives us clothing to cover our nakedness, than to make us without any deformity and nakedness we should be ashamed of. He rather gives us food to preserve us from famishing and wasting away and perishing miserably, to which we are continually exposed, and to satisfy our hunger, rather than to make our bodies such as should not be exposed to waste and consume, and need continual repairs, or make without hunger. So God gives us drink to satisfy our thirst, rather than to make us without thirst. He gives us means to defend us from cold and heat, and storms and the inclemencies of the weather, than to make the atmosphere to be always serene and temperate. He gives us breath, constantly to refresh and give new life to our vitals and blood, and preserve from death, that otherwise we should be exposed to every moment, rather than to make our bodies with a

6. "Images" no. 188 is written in the even, angular hand and dense black ink characteristic of most of JE's writing during the later 1740s and early '50s. This entry was probably written no earlier than the end of 1746 (see above, p. 44).

permanent life, and so that our vital and animal juices should not need continual refreshment and revival. He gives us sleep to relieve us and gives us comfortable rest when weary, rather than that we should not be liable to weariness. He gives us means to enlighten us in the night, as by the light of a candle, etc. rather than that we should have no darkness, or no more than during the necessary time of sleep. He gives means of defense from wild beasts, from noisome vermin and insects, rather than there should be no such noxious things that we should be exposed to. He has provided many things of medicinal and sanative virtue as a remedy in ease of wounds and sickness, rather than that we should be liable to none of these maladies.

But here it is observable, that though these mercies are thus given us [as] a protection or remedy from evils and calamities we are subject to or exposed [to], yet they are, many of them, something beyond a mere remedy. Thus we have food, not only to keep us from famishing[7] and remove the pain of hunger, but to entertain and delight us. So we have not only clothing to cover our nakedness, but to adorn us. And so of other things: as God, in the redemption of Christ, don't only provide for our salvation from misery, but provides for us positive blessedness and glory.

189. (Vid. [nos.] 68 and 48.) The seeming suffering of our food, by being boiled, roasted, etc. to cleanse it from its crudities and impurities, to fit it to be wholesome, pleasant food for us, also represents God's dealings with his people, with particular persons and elect nations, and his visible church, to fit it to be as it were food for him. See Jer. 2:3.

190. In the conception of an animal and formation of the embryo, the first thing appearing is the *punctum saliens* or the heart, which beats as soon as it exists. And from thence the other parts gradually appear, as though they all gradually proceeded and branched forth from that beating point. This is a lively image of the manner of the formation of the new creature. The first thing is a new heart, a new sense and inclination, that is a principle of new life; a principle that, however small, is active and has vigor and power, and as it were beats and struggles, thirsts after holiness, aims at and tends to everything that belongs to the new creature, and has within it the foundation and

7. MS: "Family."

source of the whole. It aims at perfection. And from thence are the issues of life: from thence the various things that belong to the new creature all proceed and branch forth, and gradually appear, and that more and more. And this principle, from its first existence, never ceases to exert itself,[8] until the new creature be complete and comes to its proper perfection.

191. A bubble that is blown up, when it is come to be largest of all and full of fine colors, is near breaking, which is a lively image of earthly glory, which very commonly when it is come to the height is near its end, and commonly goes out and vanishes away in a moment; and a proper type[9] of the men of this world who place their happiness in the things of this life, who, when they are most swollen with worldly prosperity, and are in the midst of their honors, wealth and pleasures, and glory most in these things, do commonly die. Death dashes all their glory to pieces in a moment. Ps. 37:35–36, "I have seen the wicked in great power, and spreading himself like a green bay tree. Yet he passed away, and, lo, he was not: yea, I sought him, but he could not be found"; and many places in Job. Hos. 10:7, "As for Samaria, her king is cut off as the foam upon the water."

192. When the fruit is ripe, it is easily gathered. It don't cleave fast to the tree, but is ready to quit it, and is picked without rending or making any wound. So is a saint that is ripe for heaven; he easily quits this world (Job 5:26).

193. The head supplies, animates and directs the body, but the body supports and bears the weight of the head. This is an image of what should be between civil and ecclesiastical heads of societies and their people.

194. Many hypocrites are like wood that lies above ground, and has no root at all in the ground, that yet will grow in the spring and put forth boughs like a living plant. But this growth is short-lived; it will not endure the trial of the burning heat of midsummer. See Matt. 13:6.

195. We can't go about the world but our feet will grow dirty. So in

8. MS: "it self it."
9. MS: "Time."

whatever sort of worldly business men do with their hands, their hands will grow dirty, and will need washing from time to time, which is to represent the fullness of this world of pollution. It is full of sin and temptations. In all their goings they are imperfect and polluted with sin; every step they take is attended with sin, so all the works that they do are polluted. They can perform no service, no business, but they contract their guilt and defilement, that they need the renewed washing of the blood of Christ.

196. The meat and drink of mankind comes down from heaven in the rain, and even our clothing and habitations, and even the substance of our bodies, is mostly of the very substance of the rain; which very naturally leads us to the fountain of all our mercies, and teaches us that we are fed and maintained by those things that are wholly the fruits of God's bounty, and are universally and entirely dependent on him.

197. (See no. 187.) 'Tis evident the baking of bread is a type of the sufferings of Christ, because the shew bread is said to be "an offering made by fire unto the Lord" (Lev. 24:7, 9); but it was an offering made by fire no otherwise than it was baked with fire. But all the offerings made by fire by the Mosaic law were types of Christ, undoubtedly, and their suffering the fire was also undoubtedly a type of Christ's suffering.[1]

198. As the silkworm, so the bee seems to be designed as a type of Christ who, having spent his life with ingathering with the greatest labor and industry, and laying up in store the most delicious food, having completed his work, is killed; and by his death yields all his stores for the refreshment and delight of his murderers. (See Hervey's *Meditations*, vol. 1, pp. 269–70.)[2]

---

1. On the ceremonial law, see "Types of the Messiah," pp. 305–22.

2. James Hervey, *Meditations and Contemplations*, *1*, 269–70, in "Reflections on a Flower-Garden." JE's thoughts take a different course from Hervey, who attends to the bees' industry: "While the gay *Butterfly*, flutters her painted Wings; and sips a little fantastic Delight, only for the present Moment. While the gloomy *Spider*, worse than idly busied, is preparing his insidious Nets for destruction; or sucking Venom, even from the most wholesome Plants. This frugal Community, are wisely employed in providing for Futurity; and collecting a copious Stock, of the most balmy Treasures." From references to Hervey's work in his "Catalogue," it appears that JE wrote "Images" no. 198 in the first part of 1750, before he left Northampton to take up his Stockbridge pastorate (see above, p. 45).

199. See "Blank Bible," p. 656, col. 1, at the top of the column.[3]

200. That machines for the measuring of time are by wheels, and wheels within wheels, some lesser, some greater; some of quicker, others of slower revolution; some moving one way, others another; some wheels dependent on others and all connected together, all adjusted one to another and all conspiring to bring about the same effect, livelily[4] represents the course of things in time from day to day, from year to year, and from age to age, as ordered and governed by divine providence.

201. 'Tis observed by the prophet Jeremiah (ch. 32:8), concerning only a common providential occurrence, that it *"was the word of the Lord,"* that is, that it was designedly ordered to be a special signification of God's mind and will, as much as his Word. By which it appears that God don't think this a thing improper, or unbecoming of his wisdom, thus designedly to contrive his works and to dispose things in the common affairs of the world in such a manner as [to] represent divine things and signify his mind as truly as his Word.

202. If even the most GLORIOUS HEAVENLY BODIES are viewed narrowly, as when we view 'em with glasses, they appear with spots; even that most bright and glorious of all visible things, the sun. Which denotes the imperfection of the most excellent of created beings. Job 25:5, "Behold even to the moon, and it shineth not; yea, the stars are not pure in his sight."

203. EXTERNAL THINGS are intended to be IMAGES of things spiritual, moral and divine. The following words are taken from Turnbull's *Moral Philosophy*, pp. 54–55:

> Now it has been often observed that such is the analogy between sensible and moral objects, that there is none of the latter sort that may not be clothed with a sensible form or image, and represented to us as it were in a material shape and hue. So true is [this], that not only are wit and poetry owned to take place only in consequence of

3. "Blank Bible," p. 656 top, at the beginning of the New Testament: "'Tis evident by John 11:50–52 that occurrences in the history of the New Testament as well as Old, have a mystery in them, and that they are ordered on purpose to represent and shadow forth spiritual things."
4. MS: "lively."

this analogy or resemblance of moral and natural ideas; but even all language is confessed to be originally taken from sensible objects, or their properties and effects.... Words cannot express any moral objects, but by exciting pictures of them in our minds. But all words being originally expressive of sensible qualities, no words can express moral ideas, but so far as there is such an analogy betwixt the natural and moral world, that objects in the latter may be shadowed forth, pictured or imaged to us by some resemblances to them in the former.... And so far as language can go in communicating sentiments, so far we have an indisputable proof of analogy between the sensible and the moral world; and consequently of wonderful wisdom and goodness, in adjusting sensible and moral relations and connections one to another; the sensible world to our minds, and reciprocally the connections of things relative to our moral powers to the connection of things that constitute the sensible world. It is this analogy that makes the beauty, propriety, and force of words, expressive of moral ideas, by conveying pictures of them into the mind.

All the phrases among the ancients, used to signify the beauty, harmony and consistency of virtuous manners, are taken from the beauty of sensible forms in nature, or in the arts which imitate nature, music, painting, etc.... So that here we have a clear proof of that analogy between the moral world or moral effects, and the natural world or sensible effects, without which language could not be a moral paintress, or paint moral sentiments, and affections and their effects (*ibid.*, pp. 145–46).

And the same author, in his second volume entitled *Christian Philosophy*, pp. 178–79, says: "There is a much more exact correspondence and analogy between the natural and moral world than superficial observers are apt to imagine or take notice of." Again, *ibid.*, pp. 180–81,

No one can be acquainted with nature, or indeed with the imitative arts, with poetry in particular, without perceiving and admiring the correspondence between the sensible and moral world, from which arises such a beautiful rich source of imagery in poetry, and without which there could be no such thing.[5]

5. These passages are virtually direct quotes from George Turnbull's *The Principles of Moral Philosophy* and *The Principles of Moral and Christian Philosophy*. Miller comments: "Turn-

204. There is a sort of OWLS that make a screaming, shrieking, dolorous noise. These are birds of the night, that shun daylight and live in darkness. And those creatures that are in Scripture called dragons, it seems used to make a doleful, screaming, wailing noise. Both which are referred to in Mic. 1:8, "I will make a wailing like dragons, and mourning as the owls"; Job 30:28–29, "I went mourning without the sun: I stood up and I cried in the congregation. I am a brother to dragons, and a companion to owls." The wailing of those dragons and owls represents the misery and wailing of devils, who are often called dragons, and of other spirits that dwell in eternal darkness.

205. The time for WEEDING a GARDEN is when it has newly rained upon it. Otherwise, if you go to pull up the weeds, you will pull up the good herbs and plants with them. So the time for purging the church of God is a time of revival of religion. It can't be so well done at another time; the state of the church of God will not so well bear it. It will neither so well bear the searching, trying doctrines of religion in their close application, nor a thorough ecclesiastical administration and discipline; nor will it bear at another time to be purged from its old corrupt customs, ceremonies, etc.

206. IMAGES of divine things in God's works:

It is certain, that the word "hieroglyphics," which the Greeks made use of to design these symbolical characters (used by the ancients), signifies a sacred graving or sculpture, because this way of writing was first consecrated to preserve and transmit to posterity some idea of the mysteries of religion. The first sages of the most remote antiquity made use of sensible signs [...] to represent intellectual and spiritual truths. All the different parts of nature are employed in this sacred language.... The source of this primitive hieroglyphical language seems to have been the persuasion of that great truth [...] that the visible world is representative of the invisible; that the properties, forms and motions of the one were copies, images, and

bull was one of the opponents singled out for attack in Edwards' *Freedom of the Will* as being 'a great enemy to the doctrine of necessity.' Yet he was a disciple of Newton and Locke, and still more of Shaftesbury and Hutcheson, so that Edwards could find in him many of the premises from which his own arguments commenced.... In this passage Edwards is picking out remarks in Turnbull that seem to fall in with his conception of language" (*Images or Shadows*, p. 148, n. 21).

shadows of the attributes, qualities and laws of the other (Ramsay's *Principles*, vol. 2, pp. 11–12).[6]

207. "Creaturæ rationales sumptæ vocantur mundus spiritualis, opposite ad mundum aspectabilem sive corporeum, etiam respublica spirituum et civitas dei.

"Hic [...] fundamenta theologiæ emblematicæ ostendere possemus, indicando nempe, non ninimam sapientiæ divinæ partem esse, quod tam admirabilem harmoniam atque comformitatem intet mundum illum aspectabilem et alterum illum, qui mundus spiritualis est, instituerit, ut ea, quæ in uno fiunt, etiam in altero, modo licet differente, fiant; et uti mundus ille visibilis existentiæ et attributorum divinorum speculum est, ita non minus illarum rerum, quæ in mundo spirituali eveniunt, speculum esse. Ex sapienti hac atque admirabili omnium divinorum operum harmonia atque conformitate nullo diende negatio totam illam de emblematibus doctrinam deducere nobis liceret. Neque etiam instituti nostri ratio nobis permittit, ut multa [hic] de præstantia civitatis illius Dei, sive respublicæ spirituum peroremus; non tamen a me impetrare possum, quin, brevissima licet sed elegantissima illust. Leibnitii verba de hac re adducam, quæ extant *in Causa Dei adserta per Justitiam ejus.* [...] 'Ipsum autem Βάθος in divinæ sapientiæ thesauris, vel in Deo abscondito, et in universali rerum harmonia latet.... Thesaurum mundi corporei magis magisque ipso naturæ lumine in hac vita elegantiam suam nobis ostendit, dum systemata macrocosmi et microcosmi recentiorum inventis aperiri cœpere. Sed pars rerum præstantissima civitas Dei spectaculum est, cujus ad pulchritudinem noscendam aliquando demum illustrati divinæ [gloriæ] lumine propius admittemur, etc'" (Stapferus, *Theologia Polemicæ*, Tome I, 181–82).[7]

---

6. Andrew Ramsay, *The Philosophical Principles of Natural and Revealed Religion*, 2, 11–12. An entry in JE's "Catalogue" gives evidence that he read Ramsay's work, at least vol. 2, in 1754 (see above, pp. 45–46).

7. Stapfer, *Institutiones Theologiæ Polemicæ*, vol. 1, ch. 3, no. 686. The passage reads: "Those rational beings, once they are taken up, are called the Spiritual World, as opposed to the visible or corporeal world; also the Republic of Spirits, or the City of God.

"At this point we are able to reveal the foundations of emblematic theology, by pointing out that it is not the least part of divine wisdom that it established such wonderful harmony and conformity between the visible world and that other, the spiritual world; with the result that those things that are done in one are also done in the other, although in a different manner; and that, just as this world of visible existence is a mirror of the divine attributes, so it is no less a mirror of those things which occur in the spiritual world. From this wisdom and marvelous harmony and conformity of all divine works it would be possible for us, with no

208. Our BREATH to support life, a representation of our dependence on the Spirit of God for spiritual life. Cudworth (*Intellectual System*, p. 428) mentions this saying of M. Antoninus: "That as our bodies breathe the common air, so should our souls suck and draw in vital breath, from the great Mind that comprehends the universe, becoming as it were one spirit with the same."[8]

209. The sun, a type of Christ. Cudworth's *Intellectual System*, p. 25: "The writer *de Placites Philosophorum* observes, *that Empedocles made two suns, the one archetypal and intelligible, the other apparent or sensible.*"

210. Cudworth's *Intellectual System*, p. 25: "Simplicius acquaints us, that Empedocles made two worlds, the one intellectual, and the other sensible; and the former of these to [be] the exemplar and archetype of the latter."

211. In the night the beasts of prey range abroad to destroy and devour, but when the sun rises they lie down in their dens. So in a dark time in the moral world, devils, as roaring lions, walk about seeking whom he may devour; but when the Sun of Righteousness shall arise, he shall be confined to the bottomless pit. Ps. 104:21–22.

212. The immense magnificence of the visible world, its inconceivable vastness, the incomprehensible height of the heavens, etc. is but a type of the infinite magnificence, height and glory of God's work in the spiritual world: the most incomprehensible expression of his power, wisdom, holiness and love, in what is wrought and brought to pass in

---

further effort, to deduce the whole doctrine of emblematics. Yet the reason of our plan does not allow us to speak much here concerning the superiority of the City of God, or the Republic of Spirits. I cannot, however, keep myself from citing those most elegant, if very brief, words of W. Leibniz, which appear in *in Causa Dei adserta per Justitiam ejus*, § 142, 143, 144: 'This Βάθος is concealed in the treasury of divine wisdom, or in the hidden God, and hidden in the universal harmony of things.... The treasury of the corporeal world more and more shows us its elegance in this life by the light of nature itself, while the systems of macrocosm and microcosm begin to be revealed by the discoveries of modern writers. But the most excellent part of things, the city of God, is a spectacle, whose beauty we will at last come closer to understanding, when we are illuminated by the light of the divine glory'" (trans. courtesy of Dr. Carl Schlam).

8. Ralph Cudworth, *The True Intellectual System of the Universe* (London, 1678). In addition to this and the two following entries, JE quotes Cudworth at length in "Miscellanies" no. 1359, and in "The Mind" no. 40. References to commendations of Cudworth's work in his "Catalogue" suggest that JE had not read it as late as near the end of his Stockbridge pastorate. "Images" nos. 208–12 were probably written in late 1756 or afterwards.

that world; and in the exceeding greatness of the moral and natural good, the light, knowledge, holiness and happiness which shall be communicated to it. And therefore to that magnificence of the world, height of heaven, those things are often compared in such expressions, "Thy mercy is great above the heavens, thy truth reacheth [unto the clouds]"; "Thou hast set thy glory above the heavens," etc.[9] See no. 21.

9. See Ps. 108:4 and Ps. 8:1.

# SCRIPTURES[1]

1. FLIES represent evil spirits and wicked men. The prince of the devils is called "Baalzebub," i.e. the lord of the flies [Matt. 12:24].

2. A great RIVER, with its various branches, represents the course of divine providence; thus Christ, when he appeared as the Lord and Superintendent of the course of things in providence, is represented in Daniel once and again as standing in the river Hiddekel [Dan. 10].

3. VALLEYS, in which is WATER, represents hell, or a state of death: so when it is said in Job, "the clods of the valley shall be sweet to him," or rather, "shall sweetly devour him". The word in the original[2] also signifies "brook" (Job 21:33).

4. DAWNING OF THE DAY and RISING OF THE SUN, a type of the commencement of the glorious times, Job 38:12–15.

5. LEVIATHAN, of the devil. Job 41:34.

6. A CANDLE or LAMP. II Sam. 21:17, "Thou shalt go no more out with us to battle lest thou quench the Light" (Hebrew: "candle" or "lamp") "of Israel."

7. WATERS represent misery, Job 22:11.

[8.][3] SERPENT, of the devil. Gen. 3.

1. The following series is found in a column on p. 41 of the MS, two pages below the end of the main series of entries. The items agree in ink and handwriting with "Images" no. 90, and were probably written at about that time, in 1739.
2. I. e. the Hebrew word *nachal*.
3. The following series of Scripture images is written on a separate folded sheet in the Trask Library. JE did not number the items in this series, but as they seem in every respect to be a draft of entries meant to be added to the preceding series, they are numbered and presented below as a continuation of it. These images were probably written in 1756 or early 1757.

[9.] NAKEDNESS AND EXCREMENTS, guilt, sin, etc. Gen. 3:7–11. Insufficiency, helplessness, exposedness, defenselessness, etc. See Gen. 17:10–14.

[10.] ROSES ON THORNS. Thorns, [a] type of trouble, difficulty, etc. Gen. 3:18. That the earth naturally produces in such abundance a noxious and useless growth, signifies how natural sinful and pernicious affections and actions are to the inhabitants of the world, and how naturally trouble everywhere arises in the world in its present fallen state, and full it is of affliction and vexation. See II Sam. 23:6, Cant. 2:2, Is. 33:12, Is. 55:13, Jer. 4:3 and 12:13, Ezek. 28:24, Mic. 7:4, Matt. 13:7, Ezek. 2:6, Heb. 6:8.

[11.] WOOL, SILK, SKINS. The clothes of animals, by their death, [a] type of Christ's righteousness, Gen. 3:21.

[12.] WATER, of trouble, misery. Gen. 6:17 and the two next chapters. WATERS, WAVES, FLOODS. Type of misery, wrath. II Sam. 22:5–6, 17.

[13.] FLOODS, overwhelming. Types of destruction and the wrath of God, the misery of hell. Gen. 6:16 and the two next chapters.

[14.] MOUNTAINS, of heaven. Gen. 8:4, Ex. 3, particularly v. 12; 18:5; [ch.] 19, particularly vv. 3–4; and 24:9–11 (especially v. 10; see also vv. 16–18). Ch. 25:40 and 26:30 compared with Heb. 8:5, Num. 20:22 to the end. See notes.[4] Ex. 32:30 and 33:21–23 and 34:2–7, 28–29; Num. 27. 12–13; Deut. 1:7, 19–20 and 32:49 and 34:1–5.

[15.] RAVENS, wicked men. Gen. 8:7.

[16.] DOVES, saints. Gen. 8:8.

[17.] OIL, love, grace, etc. Gen. 8:11.

4. In his "Blank Bible" note on Gen. 8:4, JE compares the Ark's coming to rest on Mt. Ararat with Christ's church arriving safe in heaven. His note on Ex. 24:10 asserts that Mt. Sinai, on which God appeared to the elders of Israel, is a type of heaven. The note on Heb. 8:5 interprets the Apostle's reference to God's instructing Moses on Mt. Sinai concerning the construction of the Tabernacle: "The Apostle means that that Mount represented heaven. He was charged to make 'em according to the pattern showed in the mount, signifying that they were to be images and shadows of heavenly things."

[18.] COLORS OF LIGHT. The various and most amiable expressions of the love and grace of God and all his moral perfections in the Gen. 9:12–17; see Ex. 25:4 and 26:1, 31, 36 and 28:5–6, 8, 15, 17–20 and 36:8, 35, 37 and 38:16 and 39:1–14, 29; II Chron. 3:14.

[19.] {COLORS OF LIGHT} and the graces of the Spirit of God in believers, ibid.

[20.] DROPS of descending rain, mortal men. Gen. 9:12–17.

[21.] TOWERS, of the pride of man. Gen. 11:4, compared with Is. 2:11–12, 15.

[22.] RAVENS, CROWS, EAGLES, VULTURES and such like birds, of evil spirits. Gen. 15:11, Lev. 11:13–19, II Sam. 21:10.

[23.] NIGHT, of times of great declension, corruption and affliction of the church. Gen. 15:12–13, 17.

[24.] FIRE, FURNACE, great misery. Gen. 15:17. See Gen. 19:24. The dreadful fire of Mt. Sinai. Ex. 19:18.

[25.] A LAMP. Light in darkness or out of darkness, comfort in affliction or deliverance from it. Gen. 15:17, II Sam. 22:29.

[26.] NAKEDNESS, native corruption. Gen. 17:10–14. See Gen. 3:7–11.

[27.] FIRE and BRIMSTONE, God's wrath. Gen. 19:24. See Gen. 15:17, II Sam. 22:9 and 23:7.

[28.] WATER, divine grace. Gen. 24:11.

[29.] WELLS OF WATER, ordinances or Word of God. Gen. 24:11.

[30.] OIL, the Spirit of God. Ex. 25:6 (see in Gen. 8:11), Ex. 30:22–33, Lev. 14:12, 15–18, 26–29. Oil supplies a lamp and enables to give light; so spiritual life and light, beauty, brightness, pleasantness and profitableness [are] from the Spirit of God.

[31.] The manner in which brightness and beautiful color is communicated by the sun to drops of water or to precious stones represent the manner in which grace, holiness and spiritual happiness is communicated from Christ to the saints. Gen. 9:12–17, Ex. 28:9–11, 17–21.

[32.] FRUITS. Types of virtues and good works. Plants with branches, flowers and fruits, of saints and of churches or the church in general. Ex. 17–22, Num. 24:6.

[33.] Lev. 2:1–2, and innumerable other places. Oil, which is by beating or pressing the olives; flour, by grinding the grain; frankincense, which is by the bleeding of a tree, were to be offered in the sacrifice, being types of the merit and benefit of the great sacrifice.

[34.] BEATING or POUNDING of olives for oil for the light. By the sufferings of Christ the church receives light by which it is enlightened and grace by which it shines. Ex. 27:20, Lev. 24:2, and other parallel places.

[35.] TREES and PLANTS with their beauty, pleasantness, growth and fruitfulness, of the saints and church of God under divine influences.

[36.] SUN, of Christ. Josh. 10:12–14. See note in loc.[5]

[37.] The MOON, the church. Josh. 10:12–14. See note.[6]

[38.] STARS, angels. Josh. 10:12–14. See note in loc.[7]

[39.] STORMS, of the wrath of God. The storms that brought on the Flood (see also Josh. 10:11); and the storm in the time of the battle against Sisera [Judg. 4]; and the storm of rain, thunder and lightning at the Red Sea [Ex. 14:12]. See Ps. 77.

---

5. "Blank Bible" note on Josh. 10:13: "In the Song of Deborah it is said 'the stars in their courses fought against Sisera' (Judg. 5:20). The angels are called stars, Christ is often compared to the sun. Here we have all the heavenly hosts, the sun, moon and all the stars, standing still to fight against the enemies of God's people, representing that Christ and all the heavenly hosts of saints (constituting the heavenly church, represented by the moon), and all the angels, are fighting against the enemies of the church. Hereby is typified that which is represented in prophecy in Rev. 19."

6. Ibid.

7. Ibid.

[40.] THUNDER AND LIGHTNING, the wrath of God. That at the Red Sea; that at Mt. Sinai; that in Egypt with the hail. II Sam. 22:14–15.

[41.] EXCREMENTS, of sin. Gen. 3:7–11. After sin, excrements began to come which made those parts appear filthy. Deut. 23:13–14, Ezek. 4:12–15.

[42.] LIONS AND BEASTS OF PREY, of the devil. Judg. 14:5–18, II Sam. 21:10.

[43.] LIGHT, of comfort, happiness. Gen. 15:17, II Sam. 22:29.

[44.] SPIDER'S WEB, of the rest, the confidence or dependence, possessions and glory of wicked men. Job 8:14.

[45.] Ps. 107, taking special notice of the forty-third verse. The chief calamities of life, such as captivity, being lost in a wilderness, suffering hunger and thirst, the sufferings of prisoners, distress in a storm at sea, distress by drought and famine, are all shadows of our spiritual misery by nature.

# EDWARDS' TABLES TO "IMAGES OF DIVINE THINGS"

1. The numbers in the subject index refer to "Images" entry numbers. It has been formed by combining the two MS tables that JE prepared for "Images." Where he refers to writings other than entries in "Images," excerpts from or paraphrases of relevant passages are given in footnotes. The subject headings, entry numbers, etc. printed in brackets were added on the MSS by Sereno Dwight, who also marked the tables to note the selection of entries from "Images" that he copied out. This copy is in the Trask Library.

2. "Blank Bible" note on John 19:39–40: "The sweet perfumed ointments with which they of old used to anoint and embalm dead bodies, as ordered in providence, betokened the happiness of departed souls of saints by being anointed with the Holy Ghost, especially the anointing and embalming the bodies of Jacob and of Jesus. The body of Jesus represented the whole church of saints which is his body, who, when they are in the state of the dead, are in Hades, are perfumed, are in a state of sweet rest by the anointings of the blessed Spirit. By this embalming, the nature of death is as it were changed. That dead body, by the nature or natural tendency of a state of death, sends forth an horrid stench and turns soon to putrefaction; but by this embalming the body is preserved from putrefaction. Death is defeated in that respect and the dead body, instead of a stench, sends forth a sweet savor. Thus is the memory of the just or blessed; but the name of the wicked shall rot and stink like the rotten corpse. So the soul of the just is blessed and perfumed, but the soul of the wicked perishes in an horrible spiritual stench and putrefaction. As the rotting and loathsomeness of the dead unburied bodies signifies the misery of damned souls, Is. 66:24 and Eccles. 6:3 (therefore it was carefully ordered that Christ's body should not see corruption), so the permanence and sweetness of the embalmed body signifies the happiness of the departed souls."

3. "Scripture" no. 397, on Gen. 2:9 and 3:22–24, concerning the Tree of Life. In a corollary to the entry JE writes of Christ as the fruit of the Tree of Life, the "food of life to either men and angels," and of man as the blossom that prepared the way for the fruit. "This

Tree of Life did as it were blossom in the sight of the angels when man was at first created in an innocent, holy, pleasant and happy state, who was that creature from whence this future fruit of the Tree of Life was to spring, the blossom out of which the fruit was to come. It was a fair and pleasant blossom, though a weak and feeble (and proved a fading) thing like a flower. When man fell then the blossom faded and fell off. Man came forth like a flower and was cut down, but the blossom fell in order to the succeeding fruit. The fall of man made way for the incarnation of Christ. It gave occasion to the production and ripening of that fruit, and to its blessed consequences."

4. See below, p. 139, n. 8.

5. Richard Bernard, Late Rector of Batcome, *Thesaurus Biblicus seu Promptuarium Sacrum; that is, the Bible's Treasury or Holy Storehouse* (London, 1644). Under the heading "Similes" Bernard gives a six-page index of biblical similes.

6. JE uses a symbol ( ⎵ ) which occurs frequently in cross-references in the later pages of his "Catalogue," where it stands for the first column of a page written in double columns. The identity of the item or passage in "The Mind" which is referred to here is problematic, because the MS of that work has been lost, and an extant index to it in JE's hand assigns nothing to its pp. 46–50. It is possible that these pages contained JE's earlier index to the series, and that he might here be referring to a related entry in that index. It is also possible that p. 49 of "The Mind" contained a continuation of his "Subjects to be handled in the treatise on the Mind" (*Works, 6,* 329, 387–93). None of these "Subjects," as presented by Sereno Dwight, is directly concerned with the natural world as representing divine things. But "The Mind" contains a relevant quotation regarding Plato's Cave from Ralph Cudworth's *Intellectual System,* which Dwight presents as an addendum to "The Mind" no. 40 (*Works of President Edwards,* Sereno Dwight, ed. (10 vols., New York, Converse, 1829), *1,* 673 [hereafter "Dwight ed."]), but which JE had almost certainly copied onto some other page of the MS. He might have included this quote among his "Subjects," and so might have written it on p. 49 of the MS. The quotation is one of the very few passages in "The Mind" that JE might appropriately cite under the topic of images of divine things. Moreover, his reference to "The Mind" in the table entry here is followed by a citation of "Images" no. 210, which gives a quotation from Cudworth.

Kernel, 163.

Lamp, 52.
Lancing a wound, 39.
Laws of nature, 16, 43.
Leviathan, 37.
Light, 58.
Light, more of in a year than dark-
ness, 103.
Lightning, 33.
Light of the sun not diminished by
wind, 97.
Lion, 131.
Love to women, 32.
Luminaries, 4.

Machines, chiefly composed of
wheels, 89.
Marriage, 5, 9, 12, 56.
Mildew, 165.
Milk, 113.
Miracles, 43.
[Mixtures that attend grace, 163.]
Mole, 179.

Moon, 76, 139.
Morning, 111.
Mountains, 29, 64, 66, 67, 107, 175;
burning, 84.
Mouse and cat, 73.

Names, 30.
Night, the time of beasts of prey
ranging and devouring, 211.
Nursing of a child, image of
nourishing grace in the heart, see
sermon on I Pet. 2:2.[7]

Olympic games, 101.
Ore, 163.
Owls, 204.

Pits, 21.
Plants, 13, 28, sermon on Heb. 6:7.[8]
Plowing, 44.
Poisonous animals, 127.
Pruning, 172.
*Punctum saliens*, 190.
Putrefaction, 1, 51, 61.

---

7. The sermon on I Pet. 2:2, "If persons have ever tasted the sweetness of the Word and grace of Christ they will be longing for more and more of it," begins with several observations on the text, especially: "3. We may observe what the Word of God is here called, viz. sincere milk. 'Tis compared to milk, for as the mother's milk is the proper nourishment of one lately born, so is the Word of God the proper food and nourishment of the soul that is new born. This is that milk which we do as it were suck from the breasts of our spiritual mother, the church (Is. 66:10–11).

"5. The new-born babe is in an imperfect state, and therefore in a growing state. It sucks its mother's breast and grows thereby: it has need of it for that end. So Christians here in this world, being in an imperfect state, they have need of growing; and the Word of God is the proper means of it.

"6. And lastly, the Apostle takes notice upon what condition they will surely follow his exhortation: 'If so be ye have tasted that the Lord is gracious.' That is, if ye have ever tasted of the grace of the Lord Jesus Christ, and experienced the sweetness of the gospel of the Word of his grace, then ye will have an appetite after the Word, and then ye will desire to grow."

8. The sermon on Heb. 6:7 (dated January/February 1746–47) develops a series of five observations, in what might have been four separate preaching units or occasions. Passages referred to in JE's tables under the entries "Ground producing plants," "Plants," and "Rain" are found in Obs. 1, "The means of grace to those that live under the gospel are like the showers that often descend on the earth," and Obs. 2, "Holiness in the saints is as it were an herb that is cultivated by God." JE makes the latter comparison in a series of points: "1.... As

the herb of the field is from a seed or principle that is not natural to the earth, but a seed implanted in it, so it is with holiness in the hearts of the saints.

"The herb of the field is a living thing in that which is wholly without life. So:

"[Holiness] beautifies and adorns that which in itself is vile and has no comeliness.... 2. It is very small in its beginning, and of a growing nature.... 3. Has all its refreshment and quickening from above. 4. Has many branches from one seed and root. 5. It is a tender thing and exposed to many injuries, easily wounded, and if not protected is easily destroyed. 6. Passes under many changes before it comes to its perfection.... 7. Comes at last to a vast increase. 8. When ripe is gathered in."

9. See above p. 139, n. 8.

## SCRIPTURE INDEX[2]

1. "Miscellanies" no. 991 is also referred to in "Images" no. 166 (see above, p. 110, n. 8).
2. On the last verso of his second table for "Images of Divine Things," JE drew up the following index of all the passages of Scripture cited in his entries. The table is arranged in canonical order, as in the MS. JE's copying and indexing errors have been corrected without comment. Citations that JE overlooked or that have been editorially interpolated have been added in brackets.

Ps.:           1:3, no. 15; [8:1, no. 212;] 19:4–6, no. 85³ [22:6, no. 46;]
               37:35–36, no. 191; [47:5,] 68:17–18, no. 81; 78:39, no.
               141; [81:10, no. 126;] 84:6, no. 35; 42:7, 88:7, no. 27;
               [104:21–22, no. 211; 108:4, no. 212]; 140:3, no. 69;
               147:18, no. 183.

Prov.:         4:23, no. 6; 5:3–6, no. 117; [10:7, no. 51;] 13:9, 24:20,
               20:20, no. 52; 16:32, no. 71; 18:8, 20:27, 30, 22:18, 26:22,
               no. 115; 30:15–16, no. 119.

Eccles.:       1:5, no. 36; 1:7, no. 22; 3:21, 12:7, no. 65.

Cant.:         2:15, no. 148 and [no. 171]; 3:11–17, no. 53 and no. 111;
               8:1, no. 166.

Is.:           2:11, 12–17, no. 74 and no. 107; 28:23, no. 44; 37:30–31,
               no. 108; [48:10, no. 163; 53:2, no. 46;] 53:7, no. 2; 54:11–
               12, no. 58; 63:1–5, no. 81 and no. 150; [63, no. 150;]
               66:17, no. 73; 66:24, [no. 1,] no. 51, no. 61.

Jer.:          2:3, no. 189; 17:8, no. 15; [32:8, no. 201].

Ezek.:         1:1, 3, no. 77; 37:9–10, 13–14, no. 62.

Dan.:          7:16, no. 45; 8:2, 3, 16 and 10:4–5 and 12:6–8, no. 77.
               Hos.:[5:10, no. 27;] 10:7, no. 191; [14:7, no. 108].

Mic.:          1:8, no. 204; 6:15, no. 68.


Matt.:         [6:22, no. 145; 12:23, no. 26;] 13:6, no. 194; 24:37–39, no.
               102; [17:2, no. 58;] 21:44, no. 48.

Luke:          15:8–10, no. 138; 22:31, no. 94; 23:44, no. 50.

John:          1:9, 6:32, no. 45; 12:24, no. 23; 15:1, no. 45; [15:5, no. 78;]
               15:6, no. 88; 20:22, no. 62.

Acts:          8:32, no. 2.

Rom.:          [3:13, no. 69; 12:4, 5, no. 130].

I Cor.:        [9:10, no. 163]; 12:4–31, no. 58; 13:11, no. 42, no. 53;
               15:36–42, no. 7, no. 20, [no. 53].

II Cor.:       12:4, 11, no. 58.

Gal.:          3:19, [16,] no. 166.

Eph.:          [2:2, no. 61;] 5:30–32, no. 9, no. 12, no. 56.

Colos.:        [2:15, no. 81].

Heb.:          7:2, no. 132; 8:2, no. 45; 9:16–17, no. 7, no. 41; 9:24, no. 45;
               [10:20, no. 185].

Jas.:          3:[6–]8, no. 69; 4:14, no. 141.

Rev.:          3:4–5, 18, 4:3, 4, 7:9, 13, 15:6, 19:8, 11, 14, [20:11,] 21:11,
               [18, 21,] no. 58; 3:5, 18, 6:11, 7:9, 19:13–14, no. 81; [12,
               no. 139;] 12:5, no. 53; [14:15, no. 171, no. 138; 16:15, no.
               121; 20:5–6, no. 108; 21:5, no. 166].

   3. JE erroneously entered here four references to the book of Proverbs, which he cited in
"Images" no. 115. These entries have been moved to their proper canonical position below.

*"TYPES"*

# NOTE ON THE MANUSCRIPT OF "TYPES"

T HE manuscript of the "Types" notebook is part of the Andover collection, and has not been previously published. It is a twenty-page octavo booklet, written mostly on used paper. It is bound in a cover of stiff blue paper, on which "Types" is written in bold letters. The first two pages are two infolded double leaves cut from letter covers, one of which bears the address, "To the Rev^d Mr. Jonathan Edwards at Northampton." These are followed by a short double leaf sewn in separately. One side of this paper contains texts of Scripture under the heading, "The answers of John Hunt's question." Edwards found space to write on the back, which became the first verso and second recto of the double leaf, and on a margin on the second verso. The last portion of the booklet consists of two more infolded double leaves of clean paper. Edwards' discussion ends on the top of the first recto and the last seven pages are blank.

From the letter cover address in the first portion of the "Types" notebook, and from the general character of the handwriting, the manuscript can be dated during the Northampton pastorate. Edwards' writing is quite uniform in hand and ink through the first eleven pages, down to his reference to a "Pamphlet entitled *Creation, the Ground-work of Revelation.*" This portion of his discussion was probably written in a brief span of time during the middle 1740s. The hand and ink are like that in "Images of Divine Things," nos. 180–87, and are particularly similar to that in the sermons on Is. 37:31 and on I Cor. 11:3, both dated March 1746.

The pamphlet to which Edwards refers, *The Creation the Ground-work of Revelation*, was published in Edinburgh in 1750. The hand and ink of this reference, and of the remainder of the "Types" notebook, indicates a still later date, probably 1755 or 1756. The writing is most similar to that in "Images" nos. 199–206.

# *TYPES*

T YPES. Texts of Scripture that seem to justify our supposing the Old Testament state of things was a typical state of things, and that not only the ceremonies of the Law were typical, but that their history and constitution of the nation and their state and circumstances were typical. It was, as it were, a typical world.

John 9:7, "Go, wash in the pool of Siloam, (which is by interpretation, Sent)." There evidently weight is laid on the interpretation of the word "signified," that there was instruction in the signification of the word, and that teaching that the pool was typical of that fount of grace and mercy that is in Christ.

Gal. 4:21–23, "Tell me, ye that desire to be under the law, do ye not hear the law? For it is written that Abraham had two sons, the one by a bondmaid, the other by a freewoman. But he who was of the bondwoman was born after the flesh; but he of the freewoman was by promise." [V.] 24, "Which things are an allegory: for these are the two covenants; the one from the mount Sinai, which gendereth to bondage, which is Agar." [V.] 25, "For this Agar is mount Sinai in Arabia, and answereth to Jerusalem which now is, and is in bondage with her children."

I Cor. 10:1–4, "I would not that ye should be ignorant, how that all our fathers were under the cloud, and all passed through the sea; And were baptized in the cloud and in the sea; And all eat of the same spiritual meat; And all drank of the same spiritual drink: for they drank of that spiritual Rock that followed them: and that Rock was Christ." V. 6, "Now these things were our examples" (or figures). V. 11, "Now all these things happened to them for ensamples" (or types).

When we are sufficiently instructed that all these things were typical

146

and had their spiritual signification, it would be on some accounts as unreasonable to say that we must interpret no more of them than the Scripture has interpreted for us, and than we are told the meaning of in the New Testament, as it would be to say that we must interpret prophecy, or prophetical visions and types, no further than the Scripture has interpreted it to our hand.

Christ blames the Jews and disciples that they don't understand his parables, that were made up of types without explication. But why so, if it be very presumption and folly to pretend to interpret any parables without explication? Matt. 13:15, "Their ears are dull of hearing," compared with Heb. 5:10–12.

Yea, Christ blames the disciples that they did not understand the types of the Old Testament without his explaining of them, as particularly he blames 'em that they did not understand that leaven was a type of hypocrisy. Matt. 16:11–12, "How is it that ye do not understand that I spake not to you concerning bread, but concerning the doctrine of the Pharisees and of the Saducees?"

These things that are called "types" used by them to be called "mysteries," and they were many of them. I Cor. 13:2, "And though I have the gift of prophecy, and understand all *mysteries*, and all knowledge."

I Cor. 9:9–10, "For it is written in the law of Moses, Thou shalt not muzzle the mouth of the ox that treadeth out the corn. Doth God take care for oxen? Or saith he it altogether for our sakes? For our sakes, no doubt, this is written: that he that ploweth should plow in hope; and that he that thresheth in hope should be partaker of his hope." And so in I Tim. 5:18, "For the scripture saith, Thou shalt not muzzle the ox that treadeth out the corn. And, The labourer is worthy of his reward."

Heb. 4:3, "As I have sworn in my wrath, if they shall enter into my rest"; [v.] 4, "For he spake in a certain place of the seventh day on this wise"; v. 9, "There remaineth therefore a rest to the people of God"; [v.] 10, "For he that entered into his rest hath ceased from his own works, as God did from his."

Of Melchizedec, ch. 5, vv. 6, 11, called "a priest forever after the order of Melchizedec. [...] Of whom we have many things to say, and hard to be uttered, seeing ye are dull of hearing." Heb. 7, throughout, concerning Melchizedec: the interpretation of his name, "King of righteousness"; the name of the city, which is by interpretation "peace"; that minute circumstance concerning him, of his having no account of his birth or death, "without beginning of days or end of life." That is declared to be typical, that Abraham paid the tenth of the spoils, and Levi in Abraham, and that Melchizedec blessed Abraham.

First, to lay down that persons ought to be exceeding careful in interpreting of types, that they don't give way to a wild fancy; not to fix an interpretation unless warranted by some hint in the New Testament of its being the true interpretation, or a lively figure and representation contained or warranted by an analogy to other types that we interpret on sure grounds.

Heb. 8:2, "A minister of the *true* tabernacle"; vv. 4–5, "There are priests that offer gifts according to the law: Who serve unto the example an shadow of heavenly things, as Moses was admonished of God when he was about to make the tabernacle: for, See, saith he, that thou make all things according to the pattern showed thee in the mount."
Whence, by the apostle's arguing, all these things and all these circumstances were typical; and if they are typical, they are for our consideration. For, for what end is a type or picture, but to give some knowledge of the antitype or thing painted?

Col. 2:16–17, "Let no man judge you in meat, or in drink, or in respect of an holyday, or of the new moon, or of the sabbath days: Which are a shadow of things to come; but the body is of Christ." Where we are told what the new moons are a shadow of, and so, of many other of their holy days and of many of their ceremonial observances about meat and drink. And, if we may not judge, how are they for our instruction? And if not for our instruction, why were these shadows appointed?

And then, how could any of these types be of any manner of instruction to the Jews to whom they were given, if they might judge nothing without interpretation, for the interpretation of none was then given? The types of the Old Testament were given, not without an aim at their instruction to whom they were given, but yet they were given much more for our instruction under the New Testament; for they understood but little, but we are under vastly greater advantage to understand them than they. That they were given chiefly for us seems to be evident by those texts, I Cor. 9:9–10, I Cor. 10:6, 11.

Heb. 9:1–4, where is mention of the various parts and utensils of the tabernacle; and then, v. 5, 'tis said, "of which we cannot now speak particularly," intimating that these have all their spiritual signification and instruction. But are these types all in vain, and must we never receive the instruction that is held forth because the Apostle did not speak of 'em particularly? Did God give 'em to hold forth to us spiritual things? And yet, is it presumption for us to endeavor to see what spiritual things are held forth in them?

Vv. 8–11, "The Holy Ghost this signifying, that the way into the holiest of all was not yet made manifest, while as the first tabernacle was yet standing: Which was a figure for the time then present, in which were offered gifts and sacrifices, that could not make him that did the service perfect, as pertaining to the conscience; Which stood in meats and drinks, and divers washings, and carnal ordinances, imposed on them until the time of reformation. But Christ being come an high priest of good things to come, by a greater and more perfect tabernacle, not made with hands, that is to say, not of this building." By this it appears that all these sacrifices and meats and drinks and ordinances were signs for that time then *present*, of good things *to come*; for the expression "to come" in v. 11 answers to the expression "the time then present" (v. 9).

Ch. 9:22–24, "And almost all things are by the law purged with blood; and without the shedding of blood is no remission. It was therefore necessary that the patterns of things in the heavens should be purified with these; but the heavenly things[1] themselves with better sacrifices than these. For Christ is not entered into the holy places made with hands, which are the figures of the true; but into heaven itself."

Ch. 10:1, "For the law having a shadow of good things to come, and not the very image of the things, can never with those sacrifices which they offered year by year continually make the comers thereunto perfect."

Ch. 11:19, "Accounting that God was able to raise him up, even from the dead; from whence he also received him in a figure."

---

1. MS: "sacrifices." In transcribing the verse, JE inadvertently confused the wording, for "things" appears in the KJV.

Ch. 13:11–13, "For the bodies of those beasts ... are burned without the camp.... Jesus ... suffered without the gate."

II Cor. 3:13–14, "Not as Moses, who put a veil over his face, that the children of Israel could not steadfastly look to the end of that which is abolished: But their minds were blinded: for until this day remaineth the same veil untaken away in the reading of the old testament; which veil is done away in Christ."

John 6:31–32, "Our fathers did eat manna in the desert; as it is written, He gave them bread from heaven to eat. Then Jesus said unto them, Verily, verily, I say unto you, Moses gave you not that bread from heaven; but my Father giveth you the true bread from heaven."

Rom. 5:14, "After the similitude of Adam's transgression, who is the figure of him that was to come."

Permutation of names. So Christ is in Scripture called "David" and "Israel" (Is. 49:3). "Christ our passover is sacrificed for us" (I Cor. 5:7). "Behold the Lamb of God, which taketh away the sin of the world" (John 1:29). The church under the New Testament is called "Jerusalem." The gospel church is called "Israel" (Gal. 6:16 and elsewhere). Gospel ministers are called "sons of Levi" (Mal. 3:3). Regeneration is called "circumcision." Heaven is called "paradise"; we read of the Tree of Life there. Christ is called "Jesus," or "Joshua."[2]

I Pet. 3:20–21, "Eight souls were saved by water. The like figure" (or, as it is in the original, "the antitype"), "whereunto baptism doth now save us."

Rev. 11:8, "Which is spiritually called Sodom and Egypt."

If we may use our own understandings and invention not at all in interpreting types, and must not conclude anything at all to be types but what is expressly said to be and explained in Scripture, then the church under the Old [Testament], when the types were given, were secluded from ever using their understanding to search into the meaning of the types given to 'em; for God did, when he gave 'em, give no interpretation.

Types are a certain sort of language, as it were, in which God is wont to speak to us. And there is, as it were, a certain idiom in that language

---

2. On the significance of names, see "Images" nos. 30 and 132, and "Types of the Messiah," pp. 294–305.

which is to be learnt the same that the idiom of any language is, viz. by good acquaintance with the language, either by being naturally trained up in it, learning it by education (but that is not the way in which corrupt mankind learned divine language), or by much use and acquaintance together with a good taste or judgment, by comparing one thing with another and having our senses as it were exercised to discern it (which is the way that adult persons must come to speak any language, and in its true idiom, that is not their native tongue).

Great care should be used, and we should endeavor to be well and thoroughly acquainted, or we shall never understand [or] have a right notion of the idiom of the language. If we go to interpret divine types without this, we shall be just like one that pretends to speak any language that han't thoroughly learnt it. We shall use many barbarous expressions that fail entirely of the proper beauty of the language, that are very harsh in the ears of those that are well versed in the language.

God han't expressly explained all the types of Scriptures, but has done so much as is sufficient to teach us the language.

I Cor. 13:2, "Though I have the gift of prophecy, and understand all mysteries, and all knowledge." This implies that there were [an] abundance of mysteries then not understood. By "mysteries" is especially meant divine truths wrapped up[3] in shadows and mysterious representations.

To show how there is a medium between those that cry down all types, and those that are for turning all into nothing but allegory and not having it to be true history; and also the way of the rabbis that find so many mysteries in letters, etc.

Types are used in the New Testament as well as the Old, as is evident by the descent of the Holy Ghost in the shape of a dove, which is a type of the Holy Ghost; and his descending on the disciples at Pentecost when there was a noise as of a rushing wind and cloven tongues as of fire.

The Apostle himself teaches us that only so small a thing as the silence of Scripture in not giving an account of Melchizedec's birth nor death was typical. If so small things in Scripture are typical, it is rational to suppose that Scripture abounds with types.

3. Conjectural reading.

I expect by very ridicule and contempt to be called a man of a very fruitful brain and copious fancy, but they are welcome to it. I am not ashamed to own that I believe that the whole universe, heaven and earth, air and seas, and the divine constitution and history of the holy Scriptures, be full of images of divine things, as full as a language is of words; and that the multitude of those things that I have mentioned are but a very small part of what is really intended to be signified and typified by these things: but that there is room for persons to be learning more and more of this language and seeing more of that which is declared in it to the end of the world without discovering all.

To say that we must not say that such things are types of these and those things unless the Scripture has expressly taught us that they are so, is as unreasonable as to say that we are not to interpret any prophecies of Scripture or apply them to these and those events, except we find them interpreted to our hand, and must interpret no more of the prophecies of David, etc. For by the Scripture it is plain that innumerable other things are types that are not interpreted in Scripture (all the ordinances of the Law are all shadows of good things to come), in like manner as it is plain by Scripture that these and those passages that are not actually interpreted are yet predictions of future events.

See the pamphlet entitled *Creation, the Ground-work of Revelation*, pp. 49–50.[4]

4. [Andrew Wilson,] *The Creation the Ground-work of Revelation, and Revelation the Language of Nature. Or, a brief attempt to demonstrate that the Hebrew Language is founded upon Natural Ideas, and that the Hebrew Writings transfer them to Spiritual Objects* (Edinburgh, 1750). Adopting an essentially Lockean conception of language, Wilson argues that, as God created the world, he also devised the Hebrew language to describe and explain the world. Names of persons and things in Hebrew were made to express the particular natures, operations, and virtues of the things named. But the material world was created a reflection of a superior spiritual order, so that "there is a mysterious harmony between this world and an invisible one; and the language of the Old Testament is the key of this mystery" (p. 24).

In the passage JE refers to, Wilson maintains that the Old and New Testaments are related in the manner of a parable and its interpretation, or a fable and its moral; the one gives a "material" representation, and the other the spiritual signification. "The whole laid together, composes that perfect original of spiritual glory, which the earthly glory under the law painted, and which the Prophets, who wrote in that style, foretold. By this means, we have the divine lineaments, and the material picture of them, which the Deity himself designed, so adjusted to one another, that every eye may trace the perfect likeness, and be judges of the true nature and value of each" (p. 49). The task of Christ and the writers of the New Testament, Wilson now argues, was not to explain the Old Testament, but "to fulfill and display that true glory, which, when completely revealed, appeared the true original of what was prefigured of old." He therefore objects to those who teach that it is dangerous to

Ps. 78:2. There the rehearsal of the story of the wonderful work God wrought for Israel, in redeeming out of Egypt, leading them through the wilderness to Canaan, instating them in the possession of that land, land, and setting up the kingdom of David, etc. is called "parables" and "dark sayings." See note on that place.[5]

That Mount Zion and Jerusalem are types of the church of saints is evident by Ps. 125:1–2.

That many more particulars in the form of the sanctuary and its various parts, vessels and utensils, than are explained is evident by Heb. 9:5, "And over it the cherubims of glory shadowing the mercy seat; of which we cannot now speak particularly," plainly intimating there [are] many particulars in those things representing heavenly things which he now thought it not expedient to explain.

---

interpret anything in the Old Testament as a type of what is revealed in the New Testament unless the New Testament expressly explains it as such. "Did the Lord fulfil the law and the prophets," Wilson responds, "and has he transmitted unto us the knowledge of what he fulfilled; and yet shall we be dared to compare the picture, of God's own designing, with the true original, which he has been pleased also to discover to us? Did all the Prophets witness unto Christ; and did the Lord himself, and his Apostles, practice the explaining, in all the scriptures, the things concerning himself; and have we these same Old Testament scriptures, with a disuasive or danger annexed unto the gift, if we attempt to make the only use of them they are useful for?" (pp. 49–50).

5. "Blank Bible" note on Ps. 78:2: "The rehearsal made of the wonderful things which God had done of old for Israel, in their redemption [out] of Egypt, settlement in Canaan, etc. are called 'a parable' and 'dark sayings,' because all these things are typical of gospel things, and with an eye to gospel things this psalm (as almost all the next) was indited by the Spirit of God." Cf. "Types of the Messiah," pp. 193–94, above.

PART TWO
*"TYPES OF THE MESSIAH"*

*Edited by*
*Mason I. Lowance, Jr. with*
*David H. Watters*

## EDITOR'S INTRODUCTION TO
## "TYPES OF THE MESSIAH"

"**M**iscellanies" no. 1069, more commonly known as "Types of the Messiah," is a long treatise on the subject of biblical typology, composed between 1744 and 1749, while Edwards was minister to the church in Northampton. It belongs with the notebook on "Types" and "Images of Divine Things" because these doctrinal statements contain theoretical declarations that are applied elsewhere in the Edwards canon. It will be helpful for anyone approaching the "Types of the Messiah" to understand the sources of the work and its relation to Edwards' other writings, especially the sermons and particularly the series of thirty sermons preached in 1739 that later comprised *A History of the Work of Redemption* (1774). "Types of the Messiah" occupies seventy-three densely inscribed folio sheets that appear to be a treatise on the subject of exegetical typology, drawing together views on the subject that had been expressed by Edwards in earlier sermons, occasional notebook entries, and in his "Types" notebook. This introduction will situate the reader by examining specific connections among these texts in the first section. Section two explores problems of interpretation in "Types of the Messiah" itself, followed by an explanation of textual and editorial procedures.

*"Types of the Messiah" and the Edwards Canon*

It is extremely important to distinguish Edwards' writings *about* typology from his other examinations of scriptural exegesis, such as the "Prophecies of the Messiah" and "Fulfillment of the Prophecies of the Messiah" ("Miscellanies" nos. 1067 and 1068), because for Edwards, typology represented an exegetical science that revealed God's progressive dispensation through history and human time while providing continuities between the Old and New Testaments and contemporary events. It is also significant that "Types of the Messiah" was one

document which represents the *process* by which Jonathan Edwards
worked from the composition of sermon literature to a "Miscellanies"
entry, albeit in this case one long enough to be considered a doctrinal
treatise. The relationship between Edwards' "Miscellanies" and his
sermons is an exact one, analogous to Ralph Waldo Emerson's use of
his *Journal* entries in the composition of his *Essays*, where use marks
and annotations indicate precise correlations between the journal
phrasing and the essay. Edwards sometimes composed a sermon by
turning to his notebooks or "Miscellanies" as a resource, though a
notebook entry could just as easily be drawn from a sermon. "Types of
the Messiah" evolved from previous writings on the same subject,
including several important sermons from Edwards' early ministry
and the *Redemption* discourse. Jonathan Edwards' writing workshop
was organized and systematic; the Bible stood at the center of his
literary and philosophical world, and its interpretation is central to his
exegetical process. As Wilson H. Kimnach has suggested, Edwards
would receive inspiration for his sermon, after which he would search
his gathered materials—notebooks, "Miscellanies," Scripture com-
mentaries, and earlier sermons—to find ideas that would illustrate or
explain his sermon text. Tables and indices became crucial ways of
organizing his thoughts, as did the "Blank Bible," an interleaved King
James text into which he would introduce interpretation and cross-
referencing.

> A sermon ... thus became an integral part of Edwards' "working
> papers" and an essential vehicle for the articulation of his thought.
> The extent to which a sermon was involved in the cycle of cross-
> references that united Edwards' notebook corpus varied.... [The]
> sermon participates in two separate cycles of reference, one involv-
> ing the interleaved Bible and the Scripture notebooks, and the
> other the "Miscellanies."[1]

The treatise "Types of the Messiah" is very much a representative
product of this compositional process; however, the general pattern
by which the sermon containing earlier "Miscellanies" expressions
would become a part of the notebook apparatus is here reversed.
"Types of the Messiah" recapitulated themes that were expressed not
only in the earlier sermon literature, but also in the earlier "Miscella-

1. Wilson H. Kimnach, "The Literary Technique of Jonathan Edwards," (Ph.D. diss., Univ.
of Pennsylvania, 1972), pp. 116–17. Excerpts from JE's sermons used in this introduction
were pointed out and transcribed by Rebecca J. Frey.

nies." For example, a sermon preached during the early 1720s, between Edwards' New York pastorate and his assistantship to Solomon Stoddard in Northampton, contained typological correspondences that were similar to those found in "Types of the Messiah." The text for the sermon was Ps. 147:1, and the subject was King David, his attributes and value as a prefiguration of Jesus the Messiah. Citing specifically David's ability as a musician, Edwards showed that:

> We have no account of any other that ever was so much or so well employed in this divine exercise as this king of Israel. Herein he was a lively type of him who is the root and the offspring of David, who so eminently glorified the Father beyond what ever was done before or by any other. By this David gained the name of the sweet psalmist of Israel (II Sam. 21:1).[2]

This early sermon argued the Old Testament anticipation of the incarnation through "types" and prophetic symbols. From his earliest writings, Edwards expressed a fascination with prefiguration and fulfillment in Scripture, and he also argued for an extension of this process to nature and history. Stephen J. Stein has shown that:

> By his willingness to employ the process of analogy liberally, Edwards was able to turn the entire text of the Old Testament into a massive anticipation of Christ and his work of redemption. The christological emphasis came at the expense of Jewish history. Edwards sounded the same note at the beginning of his collection of prophecies of the Messiah ... Prophecy therefore allowed Edwards to organize the content of the entire Bible around Christ and to bind together the two testaments as coordinate witnesses to his work of redemption.[3]

We must be careful to distinguish *prophecy* as a mode of discourse from *typology* as Edwards understood them. For example, "Miscellanies" nos. 1067 and 1068, both very long treatises separately titled "Prophecies of the Messiah" and "Fulfillments of the Prophecies of the Messiah," are filled with information about the cycles of prophecy and fulfillment in history, and they are useful in determining exactly what

2. Sermon on Ps. 147:1, L. 1v. All sermons referred to here, except as noted, are in the Beinecke Library.

3. Stephen J. Stein, "The Spirit and the Word: Jonathan Edwards and Scriptural Exegesis," in Nathan O. Hatch and Harry S. Stout, eds., *Jonathan Edwards and the American Experience* (New York, Oxford Univ. Press, 1988), p. 124.

position Edwards took in specific scriptural examples. They are not, however, writings about the subject of typology, nor are they applications of the typological reading of history as Edwards defined it in "Images of Divine Things" or the more theoretical statements, the "Types" notebook and "Types of the Messiah." It is significant that in "Miscellanies" no. 1069, Edwards was extremely careful to distinguish the typological method of relating the Old to the New Testaments from the prophetical scheme which also established a connection between the two dispensations. Broadly, the "Types of the Messiah" was a statement of theory with numerous illustrations, and it generally followed the schema outlined by Samuel Mather in *The Figures or Types of the Old Testament* (1683). Thus it was a historically anchored historiography, one in which Edwards clearly established the pattern of prefiguration and fulfillment in the persons and events of the Old Testament as they related to the life and ministry of Christ. Still, "Types of the Messiah" included departures from this strictly historical pattern of prefiguration and fulfillment, so that towards the end of document we find a long section containing "allegorical" uses of the Old Testament types and some unusually Platonic "correspondences" drawn between emblems of nature and spiritual ideas. Edwards was fond of the word "representation," and he used it not only to apply to conservative typological schemes, but also to these Platonic "correspondences" he cited late in the text.

Briefly, the problem may be summarized in the following way. For Edwards, the value and meaning of the typological associations between prefigurative types, which appeared in the pre-Christian old dispensation and foreshadowed Christ's incarnation and first appearance on earth, and the ultimate antitype, that fulfilling part of the equation which gave spiritual importance to the preceding types, was radically altered in the course of his career. Personal, ontological types, as Edwards explained in the 1739 *Redemption* discourse, were historical, linear, and real, and this conservative exegetical view was consistent with the orthodox tradition of typological exegesis extending from Paul and Augustine to the Protestant Reformation in Europe. The types were instituted by God to look forward to some future event, in this case, the coming of Christ in the first incarnation. But for Edwards, Christ had already come in Spirit, and was present as a contemporary reality for those believers and saints who had faith, so that the so-called "types"—those historical and prefigurative symbols by which Christians for centuries had understood revelation through

Scripture—came to have a new and radically different meaning as "representations," what Emerson would call "correspondences."

Edwards' types were eternal, not temporal, and the seeming tension in his typological theory never resulted in his allegorizing of nature. He showed that types, unlike mere natural symbols, participated in a scheme of adumbration and fulfillment. Often, however, his explanations suggest that this adumbration occurs through a chain of being rather than through the unfolding of time, and sometimes his interchangeable use of such terms as "type," "symbol," and especially "representation," seems to mean more reflections or analogies than anticipatory prefigurations. Edwards would propose that a new system of "types" was to be found in the world of nature, Platonic in character, not prefigurative entirely, but timeless, "in and out of time" like Yeats' gyres, so that the true believer provided with the "new sense of things"—as Edwards called the power of perception available only to the elected saint—could "read" the book of nature as previous exegetes had read the Book of Scripture for revelation of God's will. The saint would understand the mysteries of God's universe and grow increasingly aware of the direct connections between letter and spirit, Platonic essence and representation, idea and symbol.

In this context, the "type" was no longer always inferior to the forthcoming antitype; rather, it was at once a representation and an essence, precisely because it transcended time and space. John F. Wilson has argued that:

> The pattern of type and antitype provided the basic structure ... [and a] conservative practitioner would have stopped using typology at this point, because it was essential to the message that Christ fulfill all the Old Testament types—if not in the earthly life, then in the resurrection and in his anticipated coming in glory. At one level, Edwards operated with these assumptions. But he also moved beyond and transformed them, adapting a figural, even typological, framework ... The life of the redeemed was for him typified in the Old Testament, and he applied the types of the Old Testament much more generally than conservative exegesis allowed.[4]

4. *Works*, 9, 49. Other sources that review the conflict between "natural" and "historical" typology include Bercovitch, ed., *Typology and Early American Literature*; Earl Miner, ed., *Literary Uses of Typology from the Late Middle Ages to the Present* (Princeton, Princeton Univ. Press, 1977); and Lowance, *The Language of Canaan*.

Throughout his writing, Edwards maintained a central focus on eschatology, the coming of Christ and the millennial kingdom, and he looked to nature for "signs of the times" which would corroborate his lifelong belief in the revealed will of God through Scripture. It is significant that for Edwards, all history could be explained by comparing current events to biblical revelation. Through the system of types instituted by God and governed by providence, which prefigured the ultimate antitype, Christ and his kingdom, not only could human history be explained; indeed, future events could be predicted and the time of the second coming could be established in the future scheme of historical events.

> [Edwards] went a step further than many and was prepared to extend typology to utilize New Testament passages and events in the life of the Christian church as means to interpret more fully the future that the apocalyptic passages ostensibly disclosed.
>
> Even beyond this, Edwards was prepared to find types in the natural world. His antitype, in nature as well as in apocalyptic literature, was Christ. This meant that his understanding of nature was finally determined by a Christocentric construction of the world.[5]

The christocentric focus of Edwards' writing readily embraced typology as a way of linking the Old and New Testaments with each other and the Bible with contemporary history. From the beginning, Edwards exhibited a conservatism in his interpretation of Scripture passages where type and antitype appear. For example, in a sermon on I Cor. 10:8–11, preached in 1731 or 1732, Edwards argued that:

> Almost all things that pertained to the affairs of the children of Israel in the wilderness were typical, were ordered of God to be types of spiritual and eternal things. And so the judgments that God inflicted on them, as the Apostle informs us, were for types of that divine vengeance that we are in danger of in these gospel times if we are wicked.

5. *Works*, 9, 47–48. See also Galdon, *Typology and Seventeenth-Century Literature*. Galdon argues (p. 5) that "biblical typology is more than a method of interpreting Scripture which relates persons and events as type and anti-type, shadows and fulfillments of each other. It represents, in a broader sense, a world view, a way of looking at persons and events in the light of a theology of history which postulates the presence and the relevance of an eternal God at every individual moment of time."

The linear connection between type and antitype here, however, was between the hardships visited on the Israelites and their exemplary value as warnings for the New English Israel. Edwards continued:

> The Apostle says all these things happened unto them for types for our warning, which can be understood no other way than that the judgments that happened to them were shadows and resemblances of those judgments that we expose ourselves to by the like wickedness.[6]

As an example, he supplied the flood waters which destroyed the world, much as the world would be destroyed by God if men's souls were not transformed.

In another sermon, preached in New York in 1722 or 1723, Edwards turned to one of the central typology texts in the Bible, the book of Hebrews. Preaching on Heb. 9:12, he attempted to explain the role of the "blood of goats and calves" in the obtaining of eternal redemption. Again, a typological explanation was provided.

> The Jews, that one nation in the world, had more light. All the manner and different kinds of their sacrifices was instituted by God. They were so ordered as plainly figured forth to them the Messiah. They were also much enlightened by the plain prophecies which they had of Christ.

Characteristically, the Old Testament institutions were abrogated for Edwards in the New Testament and the incarnation.

> The end of these things was clearly known when the church needed no longer to be under tutors and governors but had come to adult years and fit for the more perfect dispensation. Then came the Great Sacrifice himself into the world, the end and antitype of all these things, who was the true sacrifice, the Lamb slain from the foundation of the world; that is, he was the antitype of all these sacrifices that had been slain according to God's institution from the beginning of the world ...
>
> And now, since he is come, that was the person that had been all along prefigured by those types and had entered in once, which was enough, into the holy place with his own blood. He did the business. He finished all there was to do of that kind, and left

6. Sermon on I Cor. 10:8–11, L. 2v.

nothing for men from that time to the end of the world, but only to trust in his sacrifice without offering any more of their own.[7]

The conservative position of this sermon's argument was corroborated by "Types of the Messiah," which stressed the orthodox and traditional emphasis on the historical and prefigurative value of the type in its relation to the antitype, Christ. Thematically, this association is crucial, because both the "Types" notebook and "Types of the Messiah" provide clear statements of belief about typology that may be used to interpret other texts in the Edwards canon. Together they illustrate the wide range of Edwards' thinking about typology and prophetic language. What Edwards says in the "Types" notebook and "Types of the Messiah" generally follows a traditional theory of typological prefiguration and antitypical fulfillment in the incarnation. Through a careful reading of these texts, however, particularly the more elusive passages of "Types of the Messiah" where Edwards attempted to break out of the traditional pattern, and through a cross-referencing to the more expanded typology of "Images of Divine Things," a balance is achieved between these traditional statements Edwards advanced concerning scriptural typology and the new understanding he developed of figural revelation in the natural world.

The synthesis that resulted was not static and fixed in a historical frame of reference; rather, it was organic and vital, and, like the arguments of the American Transcendentalists who would follow Edwards one hundred years later, it rendered the believer a participant in the dynamic and evolutionary process of history. For it is clear that Edwards' "new sense of things," by which the elect saint would comprehend spiritual revelation in nature, provided historians, writers, and theologians in America a new way of perceiving truth. These early sermons were recapitulated in the arguments of "Types of the Messiah" and the "Types" notebook. In both of these documents, Edwards was not allegorizing the types into static metaphors or emblems but revitalizing them by using typology as a renewed prophetic language for God's promises revealed in nature and history. These prophetic promises were revealed to the saints—not to the unregenerate—in a metaphorical language used by God's chosen people when they spoke of the kingdom of God and its realization in the last days. It was employed by the early Puritans to describe the discourse the saints will

7. *Christ's Sacrifice*, in *Sermons and Discourses, 1720–1723*, in *The Works of Jonathan Edwards*, *10*, ed. Wilson H. Kimnach (New Haven, Yale Univ. Press, 1992), p. 595.

use when the kingdom was established, so an understanding of the imperfect revelations made available through "types and figures" in Scripture was essential for the saint's comprehension of God's activity in human history.

Rules for distinguishing the instituted biblical figures—which were prophetic of Christ and his kingdom—from the Platonic, more allegorical mode were written for each succeeding generation of Puritans in England and New England. Although typology permeated earlier theological treatises by continental reformers, English Protestant and Puritan works devoted solely to the identification of typological parallels first appeared in 1620 in William Guild's *Moses Unvailed: or, those Figures which Served unto the Pattern and shadow of heavenly things*. Following Guild's example, theologians published typological guides throughout the seventeenth century, including Thomas Taylor's *Moses and Aaron, or the Types and Shadows ... Opened and Explained* (1635), Benjamin Keach's *Tropologia: A Key to Open Scripture Metaphors and Types* (1681), and the work on which Edwards depended most heavily in the composition of "Types of the Messiah," Samuel Mather's *The Figures or Types of the Old Testament*.

Edwards developed an argument about typology throughout his sermon literature and in the "Miscellanies," particularly no. 1069. Dating the entry has been made possible by the efforts of Thomas Schafer, who compared handwriting and inks in Edwards manuscripts as well as used ultra-violet light and a microscope to collate one text with another whose date is known. These methods indicate that "Types of the Messiah" was composed sometime during the mid-to-late 1740s, probably during that dark period following the "Bad Book" episode of 1744 in Northampton, through 1749, when Edwards' relationship with the congregation erupted into a full-scale controversy that resulted, ultimately, in his dismissal. The major part of the "Types" notebook was written at the same time, and it bears close resemblance to "Types of the Messiah" thematically and stylistically. The mid-1740s were an especially critical time in the development of Edwards' theology, particularly his *theory* of the types. "Types of the Messiah" represents the culmination of this development, which includes the "Types" notebook, many sermon manuscripts, the *Redemption* discourse, "Images of Divine Things," and numerous "Miscellanies."

The scholarly debate concerning Edwards' *use of types* and his *meaning in explaining types* is often confused by his sometimes interchangeable employment of "type," "image," "shadow" (as in Perry Miller's title, *Images or Shadows of Divine Things*), "correlation," "symbol," and "representation," the last of which is the most frequently used term in these documents. While this seemingly random employment of widely diverse terms is unclear to us in an age of "signs" and "signifiers," Edwards was never really confused or unclear on the subject. He was consistent in his effort to distinguish between mere "symbolic reflections," which were Platonic in character, and the ontological types, which participated in a scheme of adumbration and fulfillment. Modern readers' possible confusion about these terms arises from their own perception of the terms themselves, and not from what Edwards has said about them. Hopefully, the Edwards texts in this volume will clarify some of the theoretical language he employed to discuss the relationship between the natural world and the spiritual world. Symbols, which could be only reflections or Platonic analogies for Edwards, without any anticipatory value or ontological purpose, were always to be distinguished from "types," whether natural or personal, which were ontological and eschatological. Edwards consistently avoided the "allegorizing" of nature by illuminating those types *in* nature that were ontological and corresponded with Scripture revelation.

The scholarly debate is also concerned with the question of Edwards' changing conception of typology through his career.[8] The tension between strict conservative interpretation and a more loosely organized reading of Scripture types together with natural types would suggest a developmental model, that is, that Edwards early

8. Neither the developmental model, nor the seeming "conflict" model of JE's typological interpretation, rest easily with modern scholars of his writings. Those interested in the context of this contemporary debate should consult *Works*, 2, 5 (*Apocalyptic Writings*, in *The Works of Jonathan Edwards*, ed. Stephen J. Stein [New Haven, Yale Univ. Press, 1977]), and 6; Sacvan Bercovitch, *The Puritan Origins of the American Self* (New Haven, Yale Univ. Press, 1975); James Carse, *Jonathan Edwards and the Visibility of God* (New York, Scribner's, 1967); Delattre, *Beauty and Sensibility in the Thought of Jonathan Edwards*; R. C. De Propso, "The 'New Simple Idea' of Edwards' Personal Narrative," *Early American Literature*, 14 (Fall, 1979), 193– 204, and *Theism in the Discourse of Jonathan Edwards* (Newark, Univ. of Delaware Press, 1985); Leon Howard, ed., *"The Mind" of Jonathan Edwards: A Reconstructed Text* (Berkeley, Univ. of California Press, 1963); Norman Fiering, *Jonathan Edwardss' Moral Thought and Its British Context*; Sang H. Lee, "Mental Activity and the Perception of Beauty in Jonathan Edwards," *Harvard Theological Review*, 69 (1976), 364–96, and *The Philosophical Theology of Jonathan Edwards*; Barbara Lewalski, *Protestant Poetics and the Seventeenth-Century Religious Lyric*; Lowance, *The Language of Canaan*, esp. chs. 8, 10–11, and "Jonathan Edwards and the Platonists: Edwardsean Epistemology and the Influence of Malebranche and Norris," *Studies in Puritan American Spirituality*, 2 (Jan. 1992), 1–25.

argued a more conservative thesis of Scriptural typology that he abandoned for a persuasion focused on nature and its typological value. The developmental model is convenient and provides an easy map to Edwards' career; but it is misleading because some of Edwards' most liberal interpretations of typological value appear in entries from "Images of Divine Things" that predate by a full decade the writing of "Types of the Messiah," where some of his most conservative interpretations appear. Therefore, Edwards was clearly quite comfortable mixing the interpretative modes, without bias, and he was exceedingly careful not to cross over the Platonic line to suggest the disappearance of ontology in his reading of the natural types as they corresponded to Scripture revelation.

The "Types of the Messiah" manuscript shows clearly the importance of history for the New England Puritans, who believed the narrative of their experience to be a related series of divinely inspired events, so that the guiding hand of providence might be perceived in the drama of human experience. The record of these historical events—the Bible and subsequent Judeo-Christian history—and the language employed in biblical composition became for Edwards and the Puritans a rich source for describing their own contemporary history. The expression of historical developments in the language of the Bible became a means of associating the experience of New England with the literal, historical movements in the past record of ancient Israel, understood by Edwards to be a prefiguration of his own time, because all human history was ultimately contained between the creation in Genesis and the judgment in Revelation. The prophetic language both employed and explained in "Types of the Messiah" was essentially the language of biblical revelation and eschatology, to which the events of all human history might be related through proper exegesis of scriptural metaphor and symbol.

For example, Edwards' ultimate aim in his heretofore unpublished "Types" notebook was "to show there is a medium between those that cry down all types, and those that are for turning all into nothing but allegory and not having it be true history ..."[9] His reasoning about the distinctions between typology and allegory was always clear, and here he restored to typology its original historical and prophetic meaning while applying earlier dispensations to contemporary and future ones. He gave a cautious warning in his "Types" notebook that:

9. "Types Notebook," p. 151.

persons ought to be exceeding careful in interpreting of types, that they don't give way to a wild fancy; not to fix an interpretation unless warranted by some hint in the New Testament of its being the true interpretation, or a lively figure and representation contained or warranted by an analogy to other types that we interpret on sure grounds.[1]

However, he always regarded typology to be "a certain sort of language, as it were, in which God is wont to speak to us."[2] In "Types of the Messiah," we find similar declarations, which reflect Edwards' growing concern to understand biblical typology:

We find by the Old Testament that it has ever been God's manner from the beginning of the world to exhibit and reveal future things by symbolical representations, which were no other than types of the future things revealed. Thus when future things were made known in visions, the things that were seen were not the future things themselves, but some other things that were made use of as shadows, symbols or types of the things.[3]

Allegorical representation, a very distinct mode of discourse from typological adumbration and fulfillment, was clearly separated out both in "Types of the Messiah" and in the "Types" notebook. The types of history were for Edwards specifically focused on Christ's incarnation, as the following passage makes clear:

Now since it was, as has been observed, God's manner of old in the times of the Old Testament, from generation to generation, and even from the beginning of the world to the end of the Old Testament history, to represent divine things by outward signs, types and symbolical representations, and especially thus to typify and prefigure future events that he revealed by his Spirit and foretold by the prophets, it is very unlikely that the Messiah and things appertaining to his kingdom and salvation should not be thus abundantly prefigured and typified under the Old Testament ...[4]

If the types were a language in which God speaks to humankind, thus revealing, prophetically, his divine will in human history, there was for

1. Ibid., p. 148.
2. Ibid., p. 150.
3. "Types of the Messiah," p. 192.
4. Ibid., p. 202.

Edwards a danger when human invention and ingenuity played too prominent an interpretative role. He cautioned:

> First, to lay down that persons ought to be exceeding careful in interpreting of types, that they don't give way to a wild fancy; not to fix an interpretation unless warranted by some hint in the New Testament of its being the true interpretation, or a lively figure and representation contained or warranted by an analogy to other types that we interpret on sure grounds.

But in practice, Edwards tolerated ambiguity in the interpretation of the types, which was clearly in tension with his conservative exegetical theory:

> And there is, as it were, a certain idiom in that language which is to be learnt the same that the idiom of any language is, viz. by good acquaintance with the language, either by being naturally trained up in it, learning it by education (but that is not the way in which corrupt mankind learned divine language), or by much use and acquaintance together with a good taste or judgment, by comparing one thing with another and having our senses as it were exercised to discern it (which is the way that adult persons must come to speak any language, and in its true idiom, that is not their native tongue).

Edwards' warnings concerning excessive human inventiveness did not contradict his attempts to extend typological reasoning to natural revelation; however, they seemed to coexist with passages allowing greater creative range, such as the preceding paragraph. Still, he continued:

> Great care should be used, and we should endeavor to be well and thoroughly acquainted, or we shall never understand or have a right notion of the idiom of the language. If we go to interpret divine types without this, we shall be just like one that pretends to speak any language that han't thoroughly learnt it. We shall use many barbarous expressions....[5]

In the *Redemption* discourse, Edwards was particularly careful to maintain this crucial distinction, and he amplified its importance throughout his writings on the subject of typology. Several clear declarations of

5. "Types Notebook," pp. 148, 150–51.

typological doctrine illuminate Edwards' theory of God's revelation in cycles of historical dispensation. Edwards' writings are richly endowed with conclusions about the coming millennium, and they also abound in typological proof of its imminent fulfillment that show how the biblical figures were revitalized to strengthen the care for the coming kingdom.

This kind of millennial emphasis is exceedingly strong throughout Edwards' writing. For example, in *Some Thoughts Concerning the Present Revival of Religion in New England* (1742), we find:

> 'Tis not unlikely that this work of God's Spirit ... is the dawning, or at least a prelude, of that glorious work of God, so often foretold in Scripture.... And there are many things that make it probable that this work will begin in America....
>
> And if we may suppose that this glorious work of God shall begin in any part of America, I think, if we consider the circumstances of the settlement of New England, it must needs appear the most likely of all American colonies....[6]

And in the same year that he had preached the *Redemption* discourse, 1739, he stated in his "Personal Narrative" that the relation he perceived between the present and the future could be determined by analyzing prophetic images in Scripture:

> My heart has been much on the advancement of Christ's kingdom in the world. The histories of the past advancement of Christ's kingdom have been sweet to me. When I have read the histories of past ages, the pleasantest thing in all my reading has been, to read of the kingdom of Christ being promoted. And when I have expected, in my reading, to come to any such thing, I have rejoiced in the prospect, all the way as I read. And my mind has been much entertained and delighted with the scripture promises and prophecies, which related to the future glorious advancement of Christ's kingdom upon earth.[7]

It should not be surprising, then, that Jonathan Edwards would develop a theology based on typological patterns, that he should apply

---

6. JE, *Some Thoughts Concerning the Present Revival of Religion in New England*, in *Works, 4*, 353, 358.

7. JE, "Personal Narrative," in *Jonathan Edwards: Representative Selections, With Introduction, Bibliography, and Notes*, ed. Clarence H. Faust and Thomas H. Johnson (New York, American Book Company, 1935), p. 62.

the "types" and "antitypes" to the natural world. The close relationship he understood to exist between Scripture, history, and nature is clearly seen in the well-known letter he wrote to the trustees of the College of New Jersey (later Princeton University) when they offered him the presidency:

> I have had on my mind and heart (which I long ago began, not with any view to publication,) a great work, which I call a *History of the Work of Redemption*, a body of divinity in an entire new method, being thrown into the form of a history ... wherein every divine doctrine will appear to the greatest advantage, in the brightest light, in the most striking manner, showing the admirable contexture and harmony of the whole.
>
> I have also, for my profit and entertainment, done much towards another great work, which I call the *Harmony of the Old and New Testaments*, in three parts. The first, considering the Prophecies of the Messiah, his redemption and kingdom ... showing the universal, precise, and admirable correspondence between predictions and events. The second part, considering the Types of the Old Testament, showing the evidence of their being intended as representations of the great things of the gospel of Christ; and the agreement of type and antitype. The third and great part, considering the Harmony of the Old and New Testament, as to doctrine and precept.[8]

Throughout his career, Edwards was concerned about situating the types historically, and these efforts were guided by his pervasive interest in showing how God used the typological system to reveal himself to his saints in nature as well as Scripture.

---

8. "To the Trustees of the College of New Jersey," in *ibid.*, pp. 411, 412. JE's "Harmony of the Gospels" (Beinecke Library) was never completed. Of his ambitious attempt to write such a harmony of Scripture, Jesper Rosenmeier remarks that "had Edwards lived to complete the Harmony, he would have made the most exhaustive compendium of biblical metaphors yet undertaken in America. His purpose, however, went far beyond working out the precise meanings and correspondences between Old Testament prefigurations and their New Testament fulfillments. Rather, Edwards was interested in the harmony and beauty of their relationships, for he was convinced that it would continue to grow in the future, and that whoever understood the present divine communications might gain a view of the harmony that would be manifest in the New Jerusalem. So dynamic did Edwards consider the process of redemption to be that he perceived not only the Bible but Nature as a prophetic part of the gyre of salvation." Jesper Rosenmeier, "Introduction to Jonathan Edwards," unpub. ms., 1971. See also Stephen J. Stein, "Providence and Apocalypse in the Early Writings of Jonathan Edwards," *Early American Literature*, 12 (1978/79), 250–67.

Edwards' assumption of the Princeton presidency and his death soon thereafter prevented his completing this ambitious work. But he did leave us the *Redemption* discourse and some manuscript fragments of the "Harmonies" in addition to the manuscripts called "Prophecies of the Messiah" and "Fulfillment of the Prophecies of the Messiah," all of which corroborate with detail those exegetical principles advanced in "Types of the Messiah" and the posthumously published *History of the Work of Redemption*. The vision of the last days provided by the *History* is yet more important, since this may be explicated by those assertions in the typology and prophecy manuscripts. Although his son, Jonathan Edwards Jr., and his friend, John Erskine, had a substantial hand in reshaping some of the sermons to complete the book, which was finally published in 1774, the views are those of Edwards since they may be checked by opinions he offered elsewhere on the same subject.

*Problems of Interpretation in "Types of the Messiah"*

The "Types of the Messiah" contains evidence of Edwards' determination to clarify his own doctrine. The original methodology by which Edwards came to understand the book of nature is represented in "Types of the Messiah," but this becomes evident only at the end of the text. Types, Edwards argued in this passage, were like Platonic emblems which could be used as a symbolic language to accommodate the doctrine of God to human understanding. The

> principles of human nature render types a fit method of instruction: it tends to enlighten and illustrate, and to convey instruction with impression, conviction and pleasure, and to help the memory. These things are confirmed by man's natural delight in the imitative arts, in painting, poetry, fables, metaphorical language and dramatic performances. This disposition appears early in children.[9]

This passage seems to disagree with some later prominent statements in "Types of the Messiah," suggesting an expansion of typological parallels beyond prefiguration by the type and fulfillment by the antitype. This is not, however, the inconsistency it appears to be. Edwards was attempting throughout his writing to reconcile the more tradi-

9. "Types of the Messiah," p. 191.

tional methods of scriptural exegesis with his expanded understanding of revelation in the book of nature, and in "Types of the Messiah" there are several places where ambiguity concerning a "fit method of instruction" is expressed. It is important to realize that for Edwards this fusion of horizons was not personal uncertainty nor intellectual confusion; rather, he sought a reconciliation between Scripture and nature as sources of revelation and the connecting link was his understanding of typology. For example, while the body of the doctrinal treatise follows closely an orthodox and conservative schema that Edwards derived from Samuel Mather's *Figures or Types of the Old Testament*, the arguments of the last sections suggest an expanded and broadened typology which would permit allegorizing of the world of nature in a Platonic fashion.

The types were no longer confined to the linear and historical scheme of typological and antitypical fulfillment; rather, the spirit of God was to be found through the process of analogy and correspondence throughout the created universe. Nowhere is this more clearly articulated than in a brief passage found at the conclusion of the "Types of the Messiah" manuscript, which carries instructions written in Edwards' hand that it should be moved to the beginning of the document, indicating that the author intended for the entire work to be read in light of the broadened typological use. "What follows is to be inserted near the beginning of the discourse on the types," Edwards requests. Its essential argument, briefly summarized as follows, gives the reader a much wider range for imaginative application while interpreting the Old Testament types than some of the early sections of the treatise would suggest.

> This may be observed concerning types in general, that not only the things of the Old Testament are typical; for this is but one part of the typical world. The system of created beings may be divided into two parts, the typical world and the antitypical world. The inferior and carnal, i. e. the more external and transitory part of the universe, that part of it which is inchoative, imperfect and subservient, is typical of the superior, more spiritual, perfect and durable part of it, which is the other end and as it were the substance and consummation of the other. Thus the material and natural world is typical of the moral, spiritual and intelligent world, or the City of God.[1]

1. Ibid.

Edwards has left no indication that would date this entry specifically;
but it begins at the conclusion of the "Types of the Messiah" manuscript, in mid-page, so that it is clear he wished to have his readers
understand the broader theory he so clearly articulated elsewhere, in
*A Treatise Concerning Religious Affections* (1746), "Images of Divine
Things," and the "Miscellanies." In this brief introductory statement,
Edwards even provided examples from literature outside the Bible
and from history and nature to corroborate his view that the types
were ultimately an image system through which the divine author
would accommodate meaning to the understanding of humankind.

> And many things in the world of mankind, as to their external
> and worldly parts, are typical of things pertaining to the City and
> kingdom of God, as many things in the state of the ancient Greeks
> and Romans, etc. And those things belonging to the City of God,
> which belong to its more imperfect, carnal, inchoative, transient
> and preparatory state, are typical of those things which belong to
> its more spiritual, perfect and durable state, as things belonging to
> the state of the church under the Old Testament were typical of
> things belonging to the church and kingdom of God under the
> New Testament. The external works of Christ were typical of his
> spiritual works.[2]

By suggesting that "things in the world of mankind" may be divinely
instituted to represent spiritual things, independent of a schema of
prefiguration and fulfillment (though there is always in Edwards' writing an eschatological emphasis present even in this passage), he argued for a broadened typology which gave new meaning to his overuse
of the word "representation." The introductory statement concludes:

> the history of the Old Testament in general is intended to be typical
> of spiritual things. The Apostle's manner of speaking seems to
> imply that it might well be expected of God that his people should
> understand such like things as representations of divine things,
> and receive the particular instruction exhibited in them, even be-
> fore they are particularly explained to 'em by God by a new revela-
> tion.[3]

When placed in this prefatory position, the "afterword" changes the

2. Ibid., pp. 191–92.
3. Ibid., p. 192.

reader's perspective on the main body of the "Types of the Messiah" argument. Essentially conservative and traditional in its recapitulation of earlier Puritan handbooks on the types such as Mather's *Figures or Types of the Old Testament*, "Miscellanies" no. 1069 commences with a statement that is misleading. One would assume that Edwards will proceed to an exegesis of the types according to the historical scheme of adumbration and fulfillment. Thus he stated that God revealed "future things" by "symbolical representations," for example, in visions, but "the things that were seen were not the future things themselves, but some other things that were made use of as shadows, symbols or types of the things."[4] In the early sections of the treatise, the emphasis on biblical types as prefigurative symbols is particularly strong, and numerous examples abound. Yet even here, Edwards interspersed his orthodox exegesis with more extravagant and allegorical representations which reflected his concern for transformed typology and new epistemology. He supplied numerous examples to reinforce his theoretical observations, including one of the most commonly found tropes in all of the typological handbooks: "God's bringing his people into Canaan, to a state of rest and happiness there, is spoken of as a resemblance of what God would do for his people through the Messiah,"[5] or the long exegesis of Old Testament types relating to Moses and the extremely full treatment of types and figures developed around Joseph as a type of Christ.

> The remarkable similitude there is between very many things in the history of Joseph and the Old Testament prophecies of the Messiah, argue the former to be a type of the latter. Joseph is said to be the son of Jacob's old age (Gen. 37:3). So the Messiah is everywhere represented in the prophecies as coming and setting up his kingdom in the latter days. He was Jacob's beloved son (Gen. 37:3). So the prophecies do represent the Messiah as the beloved Son of God. They represent him as the Son of God.[6]

This kind of parallelling of Joseph's life with messianic experience was a conventional borrowing from the traditional patterns of exegetical prefiguration and fulfillment. However, the exhaustive detail with which Edwards explored the Joseph story, and the numerous correspondences he developed between Old and New Testament represen-

4. Ibid., p. 192.
5. Ibid., p. 214.
6. Ibid., p. 228.

tations, included so much information that the reader is almost over-whelmed with evidence. Joseph, Moses, and Joshua are all examined thoroughly as typological representations of the messianic promise, and throughout these long sections, Edwards conflated the term "prophecies" with "typological representation," suggesting that his understanding of their value was linear, historical, and prefigurative. Nevertheless, even here Edwards allowed a certain latitude in drawing parallels, as when he suggested that "God's making Eve of Adam's rib was to typify the near relation and strict union of husband and wife, and the respect that is due in persons of that relation from one to another, as is manifest from the account given of it. Gen. 2:21–24 ..."[7] The typological value of Adam's rib was also given in the Puritan handbooks; however, Edwards briefly explored the notion that it may also have a more universal symbolic purpose. Similarly, when discussing Jonah's gourd, Edwards expanded the boundaries of "typological representation" beyond prefiguration and fulfillment.

> So also God miraculously caused a gourd to come up in the night over the head of Jonah, and to perish in a night, to typify the life of man. That gourd was a feeble, tender, dependent, frail vine. It came up suddenly and was very green and flourishing, and was pleasant and refreshing, and it made a fine show for one day, and then withered and dried up (Jonah 4:6–8; see note on that place).
>
> So God reproved Jonah for his so little regarding the lives of the inhabitants of Nineveh, by the type of the gourd, which was mani-festly intended as a type of the life of man, or of man with respect to this life, being exactly agreeable to the representations frequently made of man and his present frail life in other parts of the Old Testament.... It came up in a night and perished in a night, ap-peared flourishing in the morning and the next evening was smit-ten, exactly agreeable to the representation of man's life in Ps. 90:6, "In the morning it flourisheth, and groweth up; in the evening it is cut down, and withereth." The worm that smote the gourd repre-sents the cause of man's death. The gourd was killed by a worm, a little thing, as man is elsewhere said to be crushed before the moth....That this gourd was intended by God as an emblem of man's life is evident from what God himself says of it and the

7. Ibid., pp. 196–97.

application he makes of it: for God himself compares the lives of the inhabitants of Nineveh with this gourd (Jonah 4: 10–11).[8]

Here, Edwards interchanged "emblem," "type," and "representation," suggesting the use of a natural typology that was more fully explained in the brief afterword-cum-foreword to "Types of the Messiah" and in his other published works, notably *Religious Affections*. Throughout "Miscellanies" no. 1069, Edwards juxtaposed theoretical statements reflecting traditional typological exegesis with explanations of typical representation that reflected a more contemporary methodology. Most of the examples, however, came from the "personal types" of the Old Testament, with emphasis on the figures of Joseph, Moses, Joshua, David, Solomon, and Jonah. As the narrative progresses, it becomes evident that Edwards was also concerned to indicate the close proximity between the "typological" revelation and "allegorical" representation.

'Tis an argument that many of the historical events of the Old Testament are types of the great events appertaining to the Messiah's coming and kingdom, that the Spirit of God took occasion from the former to speak of the latter. He either takes occasion to speak of and foretell the Messiah, and the great events appertaining to his salvation, upon occasion of the coming to pass of these ancient events; or on his speaking of these events, celebrating or promising them, he takes occasion to speak of these latter and greater events, joining what is declared of the one with what he reveals of the other in the same discourse, which is an argument that one has relation to the other and is the image of the other.[9]

Finally, the passage already cited from Edwards' brief prefatory statement, which he would have placed at the beginning of his treatise, cannot be overemphasized. We learn that:

The system of created beings may be divided into two parts, the typical world and the antitypical world. The inferior and carnal, i. e. the ... transitory part of the universe, that part of it which is ... imperfect and subservient, is typical of the superior, more spiritual, perfect and durable part of it ...[1]

8. Ibid., p. 199.
9. Ibid., p. 217.
1. Ibid., p. 191.

In a single statement, Edwards here indicated that while typology applied on the one hand to the historical scheme established between the two testaments, it also embraced the correspondences between the external representations and the spiritual ideas they shadowed forth. "Thus the material and natural world is typical of the moral, spiritual and intelligent world ..."[2] By indicating throughout the treatise how Christ's life itself radiated a typological significance, or how the Christian ordinances were symbolic of deeper spiritual principles, Edwards consistently applied the nomenclature of orthodox typology to the broadened typology and allegorical correspondence, however proximal, and thus opened the floodgates for interpretations of the universe in terms of "types" (the symbol or signifier) and "antitype" (the idea behind the symbol or the signified). Reading the book of nature was more than an ancient, Platonic system of correspondences between the real and the figurative worlds; rather, for Edwards and his contemporaries, it required a new methodology accommodated to readers through the language of prophecy and biblical typology. The typological systems so long used by exegetes to understand the prophetic and prefigurative value of the Old Testament, were now applied to comprehend revelation through the natural world. "Types of the Messiah" is a formidable statement of the analogies and parallels between these two methods, and modern readers will find it useful to compare passages in Edwards' sermons, in his "Types" notebook, "Notes on the Scriptures," and the "Blank Bible," where he argued that objects, events, persons, places, institutions, and the like were "representations" or images of certain divine and spiritual realities. The former, he always maintained, were not merely suitable illustrations, but were "types" of the latter; they were divinely ordained to signify and in some manner to reveal or "shadow forth" the nature of those invisible and spiritual things. In "Miscellanies" no. 638, Edwards stated that "there is an harmony between the methods of God's providence in [the] natural and religious world," a passage which corroborated the reconciliation of natural and scriptural revelation. Perry Miller observed that this reconciliation was "the central perception about which Edwards strove to organize God's creation; the Bible is only one among several manifestations of the typical system; the pattern of the cosmos is infinite representation, and thereby intelligible."[3] But as the "Types" notebook makes clear, for Edwards, typol-

2. Ibid., p. 191.

ogy should always be anchored in history: he sought "to show how there is a medium between those that cry down all types, and those that are for turning all into nothing but allegory and not having it be true history..."[4]

Edwards was certainly aware that his interpretation of typology was speculative, although the system was familiar to Puritan exegetes in England and New England. Therefore, he anchored his typology in history and broadened it with great care, avoiding the pitfalls of allegorizing against which he warned his readers consistently. Nevertheless, he defended the practice of discovering types in the natural world which were validated by their analogies with the types of Scripture. In his "Types" notebook, we find the following passage, which both defends his broadened typology and asserts his awareness of its speculative character:

> I am not ashamed to own that I believe that the whole universe, heaven and earth, air and seas, and the divine constitution and history of the holy Scriptures, be full of images of divine things, as full as a language is of words; and that the multitudes of those things that I have mentioned are but a very small part of what is really intended to be signified and typified by these things ...
>
> To say that we must not say that such things are types of these and those things unless the Scripture has expressly taught us that they are so, is as unreasonable as to say that we are not to interpret any prophecies of Scripture or apply them to these and those events ... For by the Scripture it is plain that innumerable other things are types that are not interpreted in Scripture (all the ordinances of the law are all shadows of good things to come), in like manner as it is plain by Scripture that these and those passages that are not actually interpreted are yet predictions of future events.[5]

Correlating this passage with examples from "Images of Divine Things," the "Miscellanies," and especially the logically ordered "Types of the Messiah," it is possible to discern in Edwards' thinking a changing but consistent doctrine of typology, a theological and philosophical argument which gave new meaning to the more restrictive exegetical use of the Word during the Reformation.

By associating his interpretation of history in the *History of the Work*

3. Miller, ed., *Images or Shadows*, p. 27.
4. "Types Notebook," p. 151.
5. Ibid., p. 152.

*of Redemption* with the doctrinal statements provided in the "Types of the Messiah," and by sensing his awareness of the objections that would be raised to his broadening of the scriptural patterns to include a typology of nature, it is possible to perceive the consistent logic of his transformation of the types, which were always anchored in historical and eschatological ontology. Ultimately, Edwards sought a reconciliation between a strictly conservative exegetical method and a broadening of the typological spectrum, a *via media* which would accommodate the ways of God to humanity without sacrificing the more conservative scriptural readings of the Protestant Reformation. The ingenuity and imagination he utilized opened exegetical practices to the power of revelation through the human senses, and the world of nature became a vast book now available to the elect saint through the "new sense of things." This breakthrough originated in a fundamental challenge to the authority of scriptural revelation; however, by carefully showing how the natural types were always rooted in the historical process, Edwards not only gave them the authority of history but foreshadowed the theology of Ralph Waldo Emerson and the Transcendentalists. By insisting that there is a medium between the rejection of all types and the turning of Scripture into nothing but allegory, Edwards posited a challenge to those Enlightenment thinkers who would deny spiritual revelation, and he also suggested specific ways in which spirit and nature may be associated through language.

Both the spiritualizers and the rigidly conservative typologists needed to modify their positions, Edwards' argument suggested. By examining the natural world for its allegorical and interpretative possibilities, Edwards had provided a powerful extension of the system originally restricted to the Old and New Testaments. For example, he noted that "Types are used in the New Testament as well as the Old, as is evident by the descent of the Holy Ghost in the shape of a dove, which is a type of the Holy Ghost ..."[6] Scriptural typologists had restricted their interpretations to signs that were historically and actually antecedent to their referents (signifiers that precede and adumbrate that which is signified) and to events and persons that were included in the Old Testament as prefigurative of the incarnation. The allegorical meaning, by contrast, could be found in any natural object or historical event that could be shown to have tropological significance. For Edwards, neither of these extremes was acceptable. While all of his

6. Ibid., p. 151.

natural images were eschatological and prophetic of Christ, Edwards demonstrated how the events of the historical process and the language with which these events were recorded and expressed could contain spiritual significance beyond any literal meaning inherent in the text, event, or natural object. The spiritual meanings of these signs were not wholly restricted to the New Testament record of Christ, but could be supplied from any part of the post-biblical history of the work of redemption. *The ultimate antitype, after all, was Christ, who was not to be restricted to temporal boundaries, but is eternal and atemporal.* It was this bold assertion, coupled with Edwards' awareness that God was actually speaking to his saints through the representative, symbolic, *typological* language of nature, that gave Jonathan Edwards' writings on typology a transforming authority over the rigid practices that had characterized the composition of typological handbooks during the sixteenth and seventeenth centuries. The "Types" notebook, the "Miscellanies," "Images of Divine Things," and "Types of the Messiah" provide modern readers with Edwards' most consistent doctrine of typology, and they show how he transformed the exegetical system to give new meaning and a renewed prophetic power to those figures from the Bible which are recapitulated in the natural world throughout history. The restrictive, conservative patterns outlined in the early pages of "Types of the Messiah" were broadened and modified by the preface Edwards composed after he had completed the document and indicated placement at the beginning of the treatise. The "Types" notebook corroborates this alteration, as do many of the "Miscellanies" and the numerous practical applications of the new system found in "Images of Divine Things."

Christ and his kingdom were central to all of Edwards' typology, but the representations of Christ were varied, ranging from Scripture, to recorded history, to the language of historical narrative, and to sense perceptions available in nature. The "new sense of things" available to the saint would enable fallen humanity to interpret this complex and fascinating puzzle. For Edwards, neither Enlightenment empiricism nor religious allegorizing were sufficient interpretative systems; what God intended and what humankind required was a synthetic process of reading Scripture, history, and nature as one revealed expression of will, and typology provided the key to understanding that process of divine accommodation.

The lengthy folio manuscript of "Types of the Messiah" provides a full discussion of the orthodox system of typological exegesis, with complete and often complex examples from Scripture. Through the subtlety of statement so characteristic of Edwards' mature writing, the modern reader is able to discern both the orthodox and the specifically figurative use of typology reflected in Edwards' works, the tension that extended orthodox principles to a more expansive application in "Images of Divine Things." Taken together, "Types of the Messiah," along with "Images of Divine Things" and the "Types" notebook, comprise Edwards' most significant work on the *theory* of typological exegesis, and should be distinguished from the application of that theory in such writings as *A History of the Work of Redemption*, those thirty sermons preached as a series in 1739 where theoretical meaning is present in a work whose purpose is not so centrally focused on typology.

# NOTE ON THE MANUSCRIPT OF "TYPES OF THE MESSIAH"

"TYPES of the Messiah" is no. 1069 of the "Miscellanies" in the Yale collection of the manuscripts of Jonathan Edwards at the Beinecke Rare Book and Manuscript Library. It is the first item in the seventh volume of the "Miscellanies," a folio measuring 31.5 cm. x 20 cm., with a slightly larger paper cover. The volume is a single infolded signature, and no. 1069 fills the first thirty-six and one-half leaves, numbering 1–73, with an unnumbered two-page table at the end. One leaf is missing, leaving a gap between pages 22 and 25. The remainder of the volume contains "Miscellanies" nos. 1070–1155, except for 1141, 1149–52, and parts of 1153 and 1154, consisting of thirty-three and one-quarter leaves. As noted above, the sermons on which this manuscript is based were preached during 1739 and 1740, and it appears from the hand and the ink that Edwards composed the body of the manuscript within a relatively brief period in the mid-to-late 1740s. At some point after 1747, probably late in the Stockbridge period, Edwards revised the manuscript and added several entries on pp. 71–73, and made note of his revisions in the Table. We arrive at this date from the hand and from his citation of volumes by Johann Friedrich Stapfer published in Tiguri, 1743–47, since it seems unlikely that Edwards saw the books before 1747.[1]

The document, which aptly demonstrates Edwards' exhaustive study of the Bible, can readily be divided into five distinct sections. The introductory section (pp. 191–208) seeks to demonstrate how God uses things in actual existence to signify the Messiah. A lengthy section on historical figures and events (pp. 208–94) and a shorter one (pp. 294–305) on the significance of names given to Old Testament figures and things follow. Next comes a discussion of the ceremonial law and sacrifices of atonement, which in part recapitulates previous

1. See below p. 192, n. 3.

points (pp. 305–22). Finally is the brief assemblage of entries made at a
later time, most likely after 1747 (pp. 322–24).

A version of the "Types of the Messiah" appeared in Sereno
Dwight's edition of *The Works of President Edwards*, which was subse-
quently reprinted in collected Edwards sets.[2] Jonathan Edwards, Jr.
had previously worked on the manuscript, adding punctuation and
capitalization, and making numerous emendations, perhaps in preparation for a copyist, and the presence of a copy might have accounted
for Dwight's undertaking to print it. The extent of Jonathan Edwards,
Jr.'s revisions, which will be treated in more detail below, necessitated
the undertaking of a completely new edition from the manuscript.
The editing of the "Types of the Messiah" conforms to the standards
set for the Yale *Works of Jonathan Edwards* by the style manual prepared
by Wilson H. Kimnach and Thomas A. Schafer. We call to the reader's
attention several of our procedures necessitated by the special features of this manuscript. It has been the policy of the editors throughout this text to produce a readable version as close to Edwards' own
text as possible. To this end, we have kept annotation and other textual
apparatus to a minimum. We have omitted the running heads on MS
pp. 2–71. Unbracketed ellipsis dots indicate Edwards' omissions,
marked by a dash in the manuscript, and ocurring most frequently in
quotes from Scripture. We have without comment completed scripture passages when Edwards concluded a quote with a dash or with
"etc.," signals that he meant to complete the verse quoted. The manuscript, for the most part, runs sequentially, but on several pages Edwards indicates by a series of marks that the reader is to transpose
material from another place in the text. Since no lacunae is caused by
these transpositions, the editors have made the changes that Edwards
specifies without annotation.

One instance deserves special comment. Edwards directs the movement of three paragraphs from the end of his text, written after the
period of the composition of its main body, to the beginning of the
discourse.[3] These paragraphs, printed on pp. 191–92, are of great
significance, since they reveal that, in Edwards' mind, the typology of
such a text as "Images of Divine Things" is fully consistent with that of
the more traditional biblical exegesis. This movement of materials is in

2. JE, "The Types of the Messiah," in Dwight ed., *9*, 9–111.
3. See below p. 191, n. 1.

accord with Edwards' instructions, and does not disrupt the continuity of his arguments.

During the composition and correction of the manuscript, Edwards made a multitude of deletions and insertions of text. Deletions are edited without comment when the deleted phrase is repeated verbatim or with slight alteration at another point in the text without affecting its meaning, or in cases of simple substitution or scribal error. Deletions and corrections which reveal habits of composition or changes in the thought or direction of the text are printed in the notes, and these deletions are styled to conform with the principles of the edition.

Editorial difficulties and textual complexities in the matter of deletions and additions arise from the presence of Jonathan Edwards, Jr.'s hand in the manuscript. At times, his hand is nearly indistinguishable from the late hand of Jonathan Edwards. The manuscript has been thoroughly examined under a microscope to determine the additions made by Jonathan, Jr., in particular the great number of punctutation marks provided by him. Edwards' own syntax and words have been restored, and our editorial emendations are noted or enclosed in square brackets. Nevertheless, we must rely on Jonathan Edwards, Jr. and Sereno Dwight for materials on the leaf containing MS pp. 23–24, removed from the manuscript after the printing of the Dwight edition in 1829–30 and before the arrival of the manuscript at Yale in 1901.[4] There is no break in continuity between the manuscript and the Dwight text at either end of the passage, so we have inserted Dwight's text and edited it to conform with this edition.

A final category of editorial work involves a substantial number of references made by Edwards to his other manuscript works. He refers frequently to two discourses, the "Prophecies of the Messiah" and the "Fulfillment of the Prophecies of the Messiah." These lengthy numbers of the "Miscellanies" are in a much less-finished state than the "Types of the Messiah," but they bear an organic relationship to it. Together they form components of "The Harmony of the Old and New Testaments," the work to which Edwards referred in his letter to the trustees of the College of New Jersey in response to their invitation to the presidency of that institution.[5] However, the finished state of

4. See below pp. 237–40, and p. 237, n. 1.
5. See above pp. 171–72.

this text sets it apart from the others. The relevant passages in the "Prophecies of the Messiah" and the "Fulfillment of the Prophecies of the Messiah" are cited in the notes, and we quote passages that contribute to an understanding of the "Types of the Messiah." These quotations are also edited to conform with this edition. The numbering system of these passages presents some difficulty, since Edwards and Jonathan Edwards, Jr. appear to have renumbered the sections. Thus a given section may have several different numbers, and two or more sections have the same number. We provide all the numbers of a quoted passage, and when it is unclear to which section Edwards refers, we have noted the conjectural nature of our citation.

*"TYPES OF THE MESSIAH"*

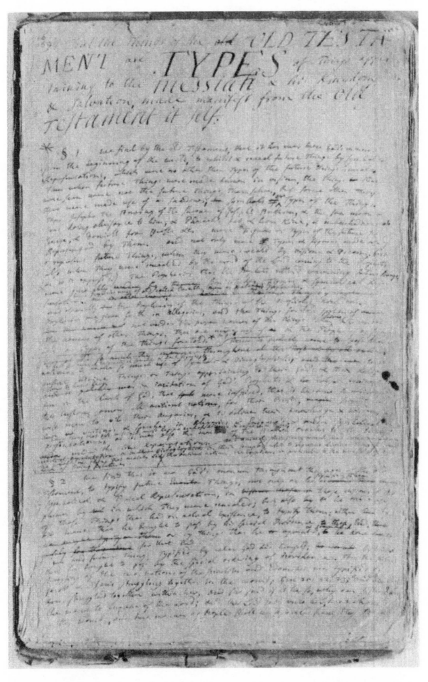

Manuscript page 1 of "Types of the Messiah," No. 1069 in Book 7 of the "Miscellanies." Beinecke Rare Book and Manuscript Library, Yale University.

# "TYPES OF THE MESSIAH"

**1069.** THAT THE THINGS OF THE OLD TESTAMENT ARE TYPES OF THINGS APPERTAINING TO THE MESSIAH AND HIS KINGDOM AND SALVATION, MADE MANIFEST FROM THE OLD TESTAMENT ITSELF.[1]

What principles of human nature render types a fit method of instruction: it tends to enlighten and illustrate, and to convey instruction with impression, conviction and pleasure, and to help the memory. These things are confirmed by man's natural delight in the imitative arts, in painting, poetry, fables, metaphorical language [and] dramatic performances. This disposition appears early in children.

This may be observed concerning types in general, that not only the things of the Old Testament are typical; for this is but one part of the typical world. The system of created beings may be divided into two parts, the typical world and the antitypical world. The inferior and carnal, i. e. the more external and transitory part of the universe, that part of it which is inchoative, imperfect and subservient, is typical of the superior, more spiritual, perfect and durable part of it, which is the end and as it were the substance and consummation of the other. Thus the material and natural world is typical of the moral, spiritual and intelligent world, or the City of God. And[2] many things in the world of mankind, as to their external and worldly parts, are typical of things pertaining to the City and kingdom of God, as many things in the state of the ancient Greeks and Romans, etc. And those things belonging to the City of God, which belong to its more imperfect, carnal, inchoative, transient and preparatory state, are typical of those things which belong to its more spiritual, perfect and durable state, as things be-

---

1. The following three paragraphs are moved from MS pp. 72–73 at JE's direction. Above the first paragraph he writes, "To show at the beginning." After this paragraph, he draws a horizontal line and writes, "Let what follows be inserted <near> in the beginning of the discourse on types." For a discussion of this transposition of text, see above, p. 184.

2. JE deletes: "even the spiritual world as to its [sic] to those things belonging to it which are more carnal and external and transitor[y], imperfect and inchoati[ve]."

longing to the state of the church under the Old Testament were typical of things belonging to the church and kingdom of God under the New Testament. The external works of Christ were typical of his spiritual works. The ordinances of the external worship of the Christian church are typical of things belonging to its heavenly state. (Here see "Miscellanies," bk. 9, pp. 82, [first column].)[3]

The manner of the Apostle's expressing himself in Gal. 4:21–22, will clearly prove that Abraham's two sons and their mothers, and Mt. Sinai and Mt. Zion, were intended to be types of those things he mentions; which is a great confirmation that the history of the Old Testament in general is intended to be typical of spiritual things. The Apostle's manner of speaking seems to imply that it might well be expected of God that his people should understand such like things as representations of divine things, and receive the particular instruction exhibited in them, even before they are particularly explained to 'em by God by a new revelation.

§1. We find by the Old Testament that it has ever been God's manner from the beginning of the world to exhibit and reveal future things by symbolical representations, which were no other than types of the future things revealed. Thus when future things were made known in visions, the things that were seen were not the future things themselves, but some other things that were made use of as shadows, symbols or types of the things. Thus the bowing of the sheaves of Joseph's brethren, and the sun, moon and stars doing obeisance to him, and Pharaoh's fat and lean kine, and Nebuchadnezzar's image, and Daniel's four beasts, etc. were figures or types of the future things represented by them. And not only were types and figures made use of to represent future things when they were revealed by visions and dreams, but also when they were revealed by the Word of the Lord coming to the prophets (as it is expressed).[4] The prophecies that the

3. Bk. 9 of the "Miscellanies," MS pp. 82–83, first column, contains the conclusion of no. 1307 and the majority of no. 1308, where JE copied passages from Stapfer, *Institutiones Theologiæ Polemicæ*, 2, 1087–88. The excerpt in no. 1307 argues that earthly, historical events are typical of the heavenly events of the church, and the one in no. 1308 maintains the self-evident nature of the prophecies of the Scripture.

When referring to the "Miscellanies," "Prophecies of the Messiah," and "Fulfillment of the Prophecies of the Messiah," JE usually provided not only an entry or section number but also specified book and pages. Because these book and page references will be rendered obsolete by subsequent publication of these works, JE's page numbers have been omitted, though the notes will indicate the MS page numbers to which he referred.

4. Possibly a reference to Acts 3:18, 21.

prophets uttered concerning future [things] were generally by similitudes, figures and symbolical representations; hence prophecies were of old called "parables," as Balaam's prophecies, and especially the prophecies of the things of the Messiah's kingdom. The prophecies are given forth in allegories, and the things foretold spoken of not under the proper names of the things them[selves], but under the names of other things that are made use of in the prophecy as symbols or types of the things foretold.

And it was the manner in those ancient times to deliver divine instructions in general in symbols and emblems, and in their speeches and discourses to make use of types and figures and enigmatical speeches, into which holy men were led by the Spirit of God. This manner of delivering wisdom was originally divine, as may be argued from that of Solomon, Prov. 1:6, "To understand a proverb" (or "parable"), "and the interpretation; the words of the wise, and their dark sayings." And from that of the psalmist, [Ps.] 49:3–4, "My mouth shall speak of wisdom; and the meditation of my heart shall be of understanding. I will incline mine ear to a parable: I will open my dark saying upon the harp." And Ps. 78:1–2, "Give ear, O my people, to my law: incline your ears to the words of my mouth. I will open my mouth in a parable: I will utter dark sayings of old" (by a parable is meant an enigmatical, symbolical speech, Ezek. 17:2 and 23:3). Hence speeches of divine wisdom in general came to be called "parables," as the speeches of Job and his friends. Hence of old the wise men of all nations, who derived their wisdom chiefly by tradition from the wise men of the church of God, who spake by inspiration, fell into that method. They received instruction that way, and they imitated it. Hence it became so much the custom in all the eastern[5] nations to deal so much in enigmatical speeches and dark figures, to make so much use of symbols and hieroglyphics to represent divine things or things appertaining to their gods and their religion. It seems to have been in imitation of God's prophets and holy and eminent persons in the church of God, that were inspired, that it became so universally the custom among all ancient nations for their priests, prophets and wise men to utter their auguries and to deliver their knowledge and wisdom, in their writings and speeches, in allegories and enigmas, and under symbolical representations. Everything that the wise said must be in a kind of allegory and veiled with types, as it was also the manner

5. MS: "East."

of the heathen oracles to utter themselves under the like representations.[6]

§2.[7] We find that it was God's manner throughout the ages of the Old Testament to typify future things, not only as he signified them by symbolical and typical representations in those visions and prophecies in which they were revealed, but also as he made use of those things that had an actual existence, to typify them either by events that he brought to pass by his special providence to that end, or by things that he appointed and commanded be done for that end.

We find future things typified by what God did himself, by things that he brought to pass by the special ordering of providence. Thus the future struggling of the two nations of the Israelites and Edomites was typified by Jacob's and Esau's struggling together in the womb. Gen. 25:22–23, "And the children struggled together within her; and

---

6. JE cancels: "And animals being very much made use [of] in these symbolical representations, and in their hieroglyphics in their temples used to represent divine things, it was probably one thing that mainly led the ancient nations, the Egyptians in particular, to the worship of all manner of living creatures."

A leaf tipped in at the end of the "Types" notebook (Trask Library) contains JE's notes for this section. The leaf, numbered "6," reads: "It was the manner in those ancient times to deliver divine instructions in symbols and emblems, in their speeches and discourses to make use of types and figures and enigmatical speeches into which holy men of old were led by the Spirit of God. Whence the wise of all nations, who derive their wisdom chiefly by tradition from those, fell into this method of teaching. They received instructions that way, and they imitated it. Hence it became so much the custom in all the east to deal so much in enigmatical speeches and symbols and dark figures; everything that the wise said must be in a kind of allegory and veiled with types. Hence the Egyptian hieroglyphics. Hence we may well suppose that God revealed divine truths in symbols and types in his institutions in his church. In those days he should represent divine things in types and symbols.

"This manner of delivering wisdom was originally divine, as may be argued from that of Solomon, to understand a proverb or parable, the words of the wise and their dark sayings. (See Ps. 49:4, Ps. 78:2, Num. 23:7–24, Ezek. 17:2.) Hence the speeches of the wise were all called "parables," as in Job, because symbolical and typical teaching were first from God by divine revelation. Hence they were looked upon by the ancient nations as sacred things, and therefore called "hieroglyphics," or "*engraven in sacreds*," or "engraven in the temple," as the word signifies.

"By a parable is meant in Scripture an enigmatical or symbolical speech, Ezek. 17:2 and 23:3.

"Show how irrefragably that prophecy, Jer. 33:17–26, proves that the Messiah is already come.

"The ancient Jewish rabbis judged that all things happened to their fathers as types and figures of the Messiah."

The entire excerpt, with the exception of the note on Jer. 33:17–26, is deleted with a vertical line, or "use" mark. JE used the final statement, regarding the Jewish rabbis, slightly later (see below, p. 208).

7. JE discontinues the use of sections with this number.

she said, If it be so, why am I thus? She went to inquire of the Lord. And the Lord said unto her, Two nations are in thy womb, and two manner of people shall be separated from thy bowels; and the one people shall be stronger than the other people; and the elder shall serve the younger." And the prevalence of Jacob over Esau, and his supplanting him so as to get away his birthright and blessing, and his posterity's prevailing over the Edomites, were typified by Jacob's hand taking hold on Esau's heel in the birth. Gen. 25:26, "And after that came his brother out, and his hand took hold on Esau's heel; and his name was called "Jacob," or "Supplanter"; ch. 27:36, "Is not he rightly named Jacob? for he hath supplanted me these two times: he took away my birthright; and, behold, now he hath taken away my blessing." Hos. 12:3, 6, "He took his brother by the heel in the womb... Therefore turn thou to thy God: keep mercy and judgment and wait on thy God continually." And as the Israelites' overcoming and supplanting their enemies, in their[8] struggling or wrestling with them, was typified by Jacob's taking hold on Esau's heel, his and his true and righteous posterity's prevailing with God, in their spiritual wrestlings with him, was typified by his wrestling with God and prevailing. Gen. 32:28, "Thy name shall no more be called Jacob, but Israel: for as a prince thou hast power with God and with men, and hast prevailed." Hos. 12:4–6, "Yea, he had power over the angel, and prevailed: he wept, and made supplication unto him: he found him in Bethel, and there he spake with us; Even the Lord God of hosts; the Lord is his memorial. Therefore turn thou to thy God: keep mercy and judgment and wait on thy God continually." The prevalence of the posterity of Pharez over Zarah, who first put forth his hand, was typified by his unexpectedly breaking forth out of the womb before him (Gen. 38:29).

So by Moses' being wonderfully preserved in the midst of great waters, though but a little helpless infant, and being drawn out of the water, seems apparently to be typified the preservation and deliverance of his people that he was made the head and deliverer of, who were preserved in the midst of dangers they were in in Egypt, which were ready to overwhelm them, when the prince and people sought to their utmost to destroy them and root them out, and they had no power to withstand them, but were like an helpless infant, and who were at last wonderfully delivered out of their great and overwhelming

8. MS: "his."

troubles and dangers, which in Scripture language is "delivering out of great waters," or "drawing out of many waters." II Sam. 22:17, "He sent from above, he took me; he drew me out of many waters." And Ps. 18:16. 'Tis the same sort of deliverance from cruel, bloodthirsty enemies that the psalmist speaks of, that the Israelites were delivered from. And so he does again, Ps. 144:7, "Send thine hand from above; rid me, and deliver me out of great waters, from the hand of strange children." And Ps. 69:2, "I sink in deep mire, where there is no standing: I am come into deep waters, where the floods overflow me"; with v. 14, "Deliver me out of the mire, and let me not sink: let me be delivered from them that hate me, and out of the deep waters."

That the king of Israel smote three times upon the ground with his arrows, was ordered in providence to be a type of his beating the Syrians three times (II Kgs. 13:18–19). The potter's working a work on the wheels, and the vessels being marred in the hand of the potter, so that he made it again another vessel as seemed good to him to make it, at the time when Jeremiah went down to the potter's house, was ordered in providence to be a type of God's dealings with the Jews (Jer. 18).

The twelve fountains of water and the threescore and ten palm trees that were in Elim (Ex. 15:27) were manifestly types of the twelve patriarchs, the fathers of the tribes, and the threescore and ten elders of the congregation. The paternity of a family, tribe or nation, in the language of the Old Testament, is called a "fountain." Deut. 33:28, "Israel shall dwell in safety alone: the fountain of Jacob shall be upon a land of corn and wine." Ps. 68:26, "Bless the Lord, from the fountain of Israel." Is. 48:1, "Hear ye this, O house of Jacob, which are called by the name of Israel, and are come forth out of the waters of Judah." And the church of God is often represented in Scripture by a palm tree or palm trees (Ps. 92:12, Cant. 7:7–8). And therefore fitly were the elders or representatives of the church compared to palm trees. God's people often [are] compared to trees (Is. 61:3 and 60:21 and elsewhere).[9]

We find that God was often pleased to bring to pass extraordinary and miraculous appearances and events to typify future things. Thus God's making Eve of Adam's rib was to typify the near relation and strict union of husband and wife, and the respect that is due in persons of that relation from one to the other, as is manifest from the account

9. JE cancels: "And the history or narrative of their being twelve fountains of water and threescore and ten palm trees in the history of Israel's travels is wholly impertinent."

given of it. Gen. 2:21–24, "And the Lord caused a deep sleep to fall upon Adam, and he [slept]:[1] and he took one of his ribs, and closed up the flesh instead thereof; And the rib, which the Lord God had taken from man, made he a woman, and brought her unto the man. And Adam said, This is now bone of my bones, and flesh of my flesh: she shall be called Woman, because she was taken out of Man. Therefore shall a man leave his father and his mother, and shall cleave unto his wife: and they shall be one flesh." And when God spoke to Moses from the burning bush concerning the great affliction and oppression of the children of Israel in Egypt, and promised to preserve and deliver them, what appeared in the bush, viz. its burning with fire and yet not being consumed, was evidently intended as a type of the same thing that God then spake to Moses about, viz. the church of Israel being in the fire of affliction in Egypt and appearing in the utmost danger of being utterly consumed there, and yet being marvelously preserved and delivered. Such a low and weak state as the people were in in Egypt, and such an inability for self-defense, we find is in the Old Testament represented by a bush or low tree, and a root out of a dry ground, as that bush in Horeb (which signifies "dry places"), Is. 53:2, Ezek. 17:22–24. Affliction and danger is in the language of the Old Testament called "fire." Zech. 13:9, "I will bring the third part through the fire."[2] Is. 48:10, "I have chosen thee in the furnace of affliction." And God's marvelously preserving his people, when in great affliction and danger, is represented by their being preserved in the fire from being burnt. Is. 43:2, "When thou passest through the fire, I will be with thee... when thou walkest through the fire, thou shalt not be burned; neither shall the flame kindle upon thee." And God's delivering that people Israel from [the] affliction and destruction they were in danger of through bondage and oppression under the hand of their enemies, is represented by their being delivered out of the fire. Zech. 3:2, "Is not this a brand plucked out of the fire?" Yea, that very thing of the deliverance of Israel out of Egypt is often represented as their being delivered from the fire. Ps. 66:12, "We went through fire and through water: but thou broughtest [us] into a wealthy place." Deut. 4:20, "The Lord hath taken you, and brought you out of the iron furnace, even out of Egypt." So I Kgs. 8:51 and Jer. 11:4.

So Moses' rod's swallowing up the magicians' rods (Ex. 7:12) is evi-

---

1. MS damage; the word is supplied from the scripture.
2. JE cancels: "Is. 43:2, 'When thou passest through the fire, I will be.'"

dently given of God as a sign and type of the superiority of God's power above the power of their gods, and that [his] power should prevail and swallow up theirs. For that rod was a token of God's power, as a prince's rod or scepter was a token of his power. Thus we read of the rods of the Messiah's strength (Ps. 110). So the turning of the water of the river of Egypt into blood, first by Moses' taking and pouring it out on the dry land and its becoming blood on the dry land, and afterwards by the river itself and all the other waters of Egypt being turned to blood in the first plague on Egypt, was evidently[3] a foreboding sign and type of what God threatened at the same time, viz. that if they would not let the people [go], God would slay their firstborn, and [of] his afterwards destroying Pharaoh and all the prime of Egypt in the Red Sea. (See Ex. 4:9 and ch. 7.) God's making a great destruction of the lives of a people is, in the language of the Old Testament, a giving them blood to drink. Is. 49:26, "And I will feed them that oppress thee with their own flesh; and they shall be drunken with their own blood." Aaron's rod's budding, blossoming and bearing fruit is given as a type of God's owning and blessing his ministry and crowning it with success. His rod was the rod of an almond tree (Num. 17:8), which God makes use [of] in Jer. 1:11–12 as a token and type of his Word, that speedily takes effect, as Moses' rod of an almond tree speedily brought forth its fruit.

God caused the corn in the land of Judah to spring again after it had been cut off with the sickle, and to bring forth another crop from the roots that seemed to be dead, and so once and again, to be a sign and type of the remnant that was escaped of the house of Judah again taking root downward and bearing fruit upward, and of his church's reviving again as it were out of its own ashes and flourishing like a plant, after it had been seemingly destroyed and past recovery, as II Kgs. 19:29–30 and Is. 37:30–31.

So God wrought the miracle of causing the shadow in the sundial of Ahaz to go backward, contrary to the course of nature, to be a sign and type of King Hezekiah's being, in a miraculous manner and contrary to the course of nature, healed of his sickness that was in itself mortal, and brought back from the grave whither he was descending, and the

---

3. MS: "evident." JE originally, and perhaps inadvertently, inserted cues to indicate that an ensuing paragraph that begins, "So God miraculously enabled David to kill the lion..." was to be inserted here. JE, Jr., sensing that the logic of JE's argument was thereby interrupted, deleted JE's instruction and placed his own cue so as to have the paragraph on Jonah come before that on David. JE, Jr.'s correction is followed here.

sun of the day of his life being made to return back again, when according to the course of nature it was just a-setting (II Kgs. 20).

So the miraculous uniting of the two sticks that had the names of Judah and Joseph written upon [them], so that they became one stick in the Prophet's hand [Ezek. 37:15–20], was to typify the future entire union of Judah and Israel.

So also God miraculously caused a gourd to come up in a night over the head of Jonah, and to perish in a night, to typify the life of man. That gourd was a feeble, tender, dependent, frail vine. It came up suddenly and was very green and flourishing, and was pleasant and refreshing, and it made a fine show for one day, and then withered and dried up (Jonah 4:6–8; see note on the place).[4]

So God reproved Jonah for his so little regarding the lives of the inhabitants of Nineveh, by the type of the gourd, which was manifestly intended as a type of the life of man, or of man with respect to this life, being exactly agreeable to the representations frequently made of man and his present frail life in other parts of the Old Testament. This gourd was a vine, a feeble, dependent plant that can't stand alone. This God therefore makes use of to represent man in Ezek. 15. This gourd was a very tender, frail plant; it sprang up suddenly and was very short-lived. Its life was but one day, as the life of man is often compared to a day. It was green and flourishing and made a fine show one day, and was withered and dried up the next. It came up in a night and perished in a night, appeared flourishing in the morning and the next evening was smitten, exactly agreeable to the representation made of man's life in Ps. 90:6, "In the morning it flourisheth, and groweth up; in the evening it is cut down, and withereth." The worm that smote the gourd represents [the cause of man's death].[5] The gourd was killed by a worm, a little thing, as man is elsewhere said to be crushed before the moth [Job 4:19]. It was that, the approach of which was not discerned; it came underground, as elsewhere man is represented as not knowing his time, but being "as the fishes that are taken in an evil net, and as the birds that are caught in the snare" [Eccles. 9:12], and smitten by an arrow that flies unseen [Job 6:4]. That this gourd was intended by God as an emblem of man's life is evident from what God himself says of it and the application he makes of it: for God himself compares the lives of the inhabitants of Nineveh with this gourd (Jonah 4:10–11). Jonah

4. "Blank Bible," note on Jonah 4:6–8, in part: "This gourd represents man, or the life of man. [...] The worm that smote the gourd represents death."

5. JE, Jr.'s insertion.

had pity on the gourd, i. e. on himself for the loss of it; for it was very pleasing and refreshing to him while it lasted, and defended him from scorching heat. So life is sweet. The Ninevites by its preservation were held back from that wrath of God that had been threatened for their sins. How much more therefore should Jonah have had pity on the numerous inhabitants of Nineveh when God had threatened them with the loss of life, which was an enjoyment so much more desirable than the gourd was to him? And if he found fault with God, that he did not spare to him the shadow of the gourd, how unreasonable was he in also finding fault with God, that he did spare to the Ninevites their sweet lives?

So God miraculously enabled David to kill the lion and the bear, and deliver the lamb out of their mouths, plainly and evidently to be a type, sign and encouragement unto him that he would enable him to destroy the enemies of his people, that were much stronger than they, and deliver his people from them. David did this as a shepherd over the flock of his father, and his acting the part of a shepherd towards them is expressly spoken of as a resemblance of his acting the part of a king and shepherd towards God's people from time to time (I Chron. 11:2, Ps. 78:70–72, Jer. 23:4–6, Ezek. 34:23–24, ch. 37:24). And God's people in places innumerable are called his flock and his sheep, and their enemies, in David's Psalms and elsewhere, are compared to the lion and other beasts of prey that devour the sheep; and David himself calls his own deliverance and the deliverance of God's people, a being saved from the lion's mouth (Ps. 7:1–2, and 17:12–13, and 22:20–21, and 35:17 and 57:3–4). And David himself thus understood and improved God's thus miraculously enabling him to conquer these wild beasts and deliver the lamb as a representation and sign of what God would enable him to do for his people against their strong enemies, as is evident from what he said to Saul when he offered to go against Goliath [I Sam. 17:37].

It was also a common thing for God to order and appoint things to be done by men in order to typify future events.[6] So Samuel poured out water in Mizpah (I Sam. 7:6) to signify their repentance; see concerning the accidental rending of Samuel's mantle, I Sam. 15:27–28.

6. The following sentence, as well as the parenthetical reference, is interlineated in a later, grayish ink. JE, Jr.'s transposition of the parts of the sentence has been followed. JE used "SSS" as a shorthand reference to Matthew Poole, *Synopsis Criticorum Aliorumque S. Scripturae Interpretum* (5 vols., London, 1669–76). Poole calls I Sam. 7:6, "Mirabilis & difficilis locus: quem explanatores non satis expediunt" (*1, pars posterior*, pp. 80–81).

(See SSS.) Thus Abijah's rending Jeroboam's garment in twelve pieces and giving him ten was to typify the rending the kingdom of Israel and giving him ten tribes (I Kgs. 11:30–31).[7] So see I Kgs. 20:35–43 and II Kgs. 13–20. The Prophet's assisting the king of Israel in shooting an arrow eastward towards Syria was appointed of God to signify that he would assist the king of Israel in fighting with the Syrians (II Kgs. 13:15–19).

The prophet Isaiah by God's appointment went naked and barefoot to typify the Egyptians and Ethiopians going naked and barefoot in their captivity (Is. 20). Jeremiah by God's appointment typified the captivity of the Jews into Babylon with many of its circumstances by taking a linen girdle and putting it on his loins, and hiding it in a hole in a rock by the river Euphrates, and returning again to take it from thence (Jer. 13). So he was commanded to typify the destruction of the people by breaking a potter's vessels (ch. 19). So by taking a wine cup and offering it to many nations, agreeable to God's appointment and direction, he typified God's causing them as it were to drink the cup of his fury (ch. 25). And he was commanded to make bonds and yokes and put them upon his neck, and send them to the neighboring [kings], to typify the yoke of bondage under Nebuchadnezzar that God was about to bring upon them (ch. 27). Nehemiah shook his lap (Neh. 5:13). So Ezekiel very often typified future events by things that he did by God's appointment, as by his eating the roll, etc. (Ezek. 3), and by lying on his side, and many other things that he was commanded to do, that we have an account [of] (Ezek. 4); and by shaving his head and beard and burning part of the hair in the fire, etc. (ch. 5), and by making a chain (ch. 7:23); and by his removing with the many circumstances that God directed him to (ch. 12:1–6); and by his eating his bread with trembling (v. 18); by setting a pot with the choice pieces of flesh onto the fire, etc.; and by his not mourning for his wife (ch. 24). So the prophet Hosea typified the things he prophesied of by taking a wife of whoredom (Hos. 1), and by marrying an adultress with the circumstances of it (ch. 3). So the prophet Zechariah was commanded to typify the things he predicted by making silver and golden crowns on the heads of those that returned from the captivity (Zech. 6); and by the two staves called "Beauty" and "Bands"; and by his casting money to the potter in the house of the Lord; and his taking the instruments of a foolish shepherd (ch. 11).

7. The following sentence is in a later, grayish ink.

It was so common a thing for the prophets to typify things that were the subjects of their prophecies by divine appointment, that the false prophets imitated 'em in it and were wont to feign directions from God to typify the subjects of their false prophecies. (See I Kgs. 22:11 and Jer. 28:10.)

Things in common use among the Israelites were spoken of by the Spirit of God as types. Thus the vine tree is spoken of, more especially of God's visible people (Ezek. 15).

It being so much God's manner from the beginning of the world to represent divine things by types, hence it probably came to pass that typical representations were looked upon by the ancient nations—the Egyptians in particular—as sacred things, and therefore called "hieroglyphics," which is a word that signifies as much as "sacred images," or "representations." And animals being very much made use of in the ancient types of the church of God, so they were very much used in the Egyptian hieroglyphics, which probably led the way to their worship of all manner of living creatures.

Now since it was, as has been observed, God's manner of old in the times of the Old Testament, from generation to generation, and even from the beginning of the world to the end of the Old Testament history, to represent divine things by outward signs, types and symbolical representations, and especially thus to typify and prefigure future events that he revealed by his Spirit and foretold by the prophets, it is very unlikely that the Messiah and things appertaining to his kingdom and salvation should not be thus abundantly prefigured and typified under the Old Testament, if the following things be considered.

It is apparent by the Old Testament (by what I have elsewhere observed of the prophecies of the Messiah),[8] that these things are the main subject of the prophecies of the Old Testament, the subject about which the Spirit of prophecy was chiefly conversant from the beginning of the world. It was the subject of the first proper prophecy that ever was uttered, and 'tis abundantly evident by the Old Testament that it is every way the chief of all prophetical events. 'Tis spoken of abundantly as the greatest and most glorious event, beyond all that eye had seen, ear heard, or had entered into the hearts of men, at the

8. JE refers to his "Prophecies of the Messiah," located in the "Miscellanies," bk. 4, nos. 891 and 922 (Beinecke Library), and bk. 6, no. 1067 (Trask Library). He argues throughout the "Prophecies of the Messiah" (hereafter "Prophecies") that all the prophecies of the Old Testament are fulfilled by Jesus Christ. In no. 1067, §98, JE states that the high style of the prophetic language of praise is only appropriate in reference to the Messiah.

accomplishment of which not only God's people and all nations should unspeakably rejoice, but the trees of the field, the hills and mountains, the sea and dry land, and all heaven and earth, should rejoice and shout for joy; and in comparison of which the greatest events of the Old Testament, and particularly those two most insisted on—the creation of the world and redemption out of Egypt—were not worthy to be mentioned or to come into mind; and in comparison of which the greatest and most sacred things of the Mosaic dispensation, even the ark itself, the most sacred of all, was worthy of no notice. And it is also abundantly evident by the Old Testament that it was the grand event that, above all other future events, was the object of the contemplations, hopes and raised expectations of God's people from the beginning of the world.

And furthermore, the introducing of the Messiah and his kingdom and salvation is plainly spoken of in the Old Testament as the great event which was the substance, main drift and end of all the prophecies of the Old Testament, to reveal which chiefly it was that the Spirit of prophecy was given, in that the angel in Dan. 9:24 speaks of this event as that in the accomplishment of which prophecies in general are summed up and have their ultimate confirmation, in which the vision and prophecy or all prophetical revelation has its last result and consummation. "Seventy weeks are determined upon thy people and upon thy holy city, to finish the transgression, and to make an end of sins, and to make reconciliation for iniquity, and to bring in everlasting righteousness, *and to seal up the vision and prophecy*, and to anoint the Most Holy." That what has been expressed is the import of the phrase of "sealing up the vision and prophecy," is evident from the drift and manner of expression of the whole verse, and also from Ezek 28:12, "Thou sealest up the sum, full of wisdom, and perfect in beauty." Mr. Basnage, in his *History of the Jews*, observes that the rabbis among the Jews still agree to this day that all the oracles of the prophets relate to the Messiah (p. 371, col. 1).[9] (See the evidence there is that the book of

9. Jacques Basnage, *The History of the Jews, From Jesus Christ to The Present Time: Containing Their Antiquities, their Religion, their Rites, The Dispersion of the Ten Tribes in the East, And The Persecutions this Nation has suffer'd in the West. Being a Supplement and Continuation of The History of Josephus*, trans. Thomas Taylor (London, 1708). P. 371 marks the beginning of a discussion of the Talmudists' and Rabbins' opinions about the Messiah. Basnage writes: "The first thing that we ought to observe, is, the Confusion and Contradictions of the *Sages*. They still agree at this day, that *all the Oracles of the Prophets relate to* Messiah; but they pretend that 'the particular Oracles, that indicate his coming, can't be distinguish'd, and that it is very difficult to find them.'"

Psalms in general relates to the Messiah, or that he and things pertaining to him are the grand subject of those sacred songs of the church of Israel, "Prophecies of the Messiah" §60 and §87.)[1]

And besides, it is to be considered that this event was that [in] which the people of God from the beginning of the world were most nearly and greatly concerned, yea, was of infinitely the greatest concern to them of all prophetical events. For 'tis evident by the Old Testament that the Messiah was not only to be the Savior of God's people that should be after his coming, but that he was the Savior of the saints in all ages from the beginning of the world; and that through his coming and what he should do at his appearing, they all should have the only true atonement for their sins, and restoration from the curse brought upon them by the Fall of Adam, the resurrection from the dead and eternal life. (See "Fulfillment of Prophecies of the Messiah" §169, together with various other parts of that discourse.)[2]

'Tis much the more reasonable to suppose that many things pertaining to the state and constitution of the nation of Israel, many things which God ordered and appointed among them, should be typical of things appertaining to the Messiah; because it is evident by the Old Testament that the very being of that people as God's people, and

1. JE begins §60 on MS p. 37 of "Prophecies," entitled "The book of Psalms in great part relates to the Messiah," by noting, "There are many other psalms or parts of psalms of which it might be made very evident that they have respect to the times of the Messiah." He argues next from 2 Sam. 23:1–5 that, of all David's works, the Psalms have particular reference to the Messiah. In §87 on MS p. 86, JE discusses those psalms which refer to captivity and affliction. He begins, "This is a great argument the book of Psalms is a great part of it prophetical, and also that very much of it relates to the times of the Messiah, even in those parts of it where the speech is in the present or preter tense, viz. that God's people are so often spoken of as being in captivity, and the temple, city and land in desolation, or as being restored from a state of captivity and desolation, in psalms that were penned at a time when no such thing was nor had lately been." In a separate five-page "Supplement to the Prophecies of the Messiah" (Trask Library), which JE notes should be used in conjunction with §60 and §87, he says, in part: "In THE BOOK OF PSALMS in general, the psalmist speaks either in the name of Christ or in the name of the church. And this is to be observed concerning a very great part of this book, that the Psalmist speaks in the name of Christ most comprehensively taken, viz. as including his body or members, or in the name of Christ mystical; and even in some of those psalms that seem to be the most direct and plain prophecies of Christ, some parts of which are most applicable to the head or Christ, other parts to the body or the church."

2. The "Fulfillment of the Prophecies of the Messiah" (hereafter "Fulfillment") is in the "Miscellanies," bk. 7, no. 1068 (Trask Library). JE probably intended a section renumbered 172 on MS pp. 134–36 which reads, in part: "The Messiah in the prophecies is represented not only as the Savior of God's people that should be then, after he should come into the world and set up his kingdom, but also the Redeemer of the saints in all ages; of those that lived many ages before his coming into the world, and even before the Mosaic dispensation."

distinguished and separated from the rest of the world, was to prepare the way for the introduction of that great blessing into the world of mankind, of the Messiah and his kingdom. It seems to be pretty plainly intimated by God at the first planting of the tree or founding that ancient church, and separating that people from the rest of the world, in the call of Abraham, in the three first verses of Gen. 12: "Now the Lord had said unto Abraham, Get thee out of thy own country, and from thy kindred, and from thy father's house, unto a land that I will show thee: And I will make of thee a great nation, and I will bless thee, and make thy name great; and thou shalt be a blessing: And I will bless them that bless thee, and curse him that curseth thee: and in thee shall all families of the earth be blessed." It here seems to be manifest that the introducing that great good which God had in view to all the families of the earth, was what God had in view in thus calling and separating Abraham, to make of him an happy nation. 'Tis therefore much the more likely that many things belonging to them should be typical of the great future things appertaining to this great blessing, which was the great end God designed by them; and especially considering that we find it to be God's manner under the Old Testament, in both persons and things, to signify and represent that which God made or separated 'em for, or the special use or design God had in view with respect to 'em. I say it was God's manner beforehand to signify and represent these things in what appertained to 'em or happened concerning them. So he often did in the signification of the names that he gave 'em, as in the names of Eve, Noah, Abraham, Isaac, Israel, Judah, Joshua, David, Solomon, etc.; and [in] things which they saw or did, or which came to pass concerning them, as Moses' being drawn out of the water, and what God showed [him] on Horeb, before [he went] into Egypt from Midian, in the burning bush; and in David, in his slaying the lion and bear and delivering the lamb.

Again, we find that many lesser redemptions, deliverances and victories of God's people, that it is plain even by the Old Testament were as nothing in comparison of the salvation and victory of the Messiah, were by God's ordering represented by types. So the redemption out of Egypt. It was much typified afterwards in institutions that God appointed in commemoration of it. And the reason given by God for his thus typifying of it, was that it was so worthy to have signs and representations to fix it in the mind. Thus concerning the representations of their coming out of Egypt in the Passover, by eating it with unleavened bread, with their staff in their hand, etc. This reason is given why they should have such representations and memorials of it: Ex. 12:42, "It is a night much to be remembered." This redemption out of Egypt was also much typified beforehand. It was typified in the smoking furnace and the burning lamp following it, which Abraham saw (Gen. 15:17; see note on the place.)[3] It was typified in Moses' being drawn out of the water, and in the burning bush that survived the flames, and Moses' rod's swallowing up the magicians' rods. So David's victory over the enemies of God's people, and his saving them out of their hands, was typified by his conquering the lion and the bear and rescuing the lamb. God's giving victory to Israel over the Syrians, and delivering them from them, was typified by the Prophet's helping the king of Israel shoot an arrow towards them (II Kgs. 13:15–17). So the salvation of Jerusalem from Sennacherib's army was typified by the springing of the corn afresh from the roots of the stubble. Hezekiah's being saved from death was typified by bringing back the sun when it was going down. Since, therefore, God did so much to typify those lesser victories and salvations, is it not exceeding likely that great victory and redemption of the Messiah, which appears by the Old Testament to be infinitely greater and that was all along so much more insisted by in the Word of the Lord to the people, be much more typified?

'Tis much more reasonably and credibly supposed that God should through the ages of the Old Testament be very much in signifying things pertaining to the Messiah and his salvation, not only in prophecies, but also in types, because we find in fact, that at the very beginning of God's revealing the Messiah to mankind, prophecies and types went together in the first prophecy of the Messiah and the first proper prophecy that ever was in the world. God foretold and typified the redemption both together when God said to the serpent, Gen. 3:15, "I will [put] enmity between thee and the woman, and between thy seed and her seed; it shall bruise thy head, and thou shalt bruise his heel." This is undoubtedly a prediction of the Messiah's victory over Satan, and his suffering from Satan, and of the Messiah's people's victory and

---

3. In the "Blank Bible" note on Gen. 15:17, JE writes, "A lamp signifies light of comfort (II Sam. 22:29)," and he directs the reader to "Scripture" nos. 75 and 353. No. 75, renumbered 129, reads, in part: "The smoking furnace signified their suffering grievous persecution and affliction in Egypt, that is called the grim furnace, and the shining lamp signified their glorious deliverance in the fourth generation and being brought into the land of Canaan." In no. 353 JE argues that Gen. 15:17 prefigures the death and sufferings of Christ.

deliverance through him. (See my discourse on the "Prophecies of the Messiah," at the beginning.)[4] And none can reasonably question but that here is also some respect had to that enmity there is between mankind and serpents, and the manner of serpents' wounding mankind and man's killing them.[5] And this state of things with respect to serpents was ordered and established in these words. But if we suppose that both these things were intended in these same words, then undoubtedly one is spoken of and ordained as the representation of the other. If God orders and speaks of the bruising of a snake's head, and thereby signifies the Messiah's conquering the devil, that is the same thing as God's ordering and speaking of the bruising of a snake's head as a sign, signification or (which is the same thing) type of his conquering the devil. And in what is said to the serpent, v. 14, "Thou art cursed above all cattle, and above every beast of the field; upon thy belly shalt thou go, and dust shalt thou eat all the days of thy life," 'tis evident God speaks concerning that serpent that was a beast of the field. And yet 'tis also evident by the Old Testament that he has a respect to something pertaining to the state of the devil that should be brought to pass by the Messiah. As by Is. 65:25, "The wolf and the lamb shall feed together, and the lion shall eat straw like the bullock: and dust shall be the serpent's meat. They shall not hurt nor destroy in all my holy mountain"; compared with Is. 11:1–9, together with Is. 27:1[6] and Zech. 3:1–4. Thus the very first thing that [was] ordered and established in this world after the Fall [was][7] a type of the Messiah, and ordered as such. Which argues that typifying of the Messiah is one principal [way][8] of God's foreshowing him. And as types and prophecies of the Messiah began together, so there is reason to think [that][9] they have kept pace one with another ever since.

'Tis the more credible that not only some particular events that came to pass among the Jews, or things appointed to be done among

---

4. JE probably intends "Miscellanies" no. 891, entitled "CHRISTIAN RELIGION. PROPHECIES OF THE MESSIAH," of which no. 922 was originally a continuation. In no. 891, §1, JE writes on Gen. 3:15, "Here it is not to suppose, that what God intended was that God would cause an aversion of nature between serpents and mankind."

5. JE, Jr. inserted: "for God is here speaking concerning a beast of the field, that was ranked with the cattle, as appears by the foregoing verse."

6. In the MS, the verse number is obliterated by damage. The verse is supplied from Dwight ed., 9, 21.

7. MS damage; reading taken from ibid.

8. Ibid.

9. Ibid.

them, should be typical, but of the state and constitution of the nation and their way of living in many things was typical; because we have an instance of an appointment of a way of living in a particular family or race to continue from generation to generation in the chief and more important things appertaining to the outward state and way of life, requiring that which was very diverse from others' manner of living and that which was very self-denying, in order to typify something spiritual. The instance I mean is that of the posterity of Jonadab, the son of Rechab, who were required by the command of Jonadab, commanding them by the Spirit of prophecy, to drink no wine, nor build any house, nor sow seed, nor plant vineyards (Jer. 35; see note on the place.)[1]

'Tis a great argument that the ancient state of the nation of Israel, and both things that appertained to their religious constitution and God's providential disposals of them, were typical of the Messiah, that the Jews themselves anciently thus understood the matter. The ancient Jewish rabbis (as Mr. Basnage in his *History of the Jews* observes, p. 367)[2] judged that all things happened to their fathers as types and figures of the Messiah. (See also Bp. Kidder's *Demonstration of the Messiah*, pt. 3, p. 40, and pt. 1, pp. 74–75; *ibid.*, pp. 111–12; *ibid.*, p. 130, and pt. 3, pp. 67e, 71b, 77c, 78b and 106c.)[3]

As to the historical events of the Old Testament, 'tis an argument that many of 'em were types of things appertaining to the Messiah's

1. "Blank Bible," note on Jer. 35:6–8, in part: "It typifies a living as pilgrims and strangers on the earth spiritually. Their not drinking any wine and living in the mortification of carnal appetites, represents a life of abstinence from sensual pleasures. Their building no houses, nor sowing seed nor planting vineyards, but dwelling in tents, signifies that God's people here have no settled dwelling place; that this world is not their country, not their home; that they have been little to do with these things, that they are to treat these things with neglect; and that they don't treat them as settling upon them, but use [them] as transient pilgrims and strangers looking for another country."

2. Basnage, *History of the Jews*, p. 367. JE is referring to the opening passage of the chapter entitled, "Of the Helps which the Jewish Church had in the Time of christ, to know the Messiah." Basnage states: "They as yet admitted the Maxim of St. *Paul*, that all things had happened to the Fathers in Types and Figures of the *Messiah*. And therefore they apply'd to him part of the Histories, and Events of the Old Testament." Basnage goes on to cite David, the book of Canticles, and the brazen serpent as containing specific images that can be interpreted as applying to the Messiah.

3. Richard Kidder, *A Demonstration of the Messias. In Which the Truth of the Christian Religion is Proved Especially Against the Jews* (London, 1684). For pt. 1, JE cited pp. 73–74, but meant pp. 74–75, in which place Kidder begins his discussion of those Old Testament texts which show that the Jews anticipated Jesus's appearance: "I shall begin, and shew what the time was in which the *Messias* was to come according to the predictions of the old Testament. And to that purpose commend to your consideration those places of Scripture which give us an account

kingdom and salvation, that these things are often in the Old Testament expressly spoken of as represented or resembled by those historical events. And those events are sometimes not only mentioned as resemblances, but as signs and pledges of these great things of the Messiah. In Is. 41, Abraham's great victory over the kings and nations of the east is spoken of [as] a resemblance of the victory of the Messiah and his people over their enemies. Abraham is here called "the righteous man" (v. 2), as the Messiah in the same discourse. In the beginning of the next chapter, the Messiah is called God's "servant that shall bring forth judgment to the Gentiles, and bring forth judgment unto truth, and set judgment in the earth" [Is. 42:1, 3–4]. God is said (ch. 41:2) to call Abraham to his foot. Ch. 42:6, 'tis said of the Messiah, "I have called thee in righteousness." Of Abraham it is said, ch. 41:2, that God "gave the nations before him as the dust to his sword, and as the driven stubble to his bow." And this is spoken of for the encouragement of God's people as a resemblance and pledge of what he would do for them in the days of the Messiah, when he [would] cause their enemies before them to be ashamed and confounded, to be as nothing and to perish, so that they should seek 'em and should not find 'em, and they that war against them should be as nothing and as a thing of nought; and they should thresh the mountains and beat them small, and make the hills as chaff, so that the wind should carry them away and the whirlwind should scatter them (vv. 11–12, 15–16).

---

of that time. And I shall begin with the words of *Jacob: The sceptre shall not depart from Judah, nor a lawgiver from between his feet, untill Shiloh come,* Gen 49:10. That those words are to be understood of the *Messias* the ancient writers of the Jews do confess, and the modern Jews know this very well: And several of them have also interpreted the place of the *Messias.*" On p. 111 he writes: "the works which our Saviour did, and to which he refers in the Epistles of *John,* were those very works which the *Messias* was to doe according to the prediction of the Prophet." Kidder continues on p. 112 to show how Christ's preaching to the poor was in accordance with prophecy. JE cited p. 150, but meant p. 130, where Kidder explicates the Jewish commentator Abravenel's works on prophecies of the Messiah in the Old Testament, with special reference to the ten characters and conditions of the Messiah, which Kidder finds fulfilled in Christ. By pt. 2, JE meant pt. 3, *A Demonstration of the Messias. In Which the Truth of the Christian Religion is Defended, Especially against the Jews. Part III* (London, 1700). Here Kidder states, "There are many prophecies in the Old Testament concerning the *peaceable* Times of the *Messias:* And the *Jews* do very frequently upbraid us Christians with our Quarrels and Wars; and from thence they infer that our Jesus is not the *Christ* that was to come" (p. 40). In a defense of the prophecies of peace, Kidder notes that prophecies of violence, as in Daniel's vision of the four beasts, often precede peace (p. 67). On p. 71, he argues that Christ himself is not the cause of evils committed by Christians, and on pp. 77–78 he defends Jesus against the attacks of Jacob Aben Amram in a manuscript entitled "Porta Veritatis." In his refutation of Amram, he points to the descent of the Holy Spirit after Christ's glorification as further proof that Christ was and is Messiah (p. 106).

The church or spouse of the Messiah is spoken of in Cant. 6:13 as being represented by the company of Mahanaim, that we have an account of (Gen. 32:1–2), made up of Jacob's family and the heavenly host that joined them.

The redemption out of Egypt is very often in the Old Testament spoken of as a resemblance of the redemption by the Messiah. Num. 23:22–23, "God brought them out of Egypt; he hath as it were the strength of an unicorn. Surely there is no enchantment against Jacob, neither is there any divination against Israel: according to this time shall it be said of Jacob and of Israel, What hath God wrought!" Mic. 7:15, "According to the days of thy coming out of the land of Egypt will I show unto him marvelous things." Is. 64:1, 3–4, "Oh that thou wouldest rend the heavens, that thou wouldest come down, that the mountains might flow down at thy presence ... When thou didst terrible things that we looked not for, the mountains flowed down at thy presence. For since the beginning of the world men have not heard, nor perceived by the ear, neither hath the eye seen, O God, beside thee, what he hath prepared for him that waiteth for him." Is. 11:11, "And it shall come to pass in that day, that the Lord shall set his hand again the second time to recover the remnant of his people, which shall be left, from Assyria, and from Egypt"; together with vv. 15–16.

This redemption out of Egypt is evidently spoken of as a resemblance of the redemption of the Messiah in Ps. 68:6, "God bringeth out them that were bound with chains." V. 13, "Though ye have lien among the pots, yet shall ye be as the wings of a dove covered with silver, and her feathers with yellow gold"; in which there is an evident reference to the people's hands being delivered from the pots in Egypt. Ps. 81:6 and the context makes this evident. And the drift and design of the psalm shows this to be a promise of the Messiah's redemption. God's dividing the Red Sea and River Jordan, and leading the people through them, are often spoken of as a resemblance [of]⁴ what God shall accomplish for his people in the days of the Messiah. Is. 11:11, "[And it]⁵ shall come to pass in that day, that the Lord shall set his hand again the second time [to recover]⁶ the remnant of his people, that shall be left from Egypt." Vv. 15–16, "And the Lord shall utterly destroy the tongue of the Egyptian sea, and shake his hand over the

---

4. MS damage; word supplied from Dwight ed., *9*, 23.
5. MS damage; words supplied from the scripture.
6. Ibid.

river, and shall smite it in the seven streams, and cause men to go over dryshod. And there shall be an highway for the remnant of his people, which shall be left, from Assyria; like as it was to Israel in the day that he came up out of the land of Egypt." Is. 43:2–3, "When thou passest through the waters, I will be with thee; and through the rivers, they shall not overflow thee ... For I ... gave Egypt for thy ransom." Vv. 16–19, "Thus saith the Lord, which maketh a way in the sea, and a path on the mighty waters; Which bringeth forth the chariot and horse, the army and the power; they shall lie down together, they shall not rise: they are extinct, they are quenched as tow. Remember not former things ... Behold I will do a new thing." Ch. 27:12, "And it shall come to pass at that day, that the Lord shall beat off from the channel of the river unto[7] the stream of Egypt" (or, "the Lord shall strike off," or "smite away," "both the channel of the river and the stream of Egypt"; see note on the place),[8] "and ye shall be gathered one by one, O ye children of Israel." Ch. 51:10–11, "Art thou not it which hath dried the sea, the waters of the great deep; that hath made the depths of the sea a way for the ransomed of the Lord to pass over? Therefore the redeemed of the Lord shall return, and come with singing unto Zion; and everlasting joy shall be upon their head: they shall obtain gladness and joy; and sorrow and mourning shall flee away." V. 15, "But I am the Lord thy God, that divided the sea, whose waves roared: The Lord of hosts is his name." Ch. 63:11–13, "Then he remembered the days of old, Moses, and his people, saying, Where is he that brought them up out of the sea with the shepherd of his flock? where is he that put his holy Spirit within him? That led them by the right hand of Moses with his glorious arm, dividing the water before them, to make himself an everlasting name? That led them through the deep, as an horse in the wilderness?" Ps. 68:22, "I will bring my people again from the depths of the sea." Zech. 10:10–11, "I will bring them again also out of the land of Egypt ... And he shall pass through the sea with affliction, and shall smite the waves in the sea, and all the deeps of the river shall dry up: and the pride of Assyria shall be brought down, and the scepter of Egypt shall depart away."

The destruction of Pharaoh and his hosts in the Red Sea is spoken of as a resemblance of the destruction of the enemies of God's people by

---

7. MS: "under."

8. In the "Blank Bible" note on Is. 27:12, JE says God will beat off Israel's enemies from "the whole land between the river of Egypt and Euphrates."

the Messiah. Is. 43:16–17, "Thus saith the Lord, which maketh a way in the sea, and a path in the mighty waters; Which bringeth forth the chariot and horse, the army and the power; they shall lie down together, they shall not rise." And particularly Pharaoh's destruction in the Red Sea is spoken of as a type of the Messiah's bruising the head of the old serpent, or dragon. Is. 51:9–11, "Awake, awake, put on thy strength, O arm of the Lord. Art thou not it that hath cut Rahab, and wounded the dragon? Art thou not it which hath dried up the sea, the waters of the great deep; that hath made the depths of the sea a way for the ransomed to pass over? Therefore the redeemed of the Lord shall return and come with singing unto Zion; and everlasting joy shall be upon their head: they shall obtain gladness and joy; and sorrow and mourning shall flee away." Pharaoh is called "Leviathan" and "the dragon" in Ps. 74:13–14, as the devil is in a like destruction in the Messiah's time (Is. 27:1). That Pharaoh is intended in those forementioned places by the dragon and Leviathan, is very manifest by Ezek. 29:3 and 32:2.

The joy and songs that the children of Israel had at their redemption out of Egypt, and their great deliverance from the Egyptians at the Red Sea, is spoken of as a resemblance of the joy God's people shall have in the redemption of the Messiah. Hos. 2:15, "And she shall sing there, as in the days of her youth, and as in the day when she came up out of the land of Egypt." The Spirit of God seems to have reference to the manner of his leading and guarding the people when they went up out of Egypt, in going before 'em to lead 'em, and behind to keep the Egyptians from hurting them, and to compare what he would do in the[9] Messiah's days thereto. Is. 52:12, "For ye shall not go out with haste, nor go by flight: for the Lord will go before you; the God of Israel will be your rereward": the God of Israel, that God that thus led Israel out of Egypt when he entered into covenant with them, and became the God of that people. (Here see SSS on Ex. 12:14.)[1] God's leading the people through the wilderness is spoken of as a resemblance of what should be accomplished towards God's people in the Messiah's times. Is. 63:13, "That led them through the deep, as an horse in the wilderness." Ps. 68:7, "O God, when thou wentest before thy people, when thou didst march through the wilderness," com-

---

9. MS: "for his." These words are cancelled by JE, Jr., who replaced them with the interpolation "in the," as given here. It seems JE was going to write "for his people," but changed his mind in mid-thought.

1. See Poole, *Synopsis, 1,* 365.

pared with the rest of the psalm. Hos. 2:14–15, "I will [allure] her, and bring her into the wilderness, and speak comfortably to her. [...] And she shall sing, as in the days of her youth, as in the day when she came up out of the land of Egypt." Ezek. 20:34–37, "And I will bring you out from the people, and gather you out of the countries wherein ye are scattered, with a mighty hand, and with a stretched out arm, and with fury poured out" (plainly alluding to God's manner of redeeming the people out of Egypt). "And I will bring you into the wilderness of the people, and there will I plead with you face to face. Like as I pleaded with your fathers in the wilderness of the land of Egypt, so will I plead with you, saith the Lord God. And I will cause you to pass under the [rod],[2] and will bring you into the bond of the covenant." Where we may also observe that God's speaking with the people face to face, and entering into covenant with them and making them his covenant people, when he brought them out of Egypt, is spoken as a resemblance of God's revealing himself to his people in the days of the Messiah and bringing them into a covenant relation to himself by him.

God's appearing with the children of Israel in a pillar of cloud and fire is spoken [of] as a resemblance of what God would do for his people in the days of the Messiah. Is. 4:5, "And the Lord will create upon every dwelling place of Mt. Zion, and upon her assemblies, a cloud and smoke by day, and the shining of a flame of fire by night: for upon all the glory shall be a defense." The earth's and mount Sinai's quaking at the time of the giving of the Law is spoken of as a resemblance of what should [be] in the Messiah's days. Ps. 68:8, "The earth shook ... even Sinai itself was moved at the presence of God, the God of Israel." So the great effect of God's presence on the mountains, and especially Mt. Sinai's being all enkindled by so great and dreadful a fire, is plainly spoken of [as] a resemblance of what should be in the days of the Messiah. Is. 64:1–4, "Oh that thou wouldest rent the heavens, that thou wouldest come down, that the mountains might flow down at thy presence, as when the melting fire burneth ... When thou didst terrible things which we looked not for, thou camest down, the mountains flowed down at thy presence. For since the beginning of the world men have not heard, nor perceived by the ear, neither hath the eye seen, O God, beside thee, what he hath prepared for him that waiteth for him."

2. MS damage; word supplied from the scripture.

And so the rain that descended on the people at the time of these thunders and lightnings at Mt. Sinai, or at the time of the great hailstones that God sent on the Amorites. Ps. 68:7–9, "O God, when thou wentest forth before thy people, when thou didst march through the wilderness; The earth shook, the heavens dropped at the presence of God ... Thou, O Lord, didst send a plentiful rain, whereby thou didst refresh thine inheritance, when it was weary."

These things do abundantly confirm that the redemption out of Egypt, and the circumstances and events that attended it, were intended by the Great Disposer of all things to be types of the redemption of God's people by the Messiah, and of things appertaining to that redemption.

'Tis an argument the manna that [God] gave the children of Israel was a type of something spiritual, because it is called "the corn of heaven" and "angels' food" (Ps. 78:24–25 and Ps. 105:40). It could be angels' food no otherwise than as representing something spiritual.

Now, by the way, I would remark that what was before made use of as an argument that the great redemption by the Messiah was very much typified beforehand, is very greatly strengthened by what has been now observed. I mean that argument that lesser redemptions were by God's ordering represented by types, and particularly that the redemption of the children of Israel out of Egypt was much typified beforehand. Now if this was so, that God was much in typifying this redemption beforehand, which itself was a type of the great redemption by the Messiah, how much more may we well suppose this great redemption itself, that is the antitype of that, should be abundantly typified? Will God do much to typify that which was itself but a shadow of the Messiah's salvation? And shall he not be much more in prefiguring the very substance, even that great redemption by the Messiah, in comparison of which the former is often in the Old Testament represented as worthy of no remembrance or notice?

God's bringing his people into Canaan, to a state of rest and happiness there, is spoken of as a resemblance of what God would do for his people through the Messiah. Jer. 31:2, "Thus saith the Lord, The people that were left of the sword found grace in the wilderness; even Israel, when I went to cause him to rest," compared with the rest of the chapter and the foregoing chapter. Is. 63:14, "As a beast goeth down into the valley, the Spirit of the Lord caused him to rest: so didst thou lead thy people, to make thyself a glorious name," together with the context. [Ps.]³ 68:10, "Thy congregation hath dwelt therein: thou, O God, hast prepared of [thy]⁴ goodness for the poor." V. 13, "Though ye have lien among the pots, ye shall be as the wings of a dove covered with silver, and her feathers with yellow gold," together with the context. The manner of God's giving Israel the possession of Canaan, viz. by a glorious conquest of the kings and nations of the land, is spoken of as a resemblance of the manner in which God would bring his people to rest and glory, by the Messiah, after his exaltation. Ps. 68:11–12, "The Lord gave the word: great was the company of them that published it. Kings of armies did flee apace: and she that tarried at home divided the spoil." V. 14, "When the Almighty scattered kings in it, it was white as snow in Salmon," taken with vv. 21–23, "But God shall wound the head of his enemies ... The Lord said, I will bring again from Bashan, I will bring my people again from the depth of the sea: That thy foot may be dipped in the blood of thine enemies, and the tongue of thy dogs in the same." V. 30, "Rebuke the company of spearmen, the multitude of bulls, with the calves of the people, till everyone submit himself with pieces of silver: scatter thou the people that delight in war," together with the rest of the psalm.

What the people of God should be brought to in the days of the Messiah is spoken of as represented by the children of Israel's slaying Achan in Joshua's time [Josh. 7]. Hos. 2:15, "And I will give her her vineyards from thence, and the valley of Achor for a door of hope: and she shall sing there, as in the days of her youth, as in the day when she came up out of the land of Egypt."

What came to pass in the time of Joshua's battle with the five kings of the Amorites, and particularly God's sending down great hailstones upon them, is spoken as a resemblance of what should be in the days of the Messiah. Is. 28:21, "For the Lord shall rise up as in mount Perazim, and be wroth as in the valley of Gibeon, that he may do his work; his strange work, and bring to pass his act, his strange act"; together with v. 2, "Behold, the Lord hath a mighty and strong one, which as a tempest of hail and a destroying storm ... shall cast down to the earth with the hand." And ch. 30:30, "And the Lord shall cause his glorious voice to be heard, and shall show the lighting down of his arm, with the indignation of his anger ... with tempest, and hailstones." And 32:19,

---

3. MS damage; supplied from Dwight ed., 9, 26.
4. MS damage; word supplied from the scripture.

"When it shall hail, coming down on the forest; and the city shall be low in a low place" (or "shall be utterly abased"). And Ezek. 38:22, "I will rain upon him ... an overflowing rain, and great hailstones."

What God did for Israel in the victory of Deborah and Barak over the Canaanites is spoken of as a resemblance of what God would do for his people against their enemies in the days of the Messiah. Ps. 83:9–10, "Do unto them ... as to Sisera, as to Jabin, at the brook of Kison: Which perished at Endor: they became as dung for the earth." For this psalm is prophetical, and these things have respect to the great things God would do against the future enemies of his church. For it don't appear that there was any such confederacy of the nations mentioned against Israel in David's or Asaph's time; and particularly it don't look probable that there was any such enmity of the inhabitants of Tyre against Israel, as is here spoken of (v. 7). And 'tis very probable that as this psalm is prophetical, so it is prophetical of the Messiah's days, as most of the Psalms are, as I have shown in my discourse on "The Prophecies of the Messiah."[5] And there is a great agreement between what is here foretold of the destruction of the enemies of the church, and what is foretold of the Messiah's days in many other places. And the last verse [v. 18], which speaks of God's being made known to all mankind as the only true God and the God of all the earth, further confirms this.

Gideon's victory over the Midianites is spoken of as a resemblance of what should be accomplished in the Messiah's days. Is. 9:4, "For thou hast broken the yoke of his burden, and the staff of his shoulder, the rod of his oppressor, as in the day of Midian." Ps. 83:9, "Do unto them as unto the Midianites." V. 11, "Make their nobles like Oreb, and like Zeeb: yea, all their princes as Zebah, and Zalmunna." As in the destruction of the Midianites every man's sword was against his brother, so it is foretold that it should be with the enemies of God's people in the Messiah's times. Ezek. 38:21, "Every man's sword shall be against his brother." Hag. 2:22, "And I will overthrow the throne of kingdoms, and I will destroy the strength of the kingdoms of the heathen; and I will overthrow the chariots, and them that ride in them; and the horses and their riders shall come down, every one by the sword of his brother."

God's wonderful appearance for David at Baal-Perazim, to fight for him against his enemies, is spoken of as a resemblance of what should

5. See above p. 204, n. 1.

be in the Messiah's times. Is. 28:21, "For the Lord shall rise up as in mount Perazim."

In Zech. 9:15, "The Lord of hosts shall defend them; and they shall devour, and subdue with sling stones," there seems to [be] a reference to David's subduing Goliath with a sling stone, as though that were a resemblance of the manner in which the enemies of God's people should be subdued in the times of the Messiah; and this is an argument that David's bruising the head of this giant and grand enemy of God's church is a type of the Messiah, the Son of David, and who is often called by the name of "David" in Scriptures, his bruising the head of Satan.

'Tis an argument the historical events of the Old Testament in the whole series of them, from the beginning of God's great works for Israel in order to their redemption out of Egypt, even to their full possession of the promised land in the days of David and the building of the temple in the days of Solomon, were typical things, and that under the whole history was hid, in a mystery or parable, a glorious system of divine truth concerning greater things than those, that a plain, summary rehearsal or narration of them is called "a parable" and "dark saying," or "enigma" (Ps. 78:2). 'Tis evident that here by "a parable" is not meant merely a set discourse of things appertaining to divine wisdom, as the word "parable" is sometimes used; but properly a mystical, enigmatical speech signifying spiritual and divine things, and figurative and typical representations, because 'tis called both "a parable" and "dark sayings."

'Tis an argument that many of the historical events of the Old Testament are types of the great events appertaining to the Messiah's coming and kingdom, that the Spirit of God took occasion from the former to speak of the latter. He either takes occasion to speak of and foretell the Messiah, and the great events appertaining to his salvation, upon occasion of the coming to pass of these ancient events; or on his speaking of these events, celebrating or promising them, he takes occasion to speak of these latter and greater events, joining what is declared of the one with what he reveals of the other in the same discourse, which is an argument that one has relation to the other and is the image of the other. Thus the Spirit of God when speaking by Balaam, took occasion, when celebrating the wonderful work of God in bringing them out of Egypt, to foretell that great salvation that God should work for his people by the Messiah (Num. 23:23). So the Spirit of God in Nathan, when speaking of the glorious reign of Solomon and his building an house to God's name, and promising these things to David (II Sam. 7), takes occasion to foretell and promise the more glorious and everlasting kingdom of the Messiah; as it is evident that David understood the words of Nathan by what he says in ch. 23 and in the book of Psalms, and as it is evident by many things in the Prophets, the Spirit of God intended them.

From the ark's being carried up into the Mt. Zion, and the great joy and privileges of Israel consequent thereupon, the Spirit took occasion to speak very much of the exaltation of the Messiah and the glorious privileges of his people consequent thereupon, as in I Chron. 16:7–36, especially from v. 22. So in the sixty-eighth psalm, which was penned or indited on occasion of the ascension of the ark into Mt. Zion, as anyone may be satisfied by duly considering the matter of the psalm, especially vv. 25–29; and by comparing the first and seventh verses of this psalm with Num. 10:35; and by comparing many passages in this psalm with many parts of that song of David on occasion of the carrying up the ark, that is recorded in I Chron. 16. Again, on this occasion the Spirit of God speaks of the things of the Messiah in Ps. 132, which was penned on that occasion, as is very plain from the matter of the psalm and by comparing vv. 8–11 with II Chron. 6:41–42.

From David's great victories over the Syrians and Edomites, the Spirit of God takes occasion to speak much of the victories of the Messiah in Ps. 60 and 108.

The seventy-second psalm, which is evidently a great prophecy of the Messiah, was written on occasion of the introducing of Solomon to the throne of Israel, as is evident by the title, together with the first verse of the psalm.

So the Spirit of God does abundantly take occasion to foretell and promise the redemption of the Messiah and the overthrow of his people's enemies by him, from these two events: the destruction of Sennacherib's army and the deliverance of Jerusalem from him, and likewise the destruction of Babylon and the redemption of the Jews from their Babylonish captivity.

Not only does God take occasion from these historical events to speak of the great events that appertain to the Messiah's coming and salvation, but with regard to several of 'em he manifestly speaks of both under one. The same words have respect to both events. One is spoken of under the other, as though one were contained in the other, or as though one were the other. Which can be no other way than by one being the type or representation of the other, in that sense wherein David said the waters of the well of Bethlehem was the blood of those men that brought it in jeopardy of their lives [II Sam. 23:17]; as the beasts Daniel saw are said to be kingdoms, and the horns to be kings [Dan. 9:20–22]; and as Ezekiel's hair is said to be Jerusalem (Ezek. 5:5).

Thus Balaam prophesied of David, who smote the four corners of Moab, and of the Messiah under one, as I have already shown ("Prophecies of the Messiah" §43).[6] So 'tis most manifest that the peace and glory of Solomon's reign, and that of the reign of the Messiah, are spoken of under one (Ps. 72); and that the ascending of the ark into Mt. Zion, and the ascension of the Messiah, are also spoken of under one in Ps. 68.

Some of the historical events of the Old Testament, if they are not typical, must needs be very impertinently taken notice of in the history, as David's sacrificing when they had gone six paces with the ark (II Sam. 6:13). It must be both insignificantly done and impertinently related in the history, unless there be some signification of some important thing in it. So the relation of there being twelve fountains of water and threescore and ten palm trees [Num. 33:9].[7]

The remarkable similitude there is between many of the events in the Old Testament, both miraculous and others, and the prophetical descriptions of events relating to the Messiah, is an argument that the

6. In "Prophecies" §43, on MS p. 7, after quoting Num. 24:17–l9, JE writes, "Undoubtedly this prophecy has some respect to David, but there is good reason to think that the prophecy looks beyond him to the great Son of David, the Branch of David so often spoken of by the prophets and that is so often by them called by David's name. He speaks of this person as one that he shall see, which is agreeable to what Job in the forementioned prophecy [says] will be true of the Messiah who shall raise the dead and every eye shall see him. But these words can't in any tolerable sense be applied to David. What is said of the destruction of Moab and Edom is agreeable to that great prophecy of the Messiah. [...] In v. 19 it is said, 'Out of Jacob shall come he that [shall] have dominion' [...] in which sense the words cannot be applied to David, or to him with his successors, for David quickly, after he had subdued the neighbor nations, died, and these nations after a little while revolted from under the dominion of the house of David. Yea, ten tribes of Israel themselves never more returned to their former subjection. The dominion of Ashur and Chittim, of which Balaam speaks in the following part of this prophecy, was much greater and of much longer continuance. Yea, the dominion of the latter over the nation of Israel was of vastly longer duration."

7. JE deletes: "And its being so much taken notice that the well of Beer in the wilderness was digged by the princes of Israel with their staves that a song was made upon it, which was sung by the whole congregation of Israel, and that these things should be recorded in the sacred history of the Book of the Law laid up in the ark holy of holies." JE leaves a blank space and resumes writing in the middle of the same page where he deletes: "There is much evidence that many of the principal persons mentioned in the history of the Old Testament were types of the Messiah."

former were designed resemblances of the latter. God's causing the light to shine out of darkness, as Moses gives us an account of it in the history of the creation, has a great similitude with what is foretold to come to pass in the Messiah's times. Is. 42:16, "I will make darkness light before 'em." Is. 9:2, "The people that walked in darkness have seen a great light: they that dwell in the land of the shadow of death, upon them hath the light shined." Is. 29:18, "The eyes of the blind shall see out of obscurity, and out of darkness." So there is a great resemblance between the account Moses gives us of a river that ran through the midst of Eden to water the trees of paradise, and the descriptions which the prophets give of what should be in the Messiah's times. As Ezek. 47:7, "Now when I had returned, behold, at the bank of the river were very many trees on the one side and on the other." V. 12, "And by the river upon the bank thereof, on this side and on that side, shall grow all trees for meat, whose leaf shall not fade, neither shall the fruit thereof be consumed." Is. 41:18–19, "I will open rivers in high places, and fountains in the midst of the valleys: I will make the wilderness a pool of water, and the dry land springs of water. I will plant in the wilderness the cedar, the shittah tree, and the myrtle, and the oil tree. I will set in the desert the fir tree, and the pine, and the box tree together." Compared with Is. 51:3, "The Lord will comfort Zion ... and he will make her wilderness like Eden, and her desert like the garden of the Lord." Ezek. 36:35, "This land that was desolate is become like the garden of Eden." And Ps. 46:4, "There is a river, [the] streams whereof make glad the city of God," taken with Num. 24:5–6, "How goodly are thy tents, O Jacob, and thy tabernacles, O Israel! As the valleys are they spread forth, *as the gardens by the river's side,* as the trees of lignaloes *which the Lord hath planted,* and as cedar trees *besides the waters.*" And Jer. 31:12, "And their soul shall be like a watered garden; and they shall not sorrow any more at all."

So between what we are told of the Tree of Life in Eden (which being in the midst of the garden, we have reason to think was by the river) and the representations made of what should be in the Messiah's times. Ezek. 47:9, 12, "Everything that liveth, which moveth, whithersoever the rivers shall come, shall live ... everything shall live whither the river cometh.... And by the river upon the bank thereof, on this side and on that side, shall grow all trees for meat, whose leaf shall [not] fade, neither shall the fruit thereof be consumed: it shall bring forth new fruit according to his months ... the fruit thereof shall be for meat, and the leaf thereof for medicine."

The things that we have an account of in Moses' history of the Deluge have a great resemblance of many of the Old Testament representations of things that shall be brought to pass in the times of the Messiah's kingdom. That destruction of the wicked world by a flood of waters is very agreeable to the Old Testament representation of the future destruction that shall come on all God's enemies, and particularly in the Messiah's days. The wicked of the old world were destroyed by a dreadful tempest.[8] So it is said concerning the ungodly, Job 27:20–21, "Terrors take hold on him as waters, a tempest stealeth him away in the night. The east wind carrieth him away, and he departeth: a storm hurleth him out of his place." Sorrow and misery is very often represented by overwhelming waters, and God's wrath by waves and billows (Ps. 42:7 and 88:7).[9] The waters of the Flood did not only overwhelm the wicked, but came into their bowels. God's wrath on the ungodly is compared to this very thing. Ps. 109:18, "As he clothed himself with cursing like as with a garment, so let it come into his bowels like water." In the time of the Flood, the waters were poured down out of heaven like spouts or cataracts of water. God's wrath is compared unto this: Ps. 42:7, "Deep calleth unto deep at the noise of thy waterspouts." The waters of the Deluge were what the ungodly of the world could not escape or hide themselves [from] by resorting to caves in the ground, or digging deep in the earth, or flying to the tops of mountains; so likewise is the matter represented with respect to God's wrath on the ungodly in Is. 28:17, "The waters shall overflow the hiding place." Amos 9:1–3, "He that fleeth of them shall not flee away; he that escapeth of them shall not be delivered. Though they dig into hell, thence shall mine hand take them; though they climb up to heaven, thence will I bring them down: And though they hide themselves in the top of Carmel, I will search and take them out thence." And so in many other places.

Particularly is there a great resemblance between the destruction that was brought on the wicked world by the Flood and what is foretold of the wicked in the Messiah's times, as in Is. 24:18–20, "And it shall come to pass, that he who fleeth from the noise of the fear shall fall into a pit; and he that cometh up out of the midst of the pit shall be taken in the snare" (so that there shall be no escaping, let 'em flee where they will, as it was in the time of the Deluge): "for the windows from on high

8. JE deletes a reference to Ps. 11:6.
9. Cf. "Images" no. 27 (p. 58) and "Scripture" nos. [12]–[13] (p. 132).

are open, and the foundations of the earth do shake. The earth is utterly broken down, the earth is clean dissolved, the earth is moved exceedingly.... And the transgression thereof shall be heavy upon it." There is not only a resemblance between this representation of the punishment of the wicked world in the Messiah's days and the history of the Flood, but here seems to be an evident allusion to the Flood and a designed comparison of that destruction of God's enemies and what was in the time of the Flood, when we are told the windows of heaven were opened and the fountains of the great deep were broken up, etc. [Gen. 7:11–24]. So the destruction of God's enemies in the Messiah's times is represented as being by a flood, Dan. 9:26, "And the end thereof shall be with a flood"; and to a flood occasioned by a mighty rain, Ezek. 38:22, "I will rain upon him, and upon his bands, and upon the many people that are with him, an overflowing rain."

There is also a remarkable agreement between what we are told in Moses' history of the preservation of those that were in the ark and what is often declared in Old Testament prophecies concerning the preservation and salvation of the church by the Messiah. Is. 32:2, "A man shall be a hiding place from the wind, a covert from the tempest." Is. 4:6, "And there shall be a place of refuge, and for a covert from storm and from rain." Is. 25:4, "Thou hast been a strength to the poor, a strength to the needy in his distress, a refuge from the storm ... when the blast of the terrible ones is as the storm against the wall." Ps. 46:1–3, "God is our refuge and strength; we will not fear, though the earth be removed, though the mountains are carried into the midst of the sea" (as they in a sense were in the flood: they were in the midst of the sea, the sea surrounded and overwhelmed them); "though the waters thereof roar and are troubled, though the mountains shake with the swelling thereof." Is. 43:2, "When thou passest through the waters, I will be with thee." Compare these texts with Ps. 32:6, "Surely in the floods of great waters they shall not come nigh thee"; and Ps. 91:7, "A thousand shall fall at thy side, and ten thousand at thy right hand; but it shall not come nigh thee."

We may suppose that there was a resorting and flocking of animals from all parts of the world, such as [are] proper to hot countries, from the south; and such as dwell in colder climates, from the north. And as there are many countries that have their peculiar kinds of animals, so we may suppose there was a resorting from every quarter, a resorting of beasts and a flocking of birds: which is a lively resemblance of what is often foretold of the gathering of God's people into his church from

Detail of Eliakim Hayden stone, Essex, Connecticut, 1797. Rubbing by R. Edwards, india ink on rice paper (courtesy Wilson H. Kimnach). In the motif, the dove typifies the Holy Spirit and the grace of God, and the ark Christ and salvation, with the all-seeing eyes of God above.

all quarters in the Messiah's days, and coming to him for salvation, when all the ends of the earth should look to him to be saved (Is. 45:22); when God [should] bring the seed of his church from the east, and gather them from the west, and would say to the north, "Give up; and to the south, Keep not back: bring my sons from far, and my daughters from the ends of the earth" (Is. 43:6–7 and many other parallel places); and God would gather his people from all countries, agreeable to many prophecies, and it shall be said, "Who are these that fly as a cloud, and as doves to their windows?" [Is. 60:8].

The gathering of all kinds of creatures to the ark, clean and unclean, tame and wild, gentle and rapacious, innocent and venomous—tigers, wolves, bears, lions, leopards, serpents, vipers, dragons—and the door of the ark standing open to 'em, and their all dwelling there peaceably together under one head, even Noah, who kindly received them and took care of them, fed and saved them, and to whom they tamely submitted, is a lively representation of what is often foretold concerning the Messiah's days, when it is foretold that not only the Jews should be saved but unclean Gentile nations, when the gates of God's church should be open to all sorts of people (Is. 60:11 with the context). When proclamation should be made to everyone to come freely (Is. 55:1–9), and God would abundantly pardon the wicked and unrighteous (vv. 6–9), and would bring again even the captivity of Sodom and her daughters (Ezek. 16:53). And those nations should be gathered to God's church to be one holy society with Israel that were wont to be their most cruel and inveterate enemies, such as the Egyptians (Ps. 87:4 and 68:31, Is. 19:18–25 and 45:14); the Philistines (Ps. 60:8 and 87:4, Zech. 9:6–7); the Chaldeans (Ps. 87:4) and Assyrians (Is. 19:23–25); and the most wild and barbarous nations, Tabor and Hermon, that were noted haunts of wild beasts (Ps. 87:12, compared with Cant. 4:8, Ps. 42:6 and Hos. 5:1); and the nations of Arabia and Ethiopia in very many places (see "Fulfillment of Prophecies of Messiah" §160),[1] countries that abounded with the most rapacious, venomous and terrible animals.

---

1. There are two sections in "Fulfillment" numbered 160, but the one renumbered 164 on MS pp. 126–29 contains a list and a description of wild countries to be converted to Christianity. JE writes, in part, "It was foretold concerning very many of the particular countries and regions of the earth that were afterwards converted to the Christian faith, that they should be brought to the true religion in the days of the Messiah's kingdom. [...]

"Besides these particular countries [of] which the Jews of old had some knowledge, it was often foretold that the ends of the earth should be subject to the Messiah and enjoy the priviledges of his kingdom. By which ends of the earth, we must understand especially to

When it is foretold that the beasts of the field should honor God, and the dragons and the owls (Is. 43:19–20), and when it is foretold that the wolf shall dwell with the lamb, and the leopard shall lie down with the kid, and the calf and the young lion and the fatling together, and a little child shall lead them; and the cow and the bear shall feed, and their young ones shall lie down together; and the lion shall eat straw like the ox; and the sucking child shall play on the hole of the asp; and the weaned child shall put his hand on the cockatrice' den, and they shall not hurt nor destroy in all God's holy mountain (Is. 11:6–9 and 65:25), [these are lively representations of the Messiah's days].[2]

The ark was a great while tossed to and fro on the face of the Flood, ready to be overwhelmed, but at last rested on a high mountain or rock, and the company in it had enlargement and liberty and were brought into a new world. So the church in the Messiah's days is long in a state of affliction, tossed with tempest and not comforted (Is. 54:11). But when she is ready to be overwhelmed, God will lead her to the rock that is higher than she (Ps. 61:2), and she shall [be] brought out of her affliction into a new world (Is. 65:17–18), and shall dwell in God's holy mountain, as is often foretold.

Another historical event between which and the Old Testament representaions of spiritual things and particular things appertaining to the Messiah's kingdom there is a great resemblance, is the destruction of Sodom and the neighbor cities. There is great resemblance between this and the future punishment of the wicked in general, as represented in the Old Testament, that is represented by fire. Fire and brimstone were poured out from God out of heaven and rained down on these cities; so the wrath of God is often in the Old Testament compared to fire, and is represented as poured out from heaven on the ungodly, and particularly to be poured out like fire (Nahum 1:6, Is. 42:25, Jer. 44:6, Lam. 2:4 and 4:11, Ezek. 22:21–22, 31). So it is threatened in allusion to the manner of Sodom's destruction (Ps. 11:6), that upon the wicked God would rain snares, fire and brimstone, and an horrible or burning tempest (as it is in the margin),[3] and it is said this should be "the portion of their cup."

---

intend those parts of the earth that were beyond the then known world or beyond that part of the earth that was known to the Jews, in the extreme parts of the continent of that old world, or far off upon the sea."

2. Instead of the interpolation that the editors have here provided, JE, Jr. inserted: "events under the Messiah's kingdom are intended."

3. "In the margin" refers to the commentary in the King James Bible of the time.

That destruction came on Sodom suddenly and unexpectedly, while the inhabitants were in the midst of their voluptuousness and wickedness, and wholly at ease and quiet, in the morning when the sun arose pleasantly on the earth and when the idle and unclean inhabitants were drowned in sloth, sleep and pleasures; which is agreeable to what is often represented in the Old Testament of the manner of God's bringing destruction on the wicked. It came on Sodom as a snare. So it is said in that eleventh psalm, "snares, fire and brimstone" shall God rain, "and an horrible tempest: this shall be the portion of their cup"; that while the wicked is about to fill [his] belly, God shall cast the fury of his wrath upon him and rain it upon him while he is eating (Job 20:23); that God hath set them in slippery places, and that they are cast down to destruction in a moment, and are utterly consumed with terrors (Ps. 73:18–19); that their destruction falls suddenly upon 'em, as the fishes are taken in an evil net (when sporting securely in the water), and as the birds are caught in the snare (when they are feeding and pleasing themselves with the bait, Eccles. 9:12). Particularly this is represented as the manner of destruction's coming on them that harden their necks when often reproved, as the inhabitants of Sodom had been by Lot, as appears by Gen. 19:9. Prov. 29:1, "He, that being often reproved hardeneth his neck, shall suddenly be destroyed, and that without remedy."

There is a special resemblance between the destruction of Sodom and the destruction that is foretold to come on the enemies of God and the Messiah under the Messiah's kingdom, which is often represented as being by fire. Mal. 3:2, "Who may abide the day of his coming? and who shall stand when he appeareth? for he is like a refiner's fire." A refiner's fire is a vehement furnace, that burns up the dross. Ch. 4:1, "For, behold, the day cometh, that shall burn as an oven; and the proud, yea, all that do wickedly, shall be as stubble: and the day that cometh shall burn them up, saith the Lord of hosts; it shall leave them neither root nor branch." Ps. 21:9, "Thou shalt make them as a fiery oven in the day of thine anger: the Lord shall swallow them up in his wrath, and the fire shall devour them." Dan. 7:11, "I beheld till the beast was slain, and his body destroyed, and given to the burning flame." Yea, that destruction is represented as effected by raining down fire and brimstone upon them. Ezek. 38:22, "And I will plead against him with pestilence and with blood; and I will rain upon him, and upon his bands, and upon the many people that are with him, an overflowing rain, and great hailstones, fire, and brimstone." Is. 30:30,

"And the Lord shall cause his glorious voice to be heard, and shall show the lighting down of his arm, with the indignation of his anger, and with the flame of devouring fire, with scattering, and tempest, and hail stones." V. 33, "For Tophet is ordained of old; for the king it is prepared; he hath made it deep and large: the pile thereof is fire and much wood; the breath of the Lord, like a stream of brimstone, doth kindle it." Ch. 29:6, "Thou shalt be visited of the Lord of hosts with thunder, and with earthquake, and great noise, with storm and tempest, and the flame of devouring fire."

The Messiah's enemies are represented as destroyed with everlasting fire. Is. 33:11–14, "The people shall be as the burnings of lime: as thorns cut up shall they be burned in the fire.... Who among us shall dwell with the devouring fire? who amongst us shall dwell with everlasting burnings?" Is. 66:15–16, "For, behold, the Lord will come with fire, and with his chariots like a whirlwind, to render vengeance with fury, and his rebuke with flames of fire. For by fire and by his sword will the Lord plead with all flesh: and the slain of the Lord shall be many." With v. 24, "And they shall go forth, and look upon the carcasses of the men that have transgressed against me: for their worm shall not die, neither shall their fire be quenched." There was something in the destruction of Sodom and Gomorrah to represent this. The fire that destroyed them was as it were everlasting fire, inasmuch as the destruction it brought upon [them] was everlasting, irreparable desolation, so that they never could be built again, and never any creature, either man or beast, could live there any more; which is often particularly remarked in Scripture (Is. 13:19–20, Jer 49:18 and ch. 50:39–40, Is. 1:9).

The place, land or lake where Sodom and its neighbor cities once were, is a place that ever since abounds with that sulphurous, inflammable matter that is called bitumen and asphaltum, and in our translation of the Bible, "pitch," which is a further representation of eternal burnings and is a remarkable resemblance of what is foretold concerning the destruction of God's enemies in the Messiah's times. Is. 34:8–10, "For it is the day of the Lord's vengeance, and the year of recompenses for the controversy of Zion. And the streams thereof shall be turned into pitch" (or "bitumen" or "asphaltum"), "and the dust thereof into brimstone, and the land thereof shall become burning pitch. It shall not be quenched night nor day; the smoke thereof shall go up forever: from generation to generation it shall lie waste; none shall pass through it forever and ever."

This destruction came on Sodom just as the sun was up and had enlightened the world by its beams. So it is manifest by many prophecies that great destruction of the enemies of the church so often spoken of is when God comes and appears gloriously for his people, and when the morning of that glorious day of the church's light, peace and triumph is come on, and the glory of the Lord shall be risen upon the church and the Sun of Righteousness with healing in his wings. Then will the day come that will burn as a oven, and the world shall be as stubble [Mal. 4:1]. Lot's being so wonderfully delivered and saved from the destruction well represents that great preservation of God's church and people so often spoken of by the prophets, in that time of God's indignation and day of his wrath and vengeance on his enemies.

The remarkable similitude there is between very many things in the history of Joseph and the Old Testament prophecies of the Messiah, argue the former to be a type of the latter. Joseph is said to be the son of Jacob's old age (Gen. 37:3). So the Messiah is everywhere represented in the prophecies as coming and setting up his kingdom in the latter days. He was Jacob's beloved son (Gen. 37:3). So the prophecies do represent the Messiah as the beloved Son of God. They represent him as the Son of God.[4] (See "Fulfillment of Prophecies of Messiah.")[5] And they also represent him as one that should be in a very peculiar and transcendent manner the beloved of God. (See "Fulfillment of Prophecies of Messiah.")[6]

Joseph was clothed with a beautiful garment. So the prophecies represent the Messiah as clothed with beautiful and glorious garments. Zech. 3:4–5, "Take away the filthy garments from him. [...] I will clothe thee with change of raiment.... So they set a fair miter on his

4. JE deletes a reference to Ps. 2:7.

5. JE refers to "Fulfillment" §16, on MS pp. 20–21, where he writes, in part, "It was the doctrine of ancient prophets that the Messiah was the Son of God. There was some divine person that was known in the church of Israel by the name of 'the Son of God,' as appears by Prov. 30:4, 'What is his name, and what is his son's name, if thou canst tell?' This divine person that they called 'the Son of God' seems to have been the same divine person that had been wont from time to time to appear in a glorious visible form."

6. JE refers to "Fulfillment" §18, renumbered §15 on MS pp. 22–23, where he writes, "It was foretold that the Messiah should be a person that was in a peculiar manner beloved of God. This is implied in a [way that] may fairly be inferred from almost all the prophecies, but is more especially and directly expressed in Is. 42:1, where the Messiah is called 'mine elect, in whom my soul delighteth.' Is. 49:6–7, 'It is a light thing that thou shouldst be my servant to raise up the tribes of Jacob....Thus saith the Lord, the Redeemer of Israel, and his Holy One, to him whom men despiseth ... Kings shall see and arise, princes also shall worship, because of the Lord that is faithful, and the Holy One of Israel, and he shall choose thee.' (See also Ps. 2, and 45, and 110 and 89.)"

head, and clothed him with garments." Is. 61:10, "He hath clothed me with the garments of salvation, he hath covered me with a robe of righteousness, as a bridegroom decketh himself with ornaments, and as a bride adorneth herself with her jewels."

The sheaves[7] of Joseph's brethren in his vision all bowed down to his sheaf. So it is prophesied of the Messiah that God would make him his firstborn, higher than the kings of the earth (Ps. 89:27). Kings are said all of them to be the sons of the Most High, but this King is represented as made the highest by God, and all the rest as being made to bow down unto him. Ps. 72:11, "Yea, all kings shall fall down before him." Is. 49:7, "Kings shall see and arise, princes also shall worship, because of the Lord that is faithful, and the Holy One of Israel, and he shall choose thee" (see also v. 23). And Ps. 45:7, "He hath anointed [thee] with the oil of gladness above thy fellows." And many other places impart the same thing.

The saints are often in the prophecies called "the children of God." (See "Fulfillment of Prophecies of Messiah" §109–11.)[8] And they are represented as the Messiah's brethren. Ps. 22:22, "I will declare thy name unto my brethren: in the midst of the congregation will I praise thee." But the Messiah is everywhere represented as their Lord and King, whom they honor and submit to and obey. Yea, 'tis promised that every knee should bow to him (Is. 45:23).

The sun, moon and stars are represented as making obeisance to Joseph. So in the prophesies the Messiah is represented as God, whom the Old Testament often speaks of as ruling sun, moon and stars. (See "Fulfillment of Prophecies" §13.)[9] And the heavens are represented as declaring the Messiah's righteousness (Ps. 97:6 and 50:6). And the

---

7. MS: "sheaf."

8. "Fulfillment" §109–11, on MS pp. 82–87, renumbered §111–13. In §111 JE notes that people will become members of the nation of Israel by reason of their righteousness and holiness. JE begins in §112, "'Tis evident by the prophecies that this spiritual birth spoken of in the last section, whereby they are begotten and created of God and become his people in the days of the Messiah, is no other than the work of God's Spirit upon their hearts, renewing them and writing God's law in them, and making them of sinful to become righteous and holy." He writes, in part, in §113, "The prophecies do represent the people of God in the days of the Messiah as being distinguishedly privileged, in being admitted to an extraordinary nearness to God, a more intimate union and more free and friendly access and converse. God treats them not so much as servants, but more as friends and children and his dear spouse."

9. "Fulfillment" §13, on MS pp. 11–18, is renumbered §14. In a lengthy discussion JE presents many texts to support his statement, "It is evident by the prophecies of the Messiah that he was to be God," and thus the ruler of Israel to be worshipped by the church.

heavens, and earth, and sea and the whole universe, is represented as rejoicing and worshipping and praising the Messiah on occasion of his coming and kingdom (Ps. 96:11–13 and 69:34, Is. 44:23 and 49:13). And the sun is represented as being ashamed, and the moon confounded, and the stars withdrawing their shining (as it were veiling their faces, as the worshipping angels do), before the Messiah at his coming to reign in the world (Is. 24:23, Joel 3:15). And the stars [as] falling from heaven (Is. 34:4).

Joseph's father and mother are represented as bowing down to him to the earth. This was never fulfilled properly with respect to Joseph. His father, when he met him in Egypt, did not, that we have any account, thus bow down to him, and his mother was dead long before; both Rachel and Leah were dead before Jacob went down into Egypt. But the Messiah's ancestors are represented as worshipping him. The Messiah is represented as the son of David, but David calls him "Lord" (Ps. 110:1).

Joseph was hated by his brethren, which is agreeable to what the prophecies represent of the Messiah. Ps. 69:8, "I am become a stranger to my brethren, and an alien unto my mother's children." Joseph was hated by the sons of the same father, Jacob. So the prophecies do represent the Messiah as a son of Jacob, one of the seed of Israel, but as hated by the generality of his seed, the Jews. (See "Fulfillment of Prophecies.")[1] Joseph's brethren sold him for a few pieces of silver; so the prophecies do represent the Jews as selling the Messiah for a few pieces of silver (Zech. 11:12–13). Joseph's brethren went about to murder him; so the prophecies represent the Messiah as being murdered by the Jews. ("Fulfillment of Prophecies" §58–59.)[2]

Joseph was the savior of his brethren and of the church of God. He saved their lives. So the Messiah is abundantly represented in the prophecies as the Savior of his brethren, the Savior of the saints, the church of God, and of the nation of the Jews, and as one that saves

---

1. "Fulfillment" §41–43, on MS pp. 49–50, recount the ways in which the Jews rejected the Messiah. In §41, JE contends, "It was foretold that the Jews should not own him to be the Messiah because of the meanness of his appearance and should be confirmed in it that he is not the Messiah by seeing the contempt and sorrows that he should be the subject of." In §42, JE writes, "It was foretold that the Jews should esteem the Messiah a wicked man, one that would not hear or regard the law."

2. "Fulfillment" §58–59, on MS pp. 54–55, review prophecies "that the Messiah should die, and that he should die a violent death and die by the hands of his cruel enemies." JE explains in §59 the "cruelty of the Jews, his brethren, and his being hated and persecuted to death by their malice against him, excited by his zeal for God."

them from death. (See "Fulfillment of Prophecies," various parts.)[3]
Joseph was the savior of the world, not only of the seed of Israel, but
the Gentile nations; yea, of all nations. "For the famine was sore in all
lands, even over all the face of the earth, and all countries came into
Egypt to Joseph to buy corn" (Gen. 41:56–57). And his name,
"Zaphnath-paaneah," in the Egyptian language signifies "the savior of
the world." This is exactly agreeable to the Old Testament representations of the Messiah. (See "Fulfillment of Prophecies," various parts
of it.)[4]

Joseph was first in a state of great humiliation and afterwards in a
state of exaltation. In his state of humiliatiion, he was a man of sorrows
and acquainted with grief. His disgrace and sufferings were very great.
He suffered all unjustly from the hands of men, being innocent and
wrongfully condemned. He suffered as being guilty of horrid crimes,
and had his place and lot among great criminals, and suffered all with
admirable meekness; all which is exactly agreeable to the prophecies
of the Messiah. (See "Fulfillment of Prophecies.")[5]

Joseph was a servant to one of the chief rulers of Egypt, Potiphar,
the captain of the guard. So the Messiah is called "servant of rulers"
(Is. 49:7).

Joseph was one of the king's prisoners under the hand of the king's
chief officer of justice, the captain of the guard and as it were high
sheriff of Egypt. So the Messiah is represented as suffering from the
hands of God, who bruised him and put him to grief, and as executing
justice upon him for man's sins, making his soul an offering for sin.
Joseph's being cast into the dungeon is a fit representation of what the
prophecies do represent of the Messiah's extreme affliction and grief,
and his being brought to the grave (often called "the pit" in the Old
Testament), and remaining some time in the state of death.

Joseph was a prophet. He had divine visions himself, and had knowl-
edge in the visions of God and could interpret the visions of others.
This is agreeable to Old Testament representations of the Messiah.
(See "Fulfillment of Prophecies.")[6] He was a revealer of secrets, as his

---

3. JE discusses the salvation offered by Christ in "Fulfillment" §20–24, 81–84, 99–100,
and 169.

4. In "Fulfillment" §84, JE presents Christ as the Savior of the world.

5. JE details the sufferings of Christ in "Fulfillment" §52–73.

6. "Fulfillment" §34, on MS p. 44, reads, in part, "His predictions were very great and
wonderful, and most various and manifold, concerning himself, his disciples, the nation of
the Jews, his own followers, and his enemies, and all sorts of persons and the world of
mankind. His predictions, many of them, respected events that were to [be] fulfilled in his

name, "Zaphnath-paaneah," signifies in the Hebrew tongue, and revealed those secrets that none other could reveal, and after the wisdom of all the wise men of Egypt had been tried and proved insufficient (Gen. 41:8–36). This is agreeable to what is represented of the Messiah in Is. 41:28–29 and 42:1, "For I beheld, and there was no man; even amongst them, and there was no counselor, that, when I asked of them, could answer a word. Behold, they are all vanity ... Behold my servant, whom I uphold; mine elect, in whom my soul delighteth; I have put my spirit upon him: he shall bring forth judgment to the Gentiles."

Joseph is spoken of as distinguished from all, in that he was one in whom the Spirit of God was. How agreeable is this to the frequent representations in the Old Testament of the Messiah as one that God puts his Spirit upon. ("Fulfillment of Prophecies" §32 and 34; also "Prophecies of the Messiah.")[7]

Joseph is spoken of as one to whom none was to be compared for wisdom and prudence and counsel, through the Spirit of God (Gen. 41:38–39). This is agreeable to what is foretold of the Messiah. Is. 9:6, "His name shall be called Wonderful, Counselor." Ch. 11:2–3, "The Spirit of the Lord shall rest upon him, the spirit of wisdom and understanding, the spirit of counsel and might, the spirit of knowledge and of the fear of the Lord; And shall make him of quick understanding in the fear of the Lord." Zech. 3:9, "Upon one stone shall be seven eyes."

---

lifetime, at his death and after his death, in that generation and future generations. Never appeared such a prophet who so abounded in such plain predictions of future events, speaking in such a manner as having a perfect view of all future things before him; speaking of himself as of the knowledge that was his own and understanding his own predictions; and his predictions never failed, but were exactly fulfilled.

7. "Fulfillment" §32 on MS p. 43, begins, "The name 'Messiah' signifies 'Anointed,' and many prophecies represent the Messiah as being in an eminent manner God's anointed. But some of those ancient prophecies do represent that anointing as being a spiritual anointing not like the anointing of the kings of Israel, but a being abundantly indued with the Spirit of God. [...] And the Messiah is represented as one that should have the Spirit of God resting on him in an extraordinary manner." "Fulfillment" §34, MS pp. 43–45, presents Jesus' abilities as a teacher, counselor, and prophet. (See above p. 231, n. 6.) JE refers next to §44 of "Prophecies" (no. 1067), MS pp. 8–15, an extended discussion of Deut. 18:15–19. He argues that the prophets of the Old Testament prefigure Christ in his role as prophet. On MS p. 11, JE writes, "And 'tis abundantly manifest by other prophecies that the Messiah was to be a great prophet. What chiefly constituted anyone a prophet was that he was to be one that had the Spirit of God put upon him in his extraordinary influences. [...] But 'tis foretold that on the Messiah, himself the head and fountain of all this glory, God would in a supereminent manner put his Spirit."

Is. 52:13, "Behold, my servant shall deal prudently." See also that forementioned, Is. 41:28–29 and 42:1.

Joseph was exalted for this his great wisdom, which is agreeable to what is said of the Messiah. Is. 52:13, "Behold, my servant shall deal prudently, he shall be exalted and extolled, and be very high." So, agreeable to this, Joseph's exaltation was very great. He was exalted by the king of the country, who we may well suppose in this case represents God, seeing 'tis evident by the Old Testament that kings in their kingly authority are the images of God (Ps. 82:1, 6). Pharaoh exalts Joseph over all his house and people. So the prophecies do often represent God as exalting the Messiah over his people and his house, or temple, and over heaven. (See "Fulfillment of Prophecies" §92.)[8] The king exalted Joseph to be next to himself in his kingdom, to ride in the second chariot which he had [Gen. 41:43]. So the prophecies represent the Messiah as the second in God's kingdom next to God the Father, and exalted by him to this dignity. Ps. 110:1, "Sit thou on my right hand." Ps. 89:27, "I will make him my firstborn, higher than the kings of the earth." Joseph was exalted over all the nobles and rulers of the land of Egypt, excepting Pharaoh himself (Ps. 105:21–22). Agreeable to this, it is often represented in the prophecies that all kings shall be made to bow and submit to the Messiah. And it is also implied that the angels of heaven, as well as all nations of the earth, should be subjected to him by God. Dan. 7:9–10, 13–14, "I beheld till the thrones were cast down, and the Ancient of days did sit ... thousand thousands ministered unto him ... I saw one in the night visions, and, behold, one like unto the Son of man came with the clouds of heaven, and came to the Ancient of days, and they brought him near before him. And there was given him dominion, and glory, and a kingdom, that all people, nations, and languages should serve him." Dan. 12:1, "Michael, the great prince which standeth for the children of thy people," together with ch. 10:13, Michael, the first of the "chief princes," with the context that speaks of angels as princes.

Pharaoh invested Joseph with his own authority and honor as his representative and vicegerent, for he took off his own ring from his hand and put it on Joseph's hand. So the prophecies do represent God as investing the Messiah with his authority and honor, seating him in

---

8. In "Fulfillment" §92, renumbered 94 on MS pp. 65–70, JE describes Christ's ascension to a throne in heaven after his death and resurrection as a fulfillment of prophecies of his ruling on a throne in the temple and over all nations.

his own throne and causing him to bear the glory (Zech. 6:12–13). And there are many other prophecies that imply the same.

Pharaoh arrayed Joseph with change of raiment, pure garments and ensigns of royalty, agreeable to what is foretold of the Messiah (Zech. 3 and Is. 61:10). Pharaoh arrayed Joseph in fine linen (Gen. 41:42), as the Messiah is represented as clothed in fine linen (Dan. 10:5). For it may, by well considering the chapter, be gathered that person there spoken [of] is the same with Michael mentioned, vv. 13 and 21, and 12:1.

Pharaoh, when he exalted Joseph, committed all his treasures and stores into Joseph's hand, to bestow on others and feed mankind (Ps. 105:21). He made him lord of his house and ruler of all his substance. And particularly Joseph received these stores and treasures to bestow on his injurious brethren, that had been mortal enemies to him, which is agreeable to what is said of the Messiah's exaltation. Ps. 68:18, "Thou hast ascended on high ... thou hast received gifts for men; yea, for the rebellious also."

When Pharaoh exalted Joseph, he gave him his wife. So the Messiah's marriage with his church is represented as following his humiliation and attending his exaltation in Is. 53 and 54. Joseph marries the daughter of Potipherah [Gen. 41:45], which signifies "destroyer of fatness," a word of the same signification with some of the names given in Scripture to the devil. This Potipherah was priest of On, which signifies "iniquity," or "sorrow." So the prophecies do represent the Messiah as bringing his church into espousals with himself from a state of sin and wickedness. Jer. 3:14, "Turn, O backsliding children, unto me; for I am married unto you"; and Hos. 2, throughout; Ps. 45:10, compared with Ezek. 16:3, 6, 8, "Thy birth and thy nativity is of the land of Canaan; thy father was an Amorite, and thy mother [an] Hittite.... When I passed by thee, and saw thee polluted in thy blood ... behold, thy time was the time of love; and I spread my skirt over thee ... and entered into covenant with thee, and thou becamest mine." And the prophecies do everywhere represent the Messiah as bringing his people into a blessed relation and union with himself from a state of sin.

Joseph's wife's name was "Asenath," which signifies "an unfortunate thing." Agreeable to this, the Messiah is represented as espousing, after his exaltation, a poor, unhappy, afflicted, disconsolate creature. Is. 54:4–6, "Fear not; for thou shalt not be ashamed: neither be thou confounded; for thou shalt not be put to shame: for thou shalt forget the shame of thy youth, and shalt not remember the reproach of thy widowhood any more. For thy Maker is thy husband ... For the Lord hath called thee as a woman forsaken and grieved in spirit, and a wife of youth, when thou wast refused." V. 11, "O thou afflicted, tossed with tempest, and not comforted, behold, I will lay thy stones with fair colors, and lay thy foundations with sapphires." Hos. 2:9–16, "I will return, and take away my corn ... none shall deliver out of my hand.... I will destroy her vines and her fig trees ... I will visit upon her the days of Baalim ... I will bring her into the wilderness, and speak comfortably unto her.... And at that day, she shall call me Ishi." Vv. 19–20, "And I will betroth thee unto me forever; yea, I will betroth thee unto me in righteousness, and in judgment, and in lovingkindness, and in mercies. I will even betroth thee unto me in faithfulness: and thou shalt know the Lord." Is. 62:4–5, "Thou shalt no more be termed Forsaken; neither shall thy land be any more termed Desolate: but thou shalt be called Hephzibah, and thy land Beulah: for the Lord delighteth in thee, and thy land shall be married.... And as the bridegroom rejoiceth over the bride, so shall thy God rejoice over thee."

Joseph's brethren are in great trouble and perplexity, and are brought to reflect on themselves for their sins and deeply to humble themselves before him, before Joseph speaks comfortably to them and makes known his love and favor to them, and receives them to the blessings and glory of his kingdom. This is agreeable to what the prophecies do often represent of the Messiah with respect to sinners. Hos. 2:14–15, "I will allure her, and bring her into the wilderness, and speak comfortably to her. And I will give her her vineyards from thence ... and she shall sing there, as in the days of her youth, and as in the day when she came up out of the land of Egypt." (See also Jer. 3:12–13, 21–22; ch. 31:18–20.)

Joseph's brethren, before they were comforted and made happy by him, are brought to cry with the greatest humility and earnestness and penitence for their abuse to Joseph, to him for mercy, agreeable to the prophecies of the Messiah. Zech. 12:10–11, "And I will pour upon the house of David, and upon the inhabitants of Jerusalem, the spirit of grace and supplication: and they shall look upon me whom they have pierced, and they shall mourn for him, as one mourneth for his only son, and shall be in bitterness for him, as one that is in bitterness for his firstborn. In that day shall there be a great mourning in Jerusalem, as the mourning of Hadadrimmon in the valley of Megiddon." Hos. 5:15, "I will go and return to my place, till they acknowledge their

offense, and seek my face: in their affliction they shall seek me early."
Ezek. 36:37, "I will yet for this be inquired of by the house of Israel, to
do it for them." Jer. 29:12–14, "Then shall ye call upon me, and ye
shall go and pray unto me, and I will hearken unto you. And ye shall
seek me, and find me, when ye shall search for me with all your heart.
And I will be found of you, saith the Lord: and I will turn away your
captivity."

When once Joseph's brethren were thoroughly humbled, then his
bowels yearned towards them with exceeding great compassion and
tenderness of heart, though before he treated them as if he was very
angry with them. See, agreeable to this, Jer. 31:18–20, "I have surely
heard Ephraim bemoaning himself thus; Thou hast chastised me, and
I was chastised, as a bullock unaccustomed to the yoke: turn thou me,
and I shall be turned; for thou art the Lord my God. Surely after I was
turned, I repented; and after that I was instructed, I smote upon my
thigh: I was ashamed, yea, even confounded, because I did bear the
reproach of my youth. Is Ephraim my dear son? is he a pleasant child?
for since I spake against him, I do earnestly remember him still: therefore my bowels are troubled for him; I will surely have mercy upon
him, saith the Lord." Joseph perfectly forgives all their past ill treatment; he blots it out, as though it had never been, and will have it
remembered no more (Gen. 45:5–8 and 50:19–21). This is agreeable
to what is often spoken of in the prophecies as a great benefit God's
people shall have by the Messiah. (See "Fulfillment of Prophecies" §79
and §86.)[9]

The manner of Joseph's comforting his brothers, and in the manifestations and fruits of his special and peculiar love; his bringing them
near to him, making known himself to them as theirs in a near relation;
his treating them with such great tenderness; his embracing them; his
manifesting so great a concern for their welfare; his putting such
honor upon them before the Egyptians; his entertaining them with a
sumptuous, joyful feast in his house and at his own table; his clothing
them with change of raiment; his bringing them into his own land and
there giving them a goodly inheritance, plentifully providing for them
in Goshen, a land of light: all is remarkably agreeable to the descrip-

---

9. "Fulfillment" §79, renumbered 80 on MS pp. 59–60, begins, "It was foretold that the
sacrifice of the Messiah should make full satisfaction to God's justice, such as should make all
other sacrifice after that needless." Sec. 86, renumbered 87 on pp. 61–62, begins, "It was
foretold that forgiveness of sin should be one great benefit by which God should wonderfully display his grace through the Messiah."

tions given in the prophecies of the manner of God's comforting, blessing, exalting and manifesting his great favor to his church, after her long-continued sin and sorrows in the days of the Messiah's kingdom, in places too many to be enumerated.

Joseph's brethren at this time are like them that dream (Gen. 45:3–15), which is agreeable to what is said of the church of God when delivered and comforted by the Messiah. Ps. 126:1, "When the Lord turned again the captivity of Zion, we were like them that dream."

There is joy in Pharaoh's court among his servants and nobles on the occasion of Joseph's reception of his brethren (Gen. 45:16). Answering to this is Is. 44:22–23, "I have redeemed thee. Sing, O ye heavens, for the Lord hath done it." And ch. 49:13, "Sing, O heavens; and be joyful, O earth ... for the Lord hath comforted his people." And Ps. 148:4, "Praise him, ye heaven of heavens, and ye waters that be above the heavens"; with vv. 13–14, "Let them praise the name of the Lord: for his name alone is excellent; his glory is above[1] the earth and heaven. He also exalteth the horn of his people."

The remarkable agreement between many things in the history of Moses and the prophecies of the Messiah, argue the former to be a type of the latter. Moses was God's elect. Ps. 106:23, "Had not Moses his chosen stood before him." In his being so wonderfully preserved and upheld by God when in great danger, preserved in the midst of many waters, when he was cast into the river. Moses was drawn out of the water when a babe. (Compare Ps. 69 and Is. 53:2.) He was preserved in his banishment, preserved and delivered from the wrath of the king of Egypt, when he from time to time went to him with messages that so much provoked him; preserved at the Red Sea, in the wilderness, and in the midst of that perverse, invidious congregation, and delivered from the strivings of the people. This is agreeable to many things said in the prophecies of the Messiah.

Moses was twice delivered out of great waters, when he was designed by his enemies for death: once in his being drawn out of the river, and another time in rising out of the Red Sea. This is agreeable to the prophecies of the Messiah's sufferings and death, and his rising from them. Misery and wrath and sore affliction are often in Scripture compared to great waters, to waves and billows and great deeps, and the like; and the Messiah's sufferings in particular, as Ps. 69:1–3, 14–

---

1. End MS p. 22; the folio leaf comprising MS pp. 23–24 has been torn from the MS. The missing passage is taken from Dwight ed., *9*, 43–46.

15, and his deliverance out of those sufferings, is represented as being delivered out of great waters (Ps. 69:14–15). The region of the dominion of death and destruction is represented as being down under the waters (Job 25:5–6).[2] These deliverances of Moses, therefore, are agreeable to the prophecies of Christ's resurrection.

Moses was not only delivered from his troubles and danger, but his deliverances were followed with great exaltation, resembling the exaltation of the Messiah that the prophecies speak of. After he was drawn out of the water, he was exalted in the king's palace as his son and heir. After his banishment he converses with God in Mount Sinai, a resemblance of heaven, and is made king over God's church. In about forty days after his resurrection out of the Red Sea, he ascends up to God in Mount Sinai.

The things that are said of the burning bush do wonderfully agree with the Old Testament representations of the Messiah. It was not a high tree, but a bush, as the Messiah is called "the low tree" (Ezek. 17:24), and elsewhere "the twig" and "the tender plant" [Ezek. 17:22, Is. 53:2]. This bush was a root out of a dry ground, for it was a bush that grew in Mt. Horeb, which was so called for the remarkable dryness of the place. The word signifies "dryness"; there was no spring about the mountain till Moses there fetched water of the dry rock. It was in a thirsty wilderness, where was wont to be no rain. Therefore the children of Israel in that wilderness were supplied with water only miraculously. Hos. 13:5, "I did know thee in the wilderness, in the land of great drought." (See Deut. 8:15.)

That bush was the growth of the earth, as the human nature of Christ in the Old Testament is represented to be. Yet it had the divine nature of Christ in it, for this angel of the Lord that is said to appear in the bush has been proved to be the same with the Messiah from the Old Testament in my discourse on "The Prophecies of the Messiah."[3] This

2. Cf. "Images" no. 27 and "Scripture" nos. [12]–[13]. See above p. 221, n. 9.

3. JE refers to "Prophecies" §44, which forms part of a lengthy commentary on Deut. 18:15–19. JE writes, in part, "The children of Israel wanted one to stand between God and them. Thus [he] should be very near and dear to God, have immediate access to God, and see and hear him for them. And this is one thing wherein God declares that the prophets of the Israelites should not be like to Moses (Num. 12), and wherein it is afterwards declared that there had arisen none like him. But the Messiah by other scriptures was to be like Moses in respect of these things, but only far beyond him. Moses approached to God and talked with him as his peculiar friend (Ex. 33:11). But according to other prophecies, the Messiah should be much more the friend of God. [...] Moses saw his backparts, but the Messiah beholds his face, for he is the angel of his Presence, as appears by Mal. 3:1. He is there called the angel of the covenant whom they delighted in, who was doubtless the angel that appeared to Moses in

angel is said to dwell in this bush (Deut. 33:16), the more to represent the divine nature of the Messiah dwelling in the human nature.

This bush burnt with fire, agreeable to what the prophecies speak of the sufferings of Christ. Great calamity and affliction in the Old Testament are often called "fire." This was especially a resemblance of the wrath of God, that is often called "fire" in the Old Testament, and which the prophecies represent the Messiah as enduring. (See "Fulfillment of Prophecies" §70.)[4]

The bush was preserved from being consumed, though it burnt with fire, agreeable to the prophecies of the preservation and upholding of the Messiah: God's not suffering his Holy One to see corruption, etc. [Ps. 16:10]. The bush emerged alive and fresh out of the fire, agreeable to the prophecies of the Messiah's resurrection from the dead and deliverance from all his sufferings. The angel that dwelt out of that bush, who was the Messiah, comes out of the fire and appears in the bush, and [is] delivered alive from the flames to work redemption for his people. (See Ex. 3:8.) So the prophecies represent the Messiah rising from the dead and exalted out of his state of humiliation to work salvation for his people.

If we consider the remarkable agreement there is between the account Moses gives of the brazen serpent (Num. 21) and the representation the Prophet makes of the Messiah, we shall see good reason to think that the former was intended to be a type of the latter. Doubtless God's appointing that way for the healing of those that were bitten with fiery serpents, by making an image of those fiery serpents and putting it on a pole, had some significancy. It was not wholly an insignificant appointment. There was doubtless some important thing that God aimed at in it. It was not an appointment without any aim or any instruction contained in it, as it seems as though it must be unless some important spiritual thing was represented and exhibited by it. And whoever considers the remarkable agreement between this appointment and its circumstances, and the things spoken concerning the Messiah, will see reason to conclude that these are doubtless the things signified and pointed forth by it.

---

the bush, and afterwards, on the same mount Sinai when God entered into covenant with the people and appeared over the ark of the covenant in the holy of holies, that is called the angel of God's presence in Is. 63:9."

4. JE writes in "Fulfillment" §70, MS p. 56, in part, "It was foretold that there should be a special hand of God in the sufferings and death of the Messiah, and that so that those sufferings should be the fruit of his indignation and wrath."

That sin, misery and death that the Messiah is represented as coming to save us from, is represented in the Old Testament as being from a serpent. (See Gen. 3:1–6 and [vv.] 15 and 20.) The Messiah is represented as saving from all hurt by the most poisonous serpents (Is. 11:8–9 and 65:25). Sin, our spiritual disease, is in the Old Testament compared to the poison of the serpent (Deut. 32:33, Ps. 58:4 and 140:3).

The brazen serpent is called "a fiery serpent" (Num. 21:8), because it was in the image of the fiery serpents. So the prophets represent the Messiah as set forth as a sinner, appearing in the form of sinners, and of a great sinner. Is. 53:6, "All we like sheep have gone astray; we have turned every one to his own way; and the Lord hath made the iniquities of us all to meet in him" (for so it is in the Hebrew). V. 9, "He made his grave with the wicked." V. 12, "He was numbered with the transgressors, and he bare the sin of many." He was treated as the greatest of sinners. The Messiah being set forth in the form of a great sinner, he was as it were exhibited in the form of a very venomous serpent, according to the manner of representing things in the Old Testament: for there great sinners are represented as poisonous serpents. Ps. 58:3–4, "The wicked are estranged from the womb: Their poison is like the poison of a serpent: they are like the deaf adder that stoppeth up her ear." Ps. 140:3, "They have sharpened their tongues like a serpent; adders' poison is under their lips."

In order to the Israelites' being saved from death through the poison of the fiery serpents, the brazen serpent was set up as an ensign to the congregation or army of Israel. For the word translated "pole," signifies "ensign," which is the much more proper English of the word. This is in exact agreeableness to the prophecies of the Messiah. Is. 11:10, "And in that day there shall be a root of Jesse, which shall stand for an ensign to the people." Here the word translated "ensign" is the very same with the word translated "pole" in the twenty-first [chapter] of Numbers. The brazen serpent was set up as an ensign that it might be exhibited to public view, and the diseased are called upon to look upon it, or behold it. Thus in the prophecies men are[5] from time to time called upon to behold the Messiah. Is. 40:9, "O Zion, that bringest good tidings, get thee up into the high mountain; O Jerusalem, that bringest good tidings, lift up thy voice with strength; lift it up, be not afraid; say unto the cities of Judah, Behold your God!" (We may well

5. Here we return to MS p. 25.

suppose that when the brazen serpent was lifted[6] up in the wilderness, there was proclamation made by heralds to that vast congregation, calling upon them to look on that.) Is. 65:1, "I said, Behold me, behold me, to a nation that was not called by my name." Ch. 62:10–11, "Lift up a standard for the people. Behold, the Lord hath proclaimed to the end of the world, Say ye to the daughter of Zion, Behold, thy salvation cometh; behold, his reward is with him, and his work before him." Zech. 9:9–12, "Rejoice greatly, O daughter of Zion; shout, O daughter of Jerusalem: behold, thy King cometh unto thee: he is just, and having salvation ... And he shall speak peace unto the heathen ... By the blood of thy covenant, I will send forth thy prisoners ... Turn ye to the stronghold, ye prisoners of hope: even today do I declare that I will render unto thee." Is. 52:7–8, "How beautiful on the mountains are the feet of him that bringeth good tidings, that publisheth peace; that bringeth good tidings of good, that publisheth salvation; that saith unto Zion, Thy God reigneth! Thy watchmen shall lift up the voice; with the voice together shall they sing: for they shall see eye to eye, when the Lord shall bring again Zion."

The way that the people were saved by the brazen serpent was by looking to it, beholding it, as seeking and expecting salvation from it, as an ensign saves an army by the soldiers looking on it and keeping it in their view. Agreeable to this, it is said concerning the Messiah, Is. 11:10, "There shall be a root of Jesse, which shall stand for an ensign of the people; *to it shall the Gentiles seek*." And Is. 45:22, "Look to me, and be ye saved, all the ends of the earth." And faith and trust in the Messiah for salvation is often spoken of in the prophecies as the great condition of salvation through him. (See "Fulfillment of Prophecies" §101.)[7] The Chaldee paraphrasts looked on the brazen serpent as a type of the Messiah and gave it the name of the *Word* (Basnage's *History of the Jews*, p. 367.)[8]

The great agreement there is between the history of Joshua and the things said of him in Scripture, and things said of the Messiah in the

---

6. MS: "lift."

7. "Fulfillment" §101, renumbered 103 on MS pp. 75–76, begins, "They represent faith, or a spiritual coming to the Messiah, and looking to him and trusting in him, and in God through him, as that which will give persons an interest in him and the benefits of his kingdom."

8. Basnage, *History of the Jews*, p. 367: "The Brazen Serpent was not only look'd upon as a Type of the *Messiah*; but the *Chaldee* Paraphrasts do even give it the Name of *Word*. It is for that reason that the Apostles have not scrupled to apply to him that Type which hath disgusted some of the Fathers."

Old Testament, strongly argues Joshua to be a type of the Messiah. There is a great agreement between the names by which he is called in Scripture and the names and things attributed to the Messiah in the Old Testament. His first name was *Oshea* (Num. 13:8, 16), which signifies "savior." So the Messiah is called by the same name, *a savior*. Is. 19:20, "He shall send them a savior, and a great one." The word is of the same root with "Oshea." So again the Messiah is called "a savior" (Is. 43:3, 11; Hos. 13:4, 9–10; Obad. 21 and other places). So he is called *salvation*. Is. 62:11, "Behold, thy salvation cometh; behold, his reward is with him, and his work before him." And this name is agreeable to what is abundantly spoken of in the Prophets as the great work and office of the Messiah, which is to be a savior and redeemer, and to work out the greatest and most eminent salvation for God's people that ever was or will be; that which is therefore often called *the salvation*. (See "Fulfillment of Prophecies" §21.)[9] This name *Oshea* was by Moses changed into *Jehoshua*. Num. 13:16, "And Moses called Oshea the son of Nun Jehoshua," i. e. *the Lord the Savior* or *Jehovah our Savior*; which makes his name still more agreeable to the name and nature of the Messiah. And it is difficult to assign any other reason why Moses thus changed his name by the direction of the Spirit of God, but that it might be so. This is agreeable to those names by which the Messiah is called in the Prophets: *Immanuel*, "God with us," and *Jehovah, our righteousness* [Is. 7:14, Is. 12:2]. So Joshua is called *the shepherd, the stone of Israel* (Gen. 49:24), agreeable to names by which the Messiah is often called by in the Prophets.

Joshua's names being the same with the Messiah's and agreeable to his office, make it the more probable that it was that he might be a type of the Messiah, because it was frequently God's manner to presignify future things by the signification of names, as is evident in many instances. Joshua was God's elect; he was called to his office and exalted to his high dignity by God's election and special designation, agreeable to what is said of the Messiah in the Prophets. He resembled the Messiah in things spoken of him by the prophets in many things wherein Moses did so, particularly in near access to God in mount Sinai and in the tabernacle (Ex. 33:11 and 24:43 and 33:17). (See how

---

9. "Fulfillment" §21, renumbered 18 on MS pp. 24–27, reads, in part, "And this great work of divine goodness thus foretold was some great salvation that God should accomplish, that by the way of eminency was called the salvation of God as being eminently so, and so much beyond all other salvations, that they were not worthy to be compared with it."

Moses in these things resembled the Messiah in my discourse on "The Prophecies of the Messiah.")[1]

Joshua was a man in whom was the Spirit in an eminent manner. Num. 27:18, "Take thee Joshua the son of Nun, a man in whom is the Spirit," agreeable to what is often said of the Messiah in the Prophets. (See "Prophecies of the Messiah.")[2] 'Tis said of Joshua that he was "full of the spirit of wisdom" (Deut. 34:9), agreeable to many prophecies of the Messiah. (See p. 232 of this discourse.)[3]

Joshua was both a king and a prophet. (See Num. 27:18, and Deut. 34:9 and Josh. 23–24.) Herein he is like the Messiah. (See "Prophecies of the Messiah.")[4]

Joshua was the captain of the host of Israel, that fought their battles for them and subdued their [enemies], though many and mighty. He was their captain in their war with Amalek and, as we may suppose, the other enemies of Israel that they encountered in the wilderness. And he conquered the numerous and mighty enemies in Canaan, agreeable to what is represented of the Messiah everywhere by the prophets. He came up out of Jordan (when it was swelled with a great flood) into Canaan, as the Messiah is spoken of by the prophets as coming up out of great affliction, terrible sufferings and death, into heaven, a land of rest and great delight. (See concerning Moses' coming up out of the Red Sea, pp. 237–38.)[5] Great sufferings are in the Old Testament represented by the swelling of the Jordan (Jer. 12:5).

Joshua brought the children of Israel out of the wilderness and out of Bashan, and out of great waters, into Canaan, a land of rest flowing with milk and honey; agreeable to Ps. 68:22, "The Lord said, I will bring again from Bashan, I will bring my people again from the depths of the sea." And Is. 11:10, "There shall be a root of Jesse, which shall stand for an ensign of the people, and his rest shall be glorious." Hos. 2:14–15, "I will allure her, and bring her into the wilderness, and speak comfortably to her. And I will give her her vineyards from thence, and the valley of Achor for a door of hope: and she shall sing there, as in the days of her youth, and as in the day when she came up

1. See above p. 238, n. 3.
2. In "Prophecies" §44, on MS p. 11, JE argues that God ordained not a succession of prophets at Mt. Sinai, but rather a particular, great Prophet, Christ, to come after other prophets. See above p. 232, n. 7.
3. JE is referring to his earlier discussion of Joseph as a man of great wisdom.
4. See above p. 238, n. 3.
5. JE compares Moses' and the Messiah's deliverance from death.

out of the land of Egypt." And agreeable to many prophecies that represent the salvation of the Messiah as a bringing God's people into a state of liberty, rest and joy in Canaan, out of a state of bondage and great affliction in foreign lands; comparing of it to God's first bringing his people through the wilderness into Canaan, which were observed before.[6] And agreeable to many prophecies which speak of God's people as delivered from great misery and brought into happy circumstances by the Messiah, and as therein partaking with the Messiah in his deliverance from his sufferings and advancement to a state of rest and glory. (See "Fulfillment of Prophecies" §90.)[7]

Joshua, in going before the children of Israel as the captain of the Lord's host and bringing them into the land of Canaan, did that which is spoken of in the books of Moses and Joshua themselves as the office of that angel of God's presence, who (as I have shown is evident by the Old Testament)[8] was the same person with the Messiah. Ex. 23:20, "Behold, I send an Angel before thee, to keep thee in the way, and to bring thee into the place which I have prepared." V. 23, "For mine Angel shall go before thee, and bring thee in unto the Amorites and the Hittites, and the Perizzites, and the Canaanites, and the Hivites, and the Jebusites: and I will cut them off." Ch. 33:14, "My presence shall go with thee, and I will give thee rest." Josh. 5:14, "Nay; but as the captain of the Lord's host am I now come."

Joshua was a most glorious conqueror, as the Messiah is everywhere represented to be in the prophecies. Joshua entered Canaan, conquered his enemies and brought in his people to their rest and inheritance by his righteousness, or strict obedience to God's commands. Josh. 1:2–8,

> Go over this Jordan, thou, and all this people, unto the land which I do give them ... Every place that the sole of your foot shall tread upon, that have I given unto you, ... From the wilderness and this Lebanon unto the great river, the river Euphrates ... There shall not a man be able to stand before thee ... unto this people shalt thou divide for an inheritance the land, which I sware unto their fathers to give them. Only be thou strong and very courageous, that thou

6. See above p. 214.

7. "Fulfillment" §90, renumbered 92 on MS pp. 62–64, begins, "By the prophecies of the Old Testament, the deliverance, joy and prosperity of the Messiah's people should depend on his deliverance and exaltation as being their head. So that in his deliverance they shall be delivered, and in his exaltation they shall be exalted, and that they shall reign with him."

8. See above pp. 238–39.

mayest observe and do according to all the law, which Moses my servant commanded thee: turn not from it to the right hand nor to the left, that thou mayest prosper whithersoever thou goest. This book of the law shall not depart out of thy mouth; but thou shalt meditate therein day and night, that thou mayest observe to do according to all that is written therein: for then thou shalt make thy way prosperous, and thou shalt have good success.

(See how this agrees with the prophecies of the Messiah, "Fulfillment of Prophecies" §27, §82–83, together with §88–89.)[9]

God promised that he would be with Joshua and would uphold him and not fail him till he had complete victory over all his enemies, agreeable to what is said of the Messiah, Is. 42:1–4, "Behold, my servant, whom I uphold ... The smoking flax shall he not quench: he shall bring forth judgment unto truth. He shall not fail nor be discouraged, till he have set judgment in the earth: and the isles wait for his law." V. 6, "I the Lord have called thee in righteousness; I will hold thine hand; I will keep thee, and give thee for a covenant of the people, for a light of the Gentiles." Ch. 49:2, "He hath made my mouth like a sharp sword; in the shadow of his hand hath he held me, and made me as a polished shaft; in his quiver hath he hid me." Vv. 7–8, "Kings shall see and arise, princes also shall worship, because of the Lord that is faithful.... In a day of salvation have I helped thee, and I will preserve thee and give thee for a covenant of the people." Ps. 89:20–24, "I have found David my servant; with my holy oil have I anointed him: With whom my hand shall be established; mine arm also shall strengthen him. The enemy shall not exact upon him; nor the son of wickedness afflict him. I will beat down his foes before his face, and plague them

---

9. "Fulfillment" §27, on MS p. 41, begins, "The prophecies represent as though the Messiah should be a person in some remarkable and peculiar manner free from sin. Yea, that he should be perfectly innocent and holy, though they represent him as being one of the race of mankind." Sec. 82, renumbered 83 on MS p. 60, begins, "It was foretold that God should be well pleased and delighted with the perfect righteousness of the Messiah, as his servant and subject to his law, as that which magnifies the law and makes it honorable." Sec. 83, renumbered 84 on MS pp. 60–61, begins, "It was foretold that the Messiah should justify others or make others righteous by his righteousness; that he should perform as God's servant, as one subject to his authority and commands, and especially the righteousness he wrought out in laying down his life." Sec. 88, renumbered 90 on MS p. 62, begins, "By the prophecies of the Old Testament, the Messiah's success in his great undertaking of saving of his people, and the conversion of his followers, and the enlargement of his kingdom, and the prosperity, honor, joy and triumph of his people, should chiefly follow the Messiah's humiliation and sufferings." Sec. 89, renumbered 91, begins on MS p. 62, and JE notes these blessings depend upon, and are the reward of, Christ's sufferings.

that hate him. But my faithfulness and my mercy shall be with him: and in my name shall his horn be exalted." And many other places.

And agreeable to the prophecies of the Messiah, God made his enemies his footstool. Josh. 1:3–5, "Every place that the sole of your foot shall tread upon, that have I given unto you, as I said unto Moses. From the wilderness and this Lebanon even unto the great river, the river Euphrates, all the land of the Hittites, and unto the great sea toward the going down of the sun, shall be your coast. There shall not any man be able to stand before thee all the days of thy life: as I was with Moses, so I will be with thee: I will not fail thee, nor forsake thee." With ch. 10:24, "Put your feet upon the necks of these kings. And they came near, and put their feet upon the necks of them." Joshua, agreeable to the prophecies of the Messiah, was an intercessor for his people (Josh. 10). (See "Fulfillment of Prophecies" §96.)[1]

The high walls of God's enemies came down before Joshua, agreeable to the prophecies of the Messiah, Is. 25:12, "And the fortress of the high fort of thy walls shall he bring down, lay low, and bring to the ground, even to the dust." Ch. 26:5, "For he bringeth down them that dwell on high; the lofty city, he layeth it low; he layeth it low, even to the ground; he bringeth it even to the dust." Ch. 30:25, "In the day of the great slaughter, when the towers fall."

Joshua destroyed the giants (Josh. 11:21). Agreeable to this, see Is. 45:14, "The Sabeans, the men of stature, shall come over to thee ... in chains shall they come over, and they shall fall down unto thee." Is. 10:33, "And the high ones of stature shall be hewn down, and the haughty shall be humbled." This seems to be connected with the prophecy in the beginning of the next chapter, in the next verse but one [Is. 11:1].

God assisted Joshua in battle by destroying his enemies by great hailstones out of heaven. (See, agreeable to this, Is. 30:30 and 32:19, Ezek. 38:22.) Joshua conquered many kings. (See "Fulfillment of Prophecies" §163.)[2] Joshua made Israel to trample their haughtiest and strongest enemies under their feet (Josh. 10:24). (See, agreeable

---

1. "Fulfillment" §96, renumbered 99 on MS p. 71, begins, "As the prophecies represent the Messiah as a priest to offer sacrifice for his people, so they represent him as an intercessor for them."

2. "Fulfillment" §163, renumbered 166 on MS p. 130, begins, "It was often foretold that the kingdom of the Messiah should be so propagated and extended as to reach thrones and palaces, and that kings and the greatest men of this world should be subject to him."

to this, Is. 26:6, ch. 49:23, Zech. 10:5, Ps. 68:23, Mic. 7:10, Ps. 47:3, Is. 60:14, Ps. 58:10.)

Joshua did as it were make the sun stand still over Israel, agreeable to those prophecies of the times of the Messiah's kingdom (Is. 60:20, Zech. 14:6–7).

Joshua houghed the horses and burnt the chariots of the enemies of God's people in the fire (Josh. 11:6, 9). Hag. 2:22, "And I will overthrow the chariots, and those that ride in them; and the horses and their riders shall come down." Ps. 46: 9, "He maketh wars to cease to the end of the earth; he breaketh the bow, and cutteth the spear in sunder; he burneth the chariot in the fire."

Joshua divided unto Israel their inheritance, as one that God had appointed to be judge, what portion belonged to every [tribe]. (See in the prophecies of the Messiah that which is agreeable to this, "Fulfillment of Prophecies" §172.)[3]

There is also such an agreement between what is said of Israel's victory over the Canaanites under Deborah and what is said in the prophecies of the church's victory over her enemies in the Messiah's times, as argues the former to be a type of the latter. The Canaanites were exceeding strong, and God's people very feeble and defenseless, having no weapons of war, and were mightily oppressed by their enemies. So are things represented between God's people and their enemies, before their glorious victory and deliverance under the Messiah, in places too many to be enumerated.

This victory was obtained by a female. So the war under the Messiah against God's enemies is spoken of as maintained by the church, and the glorious victory obtained over them by her, who is spoken [of] almost everywhere in the prophecies as a woman or female, and is represented sometimes as such in prophecies of her battle and victory over her enemies. Mic. 4:13, "Arise, thresh, O daughter of Zion: for I will make thine horn iron, and I will make thy hoofs brass: and thou shalt beat in pieces many people." Cant. 6:13, "What will ye see in the Shulamite? As it were the company of two armies." Cant. 1:9, "I have compared thee, O my love, to a company of horses in Pharaoh's chariots." Ch. 6:4, "Thou art beautiful, O my love, as Tirzah, comely as Jerusalem, terrible as an army with banners." V. 10, "Who is she that

3. "Fulfillment" §172, renumbered 175 on MS pp. 137–38, is part of a lengthy description of the establishment of Christ's kingdom in the millennium, at which time Christ is the judge of the world.

looketh forth as the morning, fair as the moon, clear as the sun, and terrible as an army with banners?" And Deborah's being a prophetess well agrees with the church's being endowed with such abundant measures of the Spirit of God at that time of the church's glorious victory over her enemies, and all her members becoming as it were prophets, agreeable to the prophecies. (See "Fulfillment of Prophecies" §118.)[4]

The assistance given by Jael, another woman, the wife of Heber the Kenite, a Gentile, who slew Sisera the captain of the host, and so is said to be blessed among women, well represents the assistance of the Gentile church in the victory over God's enemies in the Messiah's days. Deborah tells Barak, the Lord is "gone out before thee" [Judg. 4:14]; which is agreeable to Is. 42:13, "The Lord shall go forth as a mighty man, he shall stir up jealousy as a man of war; he shall cry, yea, roar; he shall prevail against his enemies." And many other places in the prophecies.

The work of God in this victory of Israel is spoken of as parallel with those things that are represented in expressions very much like those used in the prophecies to represent what shall come to pass in the time of the church's victory over her enemies under the Messiah, such as going out of Seir; his marching out of the field of Edom; and the earth's trembling, and heaven's as it were dissolving and dropping, and mountain's melting (Judg. 5:4–5). (See Is. 34:4–6, and 24:18–21, and 63:1–6 and 64:1–4.) The work of God in this victory is compared to God's great work towards Israel at their coming out of Egypt and in the wilderness, just as the glorious victory of the Messiah is in the sixty-eighth psalm, almost in the same words (compare Judg. 5:4–5 with Ps. 68:7–8); which is a clear evidence that this victory is a great image[5] of that, for those things that agree in a third thing agree among themselves. It is manifest there was a plentiful shower at the time of that victory that swelled the brook Kishon, as is manifest from Judg. 5:4 and vv. 20–21. So at the time of the great victory of the church over her enemies under the Messiah, there will be an abundant outpouring of the Spirit, which is often represented in the Prophets as a plentiful and very [great] shower of rain. And these spiritual showers are in the

---

4. In "Fulfillment" §118, renumbered 120 on MS p. 90, JE notes the "extraordinary outpouring of the Spirit of God in those days," and in §119, renumbered 121 on MS pp. 90–91, he claims that the gift of prophecy "should become common among persons of all sorts, all nations, all ages and all degrees, not only among ministers, but the common people, even the lowest and meanest of 'em."

5. JE deletes: "resemblances."

sixty-eighth psalm compared to the very same showers on Israel that this is. So the effects produced in the time of the Messiah's victories are compared to the mountain's melting in Is. 64:1–4, as the effect of this victory is (Judg. 5:5), and both [are] compared to the same effects at mount Sinai. Barak on this occasion is called upon to lead captivity captive (Judg. 5:12), in the very same expressions that are used concerning the Messiah, concerning his triumph over his enemies (Ps. 68:18). 'Tis a remnant of Israel that is spoken of as having the benefit of this salvation (Judg. 5:13), as 'tis a remnant that is often spoken of as having the benefit of the Messiah's salvation (Is. 4:3, ch. 17:3, ch. 10:21–22 and 11:11, 16; Jer. 23:3; Joel 2:32; Mic. 2:12, and 4:7, and 5:3, 7–8 and 7:18; Zeph. 3:13; Zech. 8:12).

'Tis said of the remnant of Israel in Deborah's time, Judg. 5:13, "Then he made him that remaineth to have dominion over the nobles among the people: the Lord made me have dominion over the mighty"; agreeable to the honor of the saints in the Messiah's times, spoken of, Ps. 149:6–9, "Let the high praises of God be in their mouth, and a two-edged sword in their hand; To execute vengeance upon the heathen ... To bind their kings with chains, and their nobles with fetters of iron; To execute upon them the judgment written: this honor have all the saints." And what is said (Is. 49:23) of kings licking up the dust of the church's feet. The angels of heaven are represented as fighting in this battle, as Judg. 5:20, as they are in the battle of God's people under the Messiah. Ps. 68:17, "The chariots of God are twenty thousand, even thousands of angels." Cant. 6:13, "The company of two armies," compared with Gen. 32:1–2. The enemies of Israel in Deborah's battle were swept away with a flood (Judg. 5:21). (See Dan. 9:26, Ezek. 38:22, Is. 28:17.) The church on occasion of Deborah's victory triumphs thus: "O my soul, thou hast trodden down strength" [Judg. 5:21]. This is agreeable to Is. 26:7, ch. 49:23; Zech. 10:5; Ps. 68:23; Mic. 7:10; Ps. 47:3 and 110:1; Is. 60:14; Ps. 58:10.

The great agreement there also is between the story of Gideon's victory over the Midianites and things spoken of the prophecies concerning the Messiah, is an argument that the former is typical of the latter. Gideon brought Israel out of the wilderness and from the caves, rocks and mountains where they had had their abode (Judg. 6:2). This agrees with Ps. 68:22, "The Lord said, I will bring again from Bashan." And 89:12, "Tabor and Hermon shall rejoice in thy name." Hos. 2:14, "I will bring her into the wilderness, and speak comfortably unto her." Ezek. 20:35, 37, "I will bring you into the wilderness of the people, and there will I plead with you ... I will bring you into the bond of the covenant." Is. 42:11, "Let the wilderness and the cities thereof lift up their voice ... let the inhabitants of the rock sing, let them shout from the top of the mountains." Cant. 2:14, "O my dove, that art in the clefts of the rock ... let me see thy face." And Jer. 16:16, "I will send for many hunters, and they shall hunt them from every mountain and from every hill, and out of the holes of the rocks"; taken with the two foregoing verses, and vv. 19–21 following. Is. 42:7, "To bring out the prisoners from the prison, and them that sit in darkness out of the prison house." Vv. 22, 24–25, 43:1, "This is a people robbed and spoiled; they are all of them snared in holes, and they are hid in prison houses: they are for a prey, and none delivereth; for a spoil, and none saith, Restore.... Who gave Jacob for a spoil, and Israel to the robbers? ... He hath poured upon him the fury of his anger, and the strength of battle ... But now thus saith the Lord that created thee, O Jacob ... Fear not: for I have redeemed thee, I have called thee by thy name; thou art mine." Compare this with Judg. 6:2, 4–6, "The children of Israel made them dens which are in the mountains, and caves, and strongholds.... And they destroyed the increase of the earth, and left no sustenance for Israel, neither sheep, nor ox, nor ass.... And Israel was greatly impoverished."

God, agreeable to some of these and other prophecies of the times of the Messiah, first pleaded with Israel concerning their sin and brought 'em to cry earnestly to him before he delivered them by Gideon (Judg. 6:6–10). God did not send 'em deliverance till they were brought to extremity, agreeable to Deut. 32:36–37 and many other prophecies.

The enemies of Israel that sought their destruction, that Gideon overcame, were an innumerable multitude, and many nations associated and combined together, agreeable to many prophecies of the victory and salvation of the Messiah. Gideon was appointed to the office of a savior and deliverer of God's people by the sovereign election and special designation of God, agreeable to many prophecies of the Messiah. He was endued with might, and upheld and strengthened immediately from God, and by the Spirit of God and the spirit of might resting upon him (Judg. 6:14, 16, 34), agreeable to many prophecies of the Messiah. Gideon was as it were a root [out] of a dry ground, of a poor family and the least in his father's house; a low tree, without form or comeliness (Judg. 6:15), agreeable to the prophecies of the Messiah.

Gideon was not only the captain of the host of Israel, but was immediately appointed of God to be a priest to build the altar of God and to offer sacrifice to God, to make atonement for that iniquity of Israel that had brought that sore judgment upon 'em, that he came to deliver 'em from (Judg. 6:20–21, 24, 26–28). And he offered a sacrifice acceptable unto God, and that God gave special testimony of his acceptance of by consuming his sacrifice by fire immediately enkindled from heaven (v. 21). And his sacrifice procured reconciliation and peace for Israel (v. 24). These things are exactly agreeable to the prophecies of the Messiah. Gideon destroyed idols, abolished their worship, threw down their altars and set up the worship of the true God. (See things agreeable to this in the prophecies of the Messiah, in "Fulfillment of Prophecies" §134–35 and §153.)[6]

At this time that Gideon overthrew idols and their worship, those idols and their worshippers were solemnly challenged to plead and make good their own cause (Judg. 6:31–33), agreeable to Is. 41:1–7 and [vv.] 21–29. Gideon drank of the brook in the way and was so prepared for the battle, and obtained a glorious conquest over kings and the heads of many countries, and filled the places with the dead bodies; agreeable to Ps. 110:5–7, "The Lord at thy right hand shall strike through kings in the day of his wrath. He shall judge among the heathen, he shall fill the places with the dead bodies; he shall wound the heads over many countries. He shall drink of the brook in the way: therefore shall he lift up the head."

6. "Fulfillment" §134, renumbered 137 on MS pp. 101–03, begins, "It was foretold that in the days of the Messiah's kingdom, the Gentile nations should be brought to acknowledge and worship the true God and trust in him and praise him, and should be converted to the true religion; and the prophets represent that subjection that they shall be brought into to the Lord and to the Messiah, as a voluntary, chosen subjection and not what they are reduced to by the forceable power of a conqueror against their wills." Sec. 135, renumbered 138 on MS pp. 103–04, reads, in part, "'Tis evident by the prophecies that the Gentile nations should by the Messiah be thus brought to the acknowledgment and worship of the true God and be converted to the true religion, as in the foregoing section, from a state of heathenish darkness and idolatry. [...] Therefore these two last sections do contain a great and most clear and demonstrative evidence that our Jesus is the Messiah because this grand effect is what he has brought to pass. That institution which he established has actually been the means of bringing out all the principal part of the heathen world, and all heathen nations in the then known parts of the world, from their gross, heathenish darkness and off from the worship of their idols to the acknowledgment and profession and worship of Jehovah, the God of the ancient Israel; and all those heathen nations mentioned in Scripture have long since utterly forsaken their idolatry." Sec. 153, renumbered 139 on MS pp. 121–23, begins, "It was foretold that in the times of the Messiah's kingdom, the true God would very visibly and remarkably show himself above the gods of the heathen, triumphing over them to the confounding of them and their worshippers."

The company with Gideon was a small remnant that was left after most of the people departed. So is the company represented that shall obtain victory over their enemies in the Messiah's times. Is. 10:20–26, "And it shall come to pass in that day, that the remnant of Israel ... shall stay upon the Lord, the Holy One of Israel, in truth.... For though thy people Israel be as the sand of the sea, yet a remnant shall return ... Therefore thus saith the Lord, O my people ... be not afraid of the Assyrian ... For ... the Lord shall stir up a scourge for him according to the slaughter of Midian." Mic. 5:8–9, "And the remnant of Jacob shall be among the Gentiles in the midst of many people as a lion among the beasts of the forests, a young lion among the flocks of sheep: who, if he go through, both treadeth down, and teareth in pieces, and none can deliver. Thine hand shall be lift up upon thine adversaries, and all thine enemies shall be cut off."

Gideon's company, with which he overcame his mighty enemies, was not only small but weak, and without weapons of war; agreeable to this is Is. 41:14–16, "Fear not, thou worm Jacob, and ye men" (or "few men," as it is in the margin)[7] "of Israel; I will help thee, saith the Lord, and thy redeemer, the Holy One of Israel. Behold, I will make thee a new sharp threshing instrument having teeth: thou shalt thresh the mountains, and beat them small, and make the hills as chaff. Thou shalt fan them, and the wind shall carry them away, and the whirlwind shall scatter them: and thou shalt rejoice in the Lord, and shalt glory in the Holy One of Israel." And Mic. 4:7, "I will make her that halteth a remnant, and her that was cast far off a strong nation," with v. 13, "Arise, thresh, O daughter of Zion: for I will make thine horn iron, and I will make thine hoofs brass: and thou shalt beat in pieces many people: and I will consecrate their substance unto the Lord of the whole earth." Zeph. 3:12, "I will also leave in the midst of thee an afflicted poor people, and they shall trust in the name of the Lord." Vv. 16–17, "In that day it shall be said to Jerusalem, Fear thou not: and to Zion, Let not thine hands be slack," or "faint" (as it is in the margin).[8] "The Lord thy God in the midst of thee is mighty; he will save, he will rejoice over thee with joy; he will rest in his love, he will joy over thee with singing." V. 19, "Behold, at that time I will undo all that afflict thee: and I will save her that halteth, and gather her that was driven

---

7. "In the margin" refers to the marginal commentary in the King James Bible.
8. Ibid.

out; and I will get them praise and fame in every land where they have been put to shame."

The representation of a cake of barley bread tumbling into the host of Midian, and coming unto a tent, and smiting it that it fell, and overturned it, that the tent lay along, signifying Gideon's destroying the host of Midian (Judg. 7:13), is not unlike that in Dan. 2:35 of a stone cut out of the mountains without hands, smiting the image and breaking it all in pieces, that it all became as the chaff of the summer threshing floor.

Gideon and his company overcame and destroyed the mighty host of their enemies without any other weapons than trumpets and lamps. This is agreeable to the prophecies of the Messiah, which show that the weapons by which he should ovecome his enemies should not be carnal but spiritual, and particularly that it should be by the preaching of the Word. Ps. 110:2, "The Lord shall send the rod of thy strength out of Zion: rule thou in the midst of thine enemies"; together with Is. 11:4, "He shall smite the earth with the rod of his mouth, with the breath of his lips shall he slay the wicked." Is. 49:2, "And he hath made my mouth like a sharp sword."

The Word of God is in the Old Testament compared to a lamp and a light. Prov. 6:23, "For the commandment is a lamp; and the law is a light." Ps. 119:105, "Thy word is a lamp unto my feet, and a light unto my path." And particularly it is so represented in the prophecies of the Messiah's times. Is. 51:4, "A law shall proceed from me, and I will make my judgment to rest for a light of the people."

So preaching the Word in the Old Testament is compared to blowing a trumpet. Is. 58:1, "Lift up thy voice like a trumpet, show my people their transgression, and the house of Jacob their sins." Ezek. 33:2–6, "If the people ... take a man ... and set him for their watchman: If he ... blow the trumpet, and warn the people; Then whosoever heareth the sound of the trumpet, and taketh not warning; if the sword come, and take him away, his blood shall be upon his own head. He heard the sound of the trumpet, and took not warning; his blood shall be upon him. But he that taketh warning shall deliver his soul. But if the watchman see the sword come, and blow not the trumpet, and the people be not warned; if the sword come, and take any person from among them, he is taken away in his iniquity; but his blood will I require at the watchman's hand." Particularly is it so represented in the prophecies of the Messiah's times. Is. 27:13, "And it shall come to pass in that day, that the great trumpet shall be blown, and they shall come that were ready to perish in the land of Assyria, and the outcasts in the land of Egypt, and shall worship the Lord in the holy mount at Jerusalem." Ps. 89:15, "Blessed is the people that know the joyful sound: they shall walk, O Lord, in the light of thy countenance."

God destroyed the host of Midian by setting every man's sword against his fellow. Agreeable to this is Hag. 2:22, "And the horses and their riders shall come down, every one by the sword of his brother." Ezek. 38:21, "Every man's sword shall be against his brother."

Gideon led captivity captive, agreeable to Ps. 68. He led those kings and princes in chains that before had taken them captives in chains, agreeable to Ps. 149:7–9, "To execute vengeance upon the heathen, and punishments upon the people; To bind their kings in chains and their nobles with fetters of iron; To execute upon them the judgment written: this honor have all the saints."

There is no less remarkable agreement between the things said of Samson in his history and the things said of the Messiah in the prophecies of him. His name, *Samson*, signifies *little sun*, well agreeing with a type of the Messiah, that great Sun of Righteousness so often compared[9] in the prophecies to the sun. The antitype is far greater than the type, as being its end. Therefore when the type is called by the name of the antitype, 'tis fitly with a diminutive termination. Samson and other saviors under the Old Testament, that were types of the great Savior, were but little saviors. The prophets, priests, kings, captains and deliverers of the Old Testament were indeed images of that great light of the church and the world that was to follow. But they were but images; they were little lights that shone during the night. But when Christ came, the great light arose and introduced the day. Samson's birth was miraculous; it was a great wonder in his case that a woman should compass a man, as the prophecies represent it to be in the case of the birth of the Messiah. Samson was raised up to be a savior to God's people from their enemies, agreeable to prophetical representations of the Messiah. Samson was appointed to this great work by God's special election and designation, and that in an eminent and extraordinary way, agreeable to the prophecies of the Messiah.

Samson was a *Nazarite* from the womb. The word *Nazarite* signifies "separated." This denotes holiness and purity. The Nazarite was, with

9. JE deletes: "represented."

very great and extraordinary care and strictness indeed, to abstain from the least legal defilement, as appears by Num. 6; and the reason is given in the eighth verse, "All the days of his separation he is holy unto the Lord." And with the utmost strictness he was to abstain from wine and strong drink and everything that appertained in any respect to the fruit of the vine, wine being the liquor that was especially the object of the carnal appetites of men. And he was to suffer no razor to come upon [his] head, any way to alter what he was by nature, because that would defile it, as the lifting up a tool to hew the stones of the altar would defile it. The design of these institutions concerning the Nazarite, about his hair and about wine, is declared, Num. 6:5, "He shall be holy, and shall let the locks of the hair grow." This sanctity of the Nazarite, representing a perfect holiness both negative and positive, is spoken of in Lam. 4:7, "Her Nazarites were purer than snow, they were whiter than milk, they were more ruddy in body than rubies, their polishing was of sapphire." Therefore Samson's being a Nazarite from the womb remarkably represents that perfect innocence and purity and transcendent holiness of nature and life in the Messiah, which the prophecies often speak of. (See "Fulfillment of Prophecies of the Messiah" §27.)[1]

The great things that Samson wrought for the deliverance of Israel and the overthrow of their enemies was not by any natural strength of his, [but] by the special influence and extraordinary assistance of the Spirit of God (Judg. 13:25, and 14:6, 19, and 15:14 and 16:20); agreeable to many prophecies I have already observed of the Messiah's being anointed and filled with God's Spirit, and being upheld and helped and strengthened and succeeded by God.[2]

Samson married a Philistine, and all the women that he loved were of that people that were his great enemies, agreeable to those prophecies that represent the Messiah as marrying an alien from the commonwealth of Israel, as Ps. 45; and his marrying one that was a daughter of the accursed people of Canaan (Ezek. 16:3 and 8–14, together with the latter end of the chapter); and the many prophecies that speak of Christ's calling the Gentiles and his saving sinners.

Samson was a person of exceeding great strength. Herein he is like the Messiah, as he is represented, Ps. 89:19, "I have laid help on one

1. In MS, JE cites §41, MS p. 27, but intends §27, MS p. 41. See above p. 245, n. 9.
2. See above pp. 232–33.

that is mighty." Ps. 45:3, "Gird thy sword on thy thigh, O most mighty, in thy glory and in thy majesty." Is. 63:1, "Who is this ... travelling in the greatness of his strength?"

When Samson was going to take his wife, a young lion roared against him. So the enemy of the Messiah and his people is compared to a[3] lion roaring upon him, gaping with his mouth ready to devour him. Ps. 22:13, "They gaped upon me with their mouths, as a ravening and a roaring lion." V. 21, "Save me from the lion's mouth." Samson rent the lion as the lion would have rent the kid, which is agreeable to the prophecies which represent the Messiah destroying his enemies as a strong lion devouring his prey (Gen. 49:9–33). And the prophecies that speak of his punishing Leviathan with his great and sore and strong sword, his mightily and dreadfully destroying his enemies, treading them down as the mire, treading them in his anger and trampling them in his fury, sprinkling his raiment with their blood, etc. Samson is fed with honey out of the carcass of the lion, which is agreeable to what the prophecies represent of the glorious benefits of the Messiah's conquest over his enemies, to himself and his people, his own ascension and glory and kingdom and the glory of this people. (See "Fulfillment of Prophecies of the Messiah" §88–89, §92, §98.)[4]

Samson made a feast on occasion of his marriage, which is agreeable to Is. 25:6, "And in this mountain shall the Lord of hosts make unto all the people a feast of fat things, a feast of wines on the lees, of fat things full of marrow, of wine on the lees well refined." Is. 65:13–14, "My servants shall eat ... my servants shall drink, ... my servants shall rejoice ... my servants shall sing for joy of heart." And innumerable prophecies that speak of the great plenty and joy of God's people in the Messiah's times, and this accompanying the Messiah's marriage with his spiritual spouse. (See Is. 62:4–5 and vv. 7–9, and Hos 2:19–22, and Cant. 2:4 and 5:1.)

When Samson visited his wife with a kid and would have had conjugal conversation with her, he was refused, and her younger sister, that

---

3. JE cancels a reference to Cant. 4:8.

4. For "Fulfillment" §88–89, see above p. 245, n. 9; for §92, see above p. 233, n. 8. Sec. 98, renumbered 100, p. 72, begins, "It was foretold that the enlargement and advancement of the kingdom of the Messiah, and the increase of the number of his subjects, and his success in the actual salvation of his people, and their prosperity and joy and triumph over their enemies, should be chiefly after the Messiah's ascension into heaven and dependent upon it."

was fairer than she, given to him (Judg. 15:2); which is agreeable to what the prophecies represent of the Messiah's coming to the Jews first, when he was offered up as a lamb or kid, making the first offer of the glorious benefits of his sacrifice to them and their rejecting to him, and the calling of the Gentiles, and the more glorious and beautiful state of the Gentile church than of the ancient Jewish[5] church. (See various parts of my discourse on "The Fulfillment of Prophecies of the Messiah.")[6]

In Judg. 16:1–2, we have an account how Samson loved an harlot, and from his love to her exposed himself to be compassed round by his enemies. So the prophecies represent the Messiah as loving an harlot (Hos. 1:2, 7, 10–11, ch. 2:2, 5, 14–23, and ch. 3, throughout; and Ezek. 16, throughout; Jer. 3:14, with the preceding part of the chapter; Jer. 30:14, 16–22, with ch. 31:3–4; Jer 31:22–25), and represent his love to a sinful people, and from love seeking such a people to be his spouse, as that which occasions his suffering from his enemies (Is. 53, taken with the following chapter).

Samson, while his enemies are compassing him round to destroy him, rises from sleep and from midnight darkness and takes away the strength and fortifications of the city of his enemies, the gate of the city which his enemies shut and barred fast upon him to confine him, and the two posts, bar and all, and put them on his shoulders and carried [them] up to the top of an hill (Judg. 16:3). So the prophecies represent the Messiah, when compassed round by his enemies, rising from the sleep of death and emerging out of the thick darkness of his sorrows and sufferings, spoiling his enemies, and ascending into heaven and leading captivity captive. (See "Fulfillment of Prophecies of the Messiah.")[7]

Samson was betrayed and sold by Delilah, his false spouse or companion. So the prophecies do represent the Messiah as sold by his false and treacherous people. (See "Fulfillment of Prophecies" §51, §59.)[8]

Samson was delivered up into the hands of his enemies and was mocked and derided and very cruelly treated by them, agreeable to

---

5. MS: "Gentile." JE, Jr. cancelled the word and interlineated "Jewish."

6. JE treats these topics in "Fulfillment" §25–32, MS pp. 38–43; §39–48, MS pp. 48–52; §132–45, MS pp. 99–117; and §161, MS p. 130.

7. See above p. 245, n. 9; p. 244, n. 7; p. 233, n. 8.

8. "Fulfillment" §51, on MS p. 53, begins, "It was foretold that the Messiah should suffer greatly by the cruelty of men." For §59, see above p. 230, n. 2.

what is foretold of the Messiah. (See "Fulfillment of Prophecies" §50–51, 53, 55.)[9]

Samson died partly through the cruelty and murderous malice of his enemies, and partly from his own act, agreeable to what is foretold of the Messiah. (Vid. ibid. §51, 58–59 and §72.)[1]

Samson at his death destroyed his enemies, and the destruction he made of his enemies was chiefly at his death; which is agreeable to Is. 53:10–12 and Ps. 68:18, compared with the texts mentioned ("Fulfillment of Prophecies" §87–89).[2]

Samson overthrew the temple of Dagon, which is agreeable to what the prophecies say of the Messiah's overthrowing idols and idol worship in the world. (See "Fulfillment of Prophecies" §134–35 and §153.)[3]

9. "Fulfillment" §50, on MS pp. 52–53, begins, "By the ancient prophecies, the outward meanness, abasement, disgrace and contempt that the Messiah should be the subject of, should be exceeding great, even to the utmost extreme, and that his enemies should greatly mock and deride him." For §51, see above p. 257, n. 8. In §53, on MS p. 53, JE states, "Jesus being compassed round by his enemies in his last sufferings in that manner he was, making it their business to reproach him and mock and afflict him, is agreeable to Ps. 22:12–13." Sec. 55, on MS p. 54, also declares that Christ was set upon by his enemies.

1. For "Fulfillment" §51, see above p. 257, n. 8. In §58 on MS p. 54, JE writes, "It was foretold that the Messiah should die, and that he should die a violent death, and die by the hands of his cruel enemies, and die long before he came to the age of man, and in the midst of his days." Sec. 59, on MS pp. 54–55, reads, in part, "The rulers and teachers of the Jewish church, the house of God, were prodigiously provoked by Jesus' severe reproofs for their wicked mismanagements in that church or house of God of which they had the care and charge; their false teaching in the church, making void the commandment of God; through their tradition corrupting the worship of God's house; their proud behavior in God's house, affecting the uppermost seats in the synagogues and setting up themselves in the room of God; their desiring to be called 'Rabbi, Rabbi,' and so reproaching God who alone was their master; and for shutting up the house of God against men, neither going in themselves and hindering those that were entering; and for joining long prayers in God's house with covetous practices and wicked extortion, devouring widows' houses; and teaching men that if they swear by the temple or by the altar, it is nothing, as in Matt. 23; and by [Jesus'] going into the temple a little before his crucifixion and casting out all them that sold and bought in the temple, and overthrowing the tables of the money changers and the seats of them that sold doves, charging them with making the temple a den of thieves. By these things they were greatly enraged and never left till they had imbrued their hands with his blood." Sec. 72, on MS p. 57, begins, "It was foretold that the Messiah should be active in his own sufferings and death and that he should voluntarily undergo them."

2. "Fulfillment" §87, renumbered 89 on MS p. 62, begins, "Whereas the prophecies do very often speak of [the] great honor [and] glory that the Messiah should be possessed of, and also speak of a state of great meanness, abasement and suffering, even to the ignominious death; the prophecies do signify that his low, suffering state should be first and his exaltation and glory afterwards." For §88–89, see above p. 245, n. 9.

3. See above p. 251, n. 6.

Samson destroyed his enemies suddenly in the midst of their triumph over him, so that their insulting him in the prospect of his destruction instantly issues in their own destruction, agreeable to Is. 29:5–8.

There is yet a more remarkable, manifest and manifold agreement between the things said of David in his history and the things said of the Messiah in the prophecies. His name, *David*, signifies *beloved*, as the prophecies do represent the Messiah as in a peculiar and transcendent manner the beloved of God. David was God's elect in an eminent manner. Saul was the king whom the people chose (I Sam. 8:18 and 12:13). But David was the king whom God chose, one whom he found and pitched upon according to his own mind, without any concern of man in the affair and contrary to what men would have chosen. When Jesse caused all his elder sons to pass before Samuel, God said concerning one and another of them, "The Lord hath not chosen this, neither hath the Lord chosen this," etc. [I Sam. 16:8–10]. See I Chron. 28:4: there David says, "The Lord God of Israel chose me before all the house of my father to be king over Israel forever: for he hath chosen Judah to be the ruler; and of the house of Judah, the house of my father; and among the sons of my father he liked me to make me king over all Israel." (See Ps. 78:67–70.) Ps. 89:3, "I have made a covenant with my chosen, I have sworn unto David my servant"; agreeable to Is. 42:1, "Mine elect, in whom my soul delighteth; I have put my spirit upon him: he shall bring forth judgment to the Gentiles," and 49:7, "And he shall choose thee." He was a king of God's finding and providing, and [God] speaks of him as *his* king. I Sam. 16:1, "I will send thee to Jesse ... for I have provided me a king among his sons." II Sam. 22:51, "He is the tower of salvation for his king"; agreeable to Ps. 2:6, "I have set my king on my holy hill of Zion." He is spoken of as a man after God's own heart, and one in whom God delighted. II Sam. 22:20, "He delivered me, because he delighted in me"; agreeable to Is. 42:1, "Behold my servant, whom I uphold; mine elect, in whom my soul delighteth."

David was in a very eminent manner God's anointed or *messiah* (as the word is), and is so spoken of. II Sam. 22:51, "He showeth mercy to his anointed, unto David." And 23:1, "David the son of Jesse ... the man who was raised up on high, the anointed of the God of Jacob." Ps. 89:19–20, "I have exalted one chosen out of the people. I have found David my servant; with my holy oil have I anointed him." Samuel anointed him with peculiar solemnity (I Sam. 16:13). (See how this agrees with the prophecies of the Messiah, "Prophecies of the Messiah" §91.)[4]

David's anointing remarkably agrees with what the prophecies say of the anointing of the Messiah, who speak of it as a being anointed with the Spirit of God. So David was anointed with the Spirit of God at the same time that he was anointed with oil. I Sam. 16:13, "And Samuel took the horn of oil, and anointed him in the midst of his brethren: and the Spirit of the Lord came upon David from that day forward." (See "Fulfillment of Prophecies" §32.)[5]

David is spoken of as being a poor man, of a low family and in mean circumstances. I Sam. 18:23, "I am a poor man, and lightly esteemed." II Sam. 7:18, "Who am I? and what is my house, that thou hast brought me hitherto?" Agreeable to this, it is said of the Messiah in the prophecies that he was a root out of a dry ground, that he was a low tree [Is. 52:3, Ezek. 17:24].

David is spoken of as an eminently holy person, a man after God's own heart. He is spoken of in the history of the kings of Judah as one whose heart was perfect with the Lord his God (I Kgs. 11:4); one that went fully after the Lord (I Kgs. 11:6); one that did that that was right in the eyes of the Lord (I Kgs. 15:11, II Kgs. 18:3, II Chron. 28:1 and 29:2). He is spoken of as pure and upright [and] righteous; one that

---

4. This lengthy section of "Prophecies," MS pp. 94–100, treats Dan. 9:24–27. JE begins, "I have hitherto called the person spoken of in forementioned prophecies the 'Messiah' for distinction's sake, meaning thereby no more than the great King that was spoken of in the prophecies mentioned before, which person in some of the forementioned prophecies is called God's 'Messiah' or 'Anointed.' But now it remains to be shown that the person here called by the name 'Messiah' or 'The Anointed' as his proper and distinguishing name is the same great King so often spoken of in prophecies that have been already taken notice of." JE discusses the significance of the name "Anointed," and then he writes about David, MS pp. 96–97, in part, "Again, there is no person that we read of in all the history of the Old Testament that seems to be spoken as being so eminently the Lord's anointed as David, and therefore who is so likely to be the person intended by the great future prince of God's people here spoken of, that is called by way of eminency THE ANOINTED, THE PRINCE, as that greatest of all kings so often foretold in other prophecies and spoken of there and in the name of David, being very often called by that name as being the great antitype of David; and is called 'the rod out of the stem of Jesse,' and 'the branch out of his roots,' and 'the righteous branch growing up unto David,' and 'a branch out of his roots,' and the 'great King that shall sit on the throne of his father David, of the increase of whose government and peace there should be no end,' 'the bud or branch of the house of David,' and 'the lamp God has ordained for his anointed' (Ps. 132:17).

"Lastly, the person spoken of in forementioned prophecies is expressly said to be anointed, and to be anointed above other princes, and one whom God hath anointed and spoken of as he that is by way of eminency God's anointed or messiah."

5. See above p. 232, n. 7.

had clean hands; that kept the ways of the Lord and did not wickedly depart from God (II Sam. 22:21–27). (See how this agrees with what is said in the prophecies of the Messiah, "Fulfillment of Prophecies" §27.)[6]

David was the youngest son of Jesse, as the Messiah in the prophecies is spoken of as coming in the latter days. He has frequently the appellation of "God's servant." It would be endless to mention all the places; see 'em in the Concordance under the word *Servant* DAVID."[7] So has the Messiah often this appellation in the prophecies (Is. 42:1, 19, and 49:3, 6, and 52:13 and 53:11; Zech. 3:8).

David's outward appearance was not such as would have recommended him to the esteem and choice of men as a person fit for rule and victory, but on the contrary such as tended to cause men to despise him as a candidate for such things. I Sam. 16:7, "Look not on his countenance, or on the height of his stature ... for man looketh on the outward appearance, but the Lord looketh on the heart." I Sam. 17:42, "And when the Philistine looked about, and saw David, he disdained him: for he was but a youth." V. 56, "Inquire whose son this stripling is." Eliab, his elder brother, thought him fitter to [be] with the sheep than to come to the army (I Sam. 17:28); agreeable to Is. 53:2, "He shall grow up before him as a tender plant, as a root out of a dry ground: he hath no form nor comeliness; and when we shall see him, there is no beauty that we should desire him." David appeared unexpectedly. Samuel expected a man of great stature, and appearing outwardly like a man of valor; and therefore when he saw Eliab, David's elder brother, that had such an appearance, he said, "Surely the Lord's anointed is before him" [I Sam. 16:6]. His appearance was astonishing to Goliath and to Saul. So the prophecies represent the Messiah's appearance as unexpected and astonishing, being so mean. Is. 52:14, "Many were astonished at thee; his visage was so marred more than any man."

But yet David was ruddy and of a fair countenance, and goodly to look to (I Sam. 16:12 and 17:42); agreeable to Ps. 45:2, "Thou art fairer than the children of men." Cant. 5:10, "My beloved is white and ruddy, the chiefest among ten thousands."

---

6. See above p. 245, n. 9. JE also directs the reader to his comments on Ps. 24 in "Prophecies of the Messiah" §85, MS p. 78.

7. JE used Alexander Crudens' *A Complete Concordance to the Holy Scripture of the Old and New Testaments* (London, 1738), which is listed in the "Catalogue." See "*Servant* DAVID" under the section headed "Proper Names."

He was anointed king after offering sacrifice (I Sam. 16). So the prophecies represent the Messiah's exaltation to his kingdom, after he had by his sufferings offered up a sacrifice to atone for the sins of men. (See "Fulfillment of Prophecies" §74–81 and §87–88.)[8] David says of himself, I Chron. 28:4, "The Lord God of Israel chose me to be king over Israel forever." And God says to him, II Sam. 7:16, "And thine house and thy kingdom shall be established forever before thee: thy throne shall be established forever." (See how agreeable this is to the prophecies of the Messiah, "Fulfillment of Prophecies" §166).[9]

David by occupation was a shepherd, and afterwards was made a shepherd to God's Israel. Ps. 78:70–71, "He chose David his servant, and took him from the sheepfolds: From following the ewes great with young he brought him to feed Jacob his people, and Israel his inheritance." This is agreeable to many prophecies of the Messiah, who is often spoken of in them as the shepherd of God's people, and therein is expressly compared to David. Is. 40:11, "He shall feed his flock like a shepherd." Is. 49:9–10, "They shall feed in the ways, and their pastures shall be in all high places. They shall not hunger nor thirst; neither shall the heat nor sun smite them: for he that hath mercy on them shall lead them, by the springs of water shall he guide them." Jer. 23:4–5, "And I will set up shepherds over them which shall feed them ... I will raise up unto David a righteous Branch, and a King shall reign and prosper, and shall execute judgment and justice in the earth." Ezek. 34:23, "And I will set up one shepherd over them, and he shall feed them, even my servant David; he shall feed them, and shall be their shepherd." Ezek. 37:24, "And David my servant shall be king over them; and they all shall have one shepherd." Cant. 1:7, "Tell me, O thou whom my soul loveth, where thou feedest, where thou makest thy flock to rest at noon."

David was of a humble, meek and merciful spirit (I Sam. 18:23; II Sam. 6:21–22 and 7:18; I Sam. 24, throughout, and ch. 26 through-

---

8. In these sections of the "Fulfillment," JE recounts the prophecies which describe Christ's act of atonement for sin and the exaltation he and his people receive as a result of his sacrifice.

9. "Fulfillment" §166, renumbered 169 on MS pp. 133–34, reads in part, "Though the prophecies are abundant in speaking of great and mighty opposition that should be made to the Messiah and his people and kingdom, yet it is often foretold that his kingdom should forever continue after it is once set up, and that a profession of him should ever be upheld in the world."

out; II Sam. 2:5, 21,[1] and 4:9–12 and 7:18; II Sam. 22:26; and many places in the Psalms show the same spirit, too many to be mentioned). This is agreeable to what is said of the Messiah, Zech. 9:9, "He is just, and having salvation; lowly, and riding on an ass, and a colt the foal of an ass." Is. 42:3, "A bruised reed shall he not break, and the smoking flax shall he not quench: he shall bring forth judgment unto truth." Is. 40:11, "He shall gather the lambs with his arm, and carry them in his bosom, and shall gently lead those that are with young." Is. 53:7, "He is brought as a lamb to the slaughter, as a sheep before his shearers is dumb, so he opened not his mouth."

David was a person that was eminent for wisdom and prudence. I Sam. 16:18, "Behold, I have seen a son of Jesse ... prudent in matters." And 18:5, "And David behaved himself wisely." V. 14, "And David behaved himself wisely in all his ways." V. 30, "David behaved himself more wisely than all the servants of Saul." Ps. 78:72, "He guided them by the skilfulness of his hands." This is agreeable to what is said of the Messiah (Is. 9:6, ch. 11:2–3 and 41:28–29 with 42:1, ch. 52:13, Zech. 3:7).

David is said to be "a mighty valiant man." I Sam. 16:18, "Behold, I have seen a son of Jesse, a mighty valiant man." This is agreeable to Ps. 45:3, "Gird thy sword upon thy thigh, O most mighty, with thy glory and thy majesty." Is. 63:1, "Who is this travelling in the greatness of his strength? I that speak in righteousness, mighty to save." And in this very thing the Messiah is compared to David. Ps. 89:19–20, "I have laid help upon one that is mighty; I have exalted one chosen out of the people. I have found David my servant."

David was a sweet musician, [and] was preferred as such to all that were to be found in Israel to relieve Saul in his melancholy. He is called "the sweet psalmist of Israel" (II Sam. 23:1). He lead the whole church of Israel in their praises. He instituted the order of singers and musicians in the house of [God]. He delivered to the church the book of songs they were to use in their ordinary public worship. This is most agreeable to the prophecies of the Messiah, which do everywhere represent that he should introduce the most pleasant, joyful, glorious state of the church, wherein they should abound in the praises of God,

---

1. An unclear reference, since II Sam. 2:21 contains a speech of Abner. Possibly JE meant to cite II Sam. 3:31, where David commands Joab and the people to rent their clothes and put on sackcloth and ashes after the death of Abner.

and the world [be] filled with sweet and joyful songs after sorrow and weeping; wherein songs should be heard from the utmost ends of the earth, and all nations should sing, and the mountains and trees of the field, and all creatures, sun, moon and stars, heaven and earth, should break forth into singing; and even the dead should awake and sing, and the lower parts of the earth should shout, and the tongue of the dumb should sing, and the dragons and all deeps; the barren, the prisoners, the desolate and mourners should sing; and that all nations should come and sing in the height of Zion:[2] they should sing aloud and sing a new song or in a new manner, with music and praises excelling all that ever [had] been before. The particular texts are too many to enumerate.

The patriarch from whom Christ descends, for this reason [is] called "Judah," i. e. "praise," and the Messiah is represented as leading the church of God in their sweet and joyful songs. Ps. 22:22, "I will declare thy name unto my brethren: in the midst of the congregation I will praise thee." V. 25, "My praise shall be of thee in the great congregation." Ps. 69:30, 32, "I will praise the name of God with a song, and will magnify him with thanksgiving.... The humble shall see this, and be glad." V. 34, "Let the heaven and the earth praise him, the seas, and everything that moveth therein." (See also Ps. 138:1–5.) We read in Ps. 89:15 of the joyful sound that shall be at that time, and the day of the Messiah's kingdom is compared to the spring, the time of the singing of birds (Cant. 2).

David slew a lion and bear and delivered a lamb out of their mouths. So the enemies of the Messiah and his people are in the prophecies compared to a lion, as was observed before (p. 256).[3] So the prophetical representations made of God's people, that are delivered by the Messiah, well agree with the symbol of a lamb. The prophecies represent 'em as feeble, poor and defenseless in them[selves], and as meek and harmless (Ps. 45:4, and 22:26, and 69:32, and 147:6 and 149:4; Is. 11:4 and 29:19 and 61:1).

David comes to the camp of Israel to save them from Goliath and the Philistines, just at a time when they were in special and immediate danger, when the host were going forth to the fight and shouted for the battle. So the Messiah in the prophecies is represented as appearing to save his people at the time of their extremity. So God appeared

2. See Jer. 31:13, Is. 24:16, Is. 55:12, Ps. 148:3, Ps. 88:10, Is. 44:23, Is. 35:6, Ps. 148:7, Is. 54:1, Jer. 31:12.

3. The reference is to Samson's similarities to the Messiah.

for the redemption of his people out of Egypt. But Balaam, prophesying of the redemption of the Messiah (Num. 23:23), says, "According to this time shall it be said of Jacob and of Israel, What hath God wrought!" This also is agreeable to that prophecy of the deliverance of God's people in the Messiah's times, Deut. 32:36, "The Lord shall judge his people, and repent himself for his servants, when he seeth that their power is gone, and there is none shut up, or left." (See Ps. 14, and 53, and 21:11–12, and 46, and 58:7–11, and 60, and 118:10–29 and 138:7; Is. 8:9–22; ch. 9:1–7, and 25:4–5, and 26:16–21, and 28:21–22, and 29:5–8, and 30:27–30, and 31:4–5, and 40:28–31, and 41 throughout, and 42:1–4, and 51:7–23 and many other places.)

David was hated and envied by his brethren and misused by 'em when he came to 'em on a kind errand from his father, to bring them provision. Herein he resembled the Messiah, as Joseph did. (See "Fulfillment of Prophecies," concerning the Jews' rejection of the Messiah.)[4]

David kills Goliath, who in his huge stature, great strength, with his mighty army and exceeding pride, much resembled the devil, according to the representations of the devil in the prophecies of the Messiah's conquest and destruction of him, who is called "Leviathan" (Is. 27:1); which in the Old Testament is represented as an huge and terrible creature, of vast strength and impenetrable armor, disdaining the weapons and strength of his enemies, and the king over all the children of pride (Job 41).

David went against Goliath without carnal weapons. (See "Fulfillment of Prophecies" §107.)[5] David prevailed against Goliath with a sling and a stone, which is agreeable to Zech. 9:15, "The Lord of hosts shall defend them; and they shall devour, and subdue with sling stones."

David, when going against Goliath, took strength out of the brook in the way; agreeable to that concerning the Messiah, Ps. 110:6–7, "He shall fill the places with the dead bodies; he shall wound the heads over many countries. He shall drink of the brook in the way: therefore shall he lift up the head."

David cut off the head of the Philistine with his own sword. So it may be clearly gathered from what the prophecies say of the Messiah's

4. See above p. 230, n. 1.
5. "Fulfillment" §107, renumbered 109 on MS p. 81, begins, "The prophecies do represent the weapons by which the Messiah should conquer the nations and deliver his people not to be carnal but spiritual; and particularly the main weapon to be the Word of God."

suffering, and that from the cruelty of his enemies, and the consequence of them with respect to his exaltation and victory over his enemies, that the Messiah shall destroy Satan with his own weapons. (See "Fulfillment of Prophecies" §97, and the context of the texts there referred to.)[6] David carried the head of Goliath to Jerusalem, which is agreeable to what is foretold of the Messiah. Ps. 68:18, "Thou hast ascended on high, thou hast led captivity captive," together with the context.

David put Goliath's armor in his tent, which is agreeable to Ps. 76:2–3, "In Salem is his tabernacle" (or "tent"), "and his dwelling place in Zion. There brake he the arrows of the bow, the shield, the sword, and the battle."

When Saul saw David returning from his victory, [he] says over and over with great admiration concerning him, "Whose son is this youth?" (I Sam. 17:55), "Inquire whose son this stripling is" (v. 56), "Whose son art thou?" (v. 58); agreeable to Ps. 24:8, "Who is this king of glory?" Again v. 10, and Is. 63:1, "Who is this that cometh from Edom, with dyed garments from Bosrah? this that is glorious in his apparel, travelling in the greatness of his strength?" The daughters of Israel went forth to meet King David and sang praises to him when he returned from the slaughter of the Philistine, agreeable to Ps. 24, and 68 and many other places.

David obtained his wife by exposing his life in battle with the Philistines and in destroying them, agreeable to what is prophesied of the Messiah's sufferings and death, his conflict with and victory over his enemies, and his redemption of his church by this means, and the consequent joy of espousals with the church.

David was a great savior. He saved Israel from Goliath and the Philistines, and from all their enemies round about. II Sam. 3:18, "The Lord hath spoken of David, saying, By the hand of my servant David will I save my people Israel out of the hand of the Philistines, and out of the hand of all their enemies," agreeable to the prophecies of the Messiah. David was greatly persecuted and his life sought unjustly, agreeable to prophecies of the Messiah.

David's marriage with Abigail, the wife of a son of Belial, a virtuous woman and of a beautiful countenance, is agreeable to innumerable prophecies that represent the church of the Messiah that the proph-

---

6. "Fulfillment" §97, renumbered 95 on MS pp. 71–72, begins, "It was foretold that the devil should be remarkably conquered, confounded and punished by the Messiah."

ecies speak of as his spouse, as brought into that happy state from a state of guilt and bondage to sin. (See "Fulfillment of Prophecies," in very many sections.)[7]

David was resorted to by everyone that was in distress, and everyone that was in debt, and everyone that was bitter of soul, and he became their captain; which is agreeable to innumerable prophecies that represent the Messiah as the captain and savior of the poor, afflicted, distressed, sinners and prisoners, etc. David's host is compared to the host of God (I Chron. 12:22), which is agreeable to what the prophecies represent of the divinity of the Messiah, and God's people in his times, and under him becoming as an host of mighty valiant men that shall thresh the mountains and tread down their enemies, {and shall make the hills as chaff} [Is. 41:15]. David, as it were raised from the dead, was wonderfully delivered from death when in great danger, was brought back from the wilderness and from banishment and from caves of the earth that resembled the grave. (Ps. 30:3, "O Lord, thou hast brought up my soul from the grave.") Which is agreeable to the prophecies of the Messiah's restoration from his low and suffering state and resurrection from death.

David was made king over the strong city Hebron, that had been taken from the Anakims, the gigantic enemies of God's people; which is agreeable to the prophecies of the Messiah's conquering the strong city, and bringing low the lofty city, conquering the devil and taking possession of the mightiest and strongest kingdoms of this world. (See "Fulfillment of Prophecies" §154.)[8]

David's followers, that came to him to make him king, were men of understanding, mighty men of valor, and men of a perfect heart (I Chron. 12); which is agreeable to what the prophecies represent of the followers of the Messiah. David was made king by the act and choice both of God and his people (I Chron. 11:1–3 and ch. 12; II Sam. 2:4, ch. 5:1–3). This is agreeable to the prophecies of the Messiah. Hos. 1:11, "Then shall the children of Judah and the children of Israel be gathered together, and appoint themselves one head."

7. JE refers here especially to §87–90, described above in p. 258, n. 2; p. 244, n. 7; p. 245, n. 9.

8. "Fulfillment" §154, renumbered 158 on MS pp. 123–24, reads, in part, "It was foretold that the chief nations of the world for power, arts, wealth, merchandise and seafaring should be brought into the kingdoms of the Messiah, and particularly that he should subdue and bring into subjection to him the mightiest empire that should then be in the world. [...] 'Tis particularly foretold that the Messiah should conquer the mightiest heathen empire that should be in the world."

David was made king with great feasting and rejoicing (I Chron. 12:39–40), which is agreeable to what the prophecies do abundantly represent of the joy of the introduction of the Messiah's kingdom.

David was the first king of Jerusalem, that city so often spoken of in the prophecies as a type of the church of the Messiah. David insulted the idols as lame and blind and destroyed them (II Sam. 5:21), agreeable to ["Fulfillment of Prophecies"] §132–35 and §153.[9] David conquered the strongest hold of the Jebusites and reigned there. (See what was said before concerning his reigning in Hebron.)[1] He rescued Zion from the strong possession of idols and the enemies of God's people, and reigned in Mt. Zion, agreeable to innumerable prophecies of the Messiah. David's kingdom gradually increased from small beginnings till he had subdued all his enemies. (See "[Fulfillment of] Prophecies of Messiah" §123–26 and §162–63.)[2]

It was first in David's time that God chose Him a place to put His name there. Through him God made Jerusalem His holy city, and the place of His special, gracious residence, agreeable to the prophecies of the Messiah (Ps. 132:13–18, Zech. 1:17 and 2:12, and Is. 14:1). David provided a settled habitation for God, and God is represented as through his favor to David taking up a settled abode with them, no more walking in a moveable tent and tabernacle that might be taken down, and giving Israel a constant abode, that they might no more be afflicted and carried into captivity (II Sam. 7:6, 10, 24), according to many prophecies of the Messiah. David provided a place for God's

9. "Fulfillment" §132, renumbered 135 on MS p. 99, begins, "It was foretold that the Gentiles should be brought under the dominion of the Messiah and so under the visible dominion of the God of Israel." Sec. 133, renumbered 136 on MS pp. 99–101, begins, "According to the prophecies, the Gentiles were not thus to be brought under the dominion of the Messiah to enslave them, but to enlighten and cleanse them, to save and bless them, and make them happy." For §134–35, and 153, see above p. 251, n. 6.

1. See above p. 267.

2. "Fulfillment" §123, renumbered 125 on MS pp. 92–93, begins, "It was foretold that the increase of the Messiah's kingdom and people should be small at first and should rise to such a great multitude and vast extent from small beginnings." Sec. 124, renumbered 126 on MS p. 93, begins, "It was foretold that the propagation of the Messiah's kingdom and interest, and the progress he should make in the work of his power, increasing the number of his people, should be exceeding swift." Sec. 125, renumbered 127 on MS p. 93, begins, "It was foretold that the Messiah should be greatly prospered in glorious displays of his power, vastly multiplying and increasing his people and willing subjects in the early days of his kingdom." Sec. 126, renumbered 128 on MS p. 93, begins, "It was foretold that the combined endeavors of rulers and people in opposition to the Messiah should be in vain and should not avail to hinder the prevalency of his interest and kingdom." Sec. 162, renumbered 165 on MS p. 130, reads, in part, "It was foretold that the common sort of people

habitation in Zion and in Mt. Moriah, agreeable to Zech. 6:12, "He shall build the temple of the Lord."

David brought up the ark to abide in the midst of God's people after it had departed into the land of the Philistines and had long remained in the utmost confines of the land in Kirjathjearim, which is agreeable to what the prophecies represent of the benefit the people of God in the Messiah's days shall receive in the return of the tokens of God's presence to them after long absence, and his placing his tabernacle in the midst of them, and his soul's no more abhorring them.

David ascended into the hill of the Lord with the ark at the head of all Israel, rejoicing, and gave gifts to men (II Sam. 6); but this is agreeable to what is said of the ascension of the Messiah (Ps. 68). David ascended with the ark wherein was the Law of God, as the Messiah ascended with that human nature that was the cabinet of the Law. David, after he had ascended, returned to bless his household, as the Messiah especially blessed his church after his ascension. (See "Fulfillment of Prophecies.")[3] But Michal, his first wife, despised him for his abasement and received no part in this blessing, but was as it were repudiated; as the prophecies do represent the Jews, the Messiah's first wife, as despising the Messiah for his humiliation and so as not receiving the benefits and blessings that he should bestow after his ascension, but as being repudiated.

When David came to the crown, God broke forth on his enemies as the breach of water, and in a dreadful storm of thunder, fire and hail (II Sam. 5:20, I Chron. 14:11 and Ps. 18); which is agreeable to Is. 24:18–20, Dan 9:26, Ezek. 38:22, Is. 30:30 and 32:19. Yea, the destruction of the enemies of God's people in the days of the Messiah is expressly compared to that very breaking forth of God on the enemies of David. Is. 28:21, "For the Lord shall rise up as in Mt. Perazim."

The king of Tyre (that was above all others in the world a city noted for merchandise and seafaring) built David an house (II Sam. 5:11, I Chron. 14:1). (See "Fulfillment of Prophecies" §154.)[4]

David was not only a king, but a great prophet (II Sam. 23:2), and

chiefly should be brought first to enjoy the benefits of the Messiah's kingdom, and afterwards persons in higher stations." Sec. 163, renumbered 166 on MS p. 130, begins, "It was often foretold that the kingdom of the Messiah should be so propagated and extended as to reach thrones and palaces, and that kings and the greatest men of this world should be subject to him."

3. JE refers the reader to "Fulfillment" §98, renumbered 100 on MS p. 72; see above p. 256, n. 4.

4. See above p. 267, n. 8.

also was a priest. He officiated as such on occasion of the bringing up of the ark (II Sam. 6:13–14, 17–18; I Chron. 15:27). Again, he officiated as such (II Sam. 27:17–25 and I Chron. 16:21–36), and in some respects he officiated as chief in all sacerdotal matters, ordering all things in the house of God, directing and ordering the priests in things relating to their function and disposing them into courses, etc. So the prophecies do abundantly represent the Messiah as prophet, priest and king. (See "Prophecies of the Messiah" and "Fulfillment of Prophecies," in many parts.)[5]

David is spoken of as the man that was "raised up on high" [II Sam. 23:1], which is agreeable to what is said of the Messiah in Ps. 89:19, "I have exalted one chosen out of the people." And v. 27, "I will make him my first-born, higher than the kings of the earth." Ps. 45:6, "Thy throne, O God, is forever." And Ps. 110:1, "Sit thou on my right hand," and innumerable other places. He is spoken of as eminently a just ruler, one that fed God's people in the integrity of his heart and executed judgment and justice (II Sam. 8:15, I Chron. 18:14); which is agreeable to that which is abundantly spoken of the Messiah, as the just ruler over men; the king that shall reign in righteousness; he that shall sit on the throne of his father David, to order and establish it with judgment and justice; the righteous branch that shall grow up to David, etc.[6] God made David a name like the name of the great men that are in the earth (II Sam. 7:9; see also ch. 8:13), agreeable to Is. 53:12, "Therefore will I divide him a portion with the great." "The fame of David went out into all lands; and the Lord brought the fear of him upon all nations" (I Chron. 14:17), agreeable to Ps. 45:17, "I will make thy name to be remembered"; Ps. 72:11, "All nations shall serve him"; [v.] 17, "His name shall endure forever," and innumerable other places.

David carried up the ark clothed with a robe of fine linen (I Chron.

5. David's roles as prophet, priest, and king are covered in "Prophecies" §44, 53, 74, 85, 89, and 91. "Fulfillment" §74, renumbered 75 on MS pp. 57–58, begins, "Though the prophecies almost everywhere represent the Messiah as a king, yet it was foretold that he should also be a priest." Sec. 95, renumbered 98 on MS p. 71, reads, "As the apostle Paul in his Epistle to the Hebrews represents that Jesus Christ in this differs from the high priest of old; that whereas they used to enter into the holiest of all but once a year to appear before the throne of God, Jesus Christ was a high priest that entered into the holy of holies to sit down on the throne of God, on God's right hand, there to remain continually as a royal priest. So in exact agreement with this is that prophecy in Zech. 6:13, 'Even he shall build the temple of the Lord; and he shall bear the glory, and shall sit and rule upon his throne' (i. e. upon God's throne); 'and he shall be a priest upon his throne.'"

6. JE paraphrases Jer. 3:5 and 33:15.

15:27), agreeable to Is. 61:10, "He hath clothed me with the garments of salvation, he hath covered me with a robe of righteousness." Zech. 3:4, "Take away the filthy garments from him. And unto him he said, Behold, I have caused thine iniquity to pass from thee, and I will clothe thee with change of raiment." (See also Dan. 10:5, compared with vv. 13 and 21, and ch. 12:1.)

God was with David whithersoever he went, and cut off all his enemies (II Sam. 7:9 and 8:6, 14; I Chron. 17:8, 10 and 18:6, 13; II Sam. 22: 1–20), agreeable to Ps. 2, and 45, and 110, and 89 and innumerable other places.

David subdued all the remainders of the Canaanites and the ancient heathen inhabitants of the land, and so perfected what Joshua had begun in giving the people. (See what is said of Joshua as a type of the Messiah in this respect, pp. 244–45.)[7] David brought it to pass that the Canaanites and enemies of Israel should no longer dwell with them, or [be] mixed among them in the same land. Joel 3:17, "No stranger shall pass through thee any more." Zech. 14:21, "In that day there shall be no more the Canaanite in the house of the Lord." Ps. 69:35–36, "For God will save Zion, and will build the cities of Judah: that they may dwell there, and have it in possession. The seed also of his servants shall inherit it: and they that love thy name shall dwell therein." Is. 65:9–11, "And I will bring forth a seed out of Jacob, and out of Judah an inheritor of my mountains: and mine elect shall inherit it, and my servants shall dwell there. And Sharon shall be a fold of flocks, and the valley of Achor a place for the herds to lie down in, for my people that have sought me. But ye are they that forsake the Lord, that forget my holy mountain, that prepare a table for that troop, and that furnish the drink offering unto that number." Is. 35:8, "An highway shall be there, and a way, and it shall be called The way of holiness; the unclean shall not pass over it." Ezek. 20:38, "And I will purge out from among you the rebels, and them that transgress against me: I will bring them forth out of the country where they sojourn, and they shall not enter into the land of Israel."

David subdued the Philistines, and the Moabites, and Ammonites and the Edomites, agreeable to Is. 11:14, Num. 24:17, Ps. 60:8 and 108:9, Is. 25:10, chs. 34 and 63, and Ezek. 35 and 36:5. David's kingdom reached from the river to the ends of the earth (II Sam. 8:3; I Chron. 18:3), agreeable to Ps. 72:8, Zech. 9:10.

7. Joshua's exploits as a "glorious conqueror" are recounted.

David's reign was a time of the destruction of giants. He slew all the remnant of the race of giants (I Sam. 17, II Sam. 21:18–22 and 23:20–21, I Chron. 20:4–8 and 11:22–23), agreeable to Is. 10:33, "And the high ones of stature shall be hewn down, and the haughty shall be humbled." This seems (as I observed before)[8] to be connected with the prophecy in the beginning of the next chapter, in the next verse but one. Is. 45:14, "The Sabeans, men of stature, shall come over to thee; in chains shall they come over." Ps. 76:5, "The stouthearted are spoiled, they have slept their sleep."

David destroyed the chariots and houghed the horses of the enemies of God's people (II Sam. 8:4 and 10:18, I Chron. 18:4 and 19:7), agreeable to Ps. 46:9, "He breaketh the bow, and cutteth the spear in sunder; he burneth the chariot in the fire." Ps. 76:3, "There brake he the arrows of the bow, the shield, and the sword, and the battle." V. 6, "At thy rebuke, O God of Jacob, both the chariot and horse are cast into a dead sleep." (See also Ezek. 39:9–10, 20 and Zech. 12:3–4.)

What David says (Ps. 18 and II Sam. 22) of the manner in which God appeared for him against his enemies, to destroy them in a terrible tempest with thunder, lightning, earthquake, devouring fire, etc. is agreeable to many things in the prophecies of the Messiah. (See what has before been observed, when speaking of the Deluge, and destruction of Sodom, and the destruction of the Amorites in Joshua's time.)[9]

Other kings brought presents unto David and bowed down unto him (II Sam. 5:11, I Chron. 14:1, II Sam. 8:2 and v. 10, I Chron. 18:10, II Sam. 10:19, I Chron. 22:4), agreeable to Ps. 72:10–11 and 45:12, 68:29, Is. 49:7 and 60:9. The honor, dominion and crown of David's enemies was given unto him (II Sam. 12:30 and I Chron. 20:2). Ezek. 21:26, "Thus saith the Lord; Remove the diadem, and take off the crown: this shall not be the same: exalt him that is low, and abase him that is high. Perverted, perverted, perverted will I make it, until he come whose right it is; and I will give it him."

David's sons were princes (I Chron. 28:1–8). David's sons were chief rulers or princes (as it is in the margin),[1] agreeable to Ps. 45:16, "Instead of thy fathers shall be thy children, whom thou mayest make princes in all the earth."

David brought the wealth of the heathen into Jerusalem and dedicated it to God, and as it were built the temple with it (II Sam. 8:11–12,

---

8. See above p. 246.
9. See above pp. 221–22, pp. 225–28, pp. 215–16.
1. "In the margin" refers to the marginal commentary in the King James Bible.

I Chron. 18:11 and 26:26–27, and ch. 22, throughout, and ch. 29); agreeable to Mic. 4:13, "Arise, thresh, O daughters of Zion: for I will make thine horn iron, and thy hoofs brass: and thou shalt beat in pieces many people: and I will consecrate their gain unto the Lord, and their substance unto the Lord of the whole earth." Is. 23:17–18, "The Lord will visit Tyre ... And her merchandise and hire shall be holiness to the Lord: it shall not be treasured nor laid up; for her merchandise shall be for them that dwell before the Lord, to eat suffi-ciently, and for durable clothing." (See also Is. 60:5–6, 9, 11, 13, ch. 61:6, and Zech. 14:14.)

David was a mediator to stand between God and the people, both to keep off judgments and the punishment of sin, and also to procure God's favor towards them. For his sake God granted his gracious pres-ence and favor with Israel (II Sam. 7:10). Thus we read of favor which God showed to Israel, and witholding judgments from time to time for his servant David's sake (I Kgs. 11:12–13, 32, 34, ch. 15:4; II Kgs. 8:19, ch. 19:34 and 20:6). And he stood between God and the people of Jerusalem when he saw the sword of justice drawn against it to destroy it (II Sam. 24:17–25). So the Messiah is spoken of, as in like manner, the mediator, being himself peculiarly God's elect and beloved, is given for a covenant of the people (Is. 42:6 and 49:8) and the messenger of the covenant, and a prophet like unto Moses, who was a mediator. And the prophecies speak of the forgiveness of sin, and the greatest mercy towards God's people, and an everlasting covenant, and the sure mer-cies of David, as being through the Messiah. (See "Fulfillment of Prophecies" §20–22; also §74–86, §94–96.)[2]

David as mediator saved the people of Jerusalem from destruction by offering himself to suffer and die by the sword of the destroying

2. "Fulfillment" §20–22, renumbered 17–19 on MS pp. 24–28, treat prophecies of Christ's works on earth. Sec. 19 begins, "It was foretold by the ancient prophets that God in the Messiah's days should bring to pass some very strange, mysterious and wonderful thing, an unparalleled work of wisdom, power and mercy that was altogether new, before unseen and unheard of, and that none could ever have conceived of; and therefore should greatly surprise and fill with admiration and astonishment those that should be informed of it and come to the understanding of it." For §74–86, see above p. 270, n. 5; p. 231, n. 4; p. 236, n. 9; p. 245, n. 9. Sec. 94, renumbered 97 on MS p. 71, begins, "It was foretold that the Messiah) should be a mediator to stand between an infinitely holy, great and dreadful God and weak, feeble, sinful men to screen them from the fire of God's wrath and to be a medium of their intercourse with a Being so much above them, and [of] such majesty, purity and justice that they were not fit to have access to and communicate with immediately." Sec. 95–96, renum-bered 98–99 on MS p. 91, describe the Messiah's priestly function as mediator and inter-cessor.

angel and by building [an] altar and offering sacrifice (II Sam. 24:17–
25), agreeable to the prophecies of the Messiah. (See "Fulfillment of
Prophecies" §74–86.)[3]

David not only made a tabernacle for God in Mt. Zion, and so provided an habitation for the Lord, but he in effect built the temple. He
bought the ground on which it was built, built an altar upon it. He
made provision for the building. It was in his heart to build an house to
God's name, and he directed and ordered precisely how it should be
built and ordered all its services (I Chron. 22–26), agreeable to Zech.
6:12–13. Herein David was as the Messiah, a prophet like unto Moses,
who built the tabernacle and the altar according to the pattern God
gave him (as he gave David the pattern of the tabernacle), and gave the
ordinances of the house [and] ordered all things appertaining to the
worship of the tabernacle.

God by David gave to Israel new ordinances, a new law of worship,
appointed many things that were not in the law of Moses, and some
things that superseded the ordinances of Moses. This is agreeable to
the things said of the Messiah. (See "Fulfillment of Prophecies" §146–
47.)[4]

David made all manner of preparation for the building of the temple, and that in vast abundance, an immense treasure (I Chron. 22:14
and 28:14–18, 29:2–9); agreeable to Is. 25:6, "And in this mountain
shall the Lord make unto all people a feast of fat things, a feast of wines
on the lees, of fat things full of marrow, of wines on the lees well
refined." Is. 55:1–9,

> Ho, everyone that thirsteth, come ye to the waters, and he that hath
> no money; come ye, buy, and eat; yea, come, buy wine and milk
> without money and without price. Wherefore do ye spend money
> for that which is not bread? and your labor for that which satisfieth
> not? hearken diligently unto me, and eat ye that which is good, and
> let your soul delight itself in fatness. Incline your ear, and come
> unto me: hear, and your soul shall live; and I will make an everlast-

---

3. See above p. 273, n. 2.

4. "Fulfillment" §146, renumbered 151 on MS pp. 117–18, begins, "It was foretold that in
the Messiah's times there should be given a new, divine constitution, diverse from the law or
covenant God established with Israel by Moses. This seems to be implied in the Messiah's
being a prophet like unto Moses." Sec. 147, renumbered 152 on MS pp. 118–19, begins,
"There are many things in the ancient prophecies that do show that in the times of the
Messiah's kingdom the ceremonial law should be abolished."

ing covenant with you, even the sure mercies of David. Behold, I have given him for a witness to the people, a leader and commander to the people. Behold, thou shalt call a nation that thou knowest not, and nations that knew not thee shall run unto thee because of the Lord thy God, and for the Holy One of Israel; for he hath glorified thee. Seek ye the Lord while he may be found, call upon him while he is near: Let the wicked forsake his way, and the unrighteous man his thoughts: and let him return unto the Lord, and he will have mercy upon him; and to our God, for he will abundantly pardon. For my thoughts are not your thoughts, neither are your ways my ways, saith the Lord. For as the heavens are higher than the earth, so are my ways higher than your ways, and my thoughts than your thoughts.

(See also "Fulfillment of Prophecies" §20.)[5] Hag. 2:7, "I will fill this house with glory." Jer. 33:6, "I will reveal unto them the abundance of truth and peace." Is. 64:4, eye has not seen, nor ear heard, {what God has prepared for him that waits on him}. Is. 66:12, "I will extend peace to her as a river." Ps. 72:3, "The mountains shall bring peace to the people, and the little hills, by righteousness." V. 7, there shall be "abundance of peace so long as the moon endureth." Amos 9:13, "The mountains shall drop sweet wine." Joel 3:18, "And it shall come to pass in that day, that the mountains shall drop down new wine, and the hills shall flow with milk, and all the rivers of Judah shall flow with water, and a fountain shall come forth out of the house of the Lord, and shall water the valley of Shittim." And Is. 60, throughout, besides the things which the prophecies say of the perfect satisfaction of God's justice by the sacrifice of the Messiah and the abundance of his righteousness and excellency. David made such great provision for the building of the temple in his trouble by war and exposing his own life, which is agreeable to what the prophecies represent of Christ procuring the immense blessings of his church by his extreme sufferings and precious blood.

David was the head of God's people, the prince of the congregation of Israel, not only in their civil affairs, but in ecclesiastical affairs also, and their leader in all things appertaining to religion and the worship of God. Herein he was as the Messiah is represented in the prophecies,

5. See above p. 273, n. 2.

which speak of Him as a prophet like unto Moses, and as the head of God's people, as their great king, prophet and priest. And indeed, almost all that the prophecies say of the Messiah does [imply] that he shall be the great head of God's people in their religious concerns.

David regulated the whole body of the people and brought 'em into the most exact and beautiful order (I Chron. 27), which is agreeable to what is represented of the church in the Messiah's days, as "beautiful for situation" (Ps. 48:20); "the perfection of beauty" (Ps. 50:2); "an eternal excellency, the joy of many generations" [Is. 60:15]; and what is represented in Ezekiel of the exact measures and order of all parts of the temple, the city and the whole land [Ezek. 40–48].

David built the altar in the threshing floor of Araunah the Jebusite, on Gentile ground, which is agreeable to what the prophecies represent of the church of the Messiah being erected in Gentile lands, and being made up of those that had been sinners.

The things that are said of SOLOMON fall yet if anything short of those that are said of David, in their remarkable agreement with things said of the Messiah in the prophecies. His name, "Solomon," signifies "peace" or "peaceable," and was given him by God himself from respect to the signification, because he should enjoy peace and be a means of peace to God's people. I Chron. 22:9, "Behold, a son shall be born to thee, who shall be a man of rest; and I will give him rest from all his enemies round about: for his name shall be Solomon, and I will give peace and quietness unto Israel in his days." This is agreeable to Is. 9:6–7, "For unto us a child is born, unto us a son is given: and the government shall be upon his shoulder: and his name shall be called ... The Prince of Peace. Of the increase of his ... peace there shall be no end." Ps. 110:4, "Thou art a priest forever after the order of Melchizedek," who, as the Apostle observes, was king of Salem, that is, king of peace [Heb. 7:1]. Ps. 72:3, "The mountains shall bring peace unto the people." V. 7, "In his days shall the righteous flourish; and abundance of peace so long as the moon endureth." Ps. 85:10, "Righteousness and peace have kissed each other." Is. 52:7, "How beautiful are the feet of him ... that publisheth peace." Jer. 33:6, "I will reveal unto them the abundance of truth and peace," and many other places.

When Solomon was born, it is said "the Lord loved him" (II Sam. 12:24), and the prophet Nathan for this reason called him by the name "Jedidiah," i. e. "the beloved of the Lord." He is also spoken of as the beloved son of his father. Prov. 4:3, "For I was my father's son, tender and only beloved in the sight of my mother." (See "Fulfillment of Prophecies" §18.)[6]

Solomon was the son of a woman that had [been] the wife of an Hittite, a Gentile by nation, fitly denoting the honor that the prophecies represent that the Gentiles should have by their relation to the Messiah.

God made mention of Solomon's name as one that was to be the great prince of Israel and means of their happiness from his mother's womb, agreeable to Is. 49:1, "The Lord hath called me from the womb; from the bowels of my mother hath he made mention of my name."

God promises to establish the throne of Solomon forever, in terms considerably like those used by the prophets concerning the kingdom of the Messiah. II Sam. 7:12–13, "I will set up thy seed after thee, which shall proceed out of thine own bowels, and I will establish his kingdom. He shall build an house for my name, and I will establish the throne of his kingdom forever." Also I Chron. 22:10. Is. 9:7, "Of the increase of his government there shall be no end, upon the throne of David, and his kingdom ... to establish it ... from henceforth even forever." Ps. 110:4, "Thou art a priest forever after the order of Melchizedek." Dan. 7:14, "His dominion is an everlasting dominion, which shall not pass away, and his kingdom that which shall not be destroyed."

Solomon is spoken of as God's son. I Chron. 17:13, "I will be his father, and he shall be my son." I Chron. 22:9–10, "His name shall be Solomon ... he shall be my son, and I will be his father." Ch. 28:6, "And he said unto me, Solomon thy son, he shall build my house and my courts: for I have chosen him to be my son, and I will be his father." (See "Fulfillment of Prophecies" §15.)[7] Solomon was in an eminent

---

6. "Fulfillment" §18, renumbered 15 on MS p. 22, begins, "It was foretold that the Messiah should be a person that was in a peculiar manner beloved of God."

7. In "Fulfillment" §15, renumbered 16 on MS pp. 20–21, JE offers a corollary which reads, in part, "That it indeed was the doctrine of the prophets that the Messiah was a divine person, for 'tis evident that he that was in the Old Testament called the 'Son of God' was a divine person, or one that had a divine nature. As man begets a son in his own image or nature, so the Son of God is in His image and nature. The princes of Israel of old, because they were types of the Messiah, the proper King of Israel, were called 'sons of God' figuratively, and justly so. They are figuratively called 'gods.' Ps. 82:6, 'I said, You are gods; and all of you children of the most High.' So the Messiah, the true King of Israel, the proper Son of God, is properly God."

manner God's elect. I Chron. 28:5–6, "And of all my sons (for the Lord hath given me many sons), he hath chosen Solomon my son to sit upon the throne of the kingdom of the Lord over Israel. And he said, Solomon thy son ... have I chosen to be my son." Ch. 29:1, "David the king said unto all the congregation, Solomon my son, whom alone God hath chosen."

Though David had many sons, and many born before Solomon, yet Solomon[8] was made his firstborn, higher than all the rest, and his father's heir and his brethren's prince; agreeable to Ps. 89:27, "I will make him my firstborn, higher than the kings of the earth." Ps. 45:7, "Thy God hath anointed thee with the oil of gladness above thy fellows."

The word which Nathan, the minister of the Lord, spake to Bathsheba, David's wife and Solomon's mother, and the counsel he gave her, was the occasion of the introduction of the blissful and glorious reign of Solomon (I Kgs. 1:11–13). So the prophecies represent the preaching of God's ministers as the means of introducing the glorious kingdom of the Messiah. Is. 62:6–7, "I have set watchmen upon thy walls, O Jerusalem, which shall never hold their peace day nor night ... till he make Jerusalem a praise in the earth." Ch. 52:7–8, "How beautiful upon the mountains are the feet of him that bringeth good tidings ... Thy watchmen shall lift up the voice; with the voice together shall they sing: for they shall see eye to eye, when the Lord shall bring again Zion."

This earnest, incessant preaching of ministers shall be in the first place to the visible church of God, that is represented in the Old Testament both as the wife and mother of Christ. She is represented as his mother. Mic. 4:10, "Be in pain, and labor to bring forth, O daughter of Zion, like a woman in travail"; with the next chapter, vv. 2–3, "Thou Bethlehem Ephratah ... out of thee shall he come forth unto me that is to be ruler in Israel ... Therefore will he give them up, until the time that she which travaileth hath brought forth." Is. 9:6, "Unto us a child is born, unto us a son is given." Cant. 3:11, "Behold king Solomon with the crown wherewith his mother crowned him."

Solomon's father had solemnly promised and covenanted and sworn to Bathsheba long beforehand that Solomon should reign and sit on his throne. So the sending of the Messiah and introducing the blessings of his reign was the grand promise and covenant and oath of

---

8. MS: "David." JE, Jr. cancelled the word and interlineated "Solomon."

God to his church of old, to Abraham, Isaac and Jacob, and in David's and the prophets' times (Ps. 89:3–4, 35–36, II Sam. 3–5, Jer. 33:17–26 and many other places).

The glorious reign of Solomon is introduced on the earnest petitions and pleadings of Bathsheba with his father (I Kgs. 1:15–21). So the prophecies often represent that the glorious peace and prosperity of the Messiah's reign shall be given in answer to the earnest and importunate prayers of the church. Ezek. 36:37, "I will yet for this be inquired of by the house of Israel, to do it for them" (Jer. 29:11–14, Cant. 2:14, Zech. 12:10).

Bathesheba pleads the king's promise and covenant. So the church is often represented as waiting for the fulfillment of God's promises with respect to the benefits of the Messiah's kingdom (Gen. 49:18; Is. 8:17, and 30:18, and 40:31 and 49:23; Zeph 3:8; Is. 25:9 and 26:8 and 64:4).

Solomon came to the crown after the people had set up a false heir, one that pretended to be the heir of David's crown, and for a while seemed as though they would carry all afore 'em. This is agreeable to the prophecies of the Messiah, who represent that his kingdom shall be set up on the ruins of that of others who should exalt themselves and assume the dominion. Ezek. 17:24, "I the Lord have brought down the high tree, and exalted the low tree, have dried up the green tree, and have made the dry tree to flourish: I the Lord have spoken and have done it." Ch. 21:26, "Thus saith the Lord God; Remove the diadem, take off the crown: this shall not be the same: exalt him that is low, abase him that is high." Ps. 2:2–6, "The kings of the earth set themselves, the rulers take counsel together, saying, Let us break their bands, and cast away their cords from us.... Yet have I set my king on my holy hill of Zion." Ps. 118:22, "The stone which the builders refused, the same is become the head of the corner." And particularly this is agreeable to what the prophet Daniel says of the reign of Antichrist that shall precede the glorious day of the Messiah's reign, who shall set up himself in the room of the Most High, as lawgiver in his room, shall think to change times and laws, whose reign shall continue till the Messiah comes to overthrow it by setting up his glorious kingdom.

When David understands the opposition that was made to Solomon's reign by him that had usurped the kingdom and by the rulers and great men that were with him, he solemnly declares his firm and immutable purpose and decree of exalting Solomon *that day* to his throne which was in Mt. Zion (I Kgs. 1:29–30); agreeable to Ps. 2:2–7,

"The kings of the earth set themselves, and the rulers take counsel together, against the Lord, and against his anointed, saying, Let us break their bands ... Yet have I set my king on my holy hill of Zion. I will declare the decree: the Lord hath said unto me, Thou art my son; this day have I begotten thee."

Solomon was made king by a most solemn oath of his father, that he declares he will not repent of, but fulfill. I Kgs. 1:29–30, "And the king sware, and said, As the Lord liveth, that hath redeemed my soul out of all distress, Even as I sware unto thee by the Lord God of Israel, saying, Assuredly Solomon thy son shall reign after me, and he shall sit upon my throne in my stead; even so will I certainly do this day"; agreeable to Ps. 110:4, "The Lord hath sworn, and will not repent, Thou art a priest forever after the order of Melchizedek."

When the time came for Solomon to be proclaimed king, all the opposition and interest of his competitors, though very great, and of great men (and though they seemed to have made their part strong and to have got the day), all vanished away as it were of it[self] and came to nothing at once, like a dream when one awakes; agreeable to Ps. 2:4–6, "The Lord shall laugh at them ... Yet have I set my king on my holy hill of Zion." Is. 29:7–8, "And the multitude of all the nations that fight against Ariel, even all that fight against her and her munition, shall be as a dream of a night vision. It shall be even as when a hungry man dreameth, and, behold, he eateth; and he awaketh, and his soul is empty: so shall the multitude of all the nations be, that fight against mount Zion." Ps. 68:1–2, "Let God arise, let his enemies be scattered: let them also that hate him flee before him. As smoke is driven away, as wax melteth before the fire." Is. 64:1, "Oh that thou wouldst rent the heavens, that thou wouldst come down, that the mountains might flow down at thy presence." Dan. 2:34–35, "Thou sawest till that a stone was cut out without hands, which smote the image ... Then was the iron, the clay, the brass, the silver, and the gold, broken in pieces, and became like the chaff of the summer threshing floors; and the wind carried them away."

The followers of Adonijah were dispersed without any battle, only by what they heard and saw of what David had done in exalting Solomon, and the manner in which he was introduced and instated in the kingdom; which is agreeable to Ps. 48:4–6, "For, lo, the kings were assembled, they passed by together. They saw it, and so they marvelled; they were humbled, and hasted away. Fear took hold upon them there, and pain, as of a woman in travail."

After David had declared the decree that Solomon should be king in Zion, it was dangerous for the princes and rulers not to submit themselves to Solomon and behave with suitable respect to him, lest he should be angry and they should perish. (See Ps. 2.)

Solomon in his way to the throne is made as it were to drink of the brook. He first descended from the height of Mt. Zion down into a low valley without the city, to the watercourse of Gihon. There he had a baptism to be baptized with. And then he ascended in the state and majesty of a king, agreeable to Ps. 110:7, "He shall drink of the brook in the way: therefore shall he lift up the head," and the many prophecies that speak of his humiliation and sufferings and glorious exaltation consequent thereon. (See "Fulfillment of Prophecies.")[9]

Solomon, after he had descended into the valley to the waters of Gihon, ascended up into the height of Zion in a manner resembling the ascension of the Messiah, very much after the same manner that the ascension of the ark resembled it. For he went up with the sound of the trumpet, all the people following him with songs and instruments of music and hosannas, rejoicing with great joy, so that the earth rent again (I Kgs. 1:39–40), agreeable to Ps. 68, and Ps. 47:5 and Ps. 24.

That the peaceful, happy and glorious reign of Solomon should be introduced with such extraordinary joy, shouting, songs and instruments of music in Zion, is agreeable to what is often foretold concerning the introduction of the glorious day of the Messiah's reign. Zech. 9:9, "Rejoice greatly, O daughter of Zion; shout, O daughter of Jerusalem: behold, thy King cometh unto thee." To the like purpose, ch. 2:10, Is. 40:9 and 52:7–9. Ps. 96:10–13, "Say among the heathen that the Lord reigneth: the world also shall be established that it shall not be moved: he shall judge the people righteously. Let the heavens rejoice, and let the earth be glad; let the sea roar, and the fullness thereof. Let the field be joyful, and all that is therein: then shall all the trees of the wood rejoice before the Lord." And Ps. 97:1, 8, 12, and 98:4–9 and 100:1–2; Is. 44:23 and 49:13, Is. 55:12 and many other places.

The great prosperity of Israel through the reign of Solomon was introduced with the sound of the trumpet (I Kgs. 1:34, 39, I Chron. 29:21–22), agreeable to Is. 27:13, "The great trumpet shall be blown, and they shall come which were ready to perish in the land of Assyria, and the outcasts in the land of Egypt, and shall worship the Lord in the holy mount at Jerusalem."

9. See above p. 258, n. 9; p. 258, n. 2.

Solomon was the messiah or "anointed" in an eminent manner. He was anointed by the special direction both of David and of Nathan the prophet (I Kgs. 1:13, 34, 39). He was anointed with God's holy anointing oil out of the tabernacle (v. 39).

Not only was Solomon anointed of God, but he was anointed also by the people. They made him king over them by their act (I Chron. 29:22), agreeable to Hos. 1:11, "Then shall the children of Judah and the children of Israel be gathered together, and appoint over them one head, and they shall come up out of the land: for great shall be the day of Jezreel."

David made Solomon to ride on his own mule, and he sat on his father's throne while David was yet living and was king. His father solemnly invests him with his kingly authority, and himself gives him his charge (I Kgs. 1:30, 33, 35, 47–48, ch. 2:12; I Chron. 28 and 29). This is agreeable to the account that is given of God the Father investing the Messiah with his dominion in Dan. 7. (See also Zech. 6:12–13, and Ezek. 46:1–2 with ch. 44:2; see "Prophecies of the Messiah" §74.)[1]

Solomon is spoken of as not only sitting on the throne of his father David, but also as sitting on God's throne and reigning in some respect in God's stead as his vicegerent. I Chron. 28:5, "The Lord hath chosen Solomon my son to sit upon *the throne of the kingdom of the Lord* over Israel." Ch. 29:23, "Then Solomon sat upon the throne of the Lord as king instead of David his father." II Chron. 9:8, "Blessed be the Lord thy God, which delighted in thee to set thee on his throne, to be king for the Lord thy God." So the prophecies do represent the Messiah as sitting on the throne of David his father. Is. 9:7, "On the throne of David, and upon his kingdom, to order it, and to establish it with judgment from henceforth even forever"; Jer. 33:17, 21. And also as sitting on the throne of God. Zech. 6:13, "He shall build the temple of the Lord; and he shall bear the glory, and shall sit and rule upon his throne." Also Dan. 7:13–14, and Ps. 2:6, "I have set *my king* on *my holy hill* of Zion." Ps. 110:1, "Sit thou on my right hand, till I make thine enemies thy footstool." Ps. 45:6, "Thy throne, O God, is forever and ever."

1. JE refers to "Fulfillment" §76, on MS p. 66, but almost certainly means §74, on MS pp. 62–66, a comment on the last nine chapters of Ezekiel, which he states are descriptive of the establishment of the "state of God's Israel" after the restoration from captivity. On MS p. 66, JE discusses the prophecies of the Messiah's princely office. The "Prince," he writes, "was more than a mere man, one on whom divine honor was conferred....This Prince in the prophecy may represent the rule, authority and dominion that God will set in his Israel."

The beginning of Solomon's reign was a remarkable time of vengeance on the wicked and such as had been opposers or false friends of David and Solomon. Many such were then cut off (1 Kgs. 2). So that it was as it were the righteous only that delighted themselves in that abundance of peace, and partook of the glory, prosperity and triumph of God's people that was enjoyed in that reign; which is agreeable to Is. 61:2, "To proclaim the acceptable year of the Lord, and the day of vengeance of our God." Is. 65:12–13, "Therefore will I number you to the sword, and ye shall all bow down to the slaughter ... my servants shall eat, but ye shall be hungry: behold, my servants shall drink, but ye shall be thirsty: behold, my servants shall rejoice, but ye shall be ashamed." Ch. 66:14–16, "And the hand of the Lord shall be known towards his servants, and his indignations towards his enemies. For, behold, the Lord will come with fire, and with his chariots like a whirlwind, to render his anger with fury ... and the slain of the Lord shall be many." Is. 33:14–17, "The sinners in Zion are afraid; fearfulness hath surprised the hypocrite.... He that walketh righteously ... shall dwell on high ... Thine eyes shall see the king in his beauty." Mal. 4:1–3, "All the proud, yea, all that do wickedly, shall be as stubble ... But unto you that fear my name shall the Sun of righteousness arise with healing in his wings ... And ye shall tread down the wicked." Ezek. 20:38, "And I will purge out from among you the rebels, and them that transgress against me." Ps. 37:9–11, "For evildoers shall be cut off: but those that wait upon the Lord shall inherit the earth. For yet a little while, and the wicked shall not be: yea, thou shalt diligently consider his place, and it shall not be. But the meek shall inherit the earth, and delight themselves in the abundance of peace." And many other places.

Solomon did not immediately cut off these rebels and transgressors, but gave 'em opportunity to enjoy the blessings of his reign with others, if they would turn from their evil way and submit to him and approve themselves worthy men and faithful subjects. But when they went on still in their trespasses, he cut them off, agreeable to what is foretold should be at the introduction of the glory of the Messiah's reign in Ps. 68:18–21, "Thou hast ascended on high ... thou hast received gifts for men; yea, for the rebellious also, that the Lord God might dwell among them. Blessed be the Lord, who daily loadeth us with his benefits ... But God shall wound the head of his enemies, and the hairy scalp of such an one as goeth on still in his trespasses."

Solomon was a man of great and unparalleled wisdom. This is agreeable to Is. 9:6, "His name shall be called Wonderful, Counselor."

Ch. 11:2–3, "The Spirit of the Lord shall rest upon him, the spirit of wisdom and understanding, the spirit of counsel and of might, the spirit of knowledge and of the fear of the Lord; And shall make him of quick understanding in the fear of the Lord." Zech. 3:9, "Upon one stone shall be seven eyes." (See also Is. 41:28–29 with 42:1.)

God was with Solomon and greatly established his throne (I Kgs. 2:12, II Chron. 1:1), agreeable to Is. 9:7, "Upon the throne of David, and upon his kingdom, to order it, and to establish it ... from henceforth even forever. The zeal of the Lord of hosts shall do this." Ps. 89:2–3, "Mercy shall be built up forever: thy faithfulness wilt thou establish in the very heavens. I have made a covenant with my chosen." Vv. 20–21, "With my holy oil have I anointed him: With whom my hand shall be established: mine arm also shall strengthen him." V. 25, "I will set his hand also in the sea, and his right hand in the rivers." Vv. 36–37, "His throne shall endure as the sun before me. It shall be established forever as the moon, and as a faithful witness in heaven." Ps. 2, throughout. Ps. 45:6, "Thy throne, O God, is forever and ever." Ps. 110:1, 4, "Sit thou on my right hand ... The Lord hath sworn, and will not repent, Thou art a priest forever after the order of Melchizedek." Is. 42:1, 4, "Behold my servant, whom I uphold ... He shall not fail nor be discouraged, till he have set judgment in the earth: and the isles wait for his law." And 49:8, "I have helped thee and will preserve thee, to establish the earth."

The Lord magnified Solomon exceedingly, and bestowed upon him such royal majesty as had not been on any before him in Israel (I Chron. 29:25, II Chron. 1:1); agreeable to Ps. 45:2–3, "Thou art fairer than the children of men ... Gird thy sword upon thy thigh, O most mighty, with thy glory and thy majesty." V. 6, "Thy throne, O God, is forever and ever." Is. 9:6, "Unto us a child is born, unto us a son is given: and the government shall be upon his shoulders: and his name shall be called Wonderful, Counselor, The mighty God, The everlasting father, The Prince of Peace."

Solomon married Pharaoh's [daughter], a stranger, agreeable to Ps. 45:10, "Hearken, O daughter, and consider, and incline thine ear; forget thine own people, and thy father's house." She was the daughter of a king, agreeable to Ps. 45:13, "The king's daughter is all glorious within: her clothing is of wrought gold." A Gentile, agreeable to Hos. 2:16, "Thou shalt call me Ishi" (i. e. "my husband"). Vv. 19–20, "And I will betroth thee unto me." V. 23, "And I will have mercy upon her that had not obtained mercy; and I will say unto them that were not my people, Thou art my people; and they shall say, Thou art my God," with innumerable other prophecies of the calling of the Gentiles. She was an Egyptian, and Solomon made an affinity with Pharaoh, king of Egypt; agreeable to Ps. 87:4, "I will make mention of Rahab and Babylon to them that know me." Ps. 68:31, "Princes shall come out of Egypt." Is. 19:18–25, "In that day shall five cities in the land of Egypt speak the language of Canaan ... and there shall be an altar unto the Lord in the midst of the land of Egypt ... And the Lord shall be known unto Egypt, and the Egyptians shall know the Lord ... and the Egyptians shall serve with the Assyrians.... The Lord of hosts shall bless, saying, Blessed be Egypt my people." Pharaoh's daughter, being an Egyptian, was of a swarthy complexion, agreeable to Cant. 1:5, "I am black, but comely, O ye daughters of Jerusalem."

We read of no person that ever offered such great sacrifices as Solomon did (I Kgs. 3:4 and 8:5, 63–64; I Kgs. 9:25). This is agreeable to what the prophecies represent of the Messiah, of the great priest of God, who by the sacrifices he should offer should perfectly satisfy divine justice and truly procure the favor of God for his people; his sacrifices being herein of greater value than thousands of rams and ten thousands of rivers of oil, and all the beasts of the field.

Solomon built the temple, agreeable to Zech. 6:12–13. He made the dwelling place of God, that before was only a moveable tent, to become a stable building, built on a rock or everlasting mountain; agreeable to Is. 33:20, "Look upon Zion, the city of our solemnities: thine eyes shall see Jerusalem a quiet habitation, a tabernacle that shall not be taken down; not one of the stakes thereof shall ever be removed, neither shall any of the cords thereof be broken." Ch. 28:16–17, "Behold, I lay in Zion for a foundation a stone, a tried stone, a precious cornerstone, a sure foundation ... Judgment also will I lay to the line, and righteousness to the plummet." Ezek. 37:26, "Moreover I will make a covenant of peace with them; it shall be an everlasting covenant with them: and I will place them, and multiply them, and will set my sanctuary in the midst of them forevermore"; taken together with the prophetical description of that sanctuary in the fortieth and following chapters [Ezek. 40–48].

Solomon's temple and his other buildings in Jerusalem were exceeding stately and magnificent, so that he vastly increased the beauty and glory of the city. Is. 60:13, "The glory of Lebanon shall come unto thee, the fir tree, the pine tree, and the box together, to beautify the place of my sanctuary; and I will make the place of my feet glorious."

V. 15, "I will make thee an eternal excellency." Ch. 54:11–12, "Behold, I will lay thy stones with fair colors, and lay thy foundations with sapphires. And I will make thy windows of agates, and thy gates of carbuncles, and all thy borders of pleasant stones."

The temple that Solomon built was exceeding magnifical, of fame and of glory throughout all lands (I Chron. 22:5); agreeable to Is. 2:2, "And it shall come to pass in the last days, that the mountain of the Lord's house shall be established in the top of the mountains, and shall be exalted above the hills; and all nations shall flow into it." (See also Mic. 4:1–2.) Is. 60:1–3, "Arise, shine; for thy light is come ... the Lord shall arise upon thee, and his glory shall be seen upon thee. And the Gentiles shall come to thy light, and kings to the brightness of thy rising."

Solomon enlarged the place of sacrificing, so that sacrifices were not only offered on the altar, but all the middle part of the court was made use of for that end by reason of the multitude of worshippers and the abundance of sacrifices (I Kgs. 8:64, II Chron. 7:7); which is agreeable to Jer. 3:16–17, "And it shall come to pass, when ye be multiplied and increased in the land, in those days, saith the Lord, they shall say no more, The ark of the covenant of the Lord: neither shall it come to mind: neither shall they remember it; neither shall they visit it; neither shall that be done any more. At that time they shall call Jerusalem the throne of the Lord; and all nations shall be gathered unto the name of the Lord unto Jerusalem." Mal. 1:11, "From the rising of the sun unto the going down of the same my name shall be great among the Gentiles; and in every place incense shall be offered unto my name, and a pure offering," and many other places. (See "Fulfillment of Prophecies" §147, and those numbers in "Miscellanies" there referred to.)[2]

Solomon was a great intercessor for Israel, and by his intercession he obtained that God should forgive their sins and hear their prayers, and pity 'em under their calamities and deliver 'em from their enemies, and fulfill his promises and supply all their necessities; and that they might find mercy and find grace to help in a time of need, and [that God might][3] dwell with Israel and take up his abode among them as their King, Savior and Father (I Kgs. 8, II Chron. 6). By his intercession and prayers, he brought fire down from heaven to consume their

---

2. See above p. 274, n. 4. In "Fulfillment" §147, JE refers to "Miscellanies" nos. 599, 1024, 1027, and 1040.

3. JE, Jr.'s insertion.

sacrifices, and [obtained][4] that God should come down in a cloud of glory to fill his temple (II Chron. 7:1–3, I Kgs. 8:54). His intercession was as it were continual, although he ever lived to make an intercession for his people, that they might obtain mercy and find grace to help in time of need. (See those remarkable words, I Kgs. 8:59; see "Fulfillment of Prophecies" §74 and §96.)[5]

Solomon was not only an intercessor for Israel, but for the stranger that was not of Israel, but come out of a far country for God's name's sake, when they should hear of his great name and great salvation (I Kgs. 8:41–43, II Chron. 6:32–33); which is agreeable to what the prophecies do abundantly represent of the joint interest of the Gentiles in the utmost ends of the earth with Israel in the Messiah, through hearing his great name and the report of his salvation. Solomon prayed for all the people of the earth, that they might know the true God (I Kgs. 8:60); so the prophecies do abundantly show that the Messiah should actually obtain this benefit for all nations of the world.

Solomon did the part of a priest in blessing the congregation (I Kgs. 8:14, II Chron. 6:3 with Num. 6:23), which is agreeable to the prophecies which represent the Messiah as a priest, and also to Gen. 22:18, "In thy seed shall all the families of the earth be blessed." To the like purpose, ch. 12:3 and 18:8 and 26:4, and Ps. 72:17, "And men shall be blessed in him."

Solomon made a covenant with the king of Tyre, and the servants of the king of Tyre were associated with the servants of Solomon in the building of the temple; which is agreeable to the prophecies of the Messiah's being a light of the Gentiles and covenant of the people, and the Gentiles being associated with the Jews and becoming one people with them, and their coming and building in the temple of the Lord (Zech. 6:15). Is. 60:10, "And the sons of strangers shall build up thy walls, and their kings shall minister unto thee." And particularly the prophecies that represent that the nations in the islands and ends of the earth and maritime places, the chief nations for arts, wealth, merchandise and seafaring, should be brought into the kingdom of the Messiah, bringing their silver and gold to the name of the Lord, etc. And that the Tyrians in particular should be the people of the Messiah.

4. JE, Jr.'s insertion.
5. For "Fulfillment" §74, see above p. 270, n. 5. Sec. 96, renumbered 99 on MS p. 71, begins, "As the prophecies represent the Messiah as a priest to offer sacrifice for his people, so they represent him as an intercessor for them."

(See "Fulfillment of Prophecies" §154, §158, §160.)[6] Solomon brought the glory of Lebanon, or the best and fairest of its growth, to build the temple of God, agreeable to Is. 60:13.

Solomon in an eminent manner executed judgment and justice (I Kgs. 3:9, 11, 28 and 10:9, 18). His throne of judgment was of ivory, a white, pure and precious substance, used in the Old Testament as a symbol of purity and righteousness. (See note on Ps. 45:8.)[7] This is agreeable to innumerable prophecies of the Messiah.

It was in Solomon's time that God first gave his people Israel fully to enjoy that rest in Canaan that he had promised 'em in the time of Moses, and Solomon's rest was glorious. I Kgs. 5:4, "But now the Lord my God hath given me rest on every side." And ch. 8:56, "Blessed be the Lord God, that hath given rest unto his people Israel, according to all that he promised: there hath not failed one word of all his good promise, which he promised by the hand of Moses his servant." This is agreeable to Is. 11:10, "And in that day there shall be a root of Jesse, which shall stand for an ensign of the people; to it shall the Gentiles seek: and his rest shall be glorious." Jer. 30:10, "Lo, I will save thee from afar, and thy seed from the land of their captivity; and Jacob shall return, and be in rest, and quiet, and none shall make him afraid." Is. 33:20, "Look upon Zion, the city of our solemnities: thine eyes shall see Jerusalem a quiet habitation, a tabernacle that shall not be taken down." And ch. 32:17–18, "And the work of righteousness shall be

---

6. For §154, see above p. 267, n. 8. Sec. 158, renumbered 162 on MS pp. 125–26, reads, in part, "It was abundantly foretold that the lesser Asia, and Europe in particular, should be brought into subjection to the Messiah and should belong to his kingdom, which were in the Old Testament commonly called by the name of 'the isles.' [...]

"The Israelites of old were wont to call [isles] all countries and inhabited places beyond the seas or with which the communication to and from the land of Canaan was wont to be only by sea. The chief of these countries were the lesser Asia and the countries of Europe. Indeed, these countries, all of them that were known to them, were peninsulas, as the lesser Asia, Greece, Italy and Spain. But those that were properly islands (which are not excluded from their use of the word), all of them that were known to the Jews were brought into the kingdom of Jesus Christ; as the isle of Cyprus, and Crete and the other isles in the Mediterranean Sea, and the innumerable islands in the Mediterranean Sea, and those great European islands, Ireland and Britain, the chief island in the world. And of later ages the kingdom of Jesus has extended to America, a vast continent in the ends of the earth, far off upon the sea, divided from all the old world by a vast ocean." For §160, see above p. 224, n. 1.

7. The note on Ps. 45:8 in the "Blank Bible" reads, in part, "Ivory is evidently used in Scripture as a type of spiritual purity by reason of its whiteness. So Solomon's throne of judgment was of ivory (I Kgs. 10:18) to signify the righteousness and purity of his judgment, and righteousness of his government, as Christ is represented at the day of judgment as sitting on a great white throne (Rev. 20:11)."

peace; and the effect of righteousness quietness and assurance forever. And my people shall dwell in a peaceable habitation, and in sure
dwellings, and in quiet resting places."

Judah and Israel dwelt safely, every man under his vine and under
his fig tree, from Dan even to Beersheba, all the days of Solomon (I
Kgs. 4:25); agreeable to Mic. 4:4, "But they shall sit every man under
his vine and under his fig tree; and none shall make them afraid." And
Zech. 3:10, "In that day, saith the Lord of hosts, ye shall call every man
his neighbor under his vine and under his fig tree."

In Solomon's reign there was neither adversary nor evil occurrent.
So according to the prophecies, in the Messiah's times there should be
no adversary. Is. 25:5, "Thou shalt bring down the noise of strangers,
as the heat in a dry place; even the heat with the shadow of a cloud: the
branch of the terrible ones shall be brought low." Is. 54:14, "In righteousness shalt thou be established: thou shalt be far from oppression;
for thou shalt not fear: and from terror; for it shall not come near
thee." Ch. 49:19, "They that swallowed thee up shall be far away." Is.
60:18, "Violence shall no more be heard in thy land, wasting nor
destruction within thy borders." Ch. 11:13, "The adversaries of Judah
shall be cut off." So Ezek. 36:12–13 and many other places. So by the
prophecies, in the Messiah's times there should not be evil occurrents.
Is. 25:8, "He will wipe away tears from off all faces." Ch. 35:10, "Sorrow and sighing shall flee away." Is. 33:24, "And the inhabitant shall
not say, I am sick." Is. 65:19, "And the voice of weeping shall no more
be heard in her, nor the voice of crying." V. 21, "And they shall build
houses, and inhabit them; and they shall plant vineyards, and eat the
fruit of them." Zech. 8:12, "The seed shall be prosperous; the vine
shall give her fruit, and the ground shall give her increase, and the
heavens shall give their dew; and I will cause the remnant of this
people to possess all these things." And many other places.

In Solomon's time Israel were possessed of great riches, silver and
gold, and other precious things in vast abundance (I Kgs. 10:21, 23,
27); agreeable to Is. 60:5, "The abundance of the sea shall be converted unto thee, the forces" (or "wealth") "of the Gentiles shall come
unto thee." V. 6, "The multitude of camels shall cover thee, the dromedaries of Midian and Ephah, they shall bring gold." V. 9, "The ships
of Tarshish shall bring their silver and their gold." V. 11, "Thy gates
shall be open continually; they shall not be shut day nor night; that
men may bring unto thee the forces" (or "wealth") "of the Gentiles." V.
17, "For brass I will bring gold, and for iron I will bring silver, and for

wood brass, and for stones iron." Ch. 61:6, "Ye shall eat the riches of the Gentiles, and in their glory shall ye boast yourselves." Ch. 66:11–12, "That ye may milk out, and be delighted with the abundance of her glory. For thus saith the Lord, Behold, I will extend peace to her like a river, and the glory of the Gentiles like a flowing stream: then shall ye suck, ye shall be borne upon her sides, and be dandled upon her knees." And very many other places.

Solomon's reign was a time of great feasting and rejoicing in Israel (I Kgs. 4:20, 22–23, and 8:65 and 10:5), agreeable to Is. 25:6, "And in this mountain shall the Lord of hosts make unto all people a feast of fat things, a feast of wines on the lees, of fat things full of marrow, of wines on the lees well refined." Is. 65:13–14, "Behold, my servants shall eat ... my servants shall drink ... my servants shall rejoice ... my servants shall sing for joy of heart." V. 18, "Behold, I create Jerusalem a rejoicing, and her people a joy." Jer. 31:12, "Therefore shall they come and sing in the height of Zion, and shall flow together to the goodness of the Lord, for wheat, and for wine, and for oil, and for the young of the flock and of the herd: and their soul shall be as a watered garden; and they shall not sorrow any more at all." Zech. 8:19, "Thus saith the Lord of hosts; The fast of the fourth month, and the fast of the fifth, and the fast of the seventh, and the fast of the tenth, shall be to the house of Judah joy and gladness, and cheerful feasts." Ch. 9:15, "They shall drink, and make a noise as through wine; and they shall be filled like bowls, and as the corners of the altar." Also Is. 35:1–2, 10, and 44:23, and 49:13, and 61:3, and 51:11 and very many other places.

There was a vast increase of God's people Israel in Solomon's days, so that they were as the sand of the sea, and were so many that they could not be numbered or counted for multitude (I Kgs. 3:8 and 4:20). (See "Fulfillment of Prophecies" §121.)[8]

The servants of Solomon and those that stood continually before him were pronounced happy, eminently and remarkably so. I Kgs. 10:8, "Happy are these thy men, happy are these thy servants, which stand continually before thee, and that hear thy wisdom"; agreeable to Ps. 72:17, "And men shall be blessed in him." Is. 33:17, "Thine eyes shall see the king in his beauty." Is. 2:5, "O house of Jacob, come ye, let us walk in the light of the Lord."

8. "Fulfillment" §121, renumbered 123 on MS pp. 91–92, reads, in part, "It was foretold that there should be a vast increase of the number of God's people in the days of the Messiah's kingdom. [...] The same is signified by the vast dimensions of the court of the temple in Ezekiel."

In Solomon's reign the remnant of the heathen were made bond-men, but the Israelites were for noble employments (I Kgs. 9:21–22); agreeable to Is. 61:5–6, "And strangers shall stand and feed your flocks, and the sons of the alien shall be your plowmen and your vinedressers. But ye shall be named the Priests of the Lord: men shall call you the Ministers of our God: ye shall eat the riches of the Gentiles, and in their glory shall ye boast yourselves."

Solomon made cedars to be as the sycamore trees that are in the vale for abundance, agreeable to Is. 55:13, "Instead of the thorn shall come up the fir tree, and instead of the brier shall come up the myrtle tree: and it shall be to the Lord for a name, for an everlasting sign that shall not be cut off." Ch. 41:19, "I will plant in the wilderness the cedar, the shittah tree, and the myrtle, and the oil tree; I will set in the desert the fir tree, and the pine and the box tree together." Is. 35:1–2, "The desert shall rejoice, and blossom as the rose. It shall blossom abundantly, and rejoice even with joy and singing: the glory of Lebanon shall be given unto it, the excellency of Carmel and Sharon."

In Solomon's days the house of the Lord was in a remarkable manner filled with glory (I Kgs. 8:10–11, II Chron. 5:13–14 and 7:1–2), agreeable to Hag. 2:7.

In Solomon's days a great and extraordinary Feast of Tabernacles was kept (I Kgs. 8:65, II Chron. 5:3 and 7:8–10). It was by far the greatest Feast of Tabernacles that ever was kept in Israel. This is agreeable to Zech. 14:16–19.

The blessings of Solomon's reign were the fruit of God's everlasting love to Israel. I Kgs. 10:9, "Because the Lord love Israel forever, therefore made he thee king, to do judgment and justice." Jer. 31:3, "I have loved thee with an everlasting love: therefore with lovingkindness have I drawn thee." Solomon reigned from the river Euphrates to the ends of the earth, even the utmost part of the land next to the Great Sea, as it was called (I Kgs. 4:21), agreeable to Ps. 72:8 and Zech. 9:10.

Solomon had many chariots (I Kgs. 4:26 and 10:26). This is agreeable to Ps. 68:18 and Dan. 7:10.

The exceeding greatness of Solomon's court, the vast number of his servants, ministers and attendants, which may be learned from I Kgs. 4:1–19, 22–23, ch. 9:22 [and] II Chron. 8:9–10, is agreeable to Ps. 68:18 and Dan 10:13, 21 and 12:1, compared with Dan 7:10.

Other kings and nations brought presents unto Solomon (I Kgs. 4:21 and 9:14 and 10:25). Ps. 68:29, "Because of thy temple at Jerusalem, kings shall bring presents unto thee" (Ps. 72:10 and 45:12).

The queen of Sheba came to hear the wisdom of Solomon and to be instructed by him, and brought great presents, and particularly gold and spices (I Kgs. 10:2, 10). This is agreeable to Is. 60:6, "All they from Sheba shall come: they shall bring gold and incense; and they shall show forth the praises of the Lord." Ps. 72:9–10, "The kings of Sheba and Seba shall offer gifts." V. 15, "To him shall be given of the gold of Sheba."

The queen of Sheba came bringing her presents on a multitude of camels (I Kgs. 10:2). And she came to Jerusalem with a very great train, with camels that bore spices and very much gold; agreeable to Is. 60:6, "The multitude of camels shall cover thee, the dromedaries of Midian and Ephah; all they from Sheba shall come: they shall bring gold and incense."

Solomon extended his royal bounty to the queen of Sheba and gave her all her desire, agreeable to what the prophecies represent of the blessings and favors of the Messiah to be extended to the Gentiles, and his granting the requests of those that look to him from the ends of the earth.

Israel in Solomon's time was enriched and adorned with the gold of Ophir, especially they of Solomon's courts, and we may conclude his queens and concubines; agreeable to Ps. 45:9, "On thy right hand did stand the queen in gold of Ophir."

All the kings and merchants of Arabia brought presents of gold and spices unto Solomon (I Kgs. 10:14–15). This is agreeable to Is. 45:14, "The merchandise of Ethiopia shall come over to thee." Zeph. 3:10, "From beyond the rivers of Ethiopia my suppliants." Ps. 68:31, "Ethiopia shall soon stretch out her hands to God." Ps. 72:9–10, "They that dwell in the wilderness shall bow before him ... the kings of Sheba and Seba shall offer gifts." Is. 60:6, "The multitude of camels shall cover thee, the dromedaries of Midian and Ephah; all they from Sheba shall come: they shall bring gold and incense." Is. 42:11, "Let the wilderness and the cities thereof lift up their voice, the villages that Kedar doth inhabit: let the inhabitants of the rock sing." Ch. 60:7, "All the flocks of Kedar shall be gathered together unto thee, the rams of Nebaioth shall minister unto thee."

The ships of Tarshish came bringing gold and silver and precious stones unto Solomon, and other precious things to Solomon (I Kgs. 8:26–66, ch. 9:10–11), and Solomon improved what they brought to adorn the temple (v. 12); agreeable to Ps. 72:10, "The kings of Tarshish and of the isles shall bring presents." Is. 60:5, "The abundance of the sea shall be converted unto thee." Is. 60:9, "Surely the isles shall wait for me, and the ships of Tarshish first ... their silver and their gold with them, to the name of the Lord thy God, and to the Holy One of Israel, because he hath glorified thee."

There came of all people, from all kings of the earth, to hear the wisdom of Solomon and brought presents of gold, silver, spices, etc. I Kgs. 4:34, "And there came of all people to hear the wisdom of Solomon, from all kings of the earth, which had heard of his wisdom." II Chron. 9:23–24, "And all the kings of the earth sought the presence of Solomon, to hear his wisdom, that God had put in his heart. And they brought every man his present, vessels of silver, and vessels of gold, and raiment, harness, and spices, horses, and mules, a rate year by year." Thus all kings did as it were bow down unto Solomon.[9] (See "Fulfillment of Prophecies" §163.)[1]

Solomon was a [king of] kings. II Chron. 9:26, "And he reigned over all the kings from the river even unto the land of the Philistines, and to the border of Egypt." (See "Fulfillment of Prophecies," ibid.)[2]

The labor of Egypt was brought over to Israel in Solomon's days. I Kgs. 10:28, "And Solomon had horses brought out of Egypt, and linen yarn: the king's merchants received the linen yarn at a price"; which is agreeable to Is. 45:14, "The labor of Egypt, and the merchandise of Ethiopia ... shall come over unto thee." From that, I Kgs. 10:28, 'tis manifest that fine linen was very much used for clothing in Solomon's days, at least by Solomon's court; which is a fit emblem of spiritual purity and righteousness, and was manifestly used as such by priests and princes, and was abundantly used as such in the service of the sanctuary. This is agreeable to what is often spoken of in the Prophets of the extraordinary holiness and purity of the church in Messiah's days; and to Is. 52:1, "Awake, awake; put on thy strength, O Zion; put on thy beautiful garments, O Jerusalem, the holy city: for henceforth there shall no more come unto thee the uncircumcised and the unclean."

Solomon spoke many proverbs or parables or dark sayings. I Kgs. 4:32, "And he spake three thousand proverbs." This is agreeable to what the prophets represent concerning the Messiah as an eminent teacher, and what may be learned from them of the wonderful and

9. JE cancels, "agreeable to Is. 60:3 and."
1. See above p. 246, n. 2.
2. Ibid.

mysterious things he should teach in his doctrine. (See "Fulfillment of Prophecies" §22.)[3]

Solomon was, as Joseph, a revealer of secrets. I Kgs. 10:1, 3, "The queen of Sheba came to prove Solomon with hard questions ... And Solomon told her all her questions: there was not anything hid from the king, which he told her not." This is agreeable to what the prophecies say of the Messiah's being a great teacher, and of the vast increase of light and knowledge that shall be by him. (See "Fulfillment of Prophecies" §35.)[4]

Solomon made a great number of songs. I Kgs. 4:32, "His songs were a thousand and five." This is agreeable to innumerable prophecies that represent the Messiah's times as times of extraordinary singing and melody, wherein God's people and all the world should employ themselves in joyful songs of praise; yea, wherein all creatures, the mountains, rocks, trees, the sea, the heavens and the earth, should as it were break forth into singing.

Solomon had a vast multitude of wives and concubines, fitly representing the vast number of saints in the Messiah's times, who are members of the church that is so often spoken of as the Messiah's wife.

I shall mention but one more thing under this head of things that we have an account of in the history of the Old Testament remarkably agreeing with things said in the prophecies and things relating to the Messiah's kingdom and redemption: and that is the return of the Jews from the Babylonish captivity. 'Tis manifest that the great redemption of the Messiah is abundantly represented by a redemption of Israel from captivity and bondage under the hand of their enemies, in strange and far distant lands, from the north country; and their return to their own land, and rebuilding Jerusalem and the cities of Israel, and repairing the old wastes, in places too many to be enumerated.

This redemption of the Jews was accompanied with a great destruction of those mighty and proud enemies that had carried them captive,

---

3. See above p. 273, n. 2.

4. "Fulfillment" §35, on MS pp. 45–46, reads, in part, "It was foretold that this great teacher and prophet of God should introduce a state of more glorious light, and a great increase of knowledge of the things of God and of the clearness of understanding of the doctrines and mysteries of religion. [...]

"It was foretold that at that time the light of the glory of God should be no longer hid behind curtains or concealed within the veil of the temple between the cherubims in the secret place of the Most High, but that the veil should be removed and God should shine forth openly, and there should be a plain revelation of those divine mysteries and arcana that had till [then] been kept hid."

that were stronger than they: God pleading their cause and revenging their quarrel on the greatest empire in the world, as it were causing them to tread down the loftiest city, the highest walls and towers in the world, destroying their enemies, with a very great slaughter and dreadful havoc of their enemies; agreeable to Hag. 2:22, "And I will overthrow the throne of kingdoms, and I will destroy the strength of the kingdoms of the heathen." Is. 26:5–6, "For he bringeth down them that dwell on high; the lofty city he layeth it low, he layeth it low even to the ground; he bringeth it even to the dust. The feet treadeth it down, even the feet of the poor, and the steps of the needy." Ch. 25:12, "And the fortress of the high fort of thy walls shall he bring down, lay low, and bring to the ground, even to the dust." Ch. 32:19, "When it shall hail, coming down on the forest; and the city shall be low in a low place" (or "shall be utterly abased"). Ch. 30:25, "And there shall be upon every high mountain, and upon every high hill, rivers and streams of water in the day of the great slaughter, when the towers fall." (See also Is. 34:1–8 and Joel 3:9–17, Is. 2:16–22 and many other places.)

This redemption of the Jews was attended with the final and everlasting destruction of Babylon, that great enemy of the Jewish church, that had oppressed her and carried her captive. This is agreeable to prophecies of the Messiah's redemption (Is. 34:10–17 and 41:11–12 and 43:17, Dan. 2:35, Obad. 1:10, 17–18 and many other places.)

The temple of Jerusalem was rebuilt by the countenance and authority of Gentile kings (Ezra 1:2–11, ch. 6:6–15 and 7:11–22; Neh. 2:7–9), agreeable to Is. 49:23, "And kings shall be thy nursing fathers, and their queens thy nursing mothers." It seems to be intimated that the queen of Persia, as well as the king, favored the Jews and promoted the restoring of their state in Neh. 2:6. The temple and city were rebuilt very much at the charge of Gentile kings and people, who offered silver and gold (Ezra 1:4–8, ch. 6:8 and 7:15–23; Neh. 2:7–9). This is agreeable to many places mentioned in the preceding section concerning Solomon's reign.[5]

At the time of this restoration of the Jews, strangers or Gentiles and their princes assisted with sacrifices for the house of God (Ezra 1:4, 6 and 6:9 and 7:17). This is agreeable to Ps. 22:29, "All they that be fat upon the earth shall eat and worship." Is. 49:7, "Kings shall see and arise, princes also shall worship, because of the Lord that is faithful,

5. See above, pp. 287–88, pp. 289–90, pp. 291–93.

and the Holy One of Israel, and he shall choose thee." Is. 60:6–7, "The multitude of camels shall cover thee, the dromedaries of Midian and Ephah; all they from Sheba shall come: they shall bring gold and incense. All the flocks of Kedar shall be gathered unto thee, the rams of Nebaioth shall minister unto thee: they shall come up with acceptance on mine altar, and I will glorify the house of my glory."

Gold, and silver, and sacrifices and incense were brought to the new temple at Jerusalem, especially from the nations on this side the river Euphrates (Ezra 1:4, 6, ch. 6:6–10, ch. 7:16–18, 21–23; Neh. 2:7–9), which include Tyre and Ethiopia, Midian and Ephah, Kedar, Nebaioth and other countries of Arabia, which are spoken of in prophecies that have been already mentioned in this and the foregoing section[6] as bringing presents, offering gifts, gold, incense and sacrifices.

The Jews at their return out of Babylon were redeemed without money. Is. 45:13, "He shall build my city, and he shall let go my captives, not for price nor reward"; agreeable to Is. 52:3, "Ye have sold yourselves for nought; and ye shall be redeemed without money."

The temple was built by Joshua, that signifies "Jehovah the Savior," agreeable to what is often represented of the Messiah in the prophecies. (See pp. 241–43, concerning Joshua the son of Nun.)[7]

We often read of praying, fasting, confessing sin—their own sins and the sins of their fathers—and weeping and mourning for sin that attended this restoration of the Jews (Dan. 9:1–19; Ezra 8:21–23, ch. 9, throughout, 10:1–17; Neh. 1:4–11, ch. 4:4–5, ch. 9, throughout). (See "Fulfillment of Prophecies" §102.)[8]

God gave the Jews remarkable and wonderful protection in their journey as they were returning from Babylon towards Jerusalem, and also in the midst of the great dangers and manifold oppositions they passed through in rebuilding the temple and city (Ezra 8:21–23, 31, chs. 5–7; Neh. 4 and 6). This is agreeable to Jer. 31:8–9, "Behold, I will bring them from the north country, and gather them from the coasts of the earth ... They shall come with weeping, and with supplications will I lead them: I will cause them to walk by the rivers of waters in a straight way, wherein they shall not stumble: for I am a father to Israel, and Ephraim is my firstborn." Is. 43:2, "When thou pass through the

---

6. See ibid.

7. JE argues that Joshua's many names typified the Messiah.

8. "Fulfillment" §102, renumbered 104 on MS pp. 77–78, begins, "The prophecies do represent repentance as the special condition of remission of sins in the days of the Messiah's kingdom."

waters, I will be with thee; and through the rivers, they shall not overflow thee: when thou walkest through the fire, thou shalt not be burnt; neither shall the flame kindle upon thee." (See pp. 294–95.)[9]

There was kept an extraordinary Feast of Tabernacles on occasion of this restoration of the Jews, the only one that had been kept according to the law of Moses since the time of Joshua, the son of Nun (Neh. 8:14). This is agreeable to Zech. 14:16–19.

After this return from the captivity, the Jews had extraordinary means of instruction in the law of God, much greater than they had before (Ezra 7:25, Neh. 8). After this, synagogues were set up all over the land, in each of which was kept a copy of the Law and the Prophets, which were read and explained every sabbath day; and there seems to be a great alteration as to the frequency of the solemn, public worship of God. (See "Fulfillment of Prophecies" §35, §115, §117.)[1]

Idolatry was utterly abolished among the Jews after their return from the Babylonish captivity. This is agreeable to Is. 2:18, "The idols shall be utterly abolished." Zech. 13:2, "And it shall come to pass in that day, saith the Lord of hosts, that I will cut off the names of the idols out of the land, and they shall no more be remembered." Hos. 2:17, "For I will take away the names of Baalim out of her mouth, and they shall no more be remembered by their name." Ezek. 36:25, "Then will I sprinkle clean water upon you, and ye shall be clean: from all your filthiness, and from all your idols, will I cleanse you." Ch. 37:23, "Neither shall they defile themselves anymore with their idols, nor with their detestable things." (See further, "Fulfillment of Prophecies" §153.)[2]

The remarkable agreement between what we are told of Daniel, and Shadrack, Meshack and Abednego, and what is said in the prophecies of the Messiah and his people, is such as naturally leads us to suppose

---

9. JE likens the return from Babylon to the Messiah's kingdom.

1. For "Fulfillment" §35, see above p. 000, n. 4. Sec. 115, renumbered 117 on MS p. 89, reads, in part, "It was foretold that in the time of the Messiah's kingdom, extraordinary provision should be made for the church with respect to her teachers. [...] This is fulfilled in the church of Jesus Christ. [...] But in the constitution of the Christian church, provision is made that there should be persons everywhere whose constant business it should be from week to week to instruct and guide the people in things of religion, and to explain and apply the Word of God, who should devote themselves wholly to this business, and spend and be spent in it." Sec. 117, renumbered 119 on MS p. 90, reads, in part, "It seems to be foretold that public assemblies of God's people to attend the ordinances of God's public worship, should be much more frequent in the times of the Messiah's kingdom than they were of old in the church of Israel by the appointment of the law of Moses."

2. For "Fulfillment" §153, see above p. 251, n. 6.

the former a designed type of the latter. Compare Dan. 3 and 6 with Is. 48:10 and 43:2, and Ps. 22:20–21 and 35:17, Cant. 4:8.

'Tis remarkable that it should be so ordered that so many of the chief women that we read of in the history of the Old Testament, and mothers of so many of the most eminent persons, should for so long a time be barren, and their conception afterwards of these eminent persons they were the mothers of should be through God's special mercy and extraordinary providence, as in Sarah, Rebekah, Rachel, Manoah's wife and Hannah. 'Tis reasonable to suppose that God had something special in view in thus remarkably ordering it in so many instances. Considering this, and also considering the agreement of such an event with several prophetical representations made of the church of God in the Messiah's times, there appears a great deal of reason to suppose the one of these to be designed as a type of the other. Ps. 68:6, "God setteth the solitary in families." Ps. 113:9, "He maketh the barren woman to keep house, and to be a joyful mother of children." Is. 54:1, "Sing, O barren, and thou that didst not bear; break forth into singing, and cry aloud, thou that didst not travail with child: for more are the children of the desolate than the children of the married wife, saith the Lord."

With respect to some of the principal persons spoken of in the Old Testament, there is this evidence that they were types of the Messiah, viz. that the Messiah in the prophecies is called by their names. Thus the Messiah is called by the name of *Israel*. Is. 49:3, "And he said unto me, Thou art my servant, O *Israel*, in whom I will be glorified." And he is often called in the prophecies by the name of David. Hos. 3:5, "Afterward shall the children of Israel return, and seek the Lord and David their king." Jer. 30:9, "But they shall serve the Lord their God, and David their king, whom I will raise up unto them." Ezek. 34:24, "And I the Lord will be their God, and my servant David a prince among them." Ch. 37:24–25, "And David my servant shall be king over them; and they all shall have one shepherd: they shall also walk in my judgments, and observe my statutes, and do them. And they shall dwell in the land that I have given unto Jacob my servant, wherein your fathers have dwelt; and they shall dwell therein, even they, and their children forever: and my servant David shall be their prince forever." Ps. 89:20, "I have found David my servant; with my holy oil have I anointed him." V. 27, "I will make him my firstborn, higher than the kings of the earth."

The Messiah is called by the name of Solomon (Cant. 3:7, 11, ch.

8:11–12). So the Messiah's great forerunner is called by the name of Elijah (Mal. 4), which argues that Elijah was a type of him. The Messiah is called by the name of Zerubbabel. Hag. 2:23, "In that day, saith the Lord of hosts, will I take thee, O Zerubbabel, my servant, the son of Shealtial, saith the Lord, and I will make thee a signet: for I have chosen thee, saith the Lord of hosts."

And as the Messiah is called by the proper names of some of the more eminent persons of the Old Testament, so some of them are called by names, that 'tis evident by the prophecies, do much more eminently and properly belong to the Messiah. So Joshua is called "Jehovah our Savior," as his name, "Joshua," signifies, which don't properly belong to him, but according to the prophecies does properly belong to the Messiah. So he is called "the shepherd, the stone of Israel" (Gen. 49:24), which according to the prophecies are appellations most properly belonging to the Messiah. So the name "Israel," though it was the proper name of Jacob rather than of the Messiah, yet its signification, "the prince of God," most properly and eminently belongs to the Messiah according to the prophecies. So it is with the name of Abram, "high father," and Abraham, the "father of a multitude," David, "beloved," and Solomon, "peace" or "peaceable." God also calls Solomon his son, an appellation which most properly belongs to the Messiah.

There is such a commutation of names between not only persons, but also things, that we have an account of in the histories and prophecies of the Old Testament. Thus the people of the Messiah, though 'tis plain by the prophecies that they should chiefly be of the Gentiles, yet are very generally called by the name of Jacob and Israel. So the church of the Messiah, though 'tis plain by the prophecies that they shall dwell all over the world, yet are often called by the name of "Jerusalem" and "Zion." So we read in the prophecies of the Messiah's times of all nations going up from year to year to Jerusalem to keep the Feast of Tabernacles, and of their being gathered together to the mountain of the house of the Lord, which is utterly impossible. (See "Fulfillment of Prophecies" §24.)[3] Therefore we must understand only

3. "Fulfillment" §24, renumbered 23 on MS pp. 29–38, begins, "There are a great many representations in the Prophets of wonderful things of an outward and temporal nature to be brought to pass in the Messiah's days, and of many externally glorious circumstances of the people of God in the time of his kingdom, that it is evident either from the nature of the representations them[selves], or may be made plain by the Old Testament, are not literally but figuratively and mystically to be understood." JE argues at length that it would be impossible or absurd to interpret many prophecies literally.

things that were typified by Jerusalem and the mountain of the house of the Lord, God's holy mountain, holy hill, mountain of the height of Israel, etc. and the feast of tabernacles, and Israel's going up from year to year to keep that feast. So something appertaining to the Messiah's kingdom is called by the name of "the altar of the Lord at Jerusalem" [II Kgs. 23:9], and it is represented as though all nations should bring sacrifices and offer 'em there on that altar. Yet this is utterly inconsistent with what the prophecies themselves do plainly teach of the state and worship of the church of God at that time. (See ibid.)[4] So something appertaining to the Messiah's kingdom is called by the names of the "temple," and the "tabernacle" and of God's "throne" in the temple (Zech. 6:13). But 'tis plain by the prophecies that there should indeed be no material temple or tabernacle in the kingdom of the Messiah. (See ibid.)[5]

So we read also (Ezek. 45 and 46) of the Passover, that grand memorial of the bringing the children of Israel up out of Egypt. But 'tis evident that there will be no such memorial of that event upheld in the church in the Messiah's times, by Jer. 16:14–15 and ch. 23:7–8.

Certain officers in the church of the Messiah are called "priests" and "Levites" (Is. 61:6 and Jer. 33:18), and yet 'tis plain by the prophecies that the ceremonial law should be abolished in the Messiah's times. (See "Fulfillment of Prophecies" §146–48.)[6]

A work of grace that is wrought on the hearts of men is often in the Old Testament called by the name of "circumcision," and 'tis evident by the prophecies that this should in a very eminent and distinguishing manner [be] wrought in the Messiah's times.

Something that the Messiah was to be the subject of is called in Ps. 40 by the name of *boring the ear*, as was appointed in the law concerning the servant that chose his master's service.

Something in the prophecies of the Messiah is called by the name of *oil* and *anointing* that, it is evident, is not any such outward oil[7] or

4. See above p. 299, n. 3.
5. Ibid.
6. For "Fulfillment" §146–47, see p. 274, n. 4. Sec. 148, renumbered 153 on MS p. 119, begins, "It was foretold that in the days of the Messiah's kingdom, instead of worship so much consisting in sacrifices of birds and beasts, and carnal ordinances and external performances, that worship should be appointed and maintained in the church of God that should be more simple and spiritual, consisting in prayer, praise, humility, brokenness of heart, obedience, almsgiving, etc."
7. JE deletes: "material oil."

anointing as was appointed in the ceremonial law (Ps. 45:7; Zech. 4:12, 14; Is. 61:1; Ps. 2:2, 6 and 20:6 and 89:20, with Ps. 133).

So we find something of a spiritual nature called in the prophecies by the name of the golden candlestick that was in the tabernacle and temple (Zech. 4). Something is called by the name of that cloud of glory that was above the mercy seat (Zech. 6:13), and something called by the name of God's dwelling between the cherubims (Ps. 99:1).

The name of the *incense*, and the names of the sweet spices that were used in the incense and anointing oil in the sanctuary, are made use of to signify spiritual things appertaining to the Messiah and his kingdom in the book of Canticles and Ps. 45:8. Something in the Messiah's kingdom is called by the name of the precious stones that adorned the temple.[8] Compare Is. 54:11–12 with I Chron. 29:2 and II Chron. 3:8.

And something spiritual in that prophecy, Ps. 45, is called "needle-work," the name of the work of the hangings and garments of the sanctuary (Ex. 26:36, and 27:16, and 36:37, and 38:18, and 28:39 and 39:29). The garments of the church of the Messiah are spoken under the same representation as the curtains of the tabernacle and beautiful garments of the high priest. (See also Cant. 1:5.) Something in the Messiah's kingdom is called by the name of the outward ornaments of the temple (Is. 60:13).

As the people of the Messiah are in the prophecies called by the name of God's people Israel, though they should be chiefly of the Gentiles, so likewise we find the enemies of the Messiah's people called by the names of the enemies of Israel, such as Edom, Moab, the children of Ammon, the Philistines, etc.; and the places of the abode of those enemies of the Messiah's people by the names of the countries and cities of God's enemies, as Egypt, Babylon, Bozrah, etc. And yet it is evident that these prophecies can't have respect to these nations literally, as hereafter to be such grievous and troublesome neighbors to the Messiah's people, as these nations were to Israel. For the Messiah's people were to be dispersed all over the world, and not in the neighborhood of those countries only.

Here it may be observed that the manna is called by the name of something spiritual. Ps. 78:24–25, "He had given them the corn of heaven. Men did eat angels' food." Which is an argument that it was a type of something spiritual.

8. The following sentence was written by JE at a later time in a grayish ink.

It was before observed that the things of the Messiah are in the prophecies expressly compared to many of the things of the Old Testament.[9] And I would now observe that many of them, where they are thus compared, are compared in such a manner as to be at the same time called by the same names. Thus the bondage that the Messiah should redeem his people from is called a "lying among the pots" (Ps. 68:13). And this redemption of the Messiah is expressly called a redeeming them from Egypt (Is. 11:11, Zech. 10:10). And something that God would do then is called his destroying the tongue of the Egyptian sea, and making men go over dry shod (Is. 11:15), and dividing the sea and the river. Zech. 10:10–11, "I will bring them again also out of the land of Egypt. And he shall pass through the sea with affliction, and shall smite the waves of the sea, and all the deeps of the river shall dry up." In Ps. 68:22, the redemption of the Messiah is called a "bringing God's people again from the depths of the sea."

So something that should be in the days of the Messiah is called by the name of "cloud by day and pillar of fire by night" (Is. 4:5).

Something appertaining to the kingdom of the Messiah is called by the name of the valley of Achor, the place where Achan was slain (Hos. 2:15).

So things appertaining to the destruction of the Messiah's enemies are often called by the names of things made use of in the destruction of the old world, of Sodom and Gomorrah, of the Egyptians and Canaanites, etc. as a flood of waters, rain, hailstones, fire and brimstone, a burning tempest, etc. as has been observed before.[1]

The redemption of the Messiah is called by the names by which the redemption out of Babylon was called. Jer. 16:15, "But, The Lord liveth, which brought up the children of Israel out of the land of the north." So again, ch. 23:8, that the "north country" or "land of the north" was an appellative name by which Chaldea was called is very manifest. (See Jer. 4:6, and 6:22, and 1:14 and very many other places; see the Concordance.)[2]

Things that shall be brought to pass in the Messiah's days are called by the name of what literally came to pass in the wilderness, after the redemption [out] of Egypt, in that in the prophecies we often read of waters in the wilderness; and streams in the desert and in dry places; and the Messiah's drinking of the brook in the way; and living waters

9. See above pp. 202–19.
1. Ibid.
2. See Crudens, *A Complete Concordance*, "North."

running through the desert in [the] east country, which is the desert of Arabia (Ezek. 47:8)'; waters in dry places, to give drink to God's people when ready to fail with thirst (Is. 35:7, and 41:17–18, and 32:2, and 43:19–20 and 55:1).

Sin, or corruption, which it is evident by the prophecies the Messiah comes to heal, is called by the same general names that belonged to the leprosy, as wounds and bruises and putrifying sores from the crown of the head to the soles of the feet.

Something that should be in the Messiah's times is spoken of under the name of a trumpet, an instrument much in use by God's appointment in the observances of the ceremonial law (Is. 27:13). And something seems to be spoken of under the name of that sound that was made with the trumpets on their joyful festivals, especially on the year of jubilee (Ps. 89:15).

Something that should be fulfilled in the Messiah's times is called by the name of that which the serpent is doomed to. Gen. 3:14, "Dust shalt thou eat." Is. 65:25, "Dust shalt be the serpent's meat." Something that should be done by the Messiah is spoken of under the name of the application that was made of water in the legal purifications. Is. 52:15, "So shall he sprinkle many nations." Ezek. 36:25–26, "Then will I sprinkle clean water upon you." Zech. 13:1, "In that day there [shall] be a fountain opened ... for sin and for uncleanness." Compare these with Num. 8:7 and 19:13, 18–21.

The congregation in the wilderness were in the form of an army, and an army with banners. So the church of the Messiah is often represented as an army. They are represented as being called forth to war and engaged in battle, gloriously conquering and triumphing, in places innumerable, and spoken of as being God's "goodly horse in the battle" [Zech. 10:3]; and as "a company of horses in Pharaoh's chariots" [Cant. 1:9]; and being made as "the sword of a mighty man" [Zech. 9:13]; and being gathered to an ensign (Is. 11:10, 12) and standard (Is. 49:22 and 59:19 and 62:10); and having a banner given them (Ps. 60:4); and setting up their banners in God's name (Ps. 20:5), and being terrible as an army with banners (Cant. 6:4, 10).

Something in the kingdom of the Messiah is spoken of in the prophecies under the name of pomegranates, which were represented in the work of the tabernacle and temple (Cant. 4:3, 13, and 6:7, 11, and 7:12 and 8:2).

Figures that were made in the tabernacle and temple were called cherubim, the same name by which angels are called in the Old Testament, which is an evidence that they were made as types or representations of angels.

The church and people of the Messiah are in the prophecies of the Messiah compared [to] and called a palm tree, or palm trees (Cant. 7:7–8, Ps. 92:12), which is an argument that they were typified by the figures of palm trees in the tabernacle and temple.

Something that should be in the Messiah's time is represented by what appertained to [the] manner of God's appearance in the holy of holies. Ps. 97:2, "Clouds and darkness are round about him." Compare II Sam. 22:12.[3]

Some of the persons that we have an account of in the history of the Old Testament are expressly spoken of as resembling the Messiah. So Moses: "A prophet will the Lord thy God raise up unto them, like unto thee" (Deut. 18:15, 18). So Melchizedek: Ps. 110:4, "Thou art a priest forever after the order of Melchizedek." And the account we have (Is. 7) concerning Shearjashub, the son of Isaiah the prophet, is equivalent to expressly declaring him to be a type of the Messiah. And Zerubbabel and Joshua are evidently made use of and spoken of as types of the Messiah. Hag. 2:23, "In that day, saith the Lord of hosts, will I take thee, O Zerubbabel, my servant, the son of Shealtiel, and make thee as a signet." Zech. 4:7, "Who art thou, O great mountain? before Zerubbabel thou shalt become a plain: and he shall bring forth the headstone thereof with shoutings, crying, Grace, grace unto it." V. 10, "For who hath despised the day of small things? for they shall rejoice, and shall see the plummet in the hand of Zerubbabel with those seven; they are the eyes of the Lord, which run to and fro through the whole earth." Zech. 3:1–8, "And he showed me Joshua the high priest ... And unto him he said ... I will clothe thee with change of raiment. And I said, Let them set a fair miter upon his head ... Hear now, O Joshua the high priest, thou, and thy fellows that sit before thee (for they are men wondered at): for, behold, I will bring forth my servant the Branch." Zech. 6:11–12, "Then take silver and gold, and make crowns, and set them upon the head of Joshua the son of Josedech, the high priest; And speak unto him, Behold the man whose name is The Branch."

'Tis an evidence that some of the more eminent persons that we have an account of in the history of the Old Testament are types of the Messiah, that some of them and the Messiah are plainly spoken of under one. 'Tis plain concerning David in Ps. 89, where the name of

3. JE cancels, "and Prov. 30:4; Job 11:7, and 36:26, and 37:23, and 145:3."

David is mentioned once and again, and yet the psalm evidently looks beyond David to the Messiah. 'Tis also plain concerning Solomon in the seventy-second psalm, which the title declares to have respect to Solomon, and yet the matter of the psalm most evidently shows that it has respect to the Messiah, many things in it being true of the Messiah and peculiar to him, and not true of Solomon.

And here, by the way, I would observe that to the many evidences that have already been taken notice of that David and Solomon are types of the Messiah, this may be added: that the Jews themselves looked on them as types of the Messiah. (See Basnage's *History of the Jews*, p. 367.)[4]

Many things occasionally appointed of God, if they signify nothing spiritual, must be wholly insignificant actions, and so wholly impertinent. Such as the setting up a brazen serpent for men to look upon, in order to a being healed [Num. 21:8]; God appointing the princes of the congregation to dig a well with their staves to supply the congregation, and a public record being made of [it] by divine inspiration, and its being celebrated in a song of the people that is also recorded by divine inspiration (Num. 21:17–18); Moses' holding up his hand by divine direction, that Joshua and Israel might prevail over Amalek [Ex. 17:11]; Elijah's stretching himself three times upon the widow of Zarephath's son, in order to raise him to life (I Kgs. 17:21); Elisha ordering his staff to be laid on the face of the Shunammite's dead child, and afterwards his lying upon the child, and putting his mouth on his mouth, and his eyes upon his eyes and his hands upon his hands, and stretching himself on the child, in order to raise it to life [II Kgs. 4:29, 34]. And so many other like actions that God appointed might be mentioned.[5]

But to say something more particularly concerning the ceremonial law. There is abundant evidence, even in the Old Testament, that the things that belong to that law are typical of the things of the Messiah.

---

4. Basnage, *History of the Jews*, p. 367: "[The Jewish Church] did not think *David* was that Deliverer long before promis'd, since he beg'd of God *to send him his Light and Truth;* that is, the *Messiah* as a famous Rabbi hath explain'd it. They look'd upon *David* as the Image of the Deliverer; And they had the same Notion of *Solomon.* And therefore they believ'd that the Book of *Canticles* was chiefly compos'd for the *Messiah.*"

5. JE deletes: "So some historical events, in some very minute circumstances, are manifestly typical, and God intended to signify something by 'em; otherwise it seems wholly impertinent that they should be regarded as of importance in the time that they came to pass, and afterwards in recording of 'em, such as David's offering sacrifices when the ark had gone six paces (II Sam. 2:13)."

If the things of the ceremonial law are not typical of moral and spiritual things, they are wholly insignificant and so wholly impertinent and vain. For God does abundantly declare, even in the Old Testament, that he has no delight in 'em on their own account, and that they are in his esteem worthless and vain in themselves; and therefore it will follow that they must be worthless and vain to all intents and purposes, unless they are otherwise by the relation they bear to something that God delights in on its own account, i. e. unless they are some way significant of things moral and spiritual. If the things of the ceremonial law were pleasing to God, and were not pleasing on their own account or by reason of anything that God saw in them, then it must be on account of something else that they represent, and some way stand instead of them. For instance, when God went out through the land of Egypt to smite the firstborn and saw the blood of the paschal lamb on the doorposts of an house, it is represented as being something pleasing to God, for the sake of which he would spare the inhabitants of that house. But the Old Testament reveals that that blood was not at all pleasing on its own account, for that declares that God hath no delight in the blood of beasts; and therefore the way in which it was something pleasing to God must be its being something which represented or stood instead of something that was truly in itself pleasing. So the sweet savor that was made in offering incense is spoken of as something sweet and pleasant to God, and a white, clean garment, something pure and so pleasing to God. But we know that these things were not pleasant or acceptable on their own account, and therefore it must be only as related to something else that was so. But which way is a sweet smell related to anything really sweet to God, but only as it is a type or has some signification of it? And which way has the purity of a garment any relation to spiritual purity, but as it has a representation of it?

This leads me to observe that there is an apparent and designed resemblance between those things that were instituted, that in themselves were worthless, and those moral and spiritual things that in themselves were valuable in the sight of God. Thus 'tis apparent that outward cleanness and purity resembles and shadows forth that which is in the sight of God real purity, and outward sweetness resembles real sweetness to God. So the light of the lamps in the sanctuary had a resemblance of spiritual light, and the preciousness of gold and pearls that were used in the sanctuary and priests' garments had a resemblance of some real preciousness in the sight of God. And the beauty and ornaments of the sanctuary, and its vessels and holy garments, etc. had a resemblance of real beauty and of those things that were ornaments in the sight of God. So that seeming atonement for sin that was in the legal sacrifices had a resemblance of that only true atonement the prophecies speak of. The seeming vicariousness there was in the sufferings of beasts for sinners had a resemblance of a true vicariousness and substitution.

And 'tis also manifest that God chose these things, or had respect to 'em in his choice and appointment of 'em, because they did resemble or shadow forth those correspondent spiritual things that have a real value and excellency in themselves in his sight. The very nature of the thing makes it manifest. Thus 'tis manifest that God chose pure garments rather than filthy ones, because outward purity did more resemble real purity. So he chose a sweet smell to be offered as a pleasant savor unto him, because sweet smell has more resemblance of what is really sweet to him. 'Tis manifest that he chose the suffering of beasts as an atonement for sin rather than the feeding and pampering of them, because this has more of a resemblance of a true atonement, which the prophecies speak of as being by the sufferings of a surety. 'Tis evident that God chose the blood or life of the creature to be offered to make atonement for the soul rather than the hair, because it has a greater resemblance of the life of a surety, which is a true atonement for the soul, as the prophecies of the Old Testament do represent. But if this be evident, that God in the institution of the things of the ceremonial law had respect to the resemblance that was in them of spiritual things and things of the Messiah, and appointed these rather than things of a diverse nature for the sake of that resemblance, this is the same thing as to say that the former are appointed as types of the latter.

All the people of Israel, if they exercised consideration, must[6] suppose and understand that these things pertaining to the ceremonial law were appointed and used as representations and symbols of something spiritual, and not for the sake of any innate goodness in them or any value God had for them. As, for instance, that God appointed white garments rather than yellow, green or black, not for any excellency of the color, but as a more proper representation of righteousness and spiritual purity; and the making a sweet odor with spices, not that God smelt that odor and so was pacified towards men, as though

6. JE deletes: "naturally."

he were recompensed by the great pleasure they thereby gave him, but to represent something spiritual that was highly acceptable to him. And so that God appointed them to offer the flesh of beasts and bread as the food or bread of God, as those things are called, and the drink offering of wine, not that God eat and drank those things, and was pleased with the taste of them, and received refreshment and benefit, as a hungry and thirsty man does by meat and drink, but that those things were mystical and symbolical representations of things of a higher and more divine nature.

They must know that laying hands on the head of the sacrifice, and what was called laying sins on the scapegoat, was no real laying sins on those beasts. And besides, God did expressly and abundantly teach his people under the Old Testament the contrary of those things. They must naturally therefore suppose that they were used as things significant of something of a nature higher than themselves. They must naturally suppose that the eating the Passover with the staff in the hand, and with bitter herbs, and putting the blood of the sacrifices upon the tip of the right ear, the thumb of the right hand and the great toe of the right foot, were mystical and symbolical, and so significant of something in itself of value and importance.

With respect to the legal sacrifices, the evidence that they were types of the Messiah is very strong, which will appear if we consider the following things:

'Tis evident there is some real and proper atonement for sin, which is in God's account requisite and which he insists upon, in order to the pardon of sin, and which he accepts as a true atonement and is willing to forgive sin on account of it. Otherwise God never would designedly have taken a course, by such an abundance of institutions, to bring up his people of the nation of Israel in the notion of the need of some atonement for sin, and some vicariousness and substitution of suffering for the sinner, in order to satisfy divine justice; and not only to bring up the Jews in this notion, but his church and people from the beginning of the world, insomuch that all nations received this notion from the first progenitors and founders of the nations and families of the earth. (See "Miscellanies" [no.] 912.)[7]

'Tis also very manifest that the legal sacrifices of beasts and birds

7. In "Miscellanies" no. 912, JE argues that God's requiring sacrifices in Old Testament times indicated the need for spiritual atonement. Moreover, he argues that even then it was apparent that the sacrifices offered were no real atonement for sin.

were no real atonement. This appears not only from the nature of the thing, but it is what God abundantly taught his people under the Old Testament, of whom he required these sacrifices (Ps. 40:6, Ps. 50:5–23 and 51:16, Is. 1:11–14, Is. 66:2–3, Hos. 6:6, Jer. 7:21–23 and especially Mic. 6:6–8). (See "Miscellanies" no. 912).[8]

'Tis apparent by the prophecies of the Old Testament that the Messiah was to offer a true and real atonement for the sins of men. (See "Fulfillment of Prophecies" §74–86.)[9] That the Messiah should offer up himself a sacrifice for sin is very clearly implied in many places there mentioned. But this doctrine is not only implied, but it is declared that the Messiah should atone for sin or expiate it by sacrifice. Is. 53:10, "When thou shalt make his soul an offering for sin." Dan. 9:24, "Seventy weeks are determined upon thy people and upon thy holy city ... *to make reconciliation for iniquity,*" or, "to expiate iniquity by sacrifice" or "make atonement for iniquity": for the word in the original is the very same that is used from time to time in the Law about sacrifices for making atonement. In what follows, it is declared how this atonement was to be made, viz. by the anointing the Most Holy and the coming of the Messiah, and by his being cut off, but not for himself, and making the sacrifice and oblation to cease in the last half of the seventieth week. And 'tis evident that the atonement for sin here spoken of is a proper atonement that makes real satisfaction for sin, and truly pays and finishes the debt, by the other expressions that are added: "To finish the transgression, and make an end of sin, and bring in everlasting righteousness ... and making the sacrifice and oblation to cease" [Dan. 9:24, 27]; i. e. by making sin to cease, making an end of sin and finishing the transgression, that there shall be no further occasion for sacrifice and oblation. And making atonement for sin is here prophesied of as that which was to be, but never yet was. It was a new thing, as the prophecy must be understood. But it could be a new thing in no other sense but that, viz. that a true and proper atonement for sin should be offered, for atonements in other senses but this had been abundantly offered from the beginning of the world. What is translated "to finish the transgression," might have been rendered "to consume transgression." But that expiation for sin that consumes transgression, and makes an end of sins and brings into a state of perpetual

8. Ibid.
9. For "Fulfillment" §74–86, see above p. 270, n. 5; p. 231, n. 3; p. 231, n. 4; p. 236, n. 9.

righteousness, so as to make all further sacrifices or attempts and means and representations of atonement to cease, and should abolish them as now needless, that is undoubtedly a proper atonement for sin.

Again, 'tis not only manifest by the Old Testament that the sacrifice of the Messiah is a true, real atonement for sin, but that it is the only true and real atonement for sin. For the Old Testament speaks of no other sorts of sacrifices of expiation for sin but these two, viz. the ancient legal sacrifices of beasts, and the sacrifice of the Messiah. What the prophecies sometimes say of sacrifices that should be offered by God's people after the Messiah's ascension must be understood figuratively, because it is expressly foretold that the Messiah by his sacrifice should cause the sacrifice and oblation to cease. And besides, as I observed before,[1] the Messiah's making expiation for sin is prophesied of as a new thing. And as it is foretold as a new thing, or the first thing of that nature, so it is also prophesied of as the last thing of that nature, as is implied in those expressions of his making an end of sin, finishing the transgression and making the sacrifice and oblation to cease. And these two things put together imply that this is the only truly expiatory sacrifice. (See also Zech. 3:8–9.) And then that is the only sacrifice by which the sins of God's people is atoned, and that never anyone is forgiven and accepted on account of any other atonement, is implied in that, Is. 53:6, *"All we* like sheep have gone astray; we have turned *every one* to his own way; and the Lord hath laid on him the iniquity of us *all."* ´

Another thing that is very manifest is that the legal sacrifices had a manifold resemblance and representation of the great, true and proper sacrifices that the prophecies foretell that the Messiah should offer. Thus those beasts that were offered were without blemish, as the prophecies represent the Messiah to be (Is. 53 and other places). Those sacrifices were not of unclean but clean beasts, therein representing that spiritual purity that the prophecies speak of in the Messiah. A very great part of those sacrifices were of lambs, as the paschal lambs (Ex. 29:39), and very many other of their sacrifices, which had a resemblance of what the prophecies do represent of the feebleness, innocence, meekness and gentleness of the Messiah. (See "Fulfillment of Prophecies.")[2]

Most of the sacrifices were males, as the Messiah is represented as of

1. See above p. 309.
2. JE may here refer to "Fulfillment" §27, MS p. 41, which describes the Messiah's freedom from sin; see above p. 245, n. 9.

the male sex. They were offered by a priest in white robes, representing the purity and holiness of the Messiah, who when spoken of (Dan. 9) as the great priest that should offer that atonement that should make an end of sin, is called "the Most Holy." "Seventy weeks are determined, to make reconciliation for iniquity ... and to anoint the Most Holy" [Dan. 9:24]. The priests were anointed. Herein there is a resemblance between them and the great Messiah, or "Anointed." The sacrifices suffered, as the Messiah, the great sacrifice, is represented. The sacrifices suffered death, and a violent death; the Messiah suffered death. The sacrifices were burnt by fire from heaven, as the prophecies represent the Messiah as suffering from the immediate hand of God. (See "Fulfillment of Prophecies" §70.)[3]

In most of the sacrifices, those inward parts were to be burnt on the altar, that are abundantly made use of in the Old Testament to represent the soul, which is agreeable to what the prophecies represent of the Messiah's making his soul an offering for sin. The fat of the inwards of the sacrifices was melted and consumed and burnt up in the fire, which is agreeable to Ps. 22:14–15, "I am poured out like water ... my heart is like wax; it is melted in the midst of my bowels. My strength is dried up like a potsherd." And Ps. 102:4, "My heart is smitten, and withered like grass." And Is. 53:12, "He hath poured out my soul unto death."

There was the resemblance of the substitution of the sacrificed beasts in suffering for the sinner, as the prophecies represent concerning the Messiah. There was an appearance of laying the iniquities of those for whom the sacrifice was offered, on the animal sacrificed; especially on some of the sacrifices, on the heads of which the hands of those for whom they were offered were laid, that they might lay their sins upon them. This is agreeable to Is. 53:6, "The Lord hath laid on him the iniquity of us all."

The scapegoat is represented as bearing the sins of those for whom he was offered into the wilderness, which is agreeable to Is. 53:4, "Surely he hath borne our griefs; he hath carried our sorrows."

The Messiah is expressly spoken of as being like a lamb, in his being slain and offered as a sacrifice for sin (Is. 53). The high priest made intercession for the people with the blood of the sacrifices, agreeable to Is. 53:12.

Besides all that has been already observed, this further is manifest,

---

3. See above p. 239, n. 4.

viz. that they are by God called an "atonement," and are said to be an atonement, time without number. (See the Concordance under the word "Atonement.")[4] Seeing therefore that the legal sacrifices are declared expressly and abundantly to be no real atonement, but have evidently a great resemblance of the true atonement and are plainly representations of it, and are abundantly spoken of by him that instituted 'em as being an atonement, and as instituted by him that they might be an atonement, 'tis very apparent that they were appointed figures and representations of the true atonement. For there is but these two ways of anything's being, consistent with truth, said to be such a thing, by the name of which it is called: viz. either its being that thing truly and properly, or figuratively and by representation. Either it must be that thing that it is said to be in reality, or by representation of the reality, or not at all. We have often in the law of Moses this expression used with regard to the sacrifices: *"The priest shall make an atonement for him."* Now one of these two meanings must be put upon the words: either that he shall make a real, proper atonement, or that he shall make an atonement figuratively or significantly. 'Tis either a true atonement or a seeming atonement, otherwise it would not be an atonement in any sense, nor would it be so called by God. If there be such a thing as a real atonement for sin, but the legal sacrifices are not a real atonement for sin, but yet are appointed and accepted as an atonement, then they are appointed and accepted instead of an atonement. For that is the same thing. So that it is evident that [God] appointed the legal sacrifices to stand instead of, or to represent, the real atonement. If a man be appointed to stand for another that is absent, and be accepted for an absent friend, then he is his representative.

When the prophet called the arrow that the king of Israel shot out of his window "the arrow of the Lord's deliverance" [II Kgs. 13:17], nothing else could be meant but that it was a sign of the arrow of the Lord's deliverance. So when the man that interpreted his fellow's dream, said of the barley cake, "This is the sword of Gideon, the son of Joash" [Judg. 7:14], he could mean nothing else but that this *signified* the sword of Gideon. So when Joseph said, "The seven lean kine are seven years of famine" [Gen. 41:27], and so in innumerable other instances that might be mentioned.

'Tis evident from what has been already observed, that here are certain resemblances and shadows of sacrifices and substitutions, in

4. See Crudens, *A Complete Concordance*, "Atonement."

suffering for sinners and atonements for sin. And it is manifest that it was out of regard to this resemblance there was in the shadow of the atonement that the shadow was appointed. God himself has decided it by calling the shadow by the name of the substance, and by declaring that he appointed the shadow that it might be for the substance; which he has done in declaring that he appointed it that it might be for an atonement, i. e. instead of the real atonement, which is the substance.

These shadows of atonement are not merely called by the name of an "atonement," but they are spoken of from time to time as being an atonement, and are said to be appointed that they might be an atonement. Now what other way there is of being an atonement, but either being so really, or being so in figure and significance, I don't know.

The incense appointed in the law had a sweet smell and was acceptable to the senses, and so had a shadow of that which was acceptable to God and a sweet savor to him. And seeing that it is expressly declared by God in the law that he appoints this incense for a sweet savor to him [Lev. 2:2], this demonstrates that God in the appointment has respect to that resemblance, that 'tis appointed to be a standing representation of a true, sweet savor to him. [A] sweet smell is appointed rather than [a] stinking smell, because it better resembles what is truly acceptable to God. When external whiteness and purity, that is a shadow of true purity in the sight of God, is called by the name of true purity, and is declared to be appointed that it might be for purity in the sight of God, this demonstrates that 'tis appointed to be a standing representation of true purity. So likewise when the shadows of sufferings for sinners and atonements for sin are called by the name of real sufferings for sinners and atonements for sin, and are said from time to time to be atonements for sin, and to be appointed that they might be for atonements for sin, it demonstrates clearly that these shadows of atonement are appointed out of respect to the resemblance they have to the real atonement, and that they might be instead of it and as standing representations of it; or, which is the same thing, that they might be types of it. God appointed the suffering of the creature, rather than the feeding or fatting of it, for the making atonement, because the suffering of the creature has a greater resemblance of that suffering that makes a real atonement for sin.

God in thus calling these shadows from time to time by the name of the thing resembled, and speaking of 'em from time to time as being the thing resembled, does therein plainly put 'em in their stead, and does make use of 'em as representations of 'em. As if any should on

design call one by another's name that was not his own name, and
ordinarily speak of him and treat him as being that other; this would
be the same thing as to substitute him for the other, and to make use of
him as the other's representative.

'Tis an argument that the sacrifices were types of the Messiah, that
when Manoah offered sacrifice by God's appointment, he that is called
"the angel of the Lord," and who was the Lord (and whom I have
proved to be the same person with the Messiah in my discourse on
"The Prophecies of the Messiah"),[5] ascended in the flame of the sacrifice (Judg. 13:20), and so did as it were offer up himself in the flame of
the sacrifice, intimating that he was the great sacrifice that was the
antitype of those sacrifices of beasts. The beasts that were sacrificed to
God ascended up in the flame before God for a sweet savor. So the
matter is represented in the Old Testament. But here we see that when
the sacrifice was ascending in the flame, the angel of the Lord ascends
in the same, to show that that was the end of the sacrificing fire, viz. to
cause him to ascend as a sweet savor unto God.

Again, there is clear proof that the legal sacrifices were types of the
great sacrifice of the Messiah in Dan 9:24, "Seventy weeks are determined upon thy people and upon thy holy city, to finish the transgression, and to make an end of sins, and to make reconciliation for iniquity, and to bring in everlasting righteousness, and to seal up the vision
and prophecy, and to anoint the most Holy"; taken together with v. 27,
"And he shall confirm the covenant with many for one week: and in
the midst of the week shall he cause the sacrifice and oblation to cease."
What is translated in v. 24, "and to make an end of sins," might have
been translated, "he shall seal up the sin offerings." The word translated *sins* in the original is *chattaoth*, the very same word that is made
use of in the law of Moses to signify sin offerings. So that the word
might as well be translated "sin offerings" here as there. And 'tis the
more likely that "sin offerings" should be meant here, because the
word is in the plural number; whereas if what was intended was the
same with "iniquity" in the clause preceding and "transgression" in the
clause following, thus varying the expression for eloquence's sake, it
would be more likely this word would have been in the singular number as those are. And besides, 'tis the more likely that the word signifies
sin offerings, because it is evident that this text is a prophecy of the
sacrifice that the Messiah should offer for sin. In the next words, "he

5. See above p. 238, n. 3.

shall make reconciliation for iniquity," the word rendered "reconciliation" (as has been already observed)[6] signifies "expiation by sacrifice,"
it being the same that is so often rendered *atonement* in the law of Moses
when speaking of sacrifices for sin. But what argues yet more strongly
that this should have been translated, *he shall make an end, or seal up, sin
offerings*, is that in the twenty-seventh verse there seems to be a reference to what had been said before in this verse, when it is said "in the
midst of the week" (or "in the half of the week") "he shall cause the
sacrifice and oblation to cease." In the twenty-fourth verse it had been
said that the sacrifices, or sin offerings, should be made an end of, or
sealed up, in seventy weeks. And the twenty-fifth, twenty-sixth and
twenty-seventh verses are evidently exegetical of that twenty-fourth to
explain how [the] anointed Holy One, or Messiah, should make atonement for iniquity and seal up the sin offering and sacrifices in seventy
weeks, viz. from the commandment to build Jerusalem there should
be seven weeks and threescore and two weeks, that is, sixty-nine weeks;
and then in the remaining week he should establish the covenant with
many, and in the half of the week he should make the sacrifice and
oblation to cease, or make an end of the sin offerings, as was said
before.

Now let us mind the expression. The word translated *make an end* in
the original is *he shall seal up*: "He shall seal up the sin offerings." 'Tis
the very same word that is used in the following clause concerning
vision and prophecy. He shall *"seal up* the vision and prophecy." The
same word being thus used twice in like manner in different clauses of
the same sentence, once concerning the visions and prophecy, and the
other time concerning the sin offering, there is all reason to understand it in both places in the same sense. But the plain meaning of that
clause, "to seal up the vision and prophecy," is this: then shall be
accomplished the grand event so often exhibited by the prophecies of
the prophets and so often represented and signified by the visions
which they saw, and so the vision and prophecy shall be finished and
brought to their grand accomplishment, that which they ultimately
aimed at. Then shall be fulfilled the sum of what was signified in the
vision and prophecy (Ezek. 28:12, "Thou sealest up the sum, full of
wisdom, and perfect in beauty"). So when in the same sentence it is
said, "to seal up the sin offerings and make atonement for iniquity," we
must in a like sense understand it thus: to offer that grand sacrifice or

6. See above pp. 309–10.

atonement for iniquity that is so much exhibited and represented by the sin offerings. So that the sin offerings shall be made to cease, their design being obtained and finished; that grand event, that great and true atonement for sin, which was aimed at in them and which they all signified and represented, being now accomplished.

Again, it is evident that the priests of old, in their office of offering sacrifices, were types of the Messiah in offering his sacrifice. Otherwise there is no truth in that prophecy that God declares in so solemn a manner and confirms with an oath in Jer. 33:18, "Neither shall the priests the Levites want a man before [me] to offer burnt offerings, and to kindle meat offerings, and to do sacrifice continually." See how solemnly this is confirmed and sworn in the following words [vv. 19–22]. Unless this be fulfilled in the true sacrifice or atonement which the Messiah offers, and in the accomplishment of that prophecy of the Messiah, Ps. 110:4, "The Lord hath sworn, and will not repent, Thou art a priest forever after the order of Melchizedek," it is not fulfilled at all, and is neither agreeable to fact nor to other prophecies. Unless this prophecy be fulfilled thus, it is not agreeable to fact. For the priests and Levites have no man literally to offer sacrifices literally, for a much longer time than never they had a man to offer sacrifices. And it is not agreeable to other prophecies, particularly that forementioned (Dan. 9:24 and 27), that speaks of the Messiah's causing the sacrifice and oblation to cease, and sealing them up, which is directly contrary to this prophecy of Jer. 33, if this latter be understood literally. For this very prophecy of Jeremiah is evidently a prophecy of the Messiah. See v. 15, "I will cause the Branch of righteousness to grow up to David." So that upon this supposition, Jeremiah foretells the Messiah's abundantly confirming the priests and Levites in their business of offering sacrifice and oblation, so as to perpetuate it forever. And Daniel foretells his finishing the business wholly, sealing it up and making it to cease. And 'tis elsewhere foretold that there should be no temple made with hands, no ark and no sacrifices of beasts, in the Messiah's times. (See "Fulfillment of Prophecies of the Messiah" §147–48.)[7]

From what has been now observed of the prophecies foretelling that the Messiah should abolish the legal sacrifices, it is manifest that whenever the prophecies of the Messiah's times do speak of sacrifices then to be offered, they are to be understood mystically, i. e. of spiritual

7. See above p. 274, n. 4; p. 300, n. 6.

things typified by the sacrifices, as Is. 19:21, Is. 60:7, Ezek. 20:40–41, Mal. 1:11.

The blood of the legal sacrifices is called "the blood of the covenant" by Moses. Ex. 24:8, "And Moses took the blood, and sprinkled it on the people, and said, Behold the blood of the covenant, which the Lord hath made with you concerning all these words." But God calls the blood of the Messiah the blood of the covenant that he had made with his people, or the blood [of] their covenant. Zech. 9:11, "As for thee also, by the blood of thy covenant I have sent forth thy prisoners out of the pit wherein there is no water." 'Tis evident that the blood of the Messiah is the blood by which the church will be redeemed when the Messiah comes, which is the time here spoken of. See v. 9 foregoing, "Rejoice greatly, O daughter of Zion; shout, O daughter of Jerusalem: behold, thy King cometh unto thee: he is just, and having salvation; lowly, and riding upon an ass, and upon a colt the foal of an ass." Therefore as both these, viz. the blood of the legal sacrifices and the blood of the Messiah, are called the blood of the church's covenant, 'tis manifest that one is represented by the other. The same sacrifice must be intended in that prophecy of the Messiah's times, Ps. 50:5, "Gather my saints together; those that have made a covenant with me by sacrifice."

Thus plain is it that the legal sacrifices were types of the Messiah, the great sacrifice and true atonement for sin, and appointed as such. And by some things that have been already observed, 'tis also manifest that their legal purifications were types of that spiritual purity that should be by the Messiah, and the sweet incense a type of that which is spiritual and truly sweet to God. (See pp. 305–08 and pp. 310–11.)[8] And concerning the incense, I further observe that spiritual things are expressly compared to it in the Old Testament. Ps. 141:2, "Let my prayer be set forth before thee as incense; and the lifting up of my hands as the evening sacrifice." And the Messiah is expressly compared to the cloud of incense (Cant. 3:6).

White and beautiful garments were appointed the priests by the law of Moses. These garments on the priests are expressly spoken of as representing something in the Messiah,[9] and particularly are there spoken of as representing righteousness. Again, the righteousness of

8. JE discusses how the ceremonial law was typical of the Messiah.
9. JE cancels, "Zech. 3."

the Messiah is compared to beautiful garments. Is. 61:10, "He hath covered me with the robe of righteousness, as a bridegroom decketh himself with his ornaments, and as a bride adorneth herself with her jewels." Job 29:14, "I put on righteousness, and it clothed me." God is represented as clothed with a garment white as snow (Dan. 7:9), and the Messiah appears to Daniel clothed in linen (Dan. 10:5–6 and 12:7). Spiritual purity is represented by the color white. Is. 1:18, "Though thy sins be as scarlet, they shall be white as snow." Dan. 12:10, "Many shall be purified, and made white." And 11:35, "Some shall fall, to try them, and to purge, and make them white."

The high priest had broidered garments; such are spoken of as representing righteousness. Ezek. 16:9–10, "Then I washed thee with water; I thoroughly washed away thy blood from thee, and I anointed thee with oil. I clothed thee also with broidered work ... and I girded thee about with fine linen."

'Tis manifest that the legal uncleannesses were types of sin. They are said to be an abomination to the Lord. Yea, they are called "sin" in the law of the sin offering (Lev. 6:6–8 and ch. 14:13–14, 19, 22, 24–25, 53, ch. 15:30). Moral impurities seem to [be] represented by legal impurities (Hag. 2:11–14).

One thing that was a legal pollution was blood. This is made use of by the prophets to represent sin. Ezek. 16:6, "When I saw thee polluted in thy blood." So vv. 9 and 22. Is. 1:18, "Though your sins be as scarlet ... and red like crimson." Ch. 4:4, "When the Lord shall have washed away the filth of the daughters of Zion, and shall have purged the blood of Jerusalem from the midst thereof by the spirit of judgment, and by the spirit of burning."[1]

One kind of legal uncleanness was through menstruous blood. Moral or spiritual pollution is compared to this. Is. 64:6, "All our righteousnesses are as filthy rags," or "as menstruous clothes," as it might have been rendered.

The leprosy was one kind of legal uncleanness. Sin seems to be compared to this in Is. 1:6, "From the sole of the foot even unto the head there is no soundness in it; but wounds, and bruises, and putrifying sores."

The legal purifications by washing the hands in the laver, and other parts of the body in water, is what a spiritual cleansing from sin is

---

1. JE cancels, "Joel 3:21, 'For I will cleanse their blood that I have not cleansed: for the Lord dwelleth in Zion.'"

compared to. Ps. 26:6, "I will wash my hands in innocency, and so will I compass thine altar," alluding to the priests washing their hands at the laver before they compassed God's altar. Zech. 13:1, "In that day there shall be a fountain opened to the house of David and to the inhabitants of Jerusalem for sin and for uncleanness." Ps. 51:2, "Wash me from my iniquity; cleanse me from my sin." Is. 1:16, "Wash ye, make ye clean; put away the evil of your doings." Jer. 4:14, "Wash thy heart from wickedness." Prov. 30:12, "There is a generation that are pure in their own eyes, and yet is not cleansed from their filthiness." Is. 4:4, "When the Lord shall have washed away the filth of the daughters of Zion." Ezek. 16:4, "Neither wast thou washed in water." V. 9, "Then washed I thee in water." Ezek. 36:25, "Then will I sprinkle clean waters upon you, and ye shall be clean from all your filthiness."

That the anointing under the law typified something spiritual is confirmed from that, that what is spiritual is called "anointing." Ezek. 16:9, "I anointed thee with oil." 'Tis an argument that those officers that were anointed were types of the Messiah, because his name is *Messiah*, or *The Anointed*. The holy anointing oil represented the Spirit of God, because the Holy Spirit is represented by holy anointing oil (Zech. 4:2–6, 12). And Is. 61:1, "The Spirit of the Lord God is upon me; because the Lord hath anointed me." By which last words it may also be confirmed that the anointing of the officers of the Jewish church represented the spiritual anointing of the Messiah.

Something spiritual that shall be in the Messiah's times is compared to the wine of the drink offering. Zech. 9:15, "They shall drink, and make a noise as through wine; they shall be filled like bowls, and as the corners of the altar."

We have the testimony of the Holy Spirit in the Old Testament that the golden candlestick, with its bowl on the top and its seven lamps and oil for the lamps, is a representation of the church of the Messiah (Zech. 4, taken with the preceding chapter).

The sanctuary or temple was a type of heaven, as may be argued from that, that heaven is called in the Old Testament his "dwelling place," his "holy habitation," his "sanctuary" and his "temple." I Kgs. 8:30, "Hear thou in heaven thy dwelling place." So vv. 39, 43, 49; II Chron. 6:21, 30, 39. And II Chron. 30:27, "Their prayer came up to his holy place, even unto heaven." Ps. 33:13–14, "The Lord looketh from heaven; he beholdeth all the sons of men. From the place of his habitation he looketh on all the inhabitants of the earth." Is. 63:15, "Look down from heaven, and behold from the habitation of thy holiness and thy glory." Jer. 25:30, "The Lord shall roar from on high, and utter his voice from his holy habitation." Deut. 26:15, "Look down from thy holy habitation." Ps. 68:4–5, "Sing unto the Lord, sing praises unto his name: extol him that rideth on the heavens by his name JAH ... a judge of the widows, is God in his holy habitation." Ps. 102:19, "For he hath looked down from the height of his sanctuary; from heaven did the Lord behold the earth." Ps. 11:4, "The Lord is in his holy temple, the Lord's throne is in heaven."

That the great, costly or precious stones that were the foundation of the temple, spoken of, I Kgs. 5:17, and of Solomon's house (ch. 7:10), [represented the Messiah,]² is confirmed by Is. 28:16, Ps. 118:22, Zech. 3:9 and 4:9.

'Tis a confirmation that the frame of the tabernacle and temple were typical, from the agreement there is between it and the visions under which God sometimes manifested himself. The mercy seat with the cherubims is called "the chariot of the cherubims" (I Chron. 28:18), agreeable to the vision that Ezekiel had of God riding in a chariot drawn by cherubims [Ezek. 10]. Ezekiel's vision of the chariot of the cherubims was also agreeable with the frame of the chariot in which the lavers were set, and represented as drawn by lions, oxen and cherubim, agreeable to the shapes of Ezekiel's living creatures [Ezek. 1]. (See I Kgs. 7:27–39).

But a very great and clear evidence that the city of Jerusalem, the holy city and the temple in all its parts and measures and its various appendages and utensils, with all its offices, services, sacrifices and ceremonies, and so all things appertaining to the ceremonial law, and indeed many things appertaining to the civil state of the people as divided into twelve tribes, were typical of things appertaining to the Messiah and his church and kingdom, is that these things are evidently made use of as such in a very particular manner in the vision of the prophet Ezekiel, that we have an account of in the nine last chapters of his prophecy [Ezek. 40–48]. Those things there mentioned, which [are] the same which were in Israel under the law of Moses, they are mentioned as resemblances, figures or symbolical representations of spirituals. (See "Prophecies of the Messiah" §74, and "Fulfillment of Prophecies" §23–24, §146–48.)³ So that God has in these chapters

---

2. JE, Jr.'s insertion.

3. In "Prophecies" §74, JE presents an extended analysis of Ezek. 40–48 to argue that they prophesy the times of the Messiah in their description of the restoration of Israel and the destruction of its enemies after captivity. JE writes on MS pp. 65–66, "This prince was to do

determined that these things are figures, symbols or types representing the things [of the Messiah's kingdom],[4] because here he plainly
makes use of 'em as such.

'Tis no argument that the things that have been treated of were not
designed as types of the Messiah and things pertaining to his kingdom,
that God, when he instituted 'em, did [not] expressly declare 'em to be
so. For there is no more necessity of supposing that all types signifying
future events, when given, should be explained, than all visions and
prophecies signifying future events. The things that [were] exhibited
in visions were truly a sort of types of future events, as Abraham's
smoking furnace and burning lamp, which was not explained nor
expressly declared to represent anything future. The twelve fountains
and threescore and ten palm trees at Elim were evidently types of the
twelve tribes and threescore and ten elders, but yet it is not expressly
said so. The like might be observed of Jacob's taking Esau by the heel at
his birth, and God's making Eve of Adam's rib, and Moses' rod's swallowing up the magicians' rods, and many other things.

*Corol.* Seeing it is thus abundantly evident by the Old Testament
itself that the things of the Old Testament were typical of the Messiah
and things appertaining to him, hence a great and most convincing
argument may be drawn that Jesus is the Messiah, seeing there is so
wonderful a correspondence and evident, manifold and great agreement between him and his gospel and these types of the Old Testament. And as it is so plain by the Old Testament that the ancient state
of things amongst the Jews was all typical of the Messiah, and the Jews
themselves acknowledged it, so 'tis a great argument that Jesus and his
kingdom were the end and antitype of these things. Because presently

---

all the part of an high priest among the people. He was to offer all the sacrifices of the nation.
They were to bring their sacrifices to him (ch. 45:13–16). They were to go through his hands
and by him to be offered to God; their daily, and their weekly and their monthly sacrifices,
and their sacrifices on all their feasts and special solemnities (ch. 45:17). And it shall be the
prince's part to give burnt offerings and meat offerings and drink offerings in the new
moons, in the sabbaths, in all solemnities of the house of Israel. He shall prepare the sin
offering and the meat offering, and the burnt offering and the sin offering, to make
reconciliation for the house of Israel." "Fulfillment" §23, renumbered 24 on MS p. 29, reads,
"'Tis evident by the Old Testament that the Messiah was not to be a temporal prince, and that
that great salvation that it is so often foretold the Messiah should work out, was not a
temporal but a spiritual salvation; and that those benefits of the Messiah, that peace and
happiness and glory so often promised under the Messiah, and so pompously represented,
don't consist in great worldly wealth, pleasures, honor and power, but is mainly a spiritual
happiness and glory." For §146–48, see above p. 274, n. 4; p. 300, n. 6.

4. JE, Jr.'s insertion.

after he comes and sets up his kingdom, God puts a total and final end to that typical state of the Jews and all thing appertaining to [it]; blots out all those types at once and wipes 'em clean away; and poured the utmost contempt upon 'em and covered 'em with the most dreadful darkness; and utterly destroyed, as by one great fatal and final blow, that whole typical world; and has now continued their abolition for so many ages, much longer than he did their existence; and has followed all that reject the antitype and would cleave to the types with so awful and continual a curse: and all this agreeably to the prophecies of what God would do when the Messiah, this great antitype, was come. (See "Fulfillment of Prophecies" §127–31 and §146–48.)[5]

That[6] typical representations were looked upon by God as no trifling matters, but things of great IMPORTANCE, is manifest in that it is spoken of in Scripture as a matter of such importance that Christ's body should not be at all corrupted, or begin to send forth any corrupt savor, before it was raised.

It was common for NAMES to be given by a spirit of prophecy. See Owen on Heb. 7:2, p. 112c, d, e.)[7]

We have reason to suppose that very many things in the Old Testament are intended as types, seeing 'tis manifest in some instances that so very minute circumstances were so ordered, such as the negative circumstances of the story of Melchizedek; there being no mention made of his father or mother, of his birth or death.

---

5. "Fulfillment" §127, renumbered 129 on MS pp. 93–95, begins, "It was foretold that in the days of the kingdom of the Messiah, the bigger part of the Jewish nation should be rejected from being God's people." Sec. 128, renumbered 131 on MS p. 95, begins, "It was foretold that the Jews, after they had rejected the Messiah and were rejected of God from being his people, should be given over to a very dreadful destruction." Sec. 129, renumbered 132 on MS pp. 95–98, details the time, manner, and means of the destruction of the Jewish nation and its people. Sec. 130, on MS p. 98, begins, "It was foretold that the Jews, for their ill treatment of the Messiah, should be in a remarkable manner given over to blindness of mind and to their own corruption and wickedness to add sin to sin." Sec. 131, renumbered 133 on MS pp. 98–99, begins, "According to the prophecies, the sins for which that people should be rejected from being God's people, and so given over to blindness of mind and hardness of heart, and at last so terribly destroyed, would be their unbelief, pride, self-righteousness, exalting themselves as better than others, their notorious hypocrisy and superstition, teaching for doctrines the commandments of men, and their perverseness and obstinacy in these things, attended with a persecuting spirit and practice."

6. The remainder of the document is written in a later hand, most likely from the Stockbridge period.

7. John Owen, *Excercitations on the Epistle to the Hebrews. Also Concerning the Messiah* (3 vols., London, 1680–88). JE refers to the third volume, *A Continuation of the Epistle of Paul the*

That everything, even to the least circumstance, prescribed by God about the tabernacle and all its services, were types of heavenly things, appears by the Apostle's manner of arguing (Heb. 8:5) from those words of God to Moses: "See that thou make all things according to the pattern showed to thee in the mount." And if they were all types, they were all for our instruction. And if they were our instruction, then we must endeavor to understand them, even those of 'em that are no-where explained in Scripture.

Heb. 9:3–5, the Apostle there mentioning the ark, mercy seat, tables of the covenant, the golden censer, pot of manna, Aaron's rod that budded, concludes thus: "*of which I cannot now speak particularly,*" i. e. "I can't now explain particularly the design of these things, and tell you particularly what evangelical and heavenly things were represented thereby"; which proves, evidently, that many things in the tabernacle were typical and intended to represent to God's people evangelical things, which signification is not explained to us in Scripture.

The Jews of old seemed to look on the redemption from Egypt as a type of the redemption which should be accomplished by the Messiah. (See SSS on Ex. 12:14.)[8]

'Tis an evidence that legal uncleanness was a type of sin, that they are in effect called sin. (See SSS on Lev. 12:8.)[9]

The temporal things of the Old Testament, types of the spiritual things of the New. (See SSS on I Sam. 2:10.)[1]

*Obj.* From the abuse that will be made of this doctrine of types.

*Ans.* I don't know that the types of Scripture are more abused by people that are enthusiastic and of teeming imagination than the visionary representations of the book of Revelation. And yet none makes that an objection against all attempts to understand that book.

---

*Apostle to the Hebrews* (London, 1688), pp. 112, where Owen is discussing the names that Paul gives Christ in Heb. 7:2, "King of righteousness" and "King of peace": "It may be enquired what *Ground* the apostle had to Argue from the *Signification of these Names*. [...] The apostle takes it for granted in general that every thing in the story of *Melchisedec* was *Mystical* and Figurative. [...] It was usual under the Old Testament to have Names given unto Children by a Spirit of Prophecy, as to *Noah, Peleg,* and others, yea, it may be most of the Patriarchs. It was so also to have Mens names changed upon some great and Solemn occasions, whence it was highly significant. [...] But where this was done by *Divine Warranty*, it was Doctrinal and Prophetically instructive." Owen goes on to state that the name "Immanuel" was given to Jesus by "*Divine Direction.*"

8. See above p. 212, n. 1.

9. See Poole, *Scripturae, 1,* 556.

1. *Ibid., 1, pars posterior,* cols. 23–25.

We have as good warrant from the Word of God to suppose the whole ceremonial law to be given in order to a figurative representing and signifying spiritual and evangelical things to mankind, as we have to suppose that prophetical representations are to represent and signify the events designed by them, and therefore as good reason to endeavor to interpret them.[2]

2. The remaining materials on MS pp. 72–73 have been moved to the beginning of the document (pp. 191–92) at JE's direction.

# EDWARDS' TABLE TO "TYPES OF THE MESSIAH"

## THE TABLE[1]

Aaron's rod blossoming, 198

Abraham, called by a name of the
Messiah, 299; his victory over the
kings, 208–09

Achan, the slaying of him, 215, 302

Allegories among the heathen,
193–94

Altar in the sanctuary, 299–300

Anointing, 310–11, 318–19

Anointing oil, 300–01

Arrows, the king of Israel's smiting
the ground with them, 196; his
shooting them out of his eastern
window, 206

Atonement for sin, that there is some
proper and real, evident from the
Old Testament, 308; that the legal
sacrifices were no real atonement,
evident from the Old Testament,
308–09; that the Messiah makes
the real and proper and only real
atonement, evident from the Old
Testament, 309–10, 317

Baal-perazim, God's wonderful appearance for David there, 216–17

Babylonish captivity, the return
from it, 294–97, 302–03

Blood, legal pollution by it, 318; the
waters of Egypt turned into it, 198

Brazen serpent, 239

Burning bush, 197, 238–39

Canaan, God's bringing Israel in
thither, 214–15

Candlestick in the sanctuary, 301,
319

Ceremonial law, 305–13; the things
of it declared to be of no value in
the sight of God for their own
sake, 305–06; the apparent and
designed resemblance between
the things of it and the things of
the Messiah, 306–07; proved typical from the vision of Ezekiel in
the nine last chapers of his
prophecy, 320–21

Cherubims in the sanctuary, 303–
04; God's dwelling between, 301

Circumcision, 300

Cloud of glory above the mercy
seat, 301

---

1. The Table fills two unnumbered pages immediately following the text of the "Types of
the Messiah." The entries are in two columns, divided by a vertical line, and each alphabeti-
cal grouping is set off by horizontal lines. The hand dates from the same period as that of the
main body of the MS, with some later additions in the same ink and contemporary with the
bulk of the corrections made to the text. In the original, JE referred to the MS page numbers
following a subject heading; here, the page references have been converted to refer to the
page numbers of this volume.

2. This entry is in a later ink and hand. JE refers to the notebook on the "Types." See pp. 146–53, above.

*Table* 327

---

3. This entry is in a later ink and hand.
4. The last page reference is in a later ink and hand.

---

5. This entry is in a later ink and hand.
6. JE did not provide a page number in the MS.
7. This entry is in a later ink and hand.
8. This entry is in a later ink and hand.

# GENERAL INDEX

*In the following index the abbreviation JE has been used for Jonathan Edwards*

Aaron, 198
Aaron's rod, 323
Abigail, 266–67
Abijah, 201
Abraham, 80, 81, 205, 209; tree of, 81, 111, 113
Achan, 215, 302
Adam, 4, 67, 176, 196–97; fall of, 28, 204
Adonijah, 280
*Agricola* (Mather), 23
Ahaz: sundial of, 198–99
Allegory, 4–5, 11, 32; scripture as, 12; rhetorical excesses in, 21–22, 27–28; unacceptable to JE, 161–63, 180, 181. *See also* Typology
Alpha, 79
America, 101
Analogy. *See* Types
Anderson, Wallace E., xiii–xiv
Andover Collection, 48, 145
Andrewes, Lancelot, 20, 21
Angels, 100, 120, 230, 239, 303–4
Anglican exegesis, 20–24. *See also* High Church Anglicans
Animals, 225; in ark, 222, 224. *See also* Beasts; Lamb *and other individual animals*
Anointing with oil, 137n2, 300–301, 319
Antichrist, 92, 113, 118
Antiochene school, 4
Antitype, 62, 95, 160, 321; defined, 3. *See also* Christ; Type
Antoninus, M., 129
Apostates, 108
Arabia, 224
Ark, Noah's, 132n4. *See also* Flood
Ark of the covenant, 83, 84, 218, 219, 269–71
Arrow, 312
Arts, 191
Ascending high places, 58, 91, 103; as way to heaven, 72, 73
Asenath, 234
Ass, 104
Assyrians, 224
Atonement, 307–10, 312–17
Attraction. *See* Gravity

Baalzebub, 131
Babylon, 294–97
"Bad Book" episode, 165
Balaam, 217, 219, 265
Balm of Gilead, 76, 115
Barak, 216, 248, 249
Basil (theologian), 4
Basnage, Jacques, 25, 203, 305
Bathsheba, 278, 279
Beasts, 114; as type of man, 55–56, 57, 69; of prey, 98, 120, 129, 135, 200
Beauty, 29; primary and secondary, 19
*Beauty of the World, The* (JE), 28
Bee, 124
Being, 17–18
Bible: as center of JE's world, 158; history and, 167. *See also* Allegory; New Testament; Old Testament; *and individual works by JE*
Birds, 71, 84, 86, 114; singing of, 93; saints and, 96–97; as devils and evil spirits, 127, 133
Bitumen, 227
Black color, 70
"Blank Bible" (JE), 34n2, 40, 47, 158, 178; on bodies, 52n2; images in, 60nn2–3; God as husbandman, 62n8; Sun, 64–65n2, 66n5; moon, 76n4; on Job *38:13,* 93n2; on Prov. *30:15–16,* 95n8; on Deut. *20:19,* 98n6; on Cant. *2:15,* 102n5; on John *11:50–52,* 125n3; on Gen. *8:4,* 132n4; on Josh. *10:13,* 134n5; on Ps. *78:2,* 153n5; on Gen. *15:17,* 206n3; on Jer. *35:6–8,* 208
Blood, 53, 73, 93, 121; and Christ's death, 81–82; in sacrifice, 102; as pollution, 318
"Blood of the covenant," 317
Blue color, 87, 94
Bodin, Jean, 25
Body (physical) of man, 14, 56, 92, 94, 98, 123; JE's view of, 15–16, 19
Boehme, Jakob, 25
"Book of Nature and Common Providence." *See* "Images of Divine Things" (JE)

329

# INDEX OF BIBLICAL PASSAGES